GROWING UP WITH CHILDREN

GROWING UP WITH CHILDREN

An Introduction to Working with Young Children

STEWART COHEN
GWENNETH RAE
University of Rhode Island

HOLT, RINEHART AND WINSTON
New York   Chicago   San Francisco   Philadelphia
Montreal   Toronto   London   Sydney
Tokyo   Mexico City   Rio de Janeiro   Madrid

Library of Congress Cataloging-in-Publication Data

Cohen, Stewart.
  Growing up with children.

  Includes index.
   1. Child development.   2. Education, Preschool—
Study and teaching.   3. Education, Elementary—Study
and teaching.   4. Child psychology.   I. Rae, Gwenneth.
II. Title.
LB1115.C68   1987   372'.21   86-19490

ISBN 0-03-000327-X

CBS COLLEGE PUBLISHING
Holt, Rinehart and Winston
The Dryden Press
Saunders College Publishing

PREFACE

Contemporary interest in early childhood education has received varying attention. In the 1960s, with the advent of Head Start and other
experimental programs, the field experienced a surge of support. In the
1970s interest waned as many of the initial gains achieved by these programs were not further substantiated. Currently, in the 1980s, early
childhood education is once again receiving favorable attention, in part,
paradoxically, as long-term follow-up studies show that these programs
have made substantial differences in the lives of the children served by
them.

Concurrently, educators who have specialized in working with
young children have begun to better articulate professional standards
of those who enter the field. In the last 10 years increasing numbers of
colleges, universities, and state governments have revised their requirements for professional training. In October 1984, for example, the state
of Rhode Island began issuing an Early Childhood Education Teaching
Certificate for preschool through grade two. This certificate requires
five years of educational training, including a bachelor's degree, 24
units of ECE courses, and a supervised student teaching experience. In
terms of preprofessional training even today, too frequently, teachers
below the kindergarten level are hired at the discretion of an individual
school often in minimal compliance with state licensure requirements.
Fortunately, an increased rigor in standards is typical of the nationwide
trend toward some form of early childhood certificate (which 33 states
now have or are developing). In Rhode Island, as elsewhere, the initial
certificate is provisional and an additional 36 units, or a master's degree,
is required for lifetime certification. Individuals in the field, then, can
now expect to acquire graduate-level training as they plan lasting
careers (to teach for five or more years) in working with children.

The implications of this type of certification are considerable. Two-
year institutions, such as the junior or community colleges, which have
trained many of our current early childhood personnel now will train
ancillary teaching aides; those who wish to advance in the field will
need to achieve other education credentials. The four-year college and

the university, as prime movers of advances in ECE, should anticipate more students in the future who will seek advanced training.

Growing Up with Children is designed to meet the new challenges in ECE, particularly in four-year programs at our colleges and universities. The material in this text brings together theory, research, and practice in an integrated and meaningful dialogue, offering the initial foundation to students who will continue in a bachelor and, perhaps, master-level program. This text is designed to assist students in acquiring a basic understanding of the issues they will face as teachers and in becoming prepared to acquire further curriculum-related training. As an introductory text, it offers the student a broad spectrum of both theory and practice. Moreover, subjects that are not often discussed in texts of this nature, among them a chapter on families, are included. Here we do not attempt to duplicate other course offerings, but rather to provide basic information on family patterns with its varied implications for different teaching milieus. Material on infant programs, multicultural considerations, and special-needs legislation is covered as well. These topics are all facets of present teaching dictated both by law and by the economics and changes in our society. As such, they are timely and necessary for consideration among students contemplating a career in ECE.

Not everyone who completes an introductory course in ECE does so in order to teach. Some individuals will be parents or will go on to work with children in another related capacity; each needs to achieve a broad understanding of development, caregiving, and teaching.

We hope that *Growing Up with Children* will accomplish these aims and will provide a resource for professors as well. *Objectives* at the beginning of each chapter provide a ready choice for examinations and an overview of each chapter's content. *Explorations* at the end of each chapter provide a guide to class discussions and assignments. The order in which the text is presented may be varied as well, depending upon the orientation of the individual instructor. Some may wish to start, perhaps with Chapter 7, "Observing and Guiding Children," in order to emphasize a more practical orientation as a beginning, whereas others may prefer to introduce students to social policy needs (Chapter 13).

This book is a beginning, for students and for the children they will teach. As such it is a special enterprise. Above all, it is a growing one. We ask each of you to grow with our children.

Several people helped make this book a reality. Their efforts and assistance are deeply appreciated and acknowledged. They include Carolyn A. Sovet, editorial research assistant, Ethel Thompson and Elaine Wichman, typists and listeners, the children, parents, and teachers of the

University of Rhode Island Child Development Center, and the students whom we teach and who teach us. We would like to thank our photographers, Carolyn A. Sovet and Tom Chambers, whose artistry has captured a small part of the joy experienced by children and by those who work with them.

We would also like to thank our colleagues who have read the manuscript and offered many useful comments: Grace Baron, Wheaton College (MA); Joanne E. Bernstein, Brooklyn College; Patricia J. Cianciolo, Michigan State University; Marlene Hefferman, Dean Junior College (MA); G. Duwayne Keller, University of Connecticut at Storrs; Shirley Doten Oliver, University of Maine at Orono; Adelle C. Park, Vermont College of Norwich University; M.C. Pugmire-Stoy, Ricks College (ID); Maureen Mulroy Thomas, Southern Connecticut State University; and Phyllis Walt, Massachusetts Bay Community College.

CONTENTS

Chapter 6   Personality Dynamics   180

SECTION THREE
THE CHILD IN SCHOOL   231

Chapter 7   Observing and Guiding Children   233

SECTION ONE

Children and Learning

Chapter 1

PAST AND CONTEMPORARY WORLDS OF EARLY CHILDHOOD EDUCATION

Objectives

After reading this chapter the student should be able to:

1. Trace the evolution of thought concerning the education of young children from the Greeks and Romans to the present.
2. Discuss the contributions of Froebel to the kindergarten curriculum with special attention to his "gifts" and "occupations."
3. Compare and contrast the contributions of John Dewey and Maria Montessori in several aspects of their educational programs.
4. Discuss different models of education for young children which evolved from the Head Start and Follow-Through programs.
5. Define three major approaches to children's learning and offer an educational model corresponding to each.
6. Compare and contrast the two approaches to the caring of infants discussed in this chapter.
7. Summarize the major learnings from the educational experimentation and research done in the 1960s and 1970s.
8. Discuss several current issues in ECE and the current educational philosophy of the field.

"Teacher, teacher. Come push me on the swing!"

"Teacher, look at me climb. See how high I am!"

"Tie my shoe, please, teacher. I can't make it work."

So many voices calling. Each needing recognition, needing assistance, needing love. Is it possible to be there for each one? Is it realistic to expect yourself to be there 100 percent of the time? To feel the tug at your heart when a particular child cries out to you for aid and still stay available for them all?

If you watch a teacher of young children enter the play yard you will see her tie a shoe, give a child a push on the swing as she calls out her pleasure to the young lady high on the climbing bars. Each child demands, and the teacher learns to respond to those needs with a smile and a word, a hug and a hand. A moment's wait is possible, but not too long, please!

Not an easy job, that's true! But that special feeling when a child puts his or her hand in yours and leans trustingly against you, recounting an adventure or just asking for a moment's reassurance, that feeling is so precious, such a suitable reward for the busy hours of movement, concern, and care.

"You get hooked on little kids," says one student teacher. "They think you are so wonderful, and they really need you. I feel as if I have something to contribute. Like I make a difference. It's wonderful. I just love it!" This student has found the true reward of working with young children. The reward that only comes with genuine involvement in the lives and learning of young people.

From those of us who are "hooked," we invite you to enter the world of early childhood education: its past, its present, and its future. There is much to learn, much to wonder about, much to worry about. And, oh, so much to gain in personal growth and satisfaction; perhaps there is some pain along with the pleasure, but, if you are up to the adventure, come along!

Early childhood education has been called everything from "baby-sitting" to the "potential salvation of the world." The view from the outside is often highly colored by the personal and political framework of the individual's and the culture's belief about children and the purpose of education. The view from the inside is not without personal prejudice, but it is also tempered with real information based on observation, interaction, and the knowledge that comes from accumulated research. To work effectively in this field, we believe the college student needs a balanced menu of these three components. A good training program for early childhood educators will not neglect one over the other but provide varied and frequent opportunities for observation and interaction along with a rich diet of research information and many avenues for discussion and evaluation.

In this first chapter we begin with the historical context of the field. We will also look at current developments and what we have learned thus far, as well as some of what we still need to know. As we proceed, later chapters will review information derived from research, our observations, and other interactions that inform us about how infants and young children learn; the importance and place of play in the child's life; differences in family patterns and individual temperament and personality; and how these factors influence programs and teaching. We will then attempt to set the child in the context of contemporary society and within ECE settings. Finally, we ask you to look at the teaching and care of children as a career objective.

Our goals are set often in terms of learning objectives at the beginning of each chapter, not to narrow your focus of learning, but to provide milestones by which you can reflect and judge your own growth in understanding. Our own framework for education is a humanistic one; to see individuals develop to the maximum of their own potential; to move forward in the developmental tasks of life, and to find satisfaction and purpose in the pursuit of their own goals while recognizing the interrelatedness of our own life and purposes with those of others. We hope the study of early childhood environments and education will prove stimulating and exciting and that you will be "growing up with children" as we believe we have done.

THE HISTORICAL CONTEXT

The history of childhood can help us gain an understanding of the world of childhood both past and contemporary. For it is in the cultural and historical contexts within which we have viewed and taught children that the settings and habits which currently influence children have been created.

For over two thousand years, roughly the history of written records, "classical" education was our principal model of instruction. Yet, in practice, formal education within this framework was provided only for male children of the privileged classes; girls, and children of less prominent social status, in contrast, received "more practical" vocational training in skill areas preparatory for less noble roles in society.

The democratization of education has been slow and often inconsistent. Only within the past two hundred years, concurrent with the growth of modern democratic principles, has education been offered free for all children. In comparison, the period in which separate education for young children has been recognized is of more recent vintage. The following account traces this history, providing us an introductory view of some of the influences which have led to our present perspective on early childhood education.

The Early Views

The origins of contemporary educational practice are found in ancient Greece and Rome. In Greece, schooling began at the age of six or seven and reflected the influence of the philosopher Aristotle. Through his writing, by the time of the third century B.C., public education was considered a right of the people.

Aristotle (384–322 B.C.) argued that education should begin at home under maternal guidance, to be extended by formal tutoring or schooling beginning between six and seven years of age. Schools in Greece taught literature, science, and art and music. Moreover, full participation was an expectation of the curriculum. Tuition fees were low, and a high proportion of the male populace, including slaves, were educated.

Plato (427–347 B.C.) designed proposals for a utopian community on Crete. Of special interest are his proposed schools where play was to be an educational device. In views which correspond with contemporary thought, Plato believed that play should be encouraged in young children, particularly games that were spontaneously invented.

The ancient Romans had a more practical approach to education. *Quintilian* (35–95 A.D.) proposed the psychology of rewards and argued against the use of corporal punishment. He believed that a love of education should be fostered and stressed the idea that teachers needed to be aware of individual differences among their students.

During the Middle Ages, the Greek and Roman educational heritage was set aside, the church established schools, and apprenticeships dominated educational practice. However, few children participated in these programs. Education, then, was for the male elite and future clergymen of the church. Most children were viewed as small adults, inherently evil, and their value was seen principally in economic worth. Most children died before they were old enough to care for themselves.

The life of the child was difficult and dangerous during this period. There were few rewards and frequent punishments. Punishment was seen as appropriate for exacting obedience and for the "training" of unruly minds. Moreover, it has appeared this way throughout educational history. Even as public schools began to be established in the United States (in the latter half of the nineteenth century), corporal punishment was still heavily used to enforce order and frequently to "instill motivation."

A New Order

During the Reformation, which spanned the period between the fourteenth and sixteenth centuries, the first humanist educators appeared and began to work toward the education of all children, rich and poor, male and female. The invention of the printing press served to disseminate ideas and encourage the need for literacy. Philosophers such as Descartes stressed creative individuality and concern for the common man. Locke's concept of the child as a "tabula rasa" shaped by experience furthered the optimistic view that education could uplift individuals and shape them in appropriate ways.

Three contemporary figures, *Erasmus, Luther*, and *Melanchthon*, laid the basis for the German school system and, in turn, influenced European educational philosophy. Following their lead, *Comenius* (1592–1670) advocated education for all children both rich and poor. Moreover, he wrote the first picture book for children, *Orbis Pictus*, in 1658 and a curriculum guide entitled *School for Infancy* in 1633. He believed that children learned through play with constructive materials with others of their own age, and that "learning by doing" in a concentric arrangement of topics was the most appropriate approach to education.

> Comenius outlined the format that guided subsequent reformers: (1) Parents are to be in charge of rearing children during the period of infancy, (2) parents can benefit from guidance in that task, and (3) under circumstances of parental incompetence or unwillingness, the task might be taken over by others. But the persons (parents or others) and the places (home or school) represented separate and autonomous institutions connected only by the child who might travel unaided from one to another.
>
> Clarke-Stewart and Fein, 1983, p. 927

His views in *The Great Didactic* (1657) are still considered to be progressive after three hundred years.

In the 1700s a fresh view of education was proposed by *Jean-Jacques Rousseau* in the publication of *Emile or on Education* (1762). His philosophy of romantic naturalism brought the child to the center of the educational enterprise. *Claprede* (1912), on the bicentennial of Rousseau's birth, defended the proposition that *Emile* contained, either explicitly or by implication, all that was good and current in child psychology. He assigned to Rousseau the following principles of child behavior:

1. *The Law of Genetic Succession:* The child develops naturally by passing through a number of stages that succeed one another in a constant order.
2. *The Law of Genetic-Functional Exercise:*
   (a) The exercise of a function is necessary to its development
   (b) The exercise of a function is necessary to the appearance of certain other functions.
3. *The Law of Functional Adaptation:* That action will be elicited which serves to satisfy the need or interest of the moment. . . .
4. *The Law of Functional Autonomy:* The child is not, considered in himself, an imperfect being; he is a being adapted to circumstances which are appropriate to him; his mental activity is appropriate to his needs, and his mental life is integrated. . . .
5. *The Law of Individuality:* Every person differs more or less, in physical and psychological characteristics, from other people.

Thus the child emerges in the eighteenth century (Kessen, 1965) not as a creature of sin, but as a self-directed natural being who "unfolds" through the aid of a supportive environment. Through Rousseau, the concepts of individuality, age-related capabilities, and the child as an active participant in the developmental process became three of the main principles on which contemporary education was established.

Yet it took another generation before Rousseau's writings were put into practice. *Johann Pestalozzi* (1746–1827), a Swiss educator, influenced by Rousseau, wrote and taught over a 30-year span and became one of the most influential teachers of his time. In his school, punishment and rote learning were abolished. He believed that *the head, the hand,* and *the heart* must develop harmoniously and that children need to love and be loved. His school included mixed ages with older children tutoring younger children and singing and concrete learning experiences supplanting traditional rote recitations.

Pestalozzi's most startling policy, for his time, was the acceptance of poor children in his school. He believed that all children had potential, regardless of their station in life and that every child's personality was sacred. School, he argued, should foster the child's self-esteem and attention should be paid to individual differences in interests, needs, and rates of learning. Pestalozzi also instituted *the concept of readiness,* believing the child would learn with experience and over time. At one point in his career, after the village of Stanz was ravaged by Napoleon's forces, Pestalozzi established an orphanage for young war victims. With the help of one servant he spent an entire year loving, caring for, and teaching up to 80 children, aged 2 to 6, all at one time!

Pestalozzi wrote several books and established two large schools, which were visited by many distinguished leaders of the time. Yet, he was not able to systematically translate his ideas into a set of rules for others to follow. Moreover, his own personality and selfless devotion to children were difficult to replicate and others who attempted to follow his example were usually unsuccessful. The basic tenets of education that he advocated, however, have become principal bases for later developments in the field and especially for the work of Friedrick Froebel.

The Nineteenth Century

The Kindergarten

Friedrick Froebel (1770–1852), has been called the father of the kindergarten. After visiting and studying at Pestalozzi's school, he designed and instituted the first kindergarten in Blankenbury, Germany, in 1837. Froebel's philosophy of education was influenced not only by the ideas of Rousseau and the practices of Pestalozzi, but also by the new ideal of the poets and philosophers of his day. The powers of the mind and the spirit of faith were to be blended in a unity and inner harmony with God. In *A Child's Garden* he compared children to flowers that needed to be nurtured in order to grow.

Froebel's approach to education is still the foundation of most programs for young children. Here, the educator provides a stimulating environment and gentle guidance; play is the most important activity for the child; individual differences in interest and capabilities are acknowledged and accepted; and the child's personal interactions serve as the focus of the curriculum.

Froebel's contributions to curriculum are particularly notable. Most specifically, he designed programs based upon what he called "gifts" and "occupations." The *gifts* were a variety of objects that would stimulate experimentation and sensory learning. Balls, blocks, cubes, and cylinders were sequenced in complexity and invited learning by discovery. The *occupations* were tasks such as weaving, stringing, paper folding, and model construction, which were developed to enhance inventiveness. Froebel discussed these materials and educational methods in *The Education of Man*, which was published in 1877. Because of his writings and his willingness to train others, Froebel's ideas and methods spread throughout the world.

KINDERGARTEN IN THE UNITED STATES.   Kindergarten came to the United States through a former student of Froebel's, *Mrs. Carl Schurz*, who began a class in her home for her own children in 1855 and then expanded it to include other German-speaking pupils. The first English-speaking kindergarten was begun in Boston in 1860 by *Elizabeth Peabody* who had visited Mrs. Schurz's school. In 1867 Mrs. Peabody went on a lecture tour to spread the word about this new kind of education.

The first publicly supported kindergarten was founded in St. Louis, Missouri, in 1873. This signaled 30 years of growth in public and private kindergartens. In the early stages of the movement teachers worked with children in the morning and then spent their afternoons helping the families in a manner similar to present day social workers. Helping families find jobs, medical treatment, and housing were all considered part of helping the child. As the kindergarten movement grew, however, the number of children to be accommodated created the double session approach which is still practiced in most schools today. Once the kindergarten teacher taught two groups of children, one in the morning and one in the afternoon, the time to provide services to their families was no longer available. The separation of child and family contact became the norm. Other problems, such as the relationship between the kindergarten and the rest of the school grades, also emerged during this period. Should the kindergarten prepare children for first grade or should the first grade be more individualized? What kind of readiness training did the children need? Should the "three Rs" be taught? Many of these issues are still debated.

Along with kindergarten came the creation of "day nurseries," modeled after the new "nursery school," as established in London by the Macmillan sisters (1909). These programs emphasized physical well-being and emotional development. In the United States such programs were initially concerned with the Americanization of the foreign born and signaled an emerging professional identity of child care workers as "nurses."

Parent education, which was popular in the 1880s, acquired an organizational structure and leadership with *G. Stanley Hall* when he helped found the National Congress of Mothers in 1897. This organization became the Parent-Teacher Association of our contemporary school structure. Dr. Hall was also one of the first to undertake the empirical study of children through the Society for the Study of Child Nature formed in 1888.

These two contrasting concerns—parent and home versus professional teacher and institution—continued to occupy the attention of reformers in alternating fashion until recent times. Generally, institutionalized child care been recommended for the children of the poor in times of affluence and industrial expansion, while upsurges in parent education have occurred in times of economic hardship.

During World War I and later, the shifting of national interest to economic concerns, caused by the Depression, brought an abrupt end to the kindergarten movement. Some school districts dropped their kindergarten entirely, and while some districts maintained their programs, the intense interest and growth which characterized the early growth of the kindergarten movement was gone.

The Twentieth Century

Two educational leaders form the cornerstone of twentieth century early childhood education, *John Dewey* (1859–1952) and *Maria Montessori* (1870–1952). Although contemporaries with different perspectives, their basic beliefs in education suggest some fundamental and enduring parallels.

Both educators believed in the child's natural capacity to learn and that individual differences were to be respected in the child's schooling. Experiential learning, involvement, and the need for organization and continuity are key concepts in the work of both. However, Montessori's view of structured experience in the education of young children was more limited than Dewey's views. Dewey (1916; 1943), in contrast, viewed *life as an educational experience* and believed that the more children interacted with each other, and the greater their access to varied materials and relationships (including the teacher-pupil relationship), the more valid and educationally sound the experience. Gardening, building, discussing, and decision making were all activities meant to provide education through doing.

Montessori (1964), based on her experiences as a doctor working with retarded children, created an environment for the child with more specifically designed materials. Child-sized chairs and tables, cupboards at the child's eye-level, and educational material that could be demonstrated by the teacher and then used by the child to promote auto-education were her unique contributions. A minimum amount of verbal interaction was required from the teacher and social interaction with other children was less formally stressed in the curriculum.

Teachers in both approaches were expected to know the materials of their classroom, and to understand the developmental level of the child in order to match the activity and guide the learnings of each individual. In the Montessori program the teacher has the materials and activities already designed by Montessori and is extensively trained in how to observe the child, how to determine when he is ready for a particular piece of equipment, and how to present that equipment.

The teacher in a "progressive" education program, such as Dewey designed, is more active in curriculum decisions and must plan experiences that are as closely related to real life as possible. Planting a garden or building a playhouse is done in groups with the children and teacher making decisions and solving problems together. Verbal and social interactions are encouraged and the teacher's job is to guide the awareness of the group to unsolved problems and other learnings.

Both approaches to educating children have been subject to vigorous praise and criticism. Dewey's writings, especially, have been misinterpreted and at times misdirected, leading to schools that have called themselves progressive but that contrasted sharply with Dewey's model. Dewey, himself, in his 1963 edition of *Experience and Education* criticized those who used his ideas to produce a dogmatic idea of progressivism.

In analysis, it is important to remember that the children and the social cultural contexts within which these two educators worked were quite different. Maria Montessori, as the first woman physician in Italy, initially worked with retarded children and later with the children of the slums of Rome. Her Casa Bambini (Children's House) was meant to keep these children purposefully busy and provided care, as well as education, while their parents worked. A safe, respectful, and child-sized environment was a tremendous change for these "children of the street." In contrast, John Dewey's work was initiated in the United States in school environments that were highly restrictive and did little to encourage children to think and learn in creative and independent ways. Dewey believed that intelligence was the only true freedom—that is, freedom to determine purpose, judge desire, and reconstruct each into coherent plans of activity. Clearly he attempted to create programs for a democratic society.

Modern Montessori schools and educational programs that use Dewey's progressive concepts, such as the British infant schools, have modified and shaped these approaches for their current constituents. The fundamental principles of both, however, continue to have impact and relevance for early childhood education.

Day Care and Preschool Programs

The kindergarten movement in this country, as we have seen, began with the dissemination of Froebel's ideas in the 1850s and continued to grow until the "Great Depression" of 1929–35. These early kindergartens usually included children from four to six years of age, thus, "preschool" education was not, in fact, separated from the public school continuum. By 1920 about 25 percent of the nation's four to six year olds were in kindergarten. In the twenties and thirties, those public schools that did not close their kindergarten programs restricted them to five year olds and this became the typical pattern for the public schools. These restrictions encouraged the preschool movement as middle class parents began to seek other alternatives for the care and education of their children under five years of age. The term "preschool" was first introduced by *Arnold Gesell* in the 1925 winter issue of *Progressive Education.*

The Depression also saw the authorization of "WPA" nursery schools under the Federal Emergency Relief Administration. While the primary purpose of these programs was to employ adults, within a year approximately 75,000 children were enrolled in 1,900 programs across the country. These programs were distinct from, but administered by, the public schools until 1942. Thereafter, approximately 965 preschool programs remained open under other auspices. Many of these schools survived through funding under the *Lanham Act* (1943) which attempted to coordinate plans of education, welfare, and health services created by mothers participating in war-related industries. In 1946, with the end of the war, Lanham Act schools were turned over to state control or closed.

In the 1950s and 1960s changes in the family and society continued. In many two parent families, both adults were working. An increase in the divorce rate and in the number of single parent families also encouraged a large increase in day care programs across the country. Even those families with mothers who chose to stay home wanted preschool experiences for their children. Cooperative schools and play groups began to flourish. By 1964, 25 percent of the three to five year olds were in preschool programs.

Programs for young children during this period varied from those that were primarily custodial in nature, providing a supervised environment with adequate staff to attend to the child's needs, to those that incorporated a particular theory or method, such as the Montessori preschools. Many universities developed nursery schools as part of their teacher training programs and the informal play group or cooperative nursery school was often led by a mother who had participated in such training. Clearly, preschool programs were a viable part of the total educational picture.

However, the postwar technological revolution was about to spawn an educational revolution. The Soviet Union's competition in space and its success in launching the Sputnik rocket in 1957 were blows to the nation's pride. Critics of public education became increasingly vocal. In addition, research indicated that children were not learning all that they could or we thought they should. The National Defense Act of 1958 offered scholarships, loans, and grants to improve teaching in science and mathematics and to identify talented young people. In 1964, Benjamin Bloom and a number of others were demonstrating the importance of early stimulation in learning and the detrimental effects of neglect during a child's early years. Political and educational objectives aligned and in the summer of 1965 *Head Start* began.

Rest periods are an important part of each child's day.

Head Start

Head Start was designed as a prekindergarten experience for "under-privileged" children. During its first summer thousands of programs were initiated largely in public schools with elementary teachers being trained to work with young children. The following year added many programs in community settings. Many were hastily conceived and operated with meager guidelines and limited staff training. But the overwhelming political attitude was one of optimism and a sense of accomplishment. The children who attended the first 8- to 12-week summer sessions were all due to enter kindergarten the next fall, and it was generally believed that Head Start was going to help them to be "as ready" as their middle class peers. Furthermore, parent involvement, physical screening, and even psychological testing were a formal part of the overall package. For many educators, this program looked like the solution to the continuing cycles of school drop out, crime, poverty, and welfare.

These rather grandiose dreams, however, were built on shifting sands. Early gains in I.Q. (intelligence quotient as measured by standardized tests such as the *Stanford-Binet*) and readiness tests did not continue after one to two years in the standard classroom. Moreover, even full year Head Start programs did not produce consistent results. Clearly, something was not working!

Simultaneously the results of a large scale reading experiment in the Detroit public schools offered findings that gave some clues to the problems of maintaining learning gains. Children who began school with "enriched" programs only maintained their initial gains if the grades that followed altered their curriculums to accommodate these additional learnings. The path to educational improvements now seemed clear, and planned variations, also known as Project Follow-Through, were born.

Project Follow-Through

In 1968 Project Follow-Through began with 10 different models of early childhood education. Later that number was expanded and variations of the original group were devised to bring the total to 16 to 20 programs. This was the largest research endeavor ever introduced in the field of education. With one exception, every model was designed for Head Start through the third grade. This one divergent program was directed toward infant education in the home using trained paraprofessionals to work with the infant and his parent (Gordon, 1969).

Each model had a particular educational philosophy or conceptual framework and a specific set of goals and methods. Most models originated within college or university centers that specialized in education for young children or in related areas of psychology. The criteria for the models, including background of its present use with "disadvantaged" youngsters, were reviewed by teams of experts in education drawn from all parts of the country. The requirements for participation were stringent but the hope of "proving" one's model as "the right path" for educating children was an irresistible lure for educators. (Being a part of Project Follow-Through was the just reward for many educators whose work in early childhood education had often been regarded by their university colleagues as trivial or "glorified baby-sitting." The opportunity of a life-time was at hand.)

CONCEPTUAL MODELS IN PROJECT FOLLOW-THROUGH.   It is obvious by now that our beliefs on how a child learns and develops determine what is taught, how it is taught, and by whom it is taught. The models implemented in Project Follow-Through followed the philosophies of psychologists and educators whose basic tenets rested on three major approaches to learning:

1. *Socialization models*—Programs that foster self-esteem and self-actualization through peer interaction and stimulate children's intellectual curiosity by providing a wide range of experiences and materials. Children are expected to take large parts in their own education through their choice of activities and by their own active interest in the world. (S)
2. *Behavior modification or stimulus-response models*—Programs that view learning as one form of reinforced behavior. Teachers present materials that are appropriate to the learner but also reflect societies' choices of what needs to be taught. Material is learned through repetition with appropriate reinforcement. (B)
3. *Cognitive growth models*—Programs which focus on learning intellectual tasks at the level or stage of the individual's mental structures and operations. Activities and materials are chosen to maximize learning at specific stages of intellectual life. The normal stage-wise growth pattern cannot be altered significantly, so curriculum must reflect developmental criteria. (C)

The models that were chosen to participate are listed in Table 1.1 and identified by their primary emphasis on one of these frameworks. Each program was conducted in at least three school districts in various locations across the United States. The training of teachers as well as the evaluations of children's learnings and the degree to which the program was actually followed were the responsibility of the program director of that model. In addition, separate evaluators, who were recognized experts in the field, were used by federal authorities to monitor each program. The process of the final evaluation of the entire set of programs was to be devised by the external evaluators since each model had chosen evaluation techniques and tests that they believed would best reflect the goals of their own program.

EVALUATING PROJECT FOLLOW-THROUGH.   As shown in Table 1.1, the models of education selected for participation ranged from the traditional free

TABLE 1.1. Follow-Through Model Program Summary Chart

Program	Sponsor	Emphasis	Materials	Learning Approach*
Bank Street Model+	Bank Street College of Education: New York City	Optimum human interaction and development	Trade books, Bank Street Readers, teacher-made, other	S
Interdependent Learning Model+	City University of New York	Humanistic, interpersonal, noncompetitive intellectual growth	Many games, phonics-based reading, other basal readers	E
Home-School Partnership Model	Clark College: Atlanta, Georgia	Use of home environment, parents as teachers	Varied instructional materials, teacher-made materials	C
Responsive Education Program+	Far West Laboratory for Educational Research and Development: San Francisco, California	Understanding cultural differences, problem solving, promoting good self-concept	Varied materials compatible with goals	E
Parent supported application of the Behavior-Oriented Prescriptive Teaching Approach	Georgia State University: Atlanta, Georgia	Individual diagnoses and prescription for meaningful instruction	Teacher manuals, learning kits, games, other	C
Nongraded Follow-Through Model	Hampton Institute: Hampton, Virginia	Nongraded, individualized continuous progress	Varied materials, learning centers, teacher-made materials	S

Program	Sponsor/Location	Goals	Materials	
Cognitively Oriented Curriculum Model+	High/Scope Foundation: Ypsilanti, Michigan	Expansion of cognitive knowledge according to developmental abilities	Varied materials selected to fit the model	C
Cultural Linguistic Approach	Northeastern Illinois University: Chicago, Illinois	Acceptance of cultural patterns and linguistic skills and building upon them	Manuals on units and teaching strategies, ethnic objects, Sullivan Reading Program	E
Follow-Through Model	Prentice-Hall, Inc.	Attitudinal change through individualized academic growth	"Talking Typewriters," "Talking Page," "Voice Mirror," other materials	E
Language Development (Bilingual Education)	Southwest Educational Development Laboratory: Austin, Texas	Instruction in Spanish or English, increasing self-esteem, oral language stress	Six instructional kits—multimedia	E
Tucson Early Education+	University of Arizona: Tucson, Arizona	Stress on functional language competency, intellectual, and social skills	Interest centers, varied materials, teacher-made kits	S
Culturally Democratic Learning Environments	University of California at Santa Cruz: Santa Cruz, California	Appreciation of cultural identity, promote intellectual flexibility	Varied materials, Spanish reading materials, cultural heritage units	S
Florida Parent Education+	University of Florida: Gainesville, Florida	Home learning activities, parents as teachers	Home learning activities, varied instructional materials	C

TABLE 1.1. Follow-Through Model Program Summary Chart *(continued)*

Program	Sponsor	Emphasis	Materials	Learning Approach*
Mathemagenic Activities Program	University of Georgia: Athens, Georgia	Knowledge acquired through interaction with total environment, develomental-intellectual growth	Instruction units, curriculum guides, workbooks, and other materials	C
Behavior Analysis Approach[†]	University of Kansas: Lawrence, Kansas	Behavior analysis methods, positive reinforcement to promote academic progress	Model designed reading materials plus integration of other materials	B
The New School Approach to Follow Through	University of North Dakota: Grand Forks, North Dakota	Encourage curiosity, inductive learning, self-direction	Learning centers, manuals, handbooks, varied other materials	S
Engleman-Becker Model for Direct Instruction[†]	University of Oregon: Eugene, Oregon	Structured, programmed learning for optimum academic gains	DISTAR—reading, math, and language materials	B
Individualized Early Learning Program[†]	University of Pittsburgh: Pittsburgh, Pennsylvania	Individualized instruction for optimum mastery of cognitive material	PEP materials, learning centers, Sullivan Reading material, other materials	B

20

Model	Center	Description	Materials	Learning Approach
The Role-Trade Model	Western Behavioral Sciences Institute: La Jolla, California	Extension of classroom to home and neighborhood, understanding of varied roles in school, home, and community	Program produced materials, varied materials	S
EDC Open Education Model†	Educational Development Center: Newton, Mass.	Stresses independent learning	Varied instruction materials, handbooks for teachers and parents	C

*Learning Approach: S = Socialization, C = Cognitive, B = Behavior Modification, E = Eclectic.
†Indicates one of original models.
Adapted from: Early Childhood Education: An Overview by Loraine Webster and Raymond M. Schroeder (Princeton, NJ: Princeton Book Co., 1979).

play and enriched experiences approaches reminiscent of Froebel to highly structured "token economies" in which children received a plastic chip, redeemable for some reward, for each completed task or correct answer. Programs with specific teacher-directed exercises in language and mathematics vied with those in which socialization and "exposure" to concepts and materials were the primary mode of teaching. The stage was set for controversy and the battle is still being fought.

Federal evaluators found themselves with an impossible task. How do you compare different programs that use different evaluative procedures? I.Q. as a standard measure across programs was not a significant or sufficient indicator. Furthermore, many educators objected to standardized tests, which had been shown by other research to be prejudiced against children whose backgrounds differed from the white middle class norms on which the tests had been developed and standardized. Children of different backgrounds, languages, and dialects did not have sufficient "match," a concept first introduced by J. McVicker Hunt in 1961. Hunt postulated that the information brought to a task must be close enough to the requirements of the material presented to be understandable (for example, students couldn't be expected to read a story in a foreign language if they had not mastered the vocabulary of that language).

Measures of readiness, such as reading or mathematical tests, did not prove effective either, since some programs deliberately taught concepts such as numbers or letters while in other programs such learning was incidental to the goals of the programs. Attempts to measure attitudinal dimensions such as self-esteem or attitude toward school were especially difficult and tended to be unreliable over time. The arguments over measurement grew heated and *remain* unresolved.

Clearly all of these difficulties made comparisons between programs virtually impossible. Several measures within specific programs did show significant gains. But even these results were equivocal since the same program in different locations sometimes produced different results. Many directors of training programs felt their biggest challenge was the education of the teachers who were to implement their techniques with the children. Previous methodology, teacher and neighborhood attitudes, and difficulty in maintaining high levels of teacher commitment and performance were major variables in the program's effectiveness. Some teachers did not agree with the methods they were being trained to teach; old habits were strong and new methods often required more work. In addition to teacher difficulties, differences among the students appeared. These involved different cultural contexts, transiency, marital status of parents, language background, parental occupation, etc. Available means for evaluation were simply inadequate to the task.

In the last analysis, no one model proved to be consistently positive in terms of long range effects of early preschool experience upon later school performance. All models claimed gains, according to their own standards, in some areas, and with some groups of children. The most spectacular educational intervention of the century was considered by many to be a failure or at least not worth the enormous effort and funds that had been poured into the project. Educators who wanted a particular view to be validated or discredited were disappointed and the public, through their political representatives, backed away from continued involvement in large scale educational spending. Project Follow-Through quietly faded away.

The reduction in educational spending did not lead to the disappearance of these varied models. Rather, as Webster and Schroeder indicate in *Early Childhood Education: An Overview* (1979), presently at least twenty of these models are still evident across a variety of settings. Present claims of success, however, are more subdued and current programs now build on the work of earlier models.

The 1980s is shaping into a period of increasing technology in the classroom with a number of models incorporating computers and other educational "hardware" in their curriculum. However, most schools do not operate from any one model but would term themselves eclectic, choosing the approaches which best suit themselves and blending them together to meet the needs of the local populations which they serve. It is unlikely that a period of rapid and radical change such as we witnessed in the sixties and seventies will occur in this more conservative and economically difficult period. Consolidating and tightening characterizes present educational practice.

Current Issues in Early Childhood Education

INFANT EDUCATION PROGRAMS.   One type of program has drawn increased interest and seen rapid growth in the 1980s. Infant education has historically been considered the province of the child's mother or mother-substitute. Even today many states do not allow children under the age of two or three to enroll in day care or nursery settings, and most infants whose parents work are still cared for by relatives or neighbors in their homes. This prejudice against group infant care has been fermented by inadequate understanding of the infant's learning capacities and partially by our cultural bias in favor of the nuclear family concept. However, in the sixties and seventies infant research began to grow. Many new technical improvements allowed for the monitoring of infant behavior in a way that had been previously impossible. Research on infants in orphanages and other large care facilities showed that children with inadequate stimulation would suffer delay or retardation (Bowlby, 1951; Casler, 1961). Studies on maternal bonding demonstrated that infants quickly learned to identify their mother's voice and infant temperament studies found a variety of innate characteristics that could be measured even in the first days of life (see Chapter 4). It became clear that infants were learning and that they were not the totally helpless, incompetent creatures we had thought them to be.

In the models for Project Follow-Through, one program dealt with infant learning. The Florida Project was developed by Ira Gordon at the University of Florida and operated on the premise that the mothers of disadvantaged infants needed to be encouraged to interact and teach their babies more than they were doing. Paraprofessionals from the communities of the participants were trained to interact with infants and teach the child's mother Gordon's techniques. The curriculum was based on the work of Piaget and would be considered a cognitively oriented program. The parent educators and the mothers, however, had a great deal of latitude in the adaptation of these activities and were encouraged to problem solve in devising methods to work with particular children (see Chapter 9).

Meanwhile, at Syracuse University, group day care was introduced with the explicit purpose of providing an enriched environment with trained personnel to supplement the supposed "inadequate" environment of the home (Caldwell, 1970). Children from three months of age were accepted into the center and staffing involved at least one adult to every three infants. In addition to the custodial care required by the infants, activities and toys to stimulate attention and involvement were incorporated into the program on a regular basis. Early intervention was the stated goal of the center (see Chapter 9).

These two models of infant day care are still practiced, with the home teaching model attached to Head Start programs as Home Start in many states. The intervention concept has faded, however, except for youngsters with handicapping conditions. Enrichment and school oriented learning are the concepts that have replaced the term "deprived," and the concept of "different" has supplanted "disadvantaged." These new terms are, obviously, meant to resolve issues of prejudice and discrimination, which were seen as part of some of the earlier intervention models. Many groups were quick to point out that in a pluralistic society different is a more appropriate concept than disadvantaged.

CIVIL RIGHTS AND THE SCHOOLS. Beginning with the 1954 (*Brown* vs. *Board of Education*) civil rights decision invalidating the concept of "separate but equal" schools, we have seen increasing attention directed toward the plight of minority children in the school systems. Desegregation was merely the first step on the road to greater recognition of student rights and the need for more equal educational opportunities for all students. School bussing of children was a major issue in the fifties when both black and white students were taken from neighborhood schools and brought together. The hopes of providing a more heterogenous environment and better education for all children spearheaded these measures. However, in many communities they created as many problems as they attempted to solve. Long bus rides, poor acceptance in the new environment, and parental dissatisfaction, coupled with the high costs of the endeavor, created difficult problems for most school districts.

In the sixties bilingual and multicultural education commanded our interest. We already knew that too many students of ethnic minorities were failing, especially in basic skills. However, concern shifted to the difficulties encountered among children whose home language was not English. We came to recognize that learning to read in a language infrequently heard or poorly spoken created difficulties in which failure was highly likely. This knowledge helped foster programs in which children spent part of their day learning English and/or learning basic skills in their home language. In Chapter 8 we will discuss the multicultural approach—its importance and its present status. It is sufficient to note within the present context the fact that recent waves of immigration in the late 1970s and early 1980s indicate that this area of public education will continue to be an active and controversial one.

EDUCATION FOR THE HANDICAPPED

Public Law 94-142.   Another significant federal intervention into education began in 1975, with the passage of Public Law 94-142. This bill was designed to require education for all handicapped children in public schools beginning at the preschool level. A long felt need of parents with children who had special problems, this legislation has drawn attention to the importance of assessing young children and in providing individualized learning programs (IEPs) in response to special needs. Moreover, it has introduced such concepts as mainstreaming, which integrates handicapped children into regular classrooms as opposed to special segregated classes. Project Child-Find, which tests preschool children to discover those with potential learning difficulties, is also a product of this bill.

This federal mandate has had far-reaching effects on the contemporary school, especially in the financial demands necessitated by testing and providing special teachers. How to provide more services for more children with less money is a dilemma which will undoubtedly continue, at least in the near future. Providing the best education possible for *all* the children of a community is a great and exciting goal. How well we are able to achieve this ideal remains to be seen. (Chapter 12 discusses mainstreaming and programs for handicapped children in more detail.)

Technology and the Schools

The postwar technology that has led to space exploration, transistor radios, televisions, and the personal mini-computer has had a far-reaching impact on the schools, as well. The National Defense Act led not only to an increase in the emphasis and teaching of mathematics and science but also to new methodology and new hardware in the school setting. A variety of educational experiments have arisen from these innovations. Programmed instruction, education by television, and computer instruction are some of the more consistent and long-lasting results of these technological advances.

PROGRAMMED INSTRUCTION.   Originally based on behavioral learning theory, the development of small, carefully articulated "bits" of information that are learned sequentially began with some of B. F. Skinner's work after World War II (1953; 1968) and found its way into schools, first via textbooks and workbooks, and later in such innovations as O. K. Moore's "talking typewriter" and the Palo Alto programmed computer learning laboratories. (The latter two programs were used successfully for remedial instruction and for initial skill learning for young children.)

Programmed learning requires active involvement from children because each small segment of learning material requires a response. If the answer to a question or problem is correct, the student continues the learning task; if the answer is incorrect, directions either send the learner back to review material or present the material in a different manner with new examples and questions. This approach has been used extensively in beginning reading textbooks as well as a variety of other self-help materials for the schools. Short learning sequences and frequent feedback on correctness or incorrectness of response has proven a very effective learning tool for some students. Computer programming often makes use of short learning/immediate feedback teaching loops for adults as well as children who are learning how to use these machines.

TELEVISION.   As television has become a major national pastime children have so increased their viewing that they tend to spend more time watching TV than attending school. Because of the considerable number of hours spent watching TV, most often without appropriate adult guidance, television has aroused passionate critical commentary and an enormous amount of controversy. Issues vary from the efficacy of television teaching, to the behavioral effects of children viewing violence in regular programming, to the appropriateness of television advertising for children .

One of the earliest experiments with children's television was *Sesame Street*.

"Sesame Street."   In the same period that the Head Start and Follow-Through programs were initiated, a new concept in children's television programming known as "Sesame Street" was developed with federal funding. Designed as educational television for youngsters in the home, and in many areas only broadcast on educational channels, "Sesame Street" was especially designed to reach the "disadvantaged" child by offering him or her school-related learning opportunities (for example, alphabet, colors). This format became so popular with children that it quickly outstripped its educational TV base and became a regular part of conventional television programming. Workbooks and other commercial materials soon became readily available and "Sesame Street," along with its partner, "The Electric Company," are now viewed by thousands of children each day.

A number of studies of "Sesame Street" found that the program was most effective when the concepts taught were reinforced by an adult. Passive viewing, without follow-up, or viewing without focus, does not provide the same learning gains as involved learnings. Whether "Sesame Street" has accomplished its original purpose of narrowing the learning gap between poor children and middle class children in school-related concepts or whether it has, in fact, widened that gap is a subject of controversy. However, with its present commercial success, "Sesame Street" no longer requires federal funding and does not need to prove its worth. Therefore, we can expect the program to continue to grow and flourish.

Educational television, including special channels for public use and the ability to send programs through cable and satellite channels, has insured the use of television as an instructional medium. Controversy concerning TV for children currently centers on programming by commercial stations with their specially designed advertisements for children, the violence of many child-oriented programs (such as cartoons), as well as the regular adult programs viewed by children. Young children seem especially prone to the influence of commercial television because of their limitations in conceptual understanding. We will discuss some of these issues in later chapters.

COMPUTERS AND THE SCHOOLS.   With the advent of the mini-computer and the perpetuation of tax incentives to computer companies for donating machines to schools, many children are receiving instruction in this new technology. In the recent past most computers were reserved for high schools and colleges or classes for youngsters especially gifted in mathematics or technology. At the present, computers have moved into the lower elementary grades including kindergarten; children often have more expertise than their teachers in using this newest medium. Young children are generally not as intimidated as adults in trying computers and experimenting with them. Most young children use computers with software that teaches a particular skill and that is displayed on a television-like screen. This software often uses principles of programmed learning to teach the alphabet or numbers or some other related material in an interactive game-like format which children enjoy. For the child this activity is fun and it teaches! Computers will be the cutting edge of school technology in the future.

WHAT WE HAVE LEARNED

Although some politicians may view the educational innovations of the last 20 years as fiscally unsound, educators, especially those in the field of early childhood education, would strongly disagree. In fact, some of these learnings are only beginning to be seen. The most recent reports on long-term follow up of the early Head Start programs show, among those children who attended, significant positive increases in numbers entering college and a decrease in the number of high school drop-outs (Berrueta-Clement et al., 1984).

A great deal of research on infant learning and on the cognitive abilities of young children has been spurred by these programs. We now know that children are learning from the moment of birth. Various techniques of assessment have enabled us to counsel parents of "at-risk" children and to provide better education earlier for youngsters with special needs. Information concerning various learning disabilities has also greatly increased and has reached into colleges where students with learning problems can be officially diagnosed as handicapped and receive needed help.

As with all new information, new challenges and problems arise and will continue to arise. We will explore more about these methods of learning and their ramifications in the following chapters.

Explorations

PERSONAL EXPLORATIONS

These exercises are designed to help you look at your own life—attitudes, experiences, dreams, myths, and realities.

1. Think back on your first school experiences. Did you attend a pre-school or begin with kindergarten or first grade? What was that first experience like for you? Write a page describing the types of activities you did and what learning model you think that program followed.
2. What is your family's attitude toward education? Can you tell from their actions and statements what models of early childhood education would appeal to them most? How do your ideas coincide or differ from theirs? Make a small chart comparing your ideas on education and those of your parents or other relatives.
3. Froebel, Montessori, and Dewey had some ideas and attitudes in common and some that were different. These are reflected in the types of activities a child would participate in. Imagine yourself a child in each of these types of programs. What activities would appeal to you most? Why? Take a large piece of paper and fold it in thirds. In each section list the activities that you would like and the ones you would not like in each program. Write a paragraph describing what you have learned from this comparison and take the paragraph and chart to class to discuss.

INTELLECTUAL EXPLORATIONS

These exercises are designed to increase your depth of knowledge in some of the areas discussed in this chapter.

1. Find two journals in the field of education for young children at the library (for example, *Day Care, Young Children*). Find an article in each journal that discusses a particular program for young children. Can you identify the learning approach or educational model used in the program? If the programs are eclectic, what activities represent their different approaches? Write a one-page comparison of the two programs and special approaches.
2. Find a biography of a famous American of another century that discusses his or her early learning experiences. Write an essay briefly describing these experiences and compare them with a contemporary program.
3. Find some of the original writings of two of the originators of different models used in Project Follow-Through. Preferably choose two who follow different learning approaches. For example, try to find a comparable section in each discussing how children should learn or what methods teachers should use. Make a chart with quotations from each which show their similarities and differences and bring it to class for discussion.
4. Use Table 1.2 and your other readings to hypothesize the future of early childhood education in this century. Write a paragraph for discussion purposes.

TABLE 1.2. Significant Events in Early Childhood Education in the United States

1854	Dr. Henry Barnard, Secretary of Connecticut Board of Education and soon to be first National Commissioner of Education, was impressed by Froebelian display at International Education Exposition, London.
1855	First recorded U.S. kindergarten established by Mrs. Carl Schurz, pupil of Froebel's, in German language for her own children and the neighbors, using her parlor in Waterton, Wisconsin.
1856	First public use of term "kindergarten" in Barnard's July issue of *American Journal of Education.*
1860	First English language kindergarten opened in Boston by Elizabeth Peabody and her sister, Mary Mann.
1863	Day care center opened in Philadelphia for mothers involved with Civil War effort.
1869	Milton Bradley, persuaded of kindergarten value by Elizabeth Peabody, published *Paradise of Childhood* to provide manual in English; began first large scale manufacture of children's educational materials based on gifts and occupations of Froebel.
1873	John Krause, friend of Froebel, and Maria Krause-Bolte, German trained, started New York Seminary with model kindergarten for teacher training. Among first pupils was Susan Blow, who began first public school kindergarten in St. Louis in fall of the year.
1876	One-fifth of all adults in country were said to have attended Philadelphia Centennial Exhibit, which had model kindergarten on display; spread Froebelian ideas to public.
1880	Four hundred known kindergartens in 30 states, plus several hundred "home" programs run by mothers using Froebelian methods and materials. (There were only 1200 high schools in the country that year.)
1882	Froebel Institute of North America, association of kindergarten educators from United States and Canada, organized in Detroit with William Hailmann and Elizabeth Peabody as leaders.
1884	National Education Association added Kindergarten Department, led by membership of Froebel Institute.
1889	Legislature of Indiana enacted law enabling school boards to include kindergartens in the public schools.
1891	Chicago school board voted to adopt all kindergarten classes of local Froebel Association, which had developed since 1873.
1892	International Kindergarten Union formed by group of women who felt men in NEA didn't appreciate value of kindergarten education. Kindergarten Directory listed 1,429 "approved kindergartens" and 204 books dealing with teaching of young children.
1895	G. Stanley Hall, Clark University president and early advocate of child study, offered summer program for kindergarten teachers. Of 35 who began, 33 left because he criticized the way they interpreted Froebel. Remaining two, Ann E. Bryan of Chicago and Patty Smith Hill of Louisville, became crusaders for progressive movement which stressed free play and individualization, which they saw as the true Froebelian philosophy.
1906	John Dewey established laboratory school, University of Chicago, with sub-primary class of four and five year olds; emphasis upon social interaction, with retention of Froebel's kindergarten ideas.
1907	Dr. Maria Montessori opened Casa dei Bambini in San Lorenzo area of Rome; was soon visited by U.S. educators.

TABLE 1.2. Significant Events in Early Childhood Education in the United States (*continued*)

1909	Americans interested in new "nursery school" established in London by MacMillan sisters; emphasis upon physical well being, emotional development.
1912	Children's Bureau opened to coordinate federal work with families.
1915	First parent participation school developed as Chicago Cooperative Nursery School; University of Chicago location with Froebelian Alice Temple as faculty advisor.
1920	There were three nursery schools in the U.S., but about 25 percent of the nation's four to six year olds were enrolled in kindergartens, some in all day programs. Child guidance movement began to catch public interest.
1925	Most of country's 25 nursery schools established as child study centers. Term "pre-school" introduced by Gesell in winter issue of *Progressive Education*.
1929	National Committee on Nursery Schools formally organized as National Association for Nursery Education; publication of "Minimum Essentials for Nursery School Education" established basic standards for providing a learning environment through play.
1930	International Kindergarten Union and National Council of Primary Education merged to become Association for Childhood Education (now ACEI), with focus on children aged two to eight.
1931	Almost 300 known nursery schools in operation; many kindergartens in public schools closed or restricted to five year olds because of depression after 1929 economic crash.
1933	Authorization of "WPA" nursery schools under Administrator of Federal Emergency Relief Administration; primary purpose was employment of adults, but within a year about 75,000 children were enrolled in 1,900 programs administered by public schools.
1942	Last WPA nursery schools closed. Approximately 965 preschool programs remained under other auspices. About half of nation's five year olds in public kindergarten, fewer than in 1930.
1943	First funds appropriated for WWII child care, later named for Lanham Act legislation; attempt made to coordinate plans of educational, welfare, and health services to cope with problems presented by mothers going into war-related industries, with administration through public schools.
1946	With war over, mothers expected to return to home duties; Lanham Act schools turned over to state control or closed. Parent participation nursery schools began to thrive.
1954	*Brown* vs *Board of Education*. The Supreme Court ruled unanimously that racial segregation in public schools was a denial of equality of educational opportunity.
1958	National Defense Act creates scholarships, grants, and loans to improve teaching in science and mathematics.
1964	B.S. Bloom's research showing importance of intellectual stimulation during first six years of life was one impetus for increased interest in preschools. Of estimated 12.5 million three to five year olds in population, 25 percent were in preschool programs; only 4.3 percent of three year olds and 14.9 percent of four year olds, with balance in kindergarten. NANA renamed National Association for the Education of Young Children (NAEYC) and journal, *Young Children*, began.
1965	Project Head Start originated as a multidisciplinary program for children of low-income families, with 561 thousand in hastily designed summer session.

TABLE 1.2.   Significant Events in Early Childhood Education in the United States (*continued*)

1968	Project Follow-Through continued Head Start with 10 initial educational models for preschool through third grade. Number later expanded to 20.
1969	Office of Child Development created with Federal Department of Health, Education and Welfare; given responsibility for Head Start and Project Follow-Through.
1970	"Sesame Street" TV program funded as two year experiment.
1971	Comprehensive Child Care legislation passed Congress but vetoed by President Nixon.
1973	Of estimated 10.3 million three to five year olds in population, 41 percent are in preschool, including 14.5 percent of those aged three, 34.2 percent of four year olds. Almost 2 and a half million children under three had mothers employed outside the home.
1975	Public Law 94–142 passed to require education for all handicapped children ages 3 through 18 by the public schools.
1977	Office of Child Development placed with other services in new Administration for Children, Youth, and Families. Consortium on Developmental Continuity established to evaluate the long-term effects of early childhood programs designed in 1960s; publish *The Persistence of Preschool Effects*, which shows teenagers from special education less likely to be retained in current grade level and more likely to express positive attitudes about education.
1980	Fifty-three percent of mothers with children under six are working. Of the 7.5 million children this represents, 29 percent are taken care of in their own home, with 19 percent of these being taken care of by their father and mother on staggered schedules, 47 percent are taken care of in someone else's home, and some 20,000 of the 3 to 6 year olds are being left unattended as "latchkey" children. Only 15 percent are in child care institutions including Head Start programs, day care centers, and nursery school; 7 percent of these centers are run by government agencies. White-collar families in the suburbs are disproportionate consumers of day care. Predicted figures of 10.4 million children under six with working mothers needing care by 1990.
1982	Birth rate increased one half million since 1980; five million more school age children predicted by the end of century. Women are entering the work force at the rate of one million per year. Problems of day care and after school care are predicted as area of national concern.

Adapted from: Early Childhood Education: A Workbook for Administrators by Dorothy Hewes and Barbara Hartman (Palo Alto, CA: Research Assoc., 1979).

FIELD EXPLORATIONS

These exercises are designed to take you out into the world to find real examples that will illustrate and elucidate the material in this chapter.

1. Look in the yellow pages of the telephone book for nursery, preschool, and day care facilities. What information can you gather from the ads? From the names of the schools themselves? What age children do the

programs accept? Can you tell if they are socialization, cognitive, or behavior modification oriented? How many are there in your area? Make a table showing the information you gathered in this manner.

2. If there is a Montessori preschool in your area, call and see if you can arrange a visit. Try to stay for several hours and observe the activities and interactions. Write a two-page summary of your visit. Be sure to find out if the program is Italian Montessori—belongs to the international affiliate and follows their prescribed curriculum—or American Montessori—an offshoot that has modified the curriculum somewhat and is affiliated with the American Montessori Society.

3. Visit a parents' cooperative nursery, a Head Start facility, an infant/toddler program, or a university preschool or day care center. (The class may want to divide up the different possibilities available in your area.) Write a summary of your visit and bring it to class for discussion. A class chart of comparisons would be interesting.

References

Berrueta-Clement, J., Schweinhart, L. J., Barnett, W. S., Epstein, A. S., and Weikart, D. P. *Changed lives: The effects of the Perry preschool program on youths through age 19.* Ypsilanti, Mich.: High/Scope Press, 1984.

Bloom, B. S. *Stability and change in human characteristics.* New York: John Wiley & Sons, 1964.

Bowlby, J. *Maternal care and mental health.* World Health Organization Monograph Number 2. Geneva: World Health Organization, 1951.

Caldwell, B. M. "The rationale for early intervention." *Exceptional children,* 1970, 36, 717–26.

Casler, L. "Maternal deprivation: A critical review of the literature." *Monographs of the Society for Research in Child Development,* 1961, 26, 2.

Clarke-Stewart, A. and Fein, G. G. "Early childhood programs." In P. H. Mussen (Ed.), *Handbook of child psychology.* Fourth ed. (Vol. 2). New York: John Wiley & Sons, 1983.

Comenius, J. A. *The great didactic.* M. W. Keatinge, trans. London: Adams and Charles Black, 1896 (orig. publ. 1632).

Dewey, J. *Democracy and education.* New York, Macmillan, 1916.

Dewey, J. *The school and society.* Second ed. Chicago: University of Chicago Press, 1943.

Froebel, F. *The education of man.* W. N. Hailmann, trans. New York: D. Appleton, 1887.

Gordon, I. J. *Early childhood stimulation through parent education.* Final report to the Children's Bureau, Social and Rehabilitation Service, Department of Health, Education and Welfare, Gainesville, Florida, University of Florida, Institute for the Development of Human Resources, 1969, ED 038 166.

Hunt, J. McV. *Intelligence and experience.* New York: Ronald Press, 1961.

Kessen, W. *The child.* New York: John Wiley & Sons, 1965.

Montessori, M. *Dr. Montessori's own handbook.* Cambridge, Mass.: Robert Bentley, Inc. 1964.

Pestalozzi, H. *The education of man.* New York: Philosophical Library, 1951.

Plato. *Plato's dialogues.* R. E. Allen, trans. New Haven: Yale University Press, 1984.

Rousseau, J. J. *Emile or On education.* New York: Basic Books, 1979.

Skinner, B. F. *Science and human behavior.* New York: Macmillan, 1953.

Skinner, B. F. *The technology of teaching.* New York: Meredith, 1968.

Webster, L. and Schroeder, R. M. *Early childhood education: An overview.* Princeton: Princeton Book, 1979.

Chapter 2

DEVELOPMENT AND LEARNING

Objectives

After reading this chapter the student should be able to:

1. Discuss and illustrate, by example, the eight basic principles of human growth and development.
2. Compare and contrast the concepts of adequate physical and nutritional care with adequate emotional and psychological care.
3. Debate the educational ideas of Locke and Rousseau from the position of one of these two philosophies.
4. List several contributions to educational philosophy of each of the contemporary models of development: the maturational model, the psychodynamic model, the behaviorist model, and the organismic model.
5. State the basic principles and units of analysis of each of the four models of development discussed in this chapter.
6. Provide a statement for each of the educational models discussed in this chapter, including the socialization model, the behaviorist model, individuated instruction, and the cognitive-developmental model, regarding their views on:
   a. the nature of the child
   b. the goals of their programs
   c. the curriculum emphasis of each position
   d. the teaching styles appropriate to their programs

The phenomenon of human development is both a unique and complex achievement. As we observe each child grow, we bear witness to an amazing process, a restatement of a genetic plan that has proven basically true across countless generations of human beings. Yet this plan does not act alone; rather, children grow within settings and through interactions that enhance or restrict developmental opportunities and developmental outcomes. Who we are and what we will become are functions of that combination of genetic endowment and the role that both internal and external events play in the course of our lives.

In this chapter we discuss some basic principles of human growth and development. We then examine the writings of earlier theorists, particularly, the works of *Locke* and *Rousseau*, tracing how their ideas have served to influence and shape modern views of the developmental process. Finally, we extend these learnings to the development of *four* contemporary models of early childhood education.

BASIC PRINCIPLES OF HUMAN GROWTH AND DEVELOPMENT

Observations and study of the child have provided a variety of concepts that frame the developmental process. These represent basic principles that have become associated with the process of growing.

1. *Development is a function of phenotypic and genotypic expression.* Each child is born with a vast, unspecifiable, indeterminate potential to grow. As illustrated by the concept of *genotype*, the human organism, at each phase of its life, possesses the capacity for individuated/personalized growth and specific expressions of both unique and individual character. We may note, for example, that the physical appearance and characteristics that each of us assumes at different stages of our lives are phenotypically determined, and thereby predictable. We each grow taller (in most cases), older, and somewhat more clearly defined over time. Yet, the specific temper of physical expression, within this framework, for example, the grace of movement or ease of expression exhibited at each age, represents an indigenous (that is, inherent) capacity unique to the person. In children, therefore, we will observe common styles of behavioral expression, some of which are predictable, while others are specific to the child. Still others contribute to patterns of growth that unfold over time, each according to their unique pattern or program of expression. The phenotype expresses what is known and observable at the moment. The genotype represents what will come, or more accurately, the child's potential for becoming.

2. *Development is a function of interactive forces, most notably, of heredity and environment, and particularly, of maturation and learning.* The realization of specific behaviors, as well as the actualization of growth to its best potential, is a complex attainment. The child is neither a completely "free" (that is, internally programmed) nor an externally controllable being. Via the genotype, as a representative of its potential for growth, in conjunction with maturational (that is, biologically ordered) forces, the child demonstrates amazing competence toward achieving the realization of its hereditary potential. During the first five years of their lives, children will acquire more information and greater understanding of events that surround them faster than during any other period in their lives. Moreover, much of this learning will be self-initiated and spontaneous, representing indigenous activity and pursuit. However, growth, even under these circumstances cannot, and does not, occur in a vacuum. A child's immediate environment, as represented by the physical and nutritional milieu, opportunities for minimal levels of perceptual-cognitive stimulation, and the quality of person-to-person interactions—ranging from caretaking to complex social transactions—all play a critical role in providing the setting and actors critical to growth.

3. *Development is best assessed in terms of individual milestones and achievements, rather than through reference to chronological age.* Developmentally, children change as they pass from one period of life to the next. These changes occur over time. Yet time, used as a measure of developmental status (for example, age when children utter their first words, age when children achieve their first, unassisted steps, and

so on) does not offer us any information of how, why, or under what circumstances change occurs. Time merely records change. It provides us with a quick, easy reference to the appearance of change. It neither produces nor accounts for events responsible for change. We may note, for example, the grace of movement or speed evident in the cycling skills of the nine year old. These skills will surpass even those of the most sophisticated three-year-old tricylist. While we tend to report these differences by reference to age, they are more properly expressed as a function of level of development (that is, maturational status) and experiences that occur over time. This idea is important for several reasons. First, it draws our attention to the range of performances which may characterize any particular skill. In our observations and interactions with young children we must consider individual differences as a central characteristic of children's behavior. Second, by focusing on individual appraisal rather than group performance (that is, normative indices), we may account for extremes in development within, as well as across individuals and groups. Regarding the individual, this focus allows us to consider similarities and differences among children and, most critically, specialized patterns of growth marked by peaks and valleys that appear in each individual's developmental cycle.

4. *Development is a spontaneous process, facilitated, rather than controlled by experience.* Development is an observed consequence of opportunity. It is not a controlled product created through formal teachings or instructional formulas. Through the dual influence of maturational and environmental forces the child comes to experience herself through interactions with persons, events, and settings external to herself. These encounters, and those learnings derived from them, are both internally and externally motivated. The child acts upon his environment, determining, in part, the behavior of others, as well as reacting to his environment, wherein he is influenced by others. The quality of these interchanges, particularly in the young organism, might be characterized as a reflection of exploratory learning, involving curiosity, novelty seeking, and discovery. Correspondingly, in play and other spontaneously initiated activities, the child acts in tune with her emerging interests. Planned activities may be integrated into the child's established interests in ongoing activities. However, it is important to note that programmed learning among young children is secondary for the child and therefore needs to be carefully coordinated to fit within appropriate characteristics of his behavior.

5. *Development is facilitated through adequate physical and nutritional care.* The young child is not only an intellectual and emotional being, but also a physical/anatomical organism. Consequently, growth requires attention to physical, nutritional, and motor needs, as well as the more frequently cited behavioral needs. Deficiencies in health care,

diet, exercise, and nutritional intake must be addressed in themselves, as well as in terms of their consequences upon normal development. Among special-needs children, particularly, attention must be given to the unique requirements for growth posed by these children. Whether in the form of remedial services or specialized opportunities for learning, particular disabilities will influence what and how physical and motoric needs can be met.

6. *The growth and development of each child is an individual occurrence.* The process and outcome of growth stems from innumerable individual opportunities and experiences. Some of these produce learning which is universal to most children and is acquired in a similar fashion (such as, the acquisition of language), while some learning is unique to the individual child's circumstances and therefore contributes to different outcomes (such as, learning to communicate in one's native tongue). In both general and specific learning, the process of knowing and becoming is shaped *by* the child, her unique hereditary background and her individual experiences. Clearly, the principle of individual differences explains what is unique and special about each child. Why, for example, does one child learn quickly or more slowly over time? For which children is learning best facilitated through visual or auditory instruction? Why does a structured environment (for example, a cognitively-oriented curriculum) work for one child, while an unstructured setting (for example, an open classroom) appears to better enhance learning in another child?

For the adult, respect for individual differences is critical for knowing, caring, and teaching each child. Such information will help structure how we approach each child, and what techniques or methods of intervention are most likely to be effective.

7. *Development is facilitated through human interaction.* Relationships that occur within an atmosphere of positive self-regard and human support are central to the developmental process. Relationships with adults, especially primary caregivers, are critical to development. As Terkelsen (1980) observes, "If you give a living thing what it needs, it grows itself." That is, under conditions of appropriate care (need attainment), growing up is something that the organism does automatically. The heart of the matter is that need attainment is the mainspring of development. Despite our complexity, we human beings share this fundamental property with the rest of the living world. The task of caregivers, within the family and school, is to create a resource, in the form of interpersonal enactments, that matches or meets a need. When they perform this task, each member "grows up itself" (p. 32).

8. *The developmental process is sequential.* At various points we will examine the issue of whether development is best conceived of as an accumulated product subject to quantifiable analysis or a series of dis-

tinct, independent stages that are qualitatively different from each other. How we view development will affect our approach to young children—both our practices and the goals we set for the learner. Irrespective of the paths they suggest we follow, the theories that are proposed in the field of development are based on commonly validated observations.

ANTECEDENTS OF MODERN THEORY

The two roots of modern educational thought can be traced to the innovative, and antagonistic, ideas of *John Locke* (1632–1704) and *Jean-Jacques Rousseau* (1712–76). These two rather dissimilar men each independently sought a clearer vision of the natural capacities of the child and a method of instruction that could be applied to his "proper" education.

John Locke

Locke, writing in the latter part of the seventeenth century, was a physician who, although a lifelong bachelor himself, had many interactions with children and their parents, which prompted his interest in child rearing and early education. As these interests grew, Locke began to write of children in a systematic manner. He composed a series of ideas which influenced both the contemporary, emerging philosophy of his times and, most critically, the later work of modern psychological thought and educational practice. Here, for example, the origins of modern behavior theory may be found, as well as reference to observational learning, the nature of the child's curiosity, and a host of ideas that continue to address our interests.

Locke envisioned the child as a "tabula rasa" or blank slate. This novel idea was in contrast to the prevailing beliefs of the seventeenth century, which depicted the child as inherently evil. Nor did Locke view the child as inherently good, a more recent innovation. Locke, in freeing the child from the extreme philosophies that emphasized the child's demonic soul and need for salvation and, conversely, her romanticized (angelic) saintliness, proposed a truly unique doctrine. The child, as proposed by Locke, was a creation of his own experiences and training. Moreover, the process of creation was not capricious. Rather it was subject to the quality, orderliness, and rationality of the child's experiences and his exposure to others. In Locke's view each boy and girl bore the imprint and legacy of their unique opportunities and experiences.

For Locke, the child was initially unformed, neither a creature of the past nor of the future, but, rather, a contemporary being, capable of knowing and, most critically, of reasoning. Knowledge could be taught, particularly if taught properly, with understanding, and through guided tutelage. The child, according to Locke, was an eager learner; a passive-receptive knower, subject to the astute guardianship of his tutor. In contrast to his times, Locke disavowed the common practice of seventeenth century tutors that involved beating children to evoke compliance. Instead he advocated a "rational" approach to child management based upon knowledge of the child, especially understanding of the child's level of comprehension, before learning was attempted. He also believed in enhancing the child's sense of self-esteem, through reliance upon his reputation in the eyes of others (such as, peers) and by allowing the opportunity for reparation upon misconduct.

Among the varied and unique features of Locke's philosophy was the esteem in which he held the learner. He argued against rote learning, particularly of information or actions beyond the comprehension of the learner, suggesting instead the need to assess, previous to instruction, the child's capacity for knowing. In this regard he also advocated the necessity for knowing the "native Propensities, Prevalencies of Constitution" that characterized the learner. As an antecedent of present-day views, he recognized that for instruction to be effective, the tutor must solve "the problem of the match" (Hunt, 1960). That is, learning must be congruent with the learner's capability for knowing. Finally, and most commendably considering his times and the beliefs of the period, Locke encouraged children's inquiries. He wrote that, "Curiosity in children . . . is but an appetite after Knowledge; and therefore ought to be encouraged in them, not only as a good sign, but as the great Instrument Nature has provided, to remove that Ignorance they were born with; and which, without this busie Inquisitiveness, will make them dull and useless Creatures" (Kessen, 1965, p. 69). In practice, he argued that the child should be encouraged to question. Questions should be sought, not laughed at, and we need to commend, before others, the inquiring mind. Children's inquiries should not be given deceitful or elusive answers and above all, the tutor should encourage respect for inquiries into truth.

J. J. Rousseau

Approximately 70 years after the publication of Locke's thoughts on education, a new set of ideas appeared. In this work entitled *Emile*, or *On Education*, Jean-Jacques Rousseau proposed an alternative philosophy of childhood and education. Specifically, he wrote of another, different child, one which suggested a new view of childhood, as well as a radical, curiously unique, perspective of how the child was to be trained and educated.

Rousseau's work was derived from a different view of society, a view of an organized, institutionalized life that sacrificed human dignity in its treatment of people and led to the inevitable corruption of its young. This perspective is cited in the very first paragraph of *Emile*. As Rousseau writes, "Everything is good as it leaves the hands of the Author of things; everything degenerates in the hands of man. He forces one soil to nourish the products of another, one tree to bear the fruit of another. He mixes and confuses the climates, the elements, the seasons. He mutilates his dog, his horse, his slave. He turns everything upside down; he disfigures everything; he loves deformity, monsters. He wants nothing as nature made it, not even man; for him, man must be trained like a school horse; man must be fashioned in keeping with his fancy like a tree in his garden" (1979, p. 37).

In this context Rousseau saw methods of education as leading to the development of cruel and brutal adults. He observed that,

It is quite strange that since people first became involved with raising children, no instrument for guiding them has been imagined other than emulation, jealousy, envy, vanity, avidity, and vile fear—all the most dangerous passions, the quickest to ferment and the most appropriate to corrupt the soul, even before the body has been formed. With each lesson that one wants to put into their heads before its proper time, a vice is planted in the depth of their hearts. Senseless teachers think they work wonders when they make children wicked in order to teach them what goodness is. And then they solemnly tell us, "Such is man." Yes, such is the man you have made (ibid., pp. 91–92).

Rousseau viewed the child as being born pure, unspoiled, untainted. Consequently, he saw the role of the adult as one contributing to the support and maintenance of the child's inherent innocence and purity. In addressing this issue he observed that,

Although modesty is natural to the human species, naturally children have none. Modesty is born only with the knowledge of evil, and how could children, who do not and should not have this knowledge, have the sentiment which is its effect? To give them lessons in modesty and decency is to teach them that there are shameful and indecent things. It is to give them a secret desire to know these things. Sooner or later they succeed, and the first spark which touches the imagination inevitably accelerates the inflammation of the senses. Whoever blushes is already guilty. True innocence is ashamed of nothing (ibid., p. 217).

How then is the child to be taught? In a unique reformulation of this question Rousseau argued against the art, as well as the state of contemporary teaching. In place of standard instructional formulas, he envisioned a "natural plan," one in which he cautioned parents to observe nature and follow its dictates. For Rousseau saw childhood as a natural state, not a condition that adults were meant to improve upon or to finish. Rather, he viewed the learner as an *active explorer*, as an integral force in the developmental process, and as a competent discoverer who engages her environment according to her needs and interests.

The notion of the child as a natural explorer-philosopher not only placed the child in the center of the learning process but also redefined the role of the teacher. For example, we see this concern in Rousseau's caution to the adult,

> In the first place you should be well aware that it is rarely up to you to suggest to him what he ought to learn. It is up to him to desire it, to seek it, to find it. It is up to you to put it within his reach, skillfully to give birth to this desire and to furnish him with the means of satisfying it. It follows, therefore, that your questions should be infrequent but well chosen (ibid., p. 179).

The differences between Rousseau's philosophy and that of Locke were addressed by the former. Rousseau writes of his predecessor in *Emile*,

> To reason with children was Locke's great maxim. It is one in vogue today. Its success, however, does not appear to me such as to establish its reputation; and, as for me, I see nothing more stupid than these children who have been reasoned with so much. Of all the faculties of man, reason, which is, so to speak, only a composite of all the others, is the one that develops with the most difficulty and latest. And it is this one which they want to use in order to develop the first faculties. The masterpiece of a good education is to make a reasonable man, and they claim they raise a child by reason! This is to begin with the end, to want to make the product the instrument. If children understood reasons, they would not need to be raised. But by speaking to them from an early age a language which they do not understand, one accustoms them to show off with words, to control all that is said to them, to believe themselves as wise as their masters, to become disputatious and rebellious; and everything that is thought to be gotten from them out of reasonable motives is never obtained other than out of motives of covetousness or fear or vanity which are always preforce joined to the others (pp. 89–90).

Contrasting views of the child, as derived from the philosophies of Locke and Rousseau, are presented in Table 2.1.

TABLE 2.1.   Contrasting Views of the Child: Locke and Rousseau

	Locke	Rousseau
Nature of the child	Impulsive; asocial; capable of reason; responds to rational instruction, tutoring	Pure; unspoiled; responds to internal cues and external experiences
Nature of development	Gradual; cumulative; incremental-molecular	Discontinuous; stage determined; molar
Process of development	Environmentally determined by quality of experiences/ opportunity	Maturational-biologically controlled; internally regulated
Nature of learning	Passive-receptive	Active-exploratory
Role of reinforcement	To aid in acquisition (learning) and maintenance (control) of behavior	To monitor progress; as feedback/information
Developmental orientation	Attempt to identify and stress similarities among people	Attempt to identify unique qualities of the single person
Role of adult	Tutor	Guide
Teaching/ parenting strategies likely to be advocated	Structured; arranged setting; oriented interactions; behavior modification	Open; unstructured settings; verbal-cognitive approaches; parent-teacher effectiveness training
Contemporary perspectives	Behaviorist	Maturational; Organismic
Modern descendants	Watson, Skinner	Gesell, Piaget

CONTEMPORARY THEORIES OF DEVELOPMENT AND LEARNING

The legacy of Locke and Rousseau influences and continues to affect how we view, care for, and teach children. As indicated in Table 2.1, each philosophy has fostered ideas, later reformulated and expanded by modern descendants who have, in turn, created distinct contemporary perspectives that influence our practices. In this section we focus on four contemporary views of development and learning.

The Maturational Model

The maturational model of child growth is derived from the work of *Arnold Gesell* and his associates. These efforts, initiated by Gesell at Yale and continued later in the establishment of its Child Study Center, influence us even today.

Gesell, who was both a physician and a psychologist, sought to devise a natural philosophy of child care based upon the ordered developmental progression of natural, biologically controlled growth processes. Gesell and his coworkers sought to identify and describe the inherent features and characteristics of the growth process, which provide the orderly, sequential development of each human being. This process, referred to as *ontogeny*, was viewed by Gesell as not only biologically controlled but subject to the principles of evolution as well. Consequently, the order, sequence, and rate of biological development served as the primary sphere of Gesell's inquiries.

Gesell's work, which spanned a long and productive career, led to the discovery of a variety of important ideas and principles of devel-

opment. In addition, many of these ideas, which are still prominent today, were widely disseminated among parents and teachers, for Gesell was an involved scientist who attempted to address the specific concerns of the practitioner through both theory and guidance.

The basic principle of development advocated by Gesell was that *structure determines function*. This idea, derived from evolutionary theory, views behavior and learning as a consequence of established morphological (body) structures. These structures, in turn, are created through inherent principles controlling physical growth, which, in turn affect the child's readiness to act. Above all, the appearance of appropriate physical structure is assumed necessary in order for behavior to occur. One illustration of this idea is evident in the development of proper eating patterns. For example, in order for the young infant to properly chew solid food, teeth or dental structure must be present. Similarly, creeping, crawling, and walking appear, in ordered sequence, as a function of muscle and neural growth, which parallel the appearance of these behaviors. One of Gesell's most important contributions to our appreciation of growth, as well as our ability to gauge the appearance and form of various growth patterns, was his documentation of these and other growth sequences (that is, schedules of development). His survey, assessment, and publication of his research into physical growth provided important data concerning the establishment of norms on the order, sequence, and rate of development of children.

Although Gesell believed that structure dictated function, he advocated the idea that structure itself was controlled by the principle of maturation. He viewed the regularity and precision of growth as an inherently controlled, biologically ordered process, a maturing or maturational occurrence. From this principle, Gesell could refer to developmentally appropriate learning experiences in terms of the child's maturational readiness to know. Experiences that were too complex, too difficult, or beyond the child's capacity for mastery were viewed as maturationally inappropriate, in contrast to those events that were within the child's abilities. The significance of maturation, in Gesell's work, was to regulate and ensure growth (see Table 2.2).

Another important contribution of Gesell and his colleagues was the special attention they paid to the study and documentation of individual differences. In their varied studies, Gesell and his coworkers focused on four areas of human growth. These included motor behavior (that is, locomotion, coordination, and specific motor skills such as grasping), adaptive behavior (that is, alertness, intelligence, and exploration), language behavior (that is, speech and communication) and personal-social transactions (that is, social adaptations). In these studies Gesell and his colleagues repeatedly emphasized the integration of all

TABLE 2.2. Gesell's Principles of Human Growth

1. *The Principle of Developmental Direction.* Development follows a systematic, predictable sequence.
   a. *Cephalocaudal.* Development proceeds from head to toe, from neural to muscular development.
   b. *Proximal-distal.* Development proceeds from functions near (structurally closer) to the central nervous system to those further away (e.g., gross movement to fine hand coordination).
2. *The Principle of Reciprocal Interweaving.* Development proceeds from complementary or oppositional forces seeking balance (e.g., inhibition-excitation muscle action leading to coordination; flexor-extensor movement allowing for walking).
3. *The Principle of Functional Asymmetry.* Development, in contrast to the principle of reciprocal interweaving, will often incorporate periods of unbalanced or asymmetric function for select periods of time (e.g., tonic neck or fencer reflex).
4. *The Principle of Individuated Maturation.* Development follows a process of predetermined, sequential patterning.
5. *The Principle of Self-Regulatory Fluctuation.* Development fluctuates between periods of active-passive; stable-unstable; growing-consolidation phases.

four functions in appearance and purpose, suggesting that each child progresses at her own rate of development under the unerring influence of the maturational principle. Although the sequence of development is uniform across all children, the specific rate of appearance is unique.

Current educational programs that emphasize developmental readiness and assessment are outgrowths of Gesell's work.

The Psychodynamic Model

The psychodynamic model stems from the work of *Sigmund Freud*, his colleagues, and his followers. This body of writing incorporates a vast array of concerns, ranging from the normal to the disturbed, social structure and meaning, the affective-emotional domain of development, and the relations between childhood experience and adult development. It also encompasses the views of many theorists, most notably, for our interests, the writings of Anna Freud and Erik Erikson. Hence, in this section we limit our comments to the classical perspective of Sigmund Freud, particularly his observations of the developmental process, reserving consideration of the views of Anna Freud and Erik Erikson for later discussion.

Sigmund Freud's work represents, in its broadest perspective, a theory of affective-emotional development. For Freud, all facets of development, including behavior and thought were outcomes of the child's emotional life. Human development, for Freud, was the culmination of each child's efforts to resolve biologically controlled emotional needs. These needs, he believed, were essentially egocentric in nature, representing, in early life, a biologically adaptive process insuring the child's survival (such as the instinct to suck). For Freud, however, the existence of unregulated, oppressive need states or drives for gratification required adult intervention and moderation, because children had no self-controls. The nature of development, for Freud, was thereby inevitably marked by conflict and crisis. As the child matured, his needs grew, initially, from control of his self and his immediate environment, to control of others, particularly others instrumental to personal gratification and purpose. Society, correspondingly, first through the efforts of parents and later through the energies of the child's teachers, was charged with educating the child in self-control, moderation, and redirection of her needs.

Psychodynamic theory views the young infant as an instinctual organism driven by psychic energy (that is, the libido). This energy creates the fuel for activity that proceeds in a sequential, biologically ordered pattern. Channels, or outlets, in turn, control the focus of behavior displayed by the child and correspond roughly to a prearranged chronological sequence of appearance (that is, congruent with age-related experiences). This developmental sequence, for example, defines the area of primary child-adult interactions (for example, on feeding or oral activity; on elimination or anal activity; on body or sexual activity), as well as arenas of potential conflict. See Table 2.3. How the child approaches and resolves each crisis in development, relative to its caretaking (teaching) agent becomes critical for future development. Successful resolution of a given crisis frees the child to embark on the next stage of development. Unsuccessful resolution traps or fixates the child in an unresolved conflict and results in his exhibition of immature or unproductive behavior (for example, thumb sucking; ritualistic-inclusive behavior). In this regard, if failure is evident and overwhelming, then clinical symptoms may appear.

TABLE 2.3.   Psychodynamic Stages of Development

Stage	Behavior	Conflict
Oral	Feeding or oral activity	Sucking vs. biting
Anal	Elimination	Release vs. retention
Phallic	Sexual interest	Possession of others vs. acceptance of self
Latent	Sexual identification	Peer interaction vs. isolation
Genital	Sexual partnership	Love relationship vs. fixation

As the child moves from stage to stage, experiential feedback received through encounters with significant others leads to a structural transformation in the child's capacity to perceive his own and other's needs and to anticipate and resolve conflicts. Initially, the child is primarily *id*-oriented, that is, he is under the biologically controlled instinct to pursue gratification and avoid tension and pain. Yet as the child engages its environment it becomes aware of its effects upon others (for example, as the infant cries it observes that crying behavior produces changes in the behavior of others). This awareness transforms energy from the id to the infant's conscious awareness of self. This transformed energy, in turn, forms the *ego*, that is, the child's awareness of self as a separate being functioning within the realm of social and physical reality. The principles that govern such interactions (for example, falling down leads to pain; touching the stove may lead to being burned) become gradually conscious. As interactions with others increase a second transformation occurs. This change is furthered by the continuing, increasingly sophisticated differentiation of the self from others. This process leads to the formation of the *superego.*

The superego, or third structural component of the child's personality, is governed by the growing influence of significant others. Initially, the superego includes the child's parents and immediate family. Subsequently, it comes to incorporate the wider social and ethical standards of the child's culture, especially as defined by extrafamilial others such as teachers and peers. From a variety of exchanges involving these important figures, the child's behavior takes on an ethical coloration: wants become subordinate to needs, motives become subject to objective appraisal, actions become viewed in terms of their consequences. In this process two governing principles emerge. These include the *ego-ideal* and the *conscience.* The ego-ideal represents the values and judgments of parents, which the child comes to internalize as her own. Consequently, the child begins to define behavior as "good," worthy of reward, and, over time, as exemplary (for example, I *should, ought, must* ... do, be, act, etc.). This moral valuation of behavior, however, does not stand alone. That is, as the child inevitably fails at times to meet parental expectations, a second subunit of the superego emerges, a conscience. Through his conscience the child's failure to meet expectations and standards is experienced internally. Punishment is self-administered and experienced in the form of guilt. Thereafter, anticipated guilt (such as, "If I take this cookie without asking permission, I will feel bad. . . . ") forestalls or redirects the child's behavior.

The distinctions among id, ego, and superego are summarized in Table 2.4.

In the healthy personality, the development and composition of id,

TABLE 2.4.   Id, Ego, and Superego Distinctions

Id	Ego	Superego
Biological origin	Psychosocial origin	Cultural origin
Need-oriented	Person-oriented	Group-oriented
Hedonistic perspective	Factual perspective	Moralistic perspective
Subjective orientation	Reality orientation	Idealized orientation
Primitive behavioral repertoire	Integrated behavioral repertoire	Exemplary behavioral repertoire
Cognitive immaturity	Cognitive maturity	Cognitive idealization
Absence of social regard	Presence of social regard	Enhanced social regard
Absence of developmental horizons	Adequate developmental horizons	Limited developmental horizons

ego, and superego is balanced and integrated. The child comes to trust that its needs (that is, id propensities) will be met on time and relative to available resources (that is, ego properties) through the caring of responsible adults (that is, superego properties).

The inclusion of school psychologists in the schools and the use of play therapy programs stem from Freudian concepts.

The Behaviorist Model

The behaviorist model refers to a collection of differing approaches to the study of children, each of which commonly focuses on activity (that is, behavior) as the central unit of analysis. These views share a number of common assumptions about the nature of experience and the ways in which the child integrates her encounters with others in the course of development.

The legacy of behavior theory begins with the observations of Locke, who (as we have seen) saw the child as a tabula rasa and stressed the importance of rich environmental encounters, structured learning opportunities, and teacher-directed learnings.

In behavior theory, development is viewed as a consequence of learning, that is, development is a product of learning. Accordingly, in behaviorist tradition, development is the culmination, or result, of the child's experiential encounters, not a process or mediator of growth. Here, as in Locke's theory, the quality of the environment and the diversity of the learning opportunities it offers create many or few occasions for growth.

The rich and varied contributions of many researchers, most notably

Pavlov, Thorndike, Watson, Skinner, Bijou and Baer, and Bandura, now span almost a century of inquiry. From these theorists, and the work of countless others, we have recognized a second characteristic of the behaviorist model, specifically, that development may result from different kinds of learning. Learning may involve conditioning in both classical (Pavlov) and operant (Skinner) models of knowing, as well as trial and error learning (Thorndike), associate learning, such as, stimulus-response learning (Watson), and observational learning (Bandura).

The nature of development as proposed by the behaviorist model stresses the role of the child as a receptive rather than as an active learner. The behaviorist model focuses on the ways in which experiences shape or mold the child rather than on how the child structures the environment to his own level of understanding. This emphasis places considerable importance on the quality of environmental training and the role of structured learning in the developmental process. Here development results from a structured approach in which the organization of existing behaviors is crucial in the progression from simple to complex behavior. In its most basic form the behaviorist approach may be seen as a building process in which a structural foundation of primitive experiences is organized into blocks. These units, in turn, support new experiences, as well as variations in the reorganization of past experience in the light of new learnings. The process of learning is *gradual*, *additive*, and *cumulative*. New learning takes place beside older learning, some of which replaces less functional or less adaptive behaviors, whereas other learning supports existing behaviors. For example, when an infant acquires teeth, a series of new behaviors, including biting and chewing, is added to an existing repertoire of mouthing, sucking, and licking.

The role of the teacher in the behaviorist model, following Locke, is directive. Locke viewed the teacher as an enlightened tutor, serving a focused and specific task, that is, to teach. Hence, behaviorally inspired curriculum is *teacher-centered*, *goal-oriented*, and *process-specific*. In this model, specific, curriculum-designed lesson plans, behavioral objectives, and temporally spaced, teacher-defined activities often characterize learning. In addition, learnings are blocked, with emphasis placed on gradual acquisitions and continuity between new and old information.

Table 2.5 summarizes the principles and characteristics of the behavioral models.

Educational programs that are teacher directed and use concepts of "motivating" the learner to build interest are derived from these concepts.

TABLE 2.5.   Principles and Characteristics of Behavioral Models

1.   The central unit of development is behavior: its acquisition and maintenance.
2.   Development is a result of learning.
3.   Developmental learning is a function of different kinds of learning, including classical conditioning, operant conditioning, trial and error learning, associative learning (S-R learning), and observational learning (modeling).
4.   Reinforcement creates and perpetuates learning outcomes.
5.   Individual differences/outcomes in development are primarily a function of past history and experience.
6.   Biological factors set the stage for development, while environmental factors create opportunities for development.
7.   Development follows a gradual process built upon existing behavior.
8.   Development follows a gradual, continuous, cumulative process characterized by small gains or changes in the organization of existing or established behavior patterns.

The Organismic (Cognitive-Developmental) Model

The organismic model derives from the work of *Heinz Werner* (1948), and most notably, *Jean Piaget* (1950, 1957, 1963). This approach to understanding development emphasizes the role of knowing in the child's organization of experience. How children come to know their environment, including how they are able to organize and structure experience; how they transform knowledge; and finally, how they develop from concrete to abstract levels of understanding are the central questions of interest in this model.

The organismic (that is, cognitive-developmental) model, in significant measure, represents a contemporary extension of the theories and ideas of J. J. Rousseau. Specifically, Rousseau's view of the nature of the child and the processes underlying developing, as well as the child's role in the developmental enterprise clearly serve as a foundation for cognitive-developmental theory.

Piaget viewed the child, particularly, the process of "knowing" (that is, how he comes to know), which engages the child from birth to approximately 15 years of age, as an encompassing, complex, developmental experience. He termed this process, wherein understanding unfolds over time as a genetic epistemological (that is, developmentally progressive) event, which changes the course of human experience and, hence, human development, from a simple to a complex character.

The nature of development, as conceived by Piaget, was founded in part, upon a series of observations and experimental occurrences that involved naturalistic observations of his own children, as well as more formal testing of other children. These unique studies, which began in the 1920s, employed a clinical-interview approach to child interactions. In these interviews the child is given a problem task and then asked to explain his solutions. The child, in turn, reveals her understanding of the particular principle used in arriving at a solution through application of laws that govern physical properties and their appearance (for example, do two identical balls of clay remain the same when one is rolled into a long cylindrical shape?). From his observations and the recorded responses given by children of different ages, Piaget noted that children's perceptions of events, and especially their conception (such as, understanding of physical laws) differed across ages. These important observations led Piaget to view the cognitive-developmental process as being discontinuous (that is, uneven), suggesting that each child passed through four major stages of cognitive growth from early infancy to adolescence. These stages are summarized in Table 2.6.

The process of development that Piaget describes falls in part under biological control. Like Gesell, he noted the importance of an internally regulated maturational process that underlies growth. Yet, he also saw the process as being more complex depending, in large part, upon environmental opportunity and experiences, including those critical social transmissions that make up a third facet of the process. Although the potential for action is biologically mandated, the actual enactment of an idea is subject to opportunity, experience, and rehearsal. As Piaget noted, "Intelligence constitutes an organizing activity whose functioning extends that of the biological organization, while surpassing it due to the elaboration of new structures" (1963, p. 407). Moreover, he adds, "The structures are not preformed within the subject but are constructed gradually as needs and situations occur" (ibid, p. 416).

The role of the child in cognitive-developmental theory differs significantly from the behavioral model that we have just reviewed. Piaget depicts an active-exploratory child as opposed to a passive-receptive child. In Piaget's theory knowledge is acquired through activity. First, through direct motor activity (characteristic of the sensory motor stage of development), the infant actively explores and manipulates his environment. Later, through symbols such as language, the preoperational child (two to seven year old) classifies, then categorizes information. Subsequently, the concrete operational child (eight to eleven year old) learns to perform simple concrete (that is, observable) operations upon physical objects. And still later, through abstract reasoning, the formal operational child (twelve to fifteen year old) employs logical thought and solves problems through inductive reasoning. Underlying each of these achievements are two adaptive processes, *assimilation* and *accommodation*. Assimilation refers to experiences and activities that are directly learned by the child. Such information resembles previous

TABLE 2.6.   Piaget's Stages of Intellectual Development

Stage	Approximate Age	Characteristics
I. Sensorimotor	0–2 Years	Intelligence based on perceptual experiences
1. Reflexive	0–1 Month	Reflexes become more efficient, lack of differentiation
2. Primary circular reactions	1–4 Months	Repetition of certain pleasureable behaviors and the formation of habits; coordination of reflexes
3. Secondary circular reactions	4–10 Months	Intentional repetition of events discovered through chance, notion of cause and effect
4. Coordination of secondary schemes	10–12 Months	Application of old schemes to new situations; first clear signs of intelligence; instrumental activity
5. Tertiary circular reactions	12–18 Months	Discovery of new means of repetition with variation for novelty's sake; object permanence; experimentation on cause and effect situations; hypothesis testing
6. Symbolic representation	18–24 Months	Internalizes actions and begins to think before acting; represents objects and images through imagery; invention of new ideas
II. Preoperational	2–7 Years	Onset of sophisticated language system; egocentric reasoning; thinking is perception bound
III. Concrete Operational	7–10 Years	Thought is reversible, and ability to solve concrete problems develops; conservation becomes operative; logical operations develop; thinking is experience based

TABLE 2.6.   Piaget's Stages of Intellectual Development (*continued*)

Stage	Approximate Age	Characteristics
IV. Formal Operational	11 Years to Adulthood	Formulation and testing of hypotheses; abstract thought; deductive reasoning; hypothetico-deductive reasoning; thought no longer perception bound.

learnings, serving to enlarge the child's repertoire, but not leading to any qualitative changes in understanding. For example, the preoperational child may classify all four-legged animals by referring to them as "doggie." Activities illustrating assimilative processing are typically repetitive or redundant (for example, the infant who places all new objects into her mouth; the toddler who repeats sounds). The complement of assimilation is accommodation. In accommodation the child modifies and restructures existing information in order to respond to

INSET 2.1   Piaget on Assimilation and Accommodation.

Intelligence is *assimilation* to the extent that it incorporates all the given data of experience within its framework. Whether it is a question of thought which, due to judgment, brings the new into the known and reduces the universe to its own terms or whether it is a question of sensorimotor intelligence which also structures things perceived by bringing them into its schemata, in every case intellectual adaption involves an element of assimilation, that is to say, of structuring through incorporation of external reality into forms due to the subject's activity. . . . (1963, p. 6)

There can be no doubt either, that mental life is also *accommodation* to the environment. Assimilation can never be pure because by incorporating new elements into its earlier schemata, the intelligence constantly modifies the latter in order to adjust them to new elements. Conversely, things are never known by themselves, since this work of accommodation is only possible as a function of the inverse process of assimilation. We shall thus see how the very concept of the object is far from being innate and necessitates a construction which is simultaneously assimilatory and accommodating. . . . (1963, pp. 6–7).

new data. In essence, a qualitative change or alteration is made that enables the child to process new material in a "revolutionary" manner. In terms of the illustration above, for example, the preoperational child will shift his attempts at classification of animals in terms of "legged-ness" to, perhaps, sound, thereby noting that dogs make a distinct bark, whereas cows and horses do not. (Note that the child has already "learned" sounds through rehearsal, as a toddler.) Similarly, the sensorimotor infant will shake a rattle, thereby enlarging her capacity for classifying objects from taste exclusively to include sound, as well.

Adults are a child's most important resource.

The implications of Piaget's theory for teaching, of young children especially, are multiple. Some applications have embraced Rousseau's recommendations that the adult serve as guide to the child, allowing for child-centered learning with limited teacher intervention. Other recommendations have incorporated cognitively based curriculum models in which set and selected learning experiences are offered, which conform to the stage levels of learning. In our final section of this chapter we will explore the relationship between these theories and modern educational practice.

CONTEMPORARY MODELS OF EARLY CHILDHOOD EDUCATION: FROM THEORY TO PRACTICE

We initiated this chapter by listing contemporary principles of human growth and development. We then discussed the antecedents of these ideas in terms of the philosophies of Locke and Rousseau. Finally, we examined some contemporary theories of children's development and learning. We now turn our attention to contemporary models of early childhood education, specifically, *the socialization model, the behavioral model, the individualized instructional model*, and *the cognitive-developmental model* of instruction.

Each of the four programs that we have selected for discussion is founded upon the philosophies and theories we have reviewed. Two of these, the behavioral and cognitive-developmental models, respectively, are clearly direct descendants of Locke and Rousseau, with easily identifiable roots. The socialization and individuated programs, in contrast, share common origins with the philosophies of Locke and Rousseau, but offer transformations, reflecting the ideas pursued by maturational theorists such as Gesell and psychodynamic theorists such as Anna Freud and Erik Erikson. These four programs represent unique views of the child, differing programmatic emphases, and distinctions in curriculum and teaching styles. See Table 2.7.

The Socialization Model of Education

The socialization model views development and therefore learning as a function of biological-experiential interchanges. In this model, growth follows maturational principles that define and delimit the course of development. As the child matures structurally, physiological changes allow for new behavioral acquisitions and adaptations. In essence, the key to development is maturation, which prepares or readies the child to engage in biologically appropriate behavioral acquisitions. By view-

TABLE 2.7. Models of Early Childhood Education

	View of Child	Goals of Program	Curriculum	Teacher Style
Socialization	Natural unfolding of biologically tied "skills." Learning readiness flows from maturation	Peer interaction and maximum opportunity to practice social emerging skills.	Cooperation and exploration. Dramatic play, physical and emotional expression, and wide diversity of experience.	Guidance and problem solving with children. Warmth and encouragement in style.
Behavioral	Passive-receptive view of child. Learns through reinforcement of discrete units of information	Learning of academic and social skills necessary for school classroom functioning. Achievement of specific learning goals.	Language, mathematics, and early reading content with emphasis on a predetermined structured curriculum.	Directed teaching and reinforcement of responses. Enthusiasm and firmness in style.
Individualized	Individual differences in style, temperament, and experience lead to wide differences in rate of learning approach.	Learning of social and academic skills as appropriate to individual learner. Pace of learning adapted to individual	Language experience based learning with attention to production of child-generated "books" and enhancement of individual competence at level of each child.	Facilitator of experiences rich in language-expression potential. Patient and inventive in style.

| Cognitive Developmental Open Classroom (Cognitive Curriculum) | Naturally curious and innately motivated to learn. Learning occurs from interaction between learner and objects/people in environment. | Interactive learning to facilitate growth of cognitive structures. Social and academic learnings appropriate to stage. | Group and individual concrete learning experiences emphasizing planning, doing, and reporting. Special attention to seriation, classification, and temporal relationships. | Assessing cognitive functioning of child. Arranging environment to provide optimal cognitive discrepancies. Questioning to encourage child thinking. Aware and challenging style. |

ing growth as a "natural" process, interactions within the environment are seen as providing the backdrop for the practice of emerging skills. Hence, a toddler may be encouraged to play with various, multisized containers in order to acquire sorting skills.

A central feature of the socialization model is to encourage the development of children's prosocial skills (such as, cooperation, sharing, helping behaviors). These behavioral acquisitions, which represent interpersonal competencies, are viewed as important social adaptations. However, in this model social skills are not taught directly. Rather, each child is encouraged through largely self-initiated peer interactions to acquire and practice behaviors that reflect appropriate social interchange. Hence, peer interactions are not only critical for the acquisition of social skills but are mandatory for their practice as well.

The central vehicle for learning in the socialization model is play, both individually performed and group initiated. Play, as advanced in this model, offers the child important opportunities for learning through exploration and discovery, two critical antecedents of curriculum-based learning. In addition, play is seen as providing each child opportunities for emotional development, for becoming aware of his feelings and learning to accept them, and for acquiring behaviors acceptable to others in the expression of feelings.

The dual impact of maturationally based growth and nonevaluative experiential learning suggests a child-centered curriculum with emphasis on opportunities for active, creative, experientially based learning. Correspondingly, the atmosphere and role(s) played by adults in the socialization model encourage child-initiated learnings. Adults guide learning, acting as a resource to children's inquiries, and, most critically, serving as a source of emotional support and encouragement (see Table 2.8).

The Behavioral Educational Model

The behavioral model views development as a function of experience. In this model growth follows environmental opportunities, which lead to the acquisition of distinct behaviors and their maintenance over time. Although structural changes are acknowledged, the focus of concern is upon behavior—its acquisition, its maintenance, and, where appropriate, its modification.

The behavioral model views the child as an eager, receptive learner who will be "motivated" by the teacher to learn school-related skills. Hence, the classroom forms an active, *guided* setting for children's learning. Classroom processes are both formal and teacher-orchestrated. In this model, learning objectives are clearly specified with short- and long-term goals well established and under teacher direc-

TABLE 2.8.   Characteristics and Guidelines for a Socialization Instructional Program

1. Growth is a function of biological/experiential interchanges.
2. Growth follows maturational (i.e, biologically ordered) principles wherein structural development preceeds functional development.
3. Readiness determines when learning/development will occur.
4. Practice enhances proficiency in the performance of emerging skills.
5. Peer interactions are critical for the acquisition and practice of social skills.
6. Exploration and curiosity are important antecedents of curriculum-based learning.
7. Play is a central vehicle of emotional expression for affective development and learning.
8. The early "curriculum" should offer the child multiple opportunities for experientially-based learning.
9. Adults should guide and serve as a resource to children's learning.
10. The teacher is a source of emotional support and encouragement of children's exploration.

tion. Stated objectives usually reflect academic skills, and/or other appropriate classroom behaviors (for example, sitting in one's seat, raising one's hand in response to the teacher's inquiries, and so on). In this model, a business-like atmosphere, with well-delineated goals, permeates children's learnings.

Learning derived from the behavioral model follows a *step-by-step process of guided instruction.* Specifically, the behavioral model sees learning as an analytic (that is, part-oriented) undertaking, in which complex ideas may be best taught by being broken down into smaller, finer units of information or skills. Programmed learning materials, which provide carefully sequenced concepts, may be used in this type of curriculum.

As part of its predetermined, structured curriculum, the behaviorally oriented classroom places strong emphasis on formal skills acquisition; children are taught preparatory language and mathematical concepts, as well as social skills necessary for later academic success. In the behavioral model, desired learning outcomes are not only specified beforehand, but follow (that is, are produced by) well-established processes under teacher control. These appear in the form of reinforcement principles. See Table 2.9.

According to behavior theory, from which this model is derived, most human behavior, both desirable and undesirable, is learned. Moreover, behaviors are acquired and maintained, or changed, as a function of the responses that such behaviors elicit from others. Behaviors that provoke positive responses are strengthened, while behaviors that stimulate negative, especially apathetic, responses are eliminated.

TABLE 2.9.　The Behavioral Model: Principles of Children's Learning

1. Most human behavior is learned. Children learn both desirable and undesirable behavior in the same way.
2. We keep doing things that are followed by good consequences or good feelings (rewards).
3. We stop doing things that are followed by bad consequences, bad feelings, or no rewards.
4. Because each person is unique, rewards must also be unique, i.e., "tailor-made" to fit each individual.
5. We all like material rewards such as money, food, or toys. However, it is social rewards, such as attention, praise, and affection that really make us feel good about ourselves.
6. Attention is one of the most powerful social rewards, for both desirable and undesirable behavior. Even scolding a child is paying attention and may be rewarding (especially, in the absence of other rewards).
7. Much of our behavior is learned by imitating the people around us, particularly, high status people like parents and teachers.
8. Adults do not have to worry about giving "too much" love and affection to children. The way to "spoil" a child is to reward undesirable behavior.
9. One way to eliminate undesirable behavior is to consistently and permanently ignore it, never reward it, or attend to it.
10. Punishment is a way of stopping an undesirable behavior that simply cannot be ignored. If punishment is to be used, it must be clearly related to the behavior given, immediately administered, be of low to moderate intensity, and certain to occur.
11. Parents and teachers should have a "positive focus," actively looking for good behavior in their children and rewarding it.
12. Learning a new behavior is a step-by-step process. Generally, the smaller the steps, the easier the learning.
13. It is important that teacher approval or disapproval of behavior be consistent and made clear to the child.

Adapted from: Surviving with Kids by W. R. Bartz and R. B. Rasor (New York: Ballantine Books, 1980).

Consequently, the preschool child who has garnered teacher attention through tantrum-like behaviors (for example, crying, yelling) may be helped to acquire more socially appropriate behaviors (for example, asking, requesting, verbalizing needs) by the attentive adult who ceases to respond to inappropriate attention-getting behaviors and selectively attends to more socially appropriate and desirable behaviors.

Individualized Instruction in Education

The individualized instructional model views development through the intricacies and nuances of individual differences. Using biologically based distinctions as its starting point, this model seeks to address the process of growth and development and, correspondingly, the role of educational experience, for each child as a unique and individual occurrence.

In the individualized instructional model, development and learning are initially separate events. Specifically, early appearing, identifiable, individual differences (such as, temperamental distinctions; preferred learning modalities; differences in cognitive tempo and/or style) serve to define each child and set the stage for learning. As these characteristics are identified they are interrelated with appropriate experientially based learning opportunities. Through its focus upon and respect for individual differences, the learning environment comes to play a specific role, that is, to create and secure an appropriate "match" between the individual, in terms of her unique dispositional attributes and characteristics and the form and quality of educational experience best suited to enhance her growth.

In creating an effective learning environment, one in which the individual learner may achieve maximum gain, proponents of this approach view *the child as an integral component in the control of his rate of learning.* In part, this orientation follows the stress placed upon individual differences. In addition, it reflects the idea that achievements in learning are best acknowledged in terms of personal attainments.

The curriculum emphasis of individualized instruction is often linguistically based. Hence, language via communication and written models of expression is stressed. The children are encouraged to verbalize their experiences among peers and adults and to report them in written form as well. Both standard language and creative variations of language, incorporating unique and personalized modes of expression are explored.

The adult plays an indirect, less centralized, role in individualized instruction. Because learning is perceived as best accomplished within a "child-centered" curriculum, the adult plays a patient, somewhat responsive, frequently inventive, role. She is required to "facilitate" growth, especially through communication expression and, above all, to help create the unique learning opportunities special to each child. By integrating her knowledge of individual differences within a curriculum designed to stimulate specific performances, the teacher serves as the fulcrum of individually-based learning outcomes. Guidelines for an individualized instructional program are presented in Table 2.10.

The Cognitive-Developmental Model of Education: A Dual Legacy

The cognitive-developmental model, as its title suggests, is a developmental perspective that views growth as an adaptive, intellectual enterprise. This approach, which stems from the large body of research and

TABLE 2.10.　Guidelines for an Individuated Instructional Program

1. Effective teaching follows an awareness of individual uniqueness and differences.
2. Recognition of temperamental distinctions among children is most critical.
3. Recognition of differences in rate, style, and form of learning among children forms the basis for effective instruction.
4. Good teaching requires careful definition and response to the varied sensory modalities (i.e., auditory, visual, tactile, etc.) responsible for individual differences in learning among children.
5. In learning/development the child is best suited to control her or his rate of learning.
6. The adult "frames" learning goals for each child.
7. A principal goal of individuated instruction is to stress individual achievements.
8. Learning is best fostered through encouraging communication and language-based programming.
9. Learning is best accomplished with a "child-centered" curriculum.
10. The teacher "facilitates," via language/communication expression, learning opportunities for each child.

writing of Piaget and his colleagues, effectively combines three sets of ideas (that is, action-purpose; competence of performance; and stage transition). The first, derived from Rousseau, sees the child as an active and adaptive organism. The second, supported by contemporary research findings, is founded upon increased knowledge of the intellectual processes and behavioral competence of infants and children. Finally, this model views the process of development as occurring across stage-like epochs, wherein the nature of thought itself is changed over time.

Adaptations of the cognitive-developmental model to early childhood educational practices have proven both fruitful and challenging. This model's view of the child as an inquisitive and curious learner partly affirms established observations attesting to the importance of early experiences surrounding the child's growth and development. In addition, its support of both the infant and child as able learners explains, in part, the extensive learnings that typify this period of life.

The cognitive-developmental model views the child as being inherently curious and, thereby, innately motivated to learn. Knowing, however, is not simply viewed as an inherited disposition or maturational occurrence with predictable and inevitable consequences. Rather, *learning is seen as a product of active inquiry, reflecting the intimate interactions associated with the child's exploratory activity and the products of her discoveries.* Moreover, a rich milieu, reflecting multivaried opportunities to interact with people and objects in diverse settings is viewed as a necessary component for stimulating inquiry.

Two forms of childrens' programs have emerged, which incorporate cognitive-developmental principles. The first is the *open classroom*, where space and learning opportunities are specifically planned to encourage exploration and discovery learnings. Such programs, as reflected by the British Infant School, are loosely structured and are designed to facilitate curiosity and active participation by the children. Here, teachers are aware of each child's level of cognitive functioning, engage in continuous assessment of the child's progress, and create, through rearrangement of the environment, new opportunities for growth. In *the cognitive curriculum* (Weikart), materials and opportunities are more formally structured with emphasis placed on acquiring social and academic skills considered appropriate to the child's stage of development. Children, for example, are provided with opportunities to engage in seriation tasks (that is, linear ordering of objects from smallest to largest), to practice emerging classification skills, and to arrange temporal relationships. These learnings are facilitated by teachers who arrange materials that encourage more organized explorations and problem solving; children are encouraged to define, organize, carry through, and report their learnings, while watchful teachers question these guided inquiries.

Table 2.11 summarizes some aspects of the cognitive-developmental model.

SUMMARY

As we have seen, there is a direct relationship between our early theories of development, especially those of Locke and Rousseau, and contemporary theories and practices. Locke provides a model for the behavioristic view of development, which views development as the culmination of experience. Rousseau provides us a foundation for the organismic model of development, as well as maturational theory, both of which see development as a biological, unfolding process. Psychodynamic theory, although less directly influenced by these specific antecedents, still follows a biological maturation approach related to emotional development.

Contemporary theories of child development also influence educational practice. Programmed learning, teacher structured curriculum, and motivation and reinforcement are important components of many educational programs, especially those that subscribe to behavioral theory. Programs of learning that reflect student initiated learnings and

TABLE 2.11.   The Cognitive-Developmental Model: Stages, Children's Behavior/Learnings and Adult Activities/Teaching

Stage	Child's Activity	Adult's Activity
Sensorimotor (Birth to 2 years)		
Reflex activity (birth to 1 month)	Refines innate responses	Respond to and stimulate the child's senses (sight, sound, taste, touch, and smell)
Primary circular reaction (1 to 4 months)	Repeats and refines actions that once occurred by chance	Stimulate the senses through objects the child can interact with—rattles, bells, or mobiles
Secondary circular (10 months)	Manipulates objects Repeats actions by choice Develops object permanence	Provide toys with various shapes, textures, and colors to handle Partially hide a toy while child watches
Coordination of secondary schemata (10 to 12 months)	Combines previous activities for new results Imitation begins	Provide toys: familiar dolls, balls, or boxes Encourage imitation
Tertiary circular reactions (12 to 18 months)	Experiments with objects to discover new uses Locates an object with eyes and tracks it	Provide experience with water, sand, textures Include toys which can be manipulated to turn, nest, roll, open, or close
Invention through mental combination (18 to 24)	Practices deferred imitation Applies old skills in new situations	Provide opportunities to apply old skills to new experiences Provide peer contact and interaction
Preoperational (2 to 7 years)	Language appears Imaginative player, deferred imitation, egocentrism prevalent Can complete simple operations, but cannot explain why	Provide dolls, cars, blocks, crayons, paste, paper, scissors, books, musical instruments, etc. Communicate at child's level or above Provide experience with liquid, mass, and length informally Encourage decision making (red shirt or yellow, apple or orange, bath before dinner or after)

TABLE 2.11. **The Cognitive-Developmental Model: Stages, Children's Behavior/Learnings and Adult Activities/Teaching** (*continued*)

Stage	*Child's Activity*	*Adult's Activity*
Concrete operational (7 to 11 years)	Applies simple logic to arrive at conclusions Reasons deductively Performs simple operations with physical objects Conserves	Provide opportunity to pursue areas of interest Use questions to understand child's reasoning processes and to aid child's awareness of logical thinking errors
Formal operational (11 to 15 years)	Reasons abstractly Solves problems through inductive reasoning Employs logical thought	Propose hypothetical problems for the child to solve Discuss ethical questions Encourage personal decision making and problem solving

Adapted from: Thibault and McKee (1982).

more active peer involvement clearly owe their methods and approach to the organismic model.

Naturally, not all programs of education are such clear examples and most draw from a variety of theoretical roots. It is important, however, for us to understand these relationships and to recognize that we operate from a theoretical base of understandings, as we prepare to work with children and others.

Explorations

Do one or two explorations in each category to extend and enrich your understanding of this chapter.

PERSONAL EXPLORATIONS

These exercises are designed to help you look at your own life, specifically, your attitudes, dreams, myths, and realities.

1. Write about a personal experience from your early childhood in which you interacted with an adult. After you have written a description of this transaction, analyze it in relation to the basic developmental

processes discussed in this chapter, i.e., adult patterns of nurturance and stimulation; need-attainment of the child as facilitated by an adult; the appropriateness of the interaction relative to the developmental level of the child, etc.

2. Write a chronology of the developmental milestones of your own "growing up" to age seven or eight, i.e., crawling, walking, first tooth, beginning school, etc. Then discuss the "continuous, orderly process" of your development. What peaks or unusual patterns of growth were evident, and what special circumstances were characteristic of your experiences?

3. What is your concept of the nature of the child? How does your view of the child compare with the ideas of Locke and Rousseau? What similarities and differences are evident between your views and those of Locke and Rousseau?

4. Did you attend a school that followed any of the teaching models discussed in this chapter? Compare your memories of kindergarten through grade two with one or more of these approaches.

INTELLECTUAL EXPLORATIONS

These exercises are designed to increase your depth of knowledge in some of the areas discussed in this chapter.

1. In your school library find a book or article written by either Locke or Rousseau. From your reading indicate what ideas/concepts appear to "make sense" to you. Write a brief evaluation of the material you have read.

2. Learning theory is a well-researched topic in psychology and education. Find a recent journal article that illustrates findings meant to prove or disprove one of the developmental models discussed in this chapter. *Child Development, Developmental Psychology, Journal of Educational Psychology, Exceptional Children*, etc. are among the many research journals that publish in this area.

3. Gesell and his colleagues have published a series of books for parents and caregivers on the developmental expectations for children at various ages. Skim one or two of these books and list several ideas that you feel parents or teachers need to pay attention to in guiding young children. Indicate your reasons for these choices.

4. Freud, Skinner, and Piaget are three major proponents of specific approaches to child development. Read a chapter or article by one of the three and discuss with several classmates who have read articles by the other contributors, similarities and differences encountered in your readings.

FIELD EXPLORATIONS

These exercises are designed to take you out into the world to find real examples that will illustrate and elucidate the material in this chapter.

1. Visit a local preschool and observe its playtime acitivies. Write an anecdotal record (i.e., nonevaluative description of what you observed) of what you have viewed. Analyze your observations with regard to the educational models discussed in this chapter. What model is this program most like? List some ways in which the program conforms to this model. Also, indicate some ways in which the program you observed differs from the model, as presented in the text.
2. In class, compare your observations with the observations of several of your classmates. If some of you visited the same school compare your results. What did you notice that your classmates did not? How many models was the class able to find? Are there more differences or similarities between programs?
3. If you were going to teach in one of the preschool programs discussed in class, what program would appeal to you most and which would appeal least? Give reasons for your opinions that include the information from this chapter on the basic principles of development.
4. Visit a natural setting (e.g., neighborhood playground) and observe several children of approximately the same age playing. What individual differences do you observe (physical play, language use, emotional expressiveness, style of interaction, etc.)? Make several lists of these differences in development. Prepare to discuss how these differences might affect the child's learnings in the school setting.

References

Bartz, W. R. and Rasor, R. B. *Surviving with kids.* New York: Ballantine Books, 1980.

Hunt, J. McV. *Intelligence and experience.* New York: Ronald Press, 1961.

Kessen, W. *The child.* New York: John Wiley, 1965.

Locke, J. *Some thoughts concerning education.* London: A. and J. Churchill, 1699.

Piaget, J. *The psychology of intelligence.* New York: Harcourt, Brace & Co., 1950.

Piaget, J. *Logic and psychology.* New York: Basic Books, 1957.

Piaget, J. *The origins of intelligence in children.* New York: W. W. Norton, 1963.

Rousseau, J. J. *Emile or On education.* New York: Basic Books, 1979.

Terkelsen, K. G. "Toward a theory of the family life cycle." In E. A. Carter and M. McGoldrick (Eds.), *The family life cycle.* New York: Gardner Press, 1980.

Werner, H. *Comparative psychology of mental development.* Chicago: Follett, 1948.

Chapter 3

DEVELOPMENT AND PLAY

Objectives

After reading this chapter the student should be able to:

1. List and briefly describe major characteristics of children's play.
2. Describe two play activities that are primarily physiological/psycho-motor in character and that encompass the broad areas of development listed in Table 3.3.
3. Name several forms of social language play and offer two play activities that illustrate these concepts.
4. Describe a play activity in detail that illustrates one of the five areas of cognitive development indicated in Table 3.5.
5. Compare and contrast the ideas on play offered by the theories of Freud and Erikson.
6. Identify and discuss the major stages in children's play as described by Piaget.
7. Discuss the various forms of children's social play depicted by the classical research of Parten.
8. Discuss the congruence between Parten's research on the social functions of play and Piaget's cognitive-developmental orientation to play.

Play represents a universally observed mode of human experience. Although generally associated with children, play, nevertheless, constitutes a significant behavioral component of both men and women, adults and children alike. Moreover, our interest in play, particularly among children, represents neither a new nor transitory phenomenon. In historic documents, from ancient to contemporary times, we find distinct, if periodic, reference to play. To the Greek philosophers Plato (427–347 B.C.) and Aristotle (384–322 B.C.), play was seen as a necessary and critical part of a classical education. Indeed, their high regard for play was evident in educational practices throughout the Greek world, underscoring its dualistic concern for enhancing mind and body as interlocking components of the educational experience.

Other observers and philosophers sought to enlarge the image of play created within the ancient world. Comenius (1592–1670) viewed play favorably, while Rousseau (1712–78) saw play as a vehicle of exploration and discovery learning. Pestalozzi (1746–1827) established play as a central element in children's learning, and Froebel (1782–1852) stressed the importance of play as a natural vehicle of learning.

CLASSICAL THEORIES OF CHILDREN'S PLAY

During the late nineteenth and early twentieth centuries scholarly interest in play arose. This concern stemmed, in part, from the introduction and dissemination of Darwin's theories of evolution; play, in this context, served as a means for comparative analysis, since play could be viewed as a shared enterprise of animals and children alike. As such, play became a natural arena for debate and theories concerning the origin and evolution of mankind. Four theories were constructed during this period, including, the *surplus energy theory*, the *relaxation theory*, the *recapitulation theory*, and the *instinct-practice theory* of play.

The Surplus Energy Theory

This theory, associated with Spencer (1897), viewed play within a continuum of work/play relations. Behavior that was oriented and goal directed constituted work, while unfocused and goal-less activity was defined as play. He believed that in the course of organized behavioral transactions, such as seeking food or initiating activity in pursuit of selected goals, the child normally created a surplus of energy. This surplus, or overabundance of energy, provided the child a motive for continued activity in the absence of immediate needs or specific goals, thereby creating opportunity for playful (that is, surplus) behavioral transactions. While achieving some credibility as an explanation of adult play, the surplus energy theory had limited applicability to children's behavior.

The Relaxation Theory

This theory, associated with Patrick (1916), also viewed play, as did the surplus energy theory, within a work-play model. However, in this perspective, play was accorded a higher, parallel status relative to work. Here, play was seen as supplementing work. Specifically, play was viewed as a concrete, physical, unrestricted enterprise, necessitated as a complement to modern societies' demands and stressful working conditions that require abstract reasoning, intense concentration, and limited physical activity. Recreation and relaxation in this theory refocused human energy from highly channeled, restricted outlets to less directed, more flexible forms of activity. As an explanation of children's behavior, however, the theory lacked credibility since play forms the core of children's activity, does not complement work, and is characterized by activity rather than relaxation principles.

The Recapitulation Theory

This theory, as formulated by G. Stanley Hall (1920) viewed play as support for Darwin's theory of evolution. In recapitulation theory, life

...AND THEY CALL THIS PLAY...

evolved from simple and primitive forms to more complex and integrated structures through a process of individual reenactment. Play, according to Hall, recaptured this evolutionary process, wherein the young child, through play, relives various stages of ascent up the evolutionary scale. To illustrate, water play might be construed to represent the emergence of amphibian life forms, while crawling and digging in sand suggests reptilian life forms, and climbing and nesting in trees an anthropoid phase of evolution. While such rough parallels as those offered may be drawn easily between the activities of children and animals, this theory could not account for many equally obvious (and observable) differences in the play behavior of children and animals, as well. The use of language, symbols, and toys and games constitute some observable distinctions in the rich variations characteristic of human play behavior.

The Instinct-Practice Theory

This view of play was proposed by Groos (1898; 1901). As in recapitulation theory, Groos views play within the realm of human-animal evolutionary relations. However, in the instinct-practice theory, play is seen as less representative of earlier, more primitive life forms, than a form of behavior especially appropriate to animal life where the young of the species serve an extended apprenticeship period. Humans, Groos held, contrary to other life forms, experience an exceptionally long period of dependency before assuming adult status. Consequently, he depicted childhood, and play experiences especially, as offering multiple opportunities to the child for the practice/rehearsal of behaviors and roles most appropriate to attaining maturity. By viewing childhood as preparatory to adulthood, the child could pre-exercise through play, skills required for adult life. These older theories set the stage for our more modern child-oriented observations and studies of play.

MODERN THEORIES OF PLAY

Many theories have been proposed to explain the meaning and value of children's play. Some of these reflected major theories of development, while others have viewed play as a significant event in and of itself. In this section we turn our attention to several of these modern proposals, specifically, psychodynamic, cognitive-developmental, and social theories of play.

Psychodynamic Theory

A number of psychoanalytic writers have addressed the significance of children's play, particularly its role and function in the developmental process. Most prominent among these efforts have been the work of Sigmund Freud (1965; 1975) and Erik Erikson (1950; 1977; 1980).

Freud, although an extensive writer on many aspects of human development, never articulated a formal theory of children's play. However, he made frequent references to play in his writings, particularly in two specific contexts: (1) as a form of children's wish fulfillment and (2) as a means of enabling the child to resolve traumatic events.

Freud (1961) believed that play was motivated by the pleasure principle (i.e., the desire to seek pleasure and to avoid pain). Consequently, play was viewed as a technique that children use to bend reality in order to achieve pleasurable gratification. Play allowed young children to wish for, to invent, and to apply solutions to desired goal states. Through play the young child may be an astronaut flying a spacecraft, a race car driver winning an important race, or a parent dispensing nurturance or punishment to an ideal or irate child. As the reader will note, each of these roles are tailored to ensure recognition, esteem, or power in the child's construction, and control over reality.

A second aspect of play addressed by Freud is the therapeutic value of play in helping children master trauma or control anxiety. Freud believed that through play the child may reconstruct or relive, via repetition, conditions associated with a traumatic event, thereby becoming able to cope more effectively with its original consequences. For example, a child who has participated in and sustained injury in an automobile accident may, through play, reconstruct the original scene, reenact events beyond his original control, and establish a better understanding of conditions and causes of his injury. As Freud noted, play enables children to repeat events that may have "made a great impression on them in real life, and in so doing, they abreact (that is, neutralize) the strength of the impressions . . . making themselves masters of the situation" (1975, p. 11). Through repetition, the anxiety of events is lessened and brought under manageable control.

A second contribution of psychodynamic theory in its treatment of play has been proposed by Erikson. The views of Erikson differ from those offered by Freud. For Erikson the focus of play is not as a mechanism for the resolution of past trauma, but as a vehicle enhancing both present and normal (that is, nontraumatic) ego development. In this view play is timeless, enabling the child to construct "model situations in which aspects of the past are re-lived, the present represented and renewed, and the future anticipated" (1977, p. 44). Within this expanded framework, uncertainty and anxiety may be addressed and resolved. Yet play is also seen to encompass broader opportunities for growth.

In his classic work *Childhood and Society* (1950) Erikson depicts three stages of play. These stages follow a developmental progression of appearance characterized by the child's creation of new information at each stage and greater complexity overall. Erikson refers to these stages as the *autocosmic*, the *microcosmic*, and the *macrocosmic*, respectively.

The first phase of play, the autocosmic, is present at birth. Here, the child's activity consists of initial explorations that center on his own body exclusively. Perceptions, sensations, movements, vocalizations are all self-defined, child-initiated, and characterized by repetition. As the child matures, especially during the latter part of the first year of life, she directs her activities outward to include people and events external to herself. She laughs to provoke a response from her mother, or she may explore the anatomical details of her father's face, poking and squeezing a nose or ear to elicit a reaction.

The second stage of play is called the microcosmic period. This stage is distinguished by a manipulative, skill orientation and is characterized by the child's concern for small manipulative toys and objects (for example, cars and trucks). As before, play tends to be solitary, achieved through the acquisition of mastery via manageable manipulation.

The third and last stage of play described by Erikson is the macrocosmic. This stage consists of elements contained within earlier phases, but occurs in integrated and ordered form. Structure and intent now characterize the child's play. Moreover, during the macrosphere, which roughly approximates the preschool period (that is, ages 3 to 5), play begins to be social.

Cognitive-Developmental Theory

Another view of play is proposed by Jean Piaget (1962; 1967). This view focuses on intellectual development. Yet Piaget's view shares some of the important features of play suggested by Erikson, viz., play as a timeless activity, play as a pretend exercise, play activity as an instrumental behavior directed toward achieving environmental mastery, and the recognitions of play as a developmental enterprise.

The role of play, according to Piaget, is to practice new learning and to extend established learning through rehearsal of known schemes. In assimilation, the child internalizes (that is, seeks a personal understanding of) objects and events by treating them in a manner similar to previously acquired information. Hence, an infant-toddler will mouth an unknown object, such as a magnet, rather than apply a new alternative solution to its use. According to Piaget, play represents or extends, via practice, acquired information. This can be seen in the correspondence between Piaget's play categories and his stages of intellectual development as shown in Table 3.1.

Although play itself is not viewed by Piaget as adaptive, the importance of play for children, as a means of achieving mastery of the world, is recognized. To clarify, in cognitive-developmental theory, only new learnings (that is, those that require accommodation) are viewed as being adaptive. Other activity, (which does not require accommodation) is considered to be representative of play. As such, play assists the child in amplifying, augmenting, modifying, or substituting actions. For example, an infant's discovery of musical noise, produced by his banging a pot with a spoon, may be modified by introducing different sized pots, or perhaps, a drum or a xylophone for him to beat. Play creates opportunities for repetition, and through repetition actions are given broader application and attain greater proficiency.

Piaget also notes the symbolic importance of play, an important extension of original learning. Piaget analyzed sleeping games to illustrate the function of symbolism. Initially, sleeping is associated with bedtime and bedroom. Yet over time, as the rites, rituals, and symbols of "going to bed" become identified, they attain a significance apart from the event itself. The child's teddy bear, for example, or his special blanket may become symbolic of the activity and may be used to create games of sleep ("I'll put the baby to bed. Where is his teddy bear and blanket?").

A critical feature of play, as a symbolic or representational event, is the child's ability to engage in *deferred imitation*. According to Piaget, deferred imitation, which first occurs around 18 months of life, refers to the child's ability to postpone imitating the actions of another. The antecedent of deferred imitation is first evident during the sensorimotor stage, appearing as simple imitation, in which the child immediately replicates an observed action. Later, simple actions or sounds are imitated in the model's absence. At approximately 18 months of age, the child is able to imitate a complex sequence of previously observed behavior in the absence of the model. For example, a child may pick up a set of garden tools that she observed her mother using yesterday and pretend to plant a garden. Through deferred imitation Piaget sees the child's using representation in action (a sensorimotor activity) in combination with representation in thought (a preoperational activity). For Piaget, action precedes thought. And play facilitates this process.

Social Theories of Play

The importance of play in the lives of children is clearly summarized by Damon (1983). He writes,

> Because of its symbolic nature, . . . play serves several vital functions in the life of a child. First, it offers the child an opportunity to develop and exercise the symbolic skills that make possible all creative and sophisticated processes of intelligence. Second, it offers the child an opportunity to represent sentiments that are normally difficult to express, thereby enriching and stabilizing the child's emotional life. Further, the social versions of childhood play serve yet another important developmental function, a function again related to the symbolic nature of play. While constructing make-believe roles for each other to enact, children engaged in social play gain a precious opportunity to coordinate their actions and intentions in a cooperative manner. In so doing, they join together in a creative experimentation with social roles and rules. The social-cognitive rewards of this cooperative effort should not be underestimated. During such instances of "shared imagination," children not only must learn to communicate effectively with others, but they also are forced to think reflectively about the very elements of social interaction—roles and rules (p. 109).

TABLE 3.1. The Cognitive-Developmental Theory of Play: Stages, Categories, and Characteristics

Stage	Substate	Category of Play	Characteristics	Illustrations
Sensorimotor	a. Primary Circular Reaction		1. Trial and error learning 2. Absence of intentionality 3. Action centered on self/body	1. Infant engages in visual searching of thumb to suck. 2. Random movement of limbs. 3. Discriminates among sucking objects.
	b. Secondary Circular Reaction	Practice	1. Emerging notion of cause/effect relations 2. Repetition of actions 3. Action away from self/body	1. Pulls string of toy without regard to consequences/effects. 2. Will kick mobile initially moved by chance. 3. Active search for dropped/thrown objects.
	c. Tertiary Circular Reaction		1. Cause-effect experimentation 2. Intentionality 3. Discovery of new means/repetition with novelty	1. Infant explores gravity by systematically manipulating and observing the different effects produced by dropping objects from varying heights. Infant observes how a spoon lands, what noise it produces, whether it breaks or bounces, etc.

Stage	Type			
Preoperational	Symbolic	1.	Absence of rules/limitations	1. Talks to Grandma on pretend telephone
		2.	Representational	2. Uses an empty box for "house."
		3.	Creative	3. "Let's make stone soup."
		4.	Absence of fixed social rules	4. "I have the ball." "I go first."
Concrete Operational	Games with Rules	1.	Collective organization	1. "Let's play marbles."
		2.	Rule-Orientated	2. "High card wins" / "Dueces are wild"
		3.	Concrete Orientation	3. Best hitter bats clean-up.
		4.	Abstract reference	4. "You be white. I'll be black."

INSET 3.1   Piaget on the Role of Play in Childhood

Practically every form of psychological activity is initially enacted in play. At any rate, play constitutes a functional exercise of these activities. Cognitive activity thus initiates play, and play in turn reinforces cognitive activity. Well before the appearance of language, the sensorimotor functions are used in pure exercise play in which movements and percepts are activated without the intervention of thought or of socialization. At the level of collective life (seven to twelve years), by contrast, children participate in games with rules which entail certain common obligations. Between the two extremes there is a different form of play very characteristic of young children. It employs thought, but thought that is almost entirely idiosyncratic and has a minimum of collective elements. This is symbolic play or imaginative and imitative play. There are numerous examples: playing with dolls, playing house, etc. It is easy to see that this symbolic play constitutes a real activity of thought but remains essentially egocentric. Its function is to satisfy the self by transforming what is real into what is desired. The child who plays with dolls remakes his own life as he would like it to be. He relives all his pleasures, resolves all his conflicts. Above all, he compensates for and completes reality by means of a fiction . . . (1967, p. 23).

One of the earliest studies of the social functions of children's play was conducted by Mildred Parten (1933). In her research Parten observed preschool children between the ages of two and five years during free play activities. From these observations she was able to classify each child's play, based upon its degree of "social participation," into classes of primitive and more advanced categories of social interaction. Her categories, reflecting changes from isolated to participatory modes of social behavior, include the following classes and descriptions:

1. *Unoccupied behavior.* The child is not engaged in play, but watches anything of momentary interest. When there is nothing going on, he may play with his own body, get on and off chairs, stand around, perhaps, follow the teacher, or sit in one spot idly glancing around.

2. *Solitary play.* Here, the child plays alone and independently with toys that are different from those used by children within speaking distance. No effort is made to get close to other children and she pursues her own activity without regard to the behavior of others.

3. *Onlooker behavior.* The child spends most of his time watching the other children at play. He often talks to the children whom he is observ-

ing, asks questions, or gives suggestions, but he does not enter the play itself. This type of activity differs from unoccupied behavior since the onlooker is definitely observing and interacting with others. In onlooker behavior the child stands or sits within speaking distance of the group so that he can see and hear everything that takes place.

4. *Parallel play*. The child plays independent of, but near other children. He plays with toys that are like those of the other children around him, but he plays with the toys as he chooses and does not attempt to influence or modify the activity of the children near him. He plays *beside* rather than *with* other children. There is a free flow of movement among group members with no attempt made to control the coming or going of children in the group.

5. *Associative play*. In this form of play activity there is clear evidence of interaction among members of the group. Activity and verbal interchange are centered on a common interest. The children borrow play material and follow one another on bikes, in wagons, and with trains. We also find, characteristic of this form of play, mild attempts among the children to control entry into the activities of the group. While each member of the group achieves some degree of group identity by engaging in identical or similar behavior, the structure of the group is loosely organized; there is no division of labor or organization of activity in terms of some central goal or purpose. The children do not subordinate their individual interests to that of the group nor demonstrate other than superficial coordination of their behavior relative to one other.

6. *Cooperative play*. In cooperative play we find evidence of group behavior organized by some common pursuit or endeavor. Here there is a clear sense of individuals achieving identity through group membership and structured behavior. Goals, whether they take the form of participation in the achievement of some group product, or playing some formal game, are evident, as well as directive/predictive individual behavior. In cooperative play we find a division of labor, the taking of different roles among participants, and the organization of effort among children, each supplementing the work of another, often under the direction of a member of the group.

Although Parten's work does not provide us with a specific correspondence between a child's chronological age and the appearance of a particular form of social play, important trends were noted by her research. Clearly, among the two to five year old children she studied, parallel play was the most frequent form of play displayed by the children. Yet, parallel and solitary play were also most evident in the younger-aged children, while, in contrast, associative and cooperative play were more frequently observed among the older-aged children.

Although Parten's research was nondevelopmental by design (the same subjects were not studied over time), its implications for our understanding of play within a developmental framework have become apparent. In particular, her work fits neatly within a Piagetian model. As suggested by Piaget, she found that older children are more likely to engage in cooperative enterprises. Moreover, she noted that the toddler's play is characteristically solitary, while the first form of "social" play (that is, parallel play) is, as Piaget observed, highly egocentric. Finally, she observed, in correspondence with Piaget's findings, that group play appears to progress from social recognition of others (that is, associative) to organization of effort among others (that is, cooperative). Of importance, this last milestone signals the onset of "games with rules," clearly coinciding with cognitive-developmental theory and the emergence of concrete operational thought.

BASIC TENETS OF PLAY

Through naturalistic and controlled observations, the unique and distinguishing characteristics of children's play have been described and ordered (Parten, 1933; Garvey, 1977; Damon, 1983; Rubin, Fein, and Van-

INSET 3.2   The Strategic Use of Parallel Play: A Sequential Analysis

Eighteen boys and 23 girls, ranging in age from 32 to 42 months (mean age = 38 months), were individually videotaped daily for seven consecutive minutes during indoor free play over a three-week period while attending a half-day camp program. Observers unfamiliar with the objectives of the study viewed the tapes and then classified each child's play behavior for successive 15-second intervals. Coding followed a modified version of Parten's categories. The data were then subjected to a sequential analysis in which transitions into group play (Parten's associative and cooperative play) from parallel play were noted and analyzed.

Parallel play was found to occur more often then would be anticipated by chance factors alone. Moreover, all the children were observed making frequent transitions from parallel to group play. The concept and use of parallel play did not appear to be age related or developmentally characteristic of any age group. Rather, as the authors conclude, parallel play may serve a more distinct function: as a strategy that bridges the transition from solitary to group interaction.

Bakeman, R. and Brownlee, J. R. "The strategic use of parallel play: A sequential analysis." *Child Development*, 1980, 51: 873–78.

denberg, 1983). Six features of children's play, including its motivation, style or manner of expression, and its consequences have been identified. The following list represents a composite of play characteristics.

1. *Play is pursued for fun.* When a child engages in play she does so primarily because of its anticipated pleasurable significance or outcome. Thus the motive to play is the child's belief that the activity performed will in itself, offer an opportunity to have fun or attain enjoyment. In contrast, in work or other task-oriented activity, pleasure is a secondary consequence rather than the initial aim or purpose of the activity.

2. *Play is intrinsically motivated.* Play is both freely defined and pursued. In play, activity is spontaneous and self-initiated. While other behaviors may be governed by imposing internal needs (for example, hunger, thirst) or external social demands, play is neither controlled nor forceably performed in pursuit of others' interests.

3. *Play is active.* Play involves movement, energy, and performance. In contrast with passive states of imagery (for example, daydreaming) or inactivity (for example, aimless loafing; "vegging out"), play demands vigor, involvment, and active pursuit. Garvey (1977), for example, notes that play is "a state of engagement."

4. *Play involves attention to means.* Play refers to doing rather than producing. The child goes down a slide not to get to the bottom, but to experience the journey. Moreover, the child will vary her excursion (by sliding down on her stomach, or by pursuing the task hands or feet first) creating new behavioral combinations of known behaviors. This characteristic of play as a variation of experienced themes reflects Piaget's notion of play as assimilation, whereby the child engages in play not as a direct learning, exploratory, or information-seeking activity, but as a means of extending behavioral patterns that are already part of its acquired repertoire. For example, when Piaget's son, Lauent, discovers that he can see a toy by throwing his head back and then repeats this movement for its own sake, the behavior becomes play—the exercise of an acquired schema (that is, idea/concept) detached from its initial adaptive purpose of bringing an interesting object into view. Similarly, the game of peek-a-boo represents the child's extension of known (that is, previously observed) events into a "game."

5. *Play is creative and nonliteral.* Play is an imaginative activity where an "as if" strategy or "let's pretend" orientation serves as the basis for organizing interactions. In "I'll be the Mommy. You be the Daddy," reality is suspended and fantasy becomes the accepted mode of expression.

6. *Play is controlled by the players.* This idea is two-fold. First, in contrast with exploratory behavior, play is guided by the child rather than

other events or circumstances. Thus, for example, the child converts an abandoned cardboard refrigerator box into a playhouse. Second, in play, rules are usually flexible, deemphasized, or, among very young children, absent. To illustrate, in the "I'll be the Mommy" game the oldest player may choose to be "the baby", rather than to occupy the parental role, a more common adult expectation.

THE DEVELOPMENTAL FUNCTIONS OF PLAY

Play offers the young child an abundance of opportunity for advancing its growth and development. As Rubin, Fein and Vandenberg (1983) note, "many theorists, researchers, and educators strongly adhere to the belief that play relates to and, indeed, causes growth in a variety of developmental domains" (p. 747). In this section we explore the role of play in the development process.

Play as a Physiological/Psychomotor Experience

A central and generally recognized feature of play is that it occurs within a framework of action. Children at play move. They walk, run, jump, climb, and ramble about. These behaviors are physical, observable, and consequential.

On a physiological level, play creates opportunity for gross motor (that is, large limb and body movement) expression, exercise, and rehearsal. Activities such as cycling, swinging, sliding, and climbing enhance a child's gross motor competencies/coordination. Children supplement these highly expressive activities with fine motor play (that is, small/focused/specific motor behaviors), as well. Cutting with a pair of scissors will hone eye-hand coordination, as will a task in which a strand of different shaped, multicolored beads is created. Similarly, block building will enable the child to exercise spatial awareness concepts, perceptual skills, and eye-hand coordination, as well as fantasy and creative expression.

Play, as a physiological growth experience, is also evident in the creation of body awareness and body image. Climbing in, out, and on top of boxes, tunnels, passage ways, trees, tires, and so on offers the child important information pertaining to size, weight, mass, strength, and proportion. Such learnings, however, are not abstract. Rather, they reflect the child's awareness of herself in space and in relation to objects apart from herself. Informational feedback of this type possesses multiple meaning. First, it provides the child data that may serve to challenge physical exploits and accomplishments. Second, it presents an accurate picture of task difficulties, serving to adjust the child's level

TABLE 3.2. Overview of Psychomotor Domain—Some Specific Components

I. Body awareness
    A. Gross motor development
        1. Rolling
        2. Sitting
        3. Crawling
        4. Walking
        5. Running
        6. Jumping
        7. Galloping
        8. Skipping
        9. Dancing
    B. Fine-motor control
        1. Thumb-forefinger pick up
        2. Buttoning
        3. Tying shoes
        4. Drawing
           a. Circle
           b. Square
           c. Triangle
        5. Cutting with scissors
        6. Copying letters and words
    C. Body image
        1. Awareness of self
        2. Body parts of self   } Mental map of body
        3. Body parts of others
II. Spatial concepts
    A. Sensory-Motor
        1. Balance-imbalance
        2. Rhythm   } Coordination of
        3. Speed/dexterity   the body's axes
        4. Point of reference
    B. Directionality
        1. Direction of sound, movement
        2. Up-down
        3. In-out, beside, below, etc.
        4. Laterality (right-left)
III. Movement
    A. Locomotion
        1. Coordination of gait
        2. Ability to stop and start
        3. Walking up and down stairs
        4. Ability to walk a balance beam
        5. Climbing equipment
        6. Riding wheeled equipment

TABLE 3.2.   Overview of Psychomotor Domain—Some Specific Components (*continued*)

    B. Contact
        1. Estimate distance
        2. Reach out and touch and grasp objects
        3. Stop objects coming toward self
        4. Catching
        5. Tracking (following a swinging object and being able to make contact with it.)
    C. Propulsion
        1. Dropping
        2. Throwing
        3. Throwing with accuracy
IV. Perceptual skills
    A. Visual perception
        1. Perception of figure-ground
        2. Visual form discrimination
        3. Visual-motor: eye-hand coordination
        4. Visual memory
    B. Kinesthetic perception
        1. Awareness of rough-smooth, hard-soft, etc.
        2. Discrimination of form by touch
        3. Control of body in space
    C. Auditory perception
        1. Recognition of direction of sound
        2. Matching of babbling sounds to language of environment
        3. Imitation of intonation patterns of language models—pitch and stress
        4. Imitation of beat and rhythm
        5. Discrimination of minimal pair sounds—bad-dad, bad-bed, bad-bat, bad-beat

of aspiration to reflect reasonable levels of attainment. Third, through vigorous testing of physical boundaries the child experiences himself as a "doer", that is, as a participant in control of his body.

Mission Accomplished—Gross Motor Creeping

Debbie is lying on her stomach, head and upper torso elevated as she grasps a set of plastic keys. An outward thrust of her arm hurls the keys a foot in front of her grasp. Reaching and hand movements show her the object is beyond her grasp. For a moment she rocks on her stomach preparing her back muscles for forward movement. Quickly, she places her arms below her body, elbows bent, and begins to lift her torso. This movement against gravity allows her space to pull her knees, one at a time, under her body. With legs braced forward she can now place one hand on the rug and shift her weight, allowing the second hand to follow with arms now extended. In the traditional "all fours" position she now begins her forward movement with a side-to-side motion. This allows her balance to shift as she lifts one arm and moves it forward; then the opposite leg moves; her hand moves again, then her second leg. It takes Debbie three movements to reach her goal. In position, she tilts her body to pick up the keys, while simultaneously relaxing the opposite side muscles. With a soft thump she comes down on her side rolling on to her back and holds the keys above her head. Mission accomplished!

Debbie's ability to creep requires a complex combination of muscle, joint, bone, and body "sense." Bones and muscles work together to resist gravity, and therefore movement around the vertical, horizontal, and depth axes of the body becomes possible. The side-to-side motions which allow creeping are primarily around the vertical axis, whereas forward motion resists gravity primarily around the depth axis. Each body movement involves balance and imbalance that create different sensations. These sensations, in turn, become the basis for the body's spatial knowing. Directionality, laterality, convergence, and time through space are the building blocks of later concepts which allow even more complex psychomotor acts.

Over and Under—Spatial Concepts

Sam stands at the base of the climbing bars. He gazes up at the top, head tilted back, and then puts his right foot on the lowest bar and his left hand above it on the second bar. He hops on his left foot a couple of times and then quickly shifts his weight, places his right hand on the third bar from the bottom, and pulls himself off the ground. Quickly he continues his ascent placing hand and foot over and under until he sits on the top bars of the jungle gym. Two hands grasp the top of two converging bars; his bottom rests on the opposite corner; one foot on the bar is under his right hand, while the other foot swings free. "Teacher, teacher," he yells. "Look at me! I'm way up at the top. See how big I am. I'm way over you!"

What did Sam need to know in order to reach his elevated status? First, he had to use his own sense of physical self to establish a point of reference. He needed to establish up, down, left, right, between-the-bars, over and under a bar, and a concept of empty space. The point of reference for stepping, hopping, and pulling from bar to bar required an estimate of distance. A point of reference for his hand as it transferred from bar to bar was required to maintain adequate body balance. Once Sam reached the top and looked down at the playground below, a new point of reference was established. This allowed him to

Play helps children learn to share.

gauge the distance down, the appearance of shapes, length, and the area of objects and all of their relative angles. All of these sensory impressions help form the child's initial experience of "knowing" about aboveness, overness, underness, and so on. These are the pieces of fabric woven from the physical body movement of a child at play; and it is the child's repeated experience with these spontaneous concepts that forms an understanding of space and relational concepts.

Beans, Balls, and Bounces—Movement and Propulsion

Donna stands, two feet firmly placed beneath her torso, a brightly colored bean bag dangling from her right hand. Her left hand hangs by her side, and she gazes forward intently, a slight frown creasing her brow. Approximately five feet in front of her is a three-foot clown face with a wide open mouth. The face is placed on a stand so that it is vertical and the mouth is about one foot above the floor. Donna's gaze drops to her feet and then returns to the figure and her right hand begins to swing slightly back and forth. She shifts her weight slightly on to her right foot and her right hand swings further behind her. Rocking gently she guides her hand slightly in front of her body. Once more she swings her right hand back and now she shifts her weight back to allow her left foot to step forward. Her right hand swings as her foot moves, and at a point almost directly in front of her, level with her waist, her hand releases the bean bag. The bag arches upward and falls just in front of the clown. Donna makes a frustrated hissing sound and walks forward and picks up the bag and returns to her place to try again.

Bean bags are easier items for young children to throw and catch than smooth round balls. Donna's throwing performance, while not initially successful, already demonstrates considerable knowledge of balance, estimating distance, and propulsion. She has learned to scan the distance between herself and her target. Moreover, she has begun to coordinate arm and leg movement and to shift body balance so as to counter the force of throw necessary to carry an object through the air to a specific point. The force of her throw must be sufficient to overcome gravity and exact enough to reach its intended goal. In addition, timing is essential, since Donna must let go of the bean bag at the precise moment required to accurately hit the mouth of the target.

Watching Donna's attentive and involving activity, it is clear that she is determined to continue her "game" until she is successful. Adults are often astonished at the length of a child's attention span when intent on an activity. This intensity of effort seems particularly evident among activities that provide what Hunt (1961) has referred to as the "optimal learning gap." Here a task is within the child's present capabilities, but difficult enough to create challenge and new learning with limited frustration. These events are the type that teachers strive to create in their planning of curriculum materials and activities. As Donna masters her bean bag throwing, she will proceed to more difficult tasks, such as catching and throwing a bean bag with a partner (a movable target) and graduate to soft yarn and sponge balls, before attempting the large rubber ball circuit. Round, smooth balls, 9" to 12" in circumference, require considerable coordination to catch and throw, and would bounce off the clown target she is currently using, offering more frustration then success. Bouncing a rubber ball with accuracy is still beyond Donna's present level of competence and would prove discouraging. Her teacher has wisely provided the materials which encourage Donna's participation and practice.

Turn Right at the Sand Box—Kinesthetic and Perceptual Learning

Jason stands with one foot resting on the bracing of a table. On the table is a rigid plastic pool, half full of water. The water and small mounds of material indicate wet sand below the surface. Next to Jason, Lou has both hands in the water and is moving his arms to create waves and ripples on the surface. He laughs and moves his arms faster. "Stop that," demands Jason. "You'll splash me." Then in a more conciliatory tone he adds, "Let's make something."

A variety of containers, funnels, and bottles sit on one side of the table next to the pool. Lou picks up a cottage cheese container and scoops some wet sand directly into it. With his other hand he picks up more sand and heaps it on the top. He places the container down and pushes the excess sand to pack it. Jason takes a small pail and follows Lou's example. Then he crouches down with the pail and turns it upside down on the pavement next to the table. Lifting the pail, the wet sand retains its shape, and Jason looks up at Lou and announces, "There, that's my house." The two boys are engaged in cooperative, symbolic play using the mediums of water and sand as both a kinesthetic experience of the senses and as a creative representation of the world around them. Jason's house shows that he understands the properties of water and sand when they are mixed together. He "knows" that they provide an adequate molding compound, and that he can use them in conjunction with containers and instruments of various kinds to sculpt a miniature world. He also shows us that he and Lou are aware of water action in the form of waves, and that they recognize that external movement transmits a specific effect upon water, as well as that increased force escalates water motion to splashable proportions. These experiences contribute to the child's perceptions of physical properties and the consequences associated with their modification or alteration through action. Moreover, they lay the foundation for his acquisition of higher order conceptual development, especially regarding ideas involving energy, weight, organic matter, and, in social development, cooperation.

Paints, Pencils, and Pads—Fine Motor Coordination

Miguel stands brush in hand preparing to paint. He is half an arm's length from the easel, close enough to reach easily but with enough space to stretch out his arm to reach the top of his sheet. He drops his hand slightly and makes another arch on his paper leaving a white space between the two strokes. He then replaces the brush in the red carton of paint in the tray at the bottom of the easel stand and looks at the other available colors. He picks up a blue brush and gives it a slight shake spattering some drops both in the container and the tray, and then he makes a blue arch in the space between the red curves. He grins broadly, and then quickly looks around, "Teacher, come see my rainbow," he calls.

Miguel is experimenting with color and with both large and fine motor coordination. His fingers grip the brush in a "pencil" hold. At an earlier age he might well have held the brush with his fingers wrapped around in the same direction rather than with the opposing thumb across from the other fingers. The arches on his paper, however, show large muscle, whole arm use, which is the precursor to the finer lower arm and hand/finger movement necessary for drawing figures and objects and eventually of depicting letters and words. He chooses strong primary colors, and his "rainbow" makes no attempt to duplicate the sequence of colors even though a commercially produced (that is, "correct") rainbow is pinned to the bulletin board. His representation is quite adequate for his level of "knowing" and he is obviously pleased with his product.

A look at other children's paintings pinned around the room indicates a wide variation in the maturity of expression and the coordination of eye and hand movements. Some paintings appear as random squiggles, the universal beginning attempt at two-dimensional representation. Other paintings, in contrast, show figures and shapes that indicate houses, suns, and, of course, rainbows, each in various degrees of detail. Detail (that is, part-whole representation) gives us a better idea of the child's level and degree of readiness to progress to chalkboard, crayon, and finally pencil renditions. Through this sequence of activities fine motor movement and eye-hand coordination become increasingly refined. Soon the desire to copy print will emerge as the child watches and remembers her teacher and parent print the child's name. But first she must finish that rainbow!

The child's physical play leads toward more sophisticated and complicated forms of learning. All of the child's later success will depend, in part, on the amount of practice he has been encouraged to engage in during this vital period of growth. Attempts to push children into behaviors that are too difficult for their physical and cognitive abilities will inevitably lead to frustration for the children and create a negative, "I can't do it" attitude. A literate society demands many skills and the beginnings of literate expression are evident in the physical play of the young child.

Language and Play

Just as the child's initial motor behavior lies embedded in his genetic endowment, so too we may find evidence of his initial efforts at using language. The cries of the newborn, which signal the environment for needed attention and nurturance, soon give way to non-cry vocalizations that are universal in nature and expression. Cooing, babbling, and other sound patterns emerge from two to four months and reach a peak from six to ten months. Careful listening will show that these utterances are not merely random noise, but represent experimentation in matching sounds of her immediate environment. By nine months the infant holds apparent "conversations" with intonation patterns that mimic questions, declarative sentences, and all other patterns of language that she has heard. Sounds that are not a part of the child's native language, and that were earlier vocalized, are usually dropped by the end of the first year. These practice sessions are engaged in for sheer pleasure as the infant can be heard "talking" when alone as well as in response to his caregiver's attentions. Thus the actual process of making sounds, that is, articulation or phonation, is another phenomenon to be explored and enjoyed.

During the first two years language play is largely limited to sounds, controlled variations in articulation, such as whispering or rasping, syllable variations, and intonation patterns (that is, stress, pitch, and juncture). The child is still more concerned with motor behaviors and sensory learning. From two to three, language growth begins to surge and noises, syllable vocalizations, and rudimentary sentences become chants and singsong rhymes to accompany movement and fantasy play. Sound and rhythm enhance and become a part of the child's play, and action-identified "tags" begin to represent particular aspects of the environment. "Beep-beep. Watch out! My car is comin'! Beep-beep. Beep-beep," the three year old calls out as he pushes his toy car across the floor. The repeated sound/word, "beep-beep," is characteristic of an action tag. "Ruff-ruff" indicates a dog's bark, "ding-a-ling" suggests the sound of a telephone, and so on.

During this period the child also plays with the structure of linguistic strings. "See dog jump. See house jump. See Jay jump, bump, dump. Dump all out. Dump dog." These practice sessions appear when the child is alone or engaged in solitary play and mark the increasing sophistication of the child's language understanding. Whether such play is essential to the child's language growth is unclear, but the enjoyment in involvement in such experimentation can be readily observed in the child's expressions, laughter, and voice tone. The growing edge of the child's knowledge is reflected in his language play.

As the child approaches four years of age, language assumes an equal role to motor learning for most children. Social play both in parallel and cooperative form becomes more dominant, and the use of language is essential to much of the interaction. (Language in the service of play, that is, to make requests, give directions, express emotions, and so on, will be explored in other parts of this chapter.) There appear to be three main forms of social language play; spontaneous and planned *rhyming and word play*, *play with fantasy and nonsense words*, and *word play with conversation*. Each of these types of language will be used throughout the child's early school years. In fact, during this period language will be the most important area of growth for the child and become so entwined with cognitive reasoning and social interaction skills as to cause difficulty in delineating their separate components.

Language growth, however, appears to be more closely tied to environmental influences than cognitive reasoning. "Fe, fi fo, fum. Fum, fi fo, fe. Fi, fo, fum, fe," chants the four year old as she pats wet sand into a pretend castle. Her experimentation with sound and sequence is embedded in the symbolic play she is engaged in. Her "castle building" is a sensory-motor activity, but the conceptual knowledge she uses in the creation of a "castle" and the repetitive language pattern she chants are directly dependent on the experience derived from her culture and her linguistic environment. Regular doses of nursery rhymes and children's stories and fairy tales are not found in all homes and without these or other comparable enriching experiences the child's linguistic experimentation will be more limited. Language play is, as indicated, developmentally sequenced. Yet, linguistic maturity and breadth are tied to the richness and variety of words and grammatical experiences available to the child. *Words must be heard and repeated* in a variety of contexts *before they can be used* for communication or for play.

During the school years children participate in a rich linguistic culture of rhymes, insults, and songs that are passed from child to child. This tradition of verbal play has been recorded and catalogued, most notably by Iona and Peter Opie in England, and appears to stand apart from adult influence and interference. Those of us who learned Pig Latin, for example, acquired this language variant from another child.

TABLE 3.3. Language Development—Abbreviated Taxonomy of Typical Developmental Stages in Language Acquisition

Birth to two months
 Cries
 Non-cry vocalization: Grunts, coos, gurgles, squeals
Two months to four months
 Attends to others' voices
 Offers consonant-vowel utterance shapes
 May participate in vocal exchange with caretaker
Four months to seven months
 Responds to human voices by turning head toward source
 May be disturbed by angry voices
 Usually stops crying when spoken to
Seven months to nine months
 Some single syllables associated with objects
 Listens to familiar words
 Jargon with intonation that is "sentence-like"
 Imitates some sounds
Nine months to ten months
 Imitates self-perpetuated sounds that interest him or her
 Evidence of comprehension, e.g., if asked "Where is Daddy?" child will look
  toward father; will hand over toy when requested of her or him
Ten months through one year
 Imitates babbling sounds of others
 Comprehends "bye-bye" and "patacake" or similar recurrent routines
 Responds to simple commands—e.g., "No!"
 First word may appear
One year to one and one half years
 Responds to a variety of commands
 Makes self understood through reporting, requesting
 Has about 10–30 single word vocabulary
 Identifies familiar objects, some body parts when named
Eighteen months to twenty-four months
 Names objects and pictures upon request
 Two word combinations occur: may be followed by three, four, five word
  utterances
 Can follow most one and two part commands
Two years to three years
 Begins developing negative and interrogative markers: "no sit down," "why
  Sally can't come?"
 Names one to three colors
 Understands imperatives ("Sit down.")
 Uses more detailed speech to satisfy needs
 Speech used for greetings, asking questions, etc. ("Hi! Grampa"; "What's
  that?")
 Uses pronouns, but with frequent errors
 Understands concepts on-off; up-down; open-shut; in-out

TABLE 3.3.   Language Development—Abbreviated Taxonomy of Typical Developmental Stages in Language Acquisition (*continued*)

Three to four years
   Understands and uses many plural forms and some verb tenses
   Understands five colors as well as comparative concepts (little-big; fast-slow, etc.,)
   Comprehends differences in *wh* interrogatives (who, what, where) and spatial prepositions in, on, under
   Uses most pronouns correctly
   Can sequence a 3-part event
   Understands most negative forms, e.g., "the girl is not running."
Four years to five years
   Sentence length 6–8 well-ordered words sometimes employing clauses
   Usually asks for information with well-formed sentences
   Understands a picture story
   Few articulation errors
   Understands "a pair of," some, many middle, comparative words (e.g., taller, shorter, bigger) and future tense
Five years to six years
   Continued addition of pronouns, prepositions, and conjunctions
   Recites numbers to 30s
   Asks meanings of words
   Relates fanciful tales
   Names monetary units (e.g. penny, nickel, dime)
   Speech pronounciation is understandable over 90 percent of the time
   Understands passive (The boy was chased by the dog.)
   Understands concepts of half, left-right, few, fourth, same-different

Language acquisition may vary considerably across different children. Ages and stages offered refer to approximate timetables and chronological sequencing.

All of the child's linguistic play and experimentation with sound, words, and sentences are part of her need to achieve language competence. Adult encouragement of this verbal experimentation is important in ensuring the child's acquisition of an adequate linguistic foundation. Later formal academic settings will depend heavily on these language skills.

Babbles to Bubbles—Early Sound Play

Genie pulls on a ring of the mobile with an intent expression. "Ba, ba, be, bi, ba?" her voice clearly questions as the string of syllables are formed. "Ba, ba, babibi, ba, brrrrrrr. Brrrrrrrr." Her lips purse on the repeated "r" and a rasping sound is emitted with an accompanying froth of bubbles. Genie looks up momentarily to see if anyone is present to notice her new sound accomplishment. Seeing no one, her gaze drops once again to the mobile and she shakes it vigorously and laughs.

Genie is experimenting with sound and lip movement, a spontaneous activity that infants and toddlers seem to enjoy greatly. Phonemic combinations are varied with different vowel and consonant combinations as well as intonation devices of stress, pitch, and juncture (the placement of the stops and starts of sounds). These trials are random even though the variations themselves may follow a regular pattern. Such play permits Genie to practice the sound system of her home language without any artificial demands for a particular sound or word. Practice of this nature will prepare her for sounding new words as they occur in her environment and occupies her attention as she manipulates her mobile toy.

If she had found an audience to notice her sound accomplishments, she might have deliberately repeated them. This conscious repetition is a precursor to more formal language communication and can provide Genie clues to the appropriateness of the sound she is making for a specific communication sequence. Naturally, for Genie the significance of her play goes unnoticed. For her it is fun to make these silly noises and feel the vibration in her lips.

Singing Games and Jump Rope Rhymes

"One potato, two potato, three potato, four. See if you can jump in the door," Sandra chants as she swings the rope over her head and jumps with the rhythm of her words. Jo is standing with one foot poised, rocking slightly with the same rhythm. As the rope passes behind Sandra, Jo jumps in facing her, and as the rope swings overhead she is ready to join the next jump. Both girls count in unison as they jump together, "One, two, three, four, five." "Whoops," Jo suddenly yells as her feet trip on the rope. Both girls laugh as she untangles herself, and then Jo takes the rope and moves to one side to start again.

Sandra and Jo are engaged in a typical "girl's" game of jump rope. The solitary jumping to the rhythm of a chanted beat is part of an oral tradition practiced by so many generations that its origins have become obscure. Jo's ability to mark the beat and join her friend in the jumping space requires excellent coordination and can only be mastered with much practice. The chant is clearly used to facilitate this motor accomplishment and was acquired by Sandra and Jo from other children. Yet, the chant itself is also a source of play, with its rhyme and rhythm subject to change as the players improvise their jumping activity. There are no unchangeable rules in this play but rather an awareness of beat and a desire for shared activity. Rules are evident, involving "taking turns," "jumper sets the chant," "only girls allowed." Yet these are casual and may change as the play progresses. Games of "Ring-a-round-the-Rosie," or "London Bridge" will appear just as spontaneously with the players' moods. These singing games, chants, and rhythms are the most formalized of children's language play and are clearly an enjoyable and motivating aspect of play among young children.

"Let's Play Telephone"—Conversational Play

"Hello, can you come over and play?"
  "No, I'm coming to your house."
  "Aw, please come visit me."
  "Can't, I'm rushing to come, come, come." Puts down telephone and walks over to first child, leans over, and shakes her hand.

This sequence plays with the social convention of an invitation and requires that both children be aware that their response is a contradiction. The tone of the interchange is serious and the girls apparently exchange cues with ease. Only with careful listening would an observer recognize the nature of the playful exchange. To follow the meaning of verbal exchanges in social conversation requires common understandings among its participants. In this case, we find similar assumptions about the "playfulness" of the message and a willingness between the participants to join in mutual feedback. Many conversations of preschool child-pairs demonstrate this playful violation of rules appearing to be a component of play that builds on the child's developing understanding of social convention, as expressed through language. While word play becomes more elaborate with increasing age and sophistication, the underlying process of playful incongruity will remain the same. What fun, children find, to turn the world upside down, at least for awhile.

Nonny, Noony, Nonsense—Social Nonsense Play with Words

"What's your dog's name?" asks the standing child.
  "Poopydoop" is the reply and the sitting child looks up.
  "What's he eat?" asks the first child.
  "Ants and caca and dippledopple," her colleague answers.
  "Dippledopple, trippletopple, caca, yum, yum," adds the standing child.
The child with the dog rises and the two children begin to run around the outside edge of the room chanting, "caca, yum, yum," waving the dog in the air.

Silly names and nonsensical answers to apparently "straight" questions is a frequent feature of four- and five-year-old verbal exchanges. Garvey (1977) notes that "as soon as a child has learned how something is supposed to be, then it becomes a source of fun to distort it or exaggerate it in some way" (p. 70).

When the first question is asked and receives a nonsense answer, the invitation to play has been offered. The continuing inquiry in the form of another question marks this verbal play as a form of social interchange. The forthcoming second nonsense response serves to elicit futher word play and both children now become involved in the repetition and distortion, adding motor behavior to their word game.

Funny or insulting names applied to self and others and nonsense syllables that are used as part of sentences or answers to questions seem to mark a growing cognitive awareness of what is socially appropriate behavior and what constitute adult rules of conduct. The merging of social cognition and language play are hallmarks of the child's maturing awareness.

Language play appears to be a function of the child's developing understanding and expertise in the use of words. The more a child is exposed to language and encouraged to experiment and "play," the greater her linguistic maturity and competence. The once popular bromide, "Children should be seen and not heard," has no validity in fostering the language development critical to future interpersonal and school success. Language is the foundation for the expressive and receptive components of writing and reading, and word play is the child's natural avenue for the expression of this vital function. Adults who appreciate and cultivate this spontaneous language play in children will be delightfully surprised by the language growth of children they teach and nurture.

Play as an Intellectual/Cognitive Experience

Play also aids the child in cognitive learning. Through play discrimination learning, classification skills, and concept formation are enhanced. Supplementing these observations is a growing literature (Sylva, 1977; Sutton-Smith, 1968; Smith and Dutton, 1979) that suggests that play fosters problem-solving skills. Moreover, some research (Smith and Dutton, 1979) finds that play may aid the child in the identification of solutions to problems requiring innovation, as well as in enhancing motivation to engage in problem-solving behavior.

The relationship between play and cognition is an intimate one: neither exists alone or in isolation. Unfortunately, in schools, cognitive development is often translated into a dry and dusty learning process. We frequently fail to associate play with thinking and are often suspicious if a child is having "too much" fun in school. One is supposed to work at school. Yet, the child's activity is guided by other concerns. A child's play is his work and he engages in all of the forms of cognitive problem solving usually found in the school's curriculum as he pursues various play activities. Table 3.4 offers a partial listing of some of the more common cognitive tasks that reflect children's thought.

TABLE 3.4.   Some Areas of Children's Cognitive Development

A. *Classification*
 1. Relational—Grouping together items on the basis of some common function or association, i.e., same/not- same/different; some/all; naming and identifying objects; things that go together
 2. Descriptive—Grouping items on the basis of common attributes, i.e., same color, size, shape, number
 3. Generic—Grouping items on the basis of general classes or categories, i.e., tools, toys, foods.

B. *Seriation*
 1. Ordering sizes—i.e., smallest to largest; shortest to tallest
 2. Ordering quantities—i.e., ordering numbers; same/more/less
 3. Ordering qualities—i.e., soft to hard, smooth to rough, dark to light

C. *Spatial relations*
 1. Body awareness—i.e., relating body parts and functions: facial expressions with causes
 2. Position—Understanding concepts of on/off; in/on; top/bottom
 3. Direction—Understanding concepts of up/down; forward/backward; to/from; sideways/across

D. *Temporal relations*
 1. Beginning and end of time intervals, i.e., start/finish; begin/end
 2. Ordering of events, i.e., first/last; next/again; sequence of events

E. *Conservation*
 1. Realization that physical laws govern events, not our perception of them, i.e., conservation of matter—two clay balls remain the same/ equal in physical property even if one is reshaped in appearance/ presentation.

Stack It Up—Seriation

Bobby sits on a rug, toys scattered about, looking intently at a toy with a series of brightly colored wooden rings of different sizes. The rings are placed over a wooden rod that is attached to a wooden base with a curved bottom. Bobby picks up the toy and turns it upside down so that the rings fall in a heap by his feet. He then picks up the largest ring and attempts to place it over the rod while he holds the base in his other hand. After two unsuccessful attempts he places the base of the toy on the floor in front of him and again thrusts the ring toward the rod. This time he successfully places the ring and he releases the colored circle and laughs to himself.

Now Bobby once more surveys the circles on the floor and chooses another ring. Again he is successful, and he places a third ring on the rod. It is now apparent that the size of the rings is not in the appropriate graduated order. Bobby does not appear concerned, however, and places another ring on the rod.

From another room Bobby's four-year-old sister Sue enters and walks over to assess his endeavors. "No, no Bobby," she says, and taking the toy from him, she starts to remove the rings and replace them so that the order of the sizes is "correct." "See, it's easy," she says and once more dumps the rings off the rod at Bobby's feet.

In fact, Sue is wrong. For Bobby, the ordering of the rings in a seriated pattern is still an impossible task. He has the manual dexterity to pick up, place, and drop the rings and does make some discrimination in size because he puts the largest of the rings on the rod first. To compare two or more items and mentally "hold" their order, however, is too difficult an operation for him. Sue, on the other hand, has had much practice with this problem, possibly with the same toy, and is capable of comparing each ring with both its previously matched item and one adjacent to it. Her ability to seriate the rings on this toy is both a combination of her age/stage and her experience with this and other similar tasks. Helping mother stack mixing bowls in the kitchen, placing the Russian nesting dolls one inside another, stringing beads in a repeated pattern are all seriation tasks that Sue has undertaken during different play activities. All of these tasks require her to use her thinking/reasoning abilities to discriminate, compare, and above all, to order events. In the next two to three years Bobby's growth and experience will make this task equally attainable for him.

"Button, Button"—Classification

"Now you stay here and don't get into trouble," says Cecilia as she places a red button with a group of other red, but differently shaped, buttons.

"What ya doin?" Mark asks.

"These are the children. They are playing in their yard and I don't want them to go out on the street," Cecilia replies. "See this is the yard." And her finger traces a square marked by green buttons of various shapes. "And these are their toys." Cecilia holds up a button shaped like a miniature football.

"Can I play?" asks Mark.

"Sure, you make your yard over there," answers Cecilia as she points to an empty space next to her. Mark picks up the button box and begins rummaging through the collection.

"I'll make my children blue," he says and begins picking out a group of blue buttons.

Cecilia and Mark are engaged in fantasy play and they randomly designate objects as their imagination dictates. This type of symbolic play is common among young children and by four years of age can be seen in cooperative play. As the children become involved in this activity, however, they are also using classification skills and associative concepts. Classifying by color is the simplest form of classification and the earliest type of category that children typically employ. The red and blue buttons are placed in color categories. Shape and size of buttons are ignored in the face of the strong attractive quality of color. Here, Cecilia has added an association between the color green (the color of grass) and the use of green buttons to form her "yard." The football and round button, on the other hand, are placed in a category designated by function; they are "toys." The children here will likely experiment with a variety of classification schemes as they use the buttons. Yet at this age they are most likely to focus on one attribute at a time. As they mature and attain experience they will begin to employ two and three types of classification categories at the same time. Large red buttons, for example, will be used to denote a given class of objects while small blue ones will indicate a different class of objects. Classification is an important skill and requires "thinking" to occur. As adults, these children may need such skills to classify new forms of cells in medical technology or to classify different flora as botanists. In adulthood, classification involves a variety of minute and sophisticated criteria. The origin of these skills begins, as we have seen, in childhood.

It's a Puzzlement—Spatial Relationships

John picks up a green puzzle piece and looks at it for a moment. Then he places it next to a piece of similar color in the puzzle. Next, he turns the piece so that the half-circle that sticks out on one edge is meeting a similar round space of another piece of the puzzle. When this attempted match doesn't fit he moves his hand to another similar shaped piece already attached to the puzzle. After several unsuccessful tries he places the piece in his hand back among a group of other green pieces, looks at the group of pieces by his hand, and then picks up another similarly-shaped piece. Once more John matches his piece against those already in the puzzle and this time he finds a good fit. He smiles to himself and then begins his search for another part of the puzzle.

John is employing a variety of skills as he assembles the puzzle. His visual-perceptual focus helps him discriminate among different shapes, sizes, colors, and assorted parts. His fine motor coordination comes into play as he places each piece against another, carefully fitting the edges together. And his classification skills help him group pieces with similar attributes together. He is able to judge the spatial configuration and orient pieces in space so that they fit together accurately. All of these factors are used by John to solve the problem he faces; that is, assembling the puzzle from its singular parts into a complete whole. Children love puzzles and will often spend long periods of time at such activities. Naturally, the difficulty level of the task must be geared to the age and maturity of the child.

Three year olds generally like puzzles with large single pieces, pieces that fit into matching spaces in a sturdy board. By four or five the child usually graduates to five-to-twelve-piece puzzles that make up a single picture of an object. Five to six year olds enjoy puzzles with up to 50 pieces and may be able to handle a "scene," a task similar to John's achievement. Children who, because of limited attention spans, have difficulty putting together a five-piece puzzle may have difficulty concentrating on school type tasks.

When You Pass Go . . .—Rules and Roles

Jan is shaking her hand, which holds a pair of dice. She tosses them onto the board and announces her number. She then looks at the board for a minute, clearly surveying the scene. She picks up a blue piece from the board and moves it her announced number of spaces. The next child picks up the dice and throws them. "Aha!" she yells and, taking a red piece, she moves so that she passes the blue piece of her friend. With a grin she puts the blue piece back in the corner of the board.

"That's not fair. You always put me back home," the first child declares.

"Those are the rules, Molly."

"It is too fair," the third child says.

"I want a new rule!" the first child states.

These children have reached the age where they can enjoy a formal board game with established rules. Reasoning must be employed as each child calculates the route to move his pieces and to create a strategy for overtaking the other players. There are still several limitations in the quality of their play, however, particularly in their capacity to use an "if . . . then" logical plan or strategy. In addition, their reading skills are still limited, therefore games must have fairly simple rules without elaborate extra steps demanding extensive reading skills. Even meeting this criteria does not guarantee that their play will proceed smoothly. Losing is not easily accepted at this age, and Molly's sense of "fairness" relies more on her own egocentric wish to win than on the rules of the game. It is not unusual for children of this age to change the rules if they can reach a consensus on a rule that suits their interests better. Logic can be set aside at a whim. In another two or three years the rules will become extremely important, but for now they are relatively fluid.

As we can see, young children use reasoning and problem solving in a variety of ways as they play with objects and other children, and, even though the types and number of concepts available to them at any one point are limited, children proceed to employ these necessary steps before acquiring the more elaborate forms of logic to be used later. Clearly, cognitive reasoning is as much a part of the child's play as any lesson designed by a teacher to promote these abilities.

Play as an Affective Experience—Internal and Shared Interactions

To the casual observer play is synonomous with fun. And, indeed, play is frequently joyful and characterized by children's mirth and glee. Yet, play is equally often a vehicle for other forms of emotional expression as well. Play, by definition, is a process derived from and controlled by its participants. Consequently, play creates opportunities to explore feelings in a less threatening or potentially evaluative manner than reality permits. Through play, for example, the young child may act out the role of an angry parent or a restrictive teacher without fear of reprisal. To illustrate, spanking one's dolly represents a form of *dramatic play*, an important mechanism for the exploration of feelings. Here, by engaging in child-adult role reversal, the child may express a variety of adult-like emotions, including anger and sorrow, by assumption of a surrogate adult role.

Play allows for other forms of internal representational imagery and emotional exploration as well. Young children frequently confront fear and fearful objects through play. For example, "things that go bump in the dark," lurking monsters, and strange sightings often constitute principal concerns in the playful scripts composed by young children. In these explorations, the source and power of unknown entities, including potentially dangerous images, may be playfully experienced and disposed of with impunity.

Another commonly explored image, as evident in children's play, is the hero-villain theme. In this scenario, the child may examine and experiment with good and evil through the exercise of power. In such a play, moreover, right and wrong may constitute the basis for primitive explorations into morality and ethical behavior.

Finally, it is important to note that play affords the learner not only many opportunities to explore her or his own feelings, but also to observe and reflect upon the feelings of others. In a social context, particularly, he will also note those behaviors that accompany the expression of varied feeling states in others (for example, laughter-joy; crying-sadness; hiding-fear; yelling-anger). Through these observations the *matching of behavior and feelings* may be achieved.

Mastering social and emotional learnings in interactions is clearly a part of the young child's activities. In fact, play has been widely acknowledged as an instrumental factor in such learnings (Garvey, 1977; Damon, 1983). Through play children may observe others, invent and test out novel behaviors, or otherwise acquire new interpersonal skills and competencies. This testing out and refinement of old and new behaviors represent an important arena for learning among young children. Specifically, through the varied feedback received from others, ineffective behaviors may be modified or dropped and replaced by more mature responses. The child will transfer from the play arena those behaviors that best represent her learnings to new persons and settings.

Piaget proposed that children only move from *egocentric* (that is, self-defined) to *sociocentric* (that is, group-oriented) behavior through interactions with other children. Children with limited opportunity for social interaction often behave quite differently from those children with rich peer involvements. Providing creative opportunities for social interaction and play is often a central objective of nursery school and daycare programs.

"I'll Be the Baby!"—Dramatic Play

Melissa places a man's hat on her head and dons a sport coat from the "dress-up" box. She turns to her friends and asks, "Guess who I am?" Barbara looks up from the table at which she is carefully arranging dishes for the dinner party.

"You make a good Daddy," she answers. "Where do you work?" she asks.

"At the store. I'm the manger," Melissa responds.

"You mean manager," pipes up Jenny, in an annoyed tone.

"I know how to be a manager, that's more than you," Melissa responds in a louder, angrier tone of voice. "My Daddy is a manager. I know how!"

"You are being silly," says Jenny, in a tone of voice that is quiet, but clearly sarcastic.

Then Jenny's tone changes. "You'll be the Daddy. I'll be the baby!" Jenny's voice is no longer angry. She sounds and appears happy with her new thought.

"No! no! I want to be the baby." Melissa's voice is now raised to a wailing pitch.

Dramatic play is a regular feature of the interactions of young children. The girls' play is an enactment of scenes they have experienced either in their own families or through some other mode. Imitation of adults allows an important opportunity for "trying on" adult roles and provides the child with a growing sense of self and others. Melissa's adoption of the role of Daddy and her knowledge of a store manager is a reflection of her environment and experience as she understands and interprets it. It is not necessarily an exact replica of her family life, however, because she is applying her own limited but growing understanding of events around her. Jenny's and Melissa's emotional interchange is another example of the social and emotional learnings embedded in child interaction. Emotions can be expressed and reacted to with peers serving as both arbiters and interactors. Many parents hear their child "scolding" her doll or expressing anger or loving remarks to a toy or another child and recognize their own words and tone of voice in the actions of their child.

The opportunity to interact with peers provides necessary social learning during play sessions. It is not easy for the young child to give up her needs for another's. Her world is basically one that revolves around personal needs and feelings. This egocentric perspective is natural for the child but must eventually give way to more externally directed concerns. Adults tend to reinforce this type of behavior by the very nature of their caregiving role; they offer the child attention and meet her needs, sometimes almost automatically. Other children, in contrast, are more interested in their own wants and demand equal time and consideration. It becomes necessary for the child to learn to negotiate with peers if they are to play together in a satisfactory manner. It also becomes part of the child's self-interest to give up her wants at times, just as Melissa at first demands the position of baby but then allows the other children's wishes to "win" in order for the play to continue. Thus, it is largely through peers that the child learns to become more sociocentric and acquires a perspective vital to child and adult life alike.

Invisible Friends and Other Playmates—Social Imagination

Dean stands behind the swing at the playground and pulls it way above his head and then swings his arms down as he runs forward and under the swing. "That's it, Danny, push with your feet and then pull them back as they swing back. Out, then back. That's what my Daddy taught me."

Dean runs around to the back of the swing again and gives it another push as it arches over his head. "That's right, keep pumpin'." Just then a voice is heard from a distance calling Dean's name.

"Come on, Danny, Mom is callin' us for dinner." Dean runs off in the direction of the call.

Dean is a participant in a common scenario as he talks to his imaginary friend. As an only child Dean does not have siblings to play with, and his experiences with other children are limited. In his play, however, he creates the social environment he needs by inventing a "friend." Thus he meets his need for a playmate and continues to engage in a limited form of social-emotional play.

Many children create one or more invisible friends. These companions may be human or animal and generally "join" the child in most of his endeavors. Some children demand that a place be set at the table or that their "friend" be given a bed or some new toy. Sometimes parents question whether it is appropriate for a child to spend time in this way. Yet, in fact, it is much healthier for a child to spend time in this manner, using his imagination in the creation of an imaginary friend, than to be lonely and withdrawn in the absence of companionship. Only when imaginary play becomes exclusive and hinders the child from interaction with other children is there any cause for worry. Some research evidence suggests that children who have invisible friends are more creative and imaginative than children who are not prompted to do so. Most children appear to "outgrow" this practice, usually around eight years of age. Vicarious social-emotional play encourages growth toward maturity.

Let's Be Enemies—Identification through Literature

As Miss Swift finishes the book she places it face down in her lap and looks at her group. All faces are turned toward her as she asks, "Why was Max angry at his friend?"

"Because he took the crayons. Because he wants to be boss. 'Cause he didn't share," a variety of voices call out.

"Very good! You're so quick today." Miss Swift smiles at her group. "Who would like to share with us a time that they were mad at a friend and what they did to solve their problem?"

For a moment the group is silent, thinking, then Andy raises his hand and begins talking. "My sister spilled my paint and I got mad and said I was gonna stamp on her picture." Andy stops his recital.

"How did you solve the problem, Andy?" Miss Swift asks. Andy looks confused and does not continue.

"Does anyone have any ideas that might help Andy solve that kind of a problem if it happens again?" the teacher asks other children.

"Well, she might give him her paint. She could clean it up. She could ask him to not do that. She could stamp on his picture if he stamped on hers." The children's voices gather in sound as they continue their exploration.

"My goodness, so many ideas. Andy, which ones do you think would work for you and your sister?"

It is clear from the involvement and enthusiasm of the children that they have had many opportunities to explore ideas and use books as a springboard for solving problems. Only with much practice do young children engage in this kind of thinking. Miss Swift encourages the process by her warm and supportive statements and by her acceptance of all the children's responses. Children are not required to wait until they are called upon to answer (an almost impossible task for four year olds), nor are they criticized if they become confused or do not answer in the manner Miss Swift might have intended or desired. Here, there is room for divergence of opinion, and multiple solutions are quickly elicited. The teacher's skill is shown both in her leading of the discussion and in her choice of books to read. *Let's Be Enemies* is the type of book children love and can easily identify with in terms of their own experiences. The character's feelings and expressions are familiar to them and the emotional overtone of the text stimulates explorations. Emotional identification with book and TV characters is a common observation in children's play. Whether they are pretending to be Superman or one of the *Three Billy Goat's Gruff*, children enjoy being their favorite character and literature is a valuable device in aiding identification. Here, in this illustration, identification offers the group help in building and extending on the concepts presented in the story. This group discussion may not appear to be play to an observing adult, but for the children it constitutes another way of playing. This play is with ideas about social-emotional situations and, when conducted well, it can enhance the child's appreciation of books and foster group problem solving. With proper guidance, books can become a rich resource for identification and social-emotional learnings.

SUMMARY

The child's perceptions of her body image, as suggested earlier, are derived, in part, from playful activity that enhances physical awareness. These learnings are germinal and cumulative. Supplemented by other features of play, especially social interactions, they constitute events that contribute to each child's more broadly defined psychological image of herself.

The psychological/personalized component of self-awareness refers to the *self-concept* or the ideational image each of us holds about ourself. The self-concept is both a situational and a developmental accomplishment. Specifically, it is a growing system of beliefs that we attribute to ourselves and is assigned to us by others in the form of evaluations of our accomplishments and failures. In childhood, particularly, through play, we record our first achievements and our first defeats through both personal and social transactions. These events, in turn, create the form and substance for later success and failure.

It is vital for the child to experiment, practice, and create. Playful activity allows maximum opportunity for all of these expressions, thereby providing the ideal vehicle for growth and learning.

As we have seen, play has received attention throughout history because of its universal attraction for children and adults. Regardless of the education philosophy, play has been seen as a vital activity of childhood.

Play appears to have a developmental history, changing over time from the solitary play of the young child to the sophisticated cooperative play of the older child. Also, play reflects and aids in the developmental maturations of the child, clearly marking her increased abilities in psychomotor, language, cognition, and social skills. New skills can be observed, tried, practiced, and built upon at the child's discretion.

True play is a successful experience because it is child directed and motivated. This sense of control and positive feedback, this growing facility in a variety of areas, help to build the child's sense of being capable, thereby enhancing his self-image.

All in all, play constitutes the single most important child-centered activity we can foster. As adults involved with children, we can understand the value and importance of play. For the child it will always be just for "the fun of it all."

Explorations

Do one or two explorations in each category to extend and enrich your understanding of this chapter.

PERSONAL EXPLORATIONS

These exercises are designed to help you look at your own life, specifically, your attitudes, dreams, myths, and realities.

1. Think back to your early childhood experiences. What were your favorite activities? List 10 activities you enjoyed as a child. Using Parten as a reference, what social features/descriptions can you attach to each of these endeavors? Write a page describing your own "style" of play.
2. What kinds of "play" do you engage in at the present time? List some of your present favorite activities (at least five), and next to each indicate one or more types of children's play, as described in this chapter.
3. From your readings and personal experiences, what is your philosophy concerning the balance of work and play necessary for adequate functioning for both children and adults?

INTELLECTUAL EXPLORATIONS

These exercises are designed to increase your depth of knowledge in some of the areas discussed in this chapter.

1. Find one or more books in the library that describe outdoor play environments for children, such as, playgrounds, backyard equipment, etc. Make a list of at least 10 important purposes for this type of equipment and bring your list to class.
2. Find two books, chapters in books, or articles that describe play activities in two other cultures. Make a list of how these are similar and how they differ from the play of children in the United States. Summarize your findings.
3. Examine several children's picture books that show children playing. Are there any observable differences in the play activities among boys from those of girls? How do these reflect cultural images or stereotypes? Write a one-page report on your findings.
4. Find one research article that investigates some aspect of children's play. Write a brief review of this article and your opinion on its importance to the area of play for developmental inquiries.

FIELD EXPLORATIONS

These exercises are designed to take you out into the world to find real examples that will illustrate and elucidate the material in this chapter.

1. Visit an infant-toddler center or, where applicable, observe 2 or more children between 3 and 24 months of age in their homes. Write four short anecdotes of play behavior you observed in each child. Try to observe the child alone and with others.
2. Make a walking or biking trip through a "neighborhood" i.e., a local geographic area with a variety of homes and services in close proximity, between about 3 P.M. and 5 P.M. Observe:
    a. Where the children play (streets, playground, school yard, YMCA, etc.).
    b. What age groups and/or individuals are present.
    c. How many "groups" you can identify and what they are doing.
    d. What type of play behavior you find (dramatic play—cowboys and Indians; games with rules—marbles, etc.).
    Make a rough map of your environmental survey, which shows these events/activities in operation.
3. Ask some parents of young children to describe their child's bedtime activities. Possible questions include:
    a. Is there a sequence of activities that the child prefers?
    b. How do parents and child "play" together at bedtime? What role(s) do each play?

    c.   Are there any special toys the child needs/wants at bedtime?
    d.   What is the emotional tone of the bedtime ritual?
    Bring your findings to class for comparison.

4. At a local nursery school or day care center make a list of the toys and materials available for children's play. Classify your items into two lists: (1) creative, open-ended play materials and (2) specific, functional play materials. Examples included in the first list would be items such as clay or paint, whereas items on the second list would include puzzles and jump ropes. Are the lists equal or are there more of one kind of material than another? If so, what kind of philosophy and program would you anticipate at this center? Refer your response to the discussion of different models of early childhood education described in Chapter 2. What other possible learnings can you extract from your lists?

References

Bakeman, R. and Brownlee, J. The strategic use of parallel play: A sequential analysis. *Child Development*, 1980, 51, 873–78.

Damon, W. *Social and personality development*. New York: W. W. Norton, 1983.

Erikson, E. H. *Childhood and society*. New York: W. W. Norton, 1950.

———. *Toys and reasons*. New York: W. W. Norton, 1977.

———. *Identity and the life cycle*. New York: W. W. Norton, 1980.

Freud, S. *New introductory lectures on psychoanalysis*. J. Strachey (Tr. and Ed.). New York: W. W. Norton, 1965 (Org. published 1933).

———. *Beyond the pleasure principle*. J. Strachey (Tr. and Ed.) New York: W. W. Norton, 1975 (Org. published 1920).

Garvey, C. *Play*. Cambridge, Mass: Harvard University Press, 1977.

Groos, K. *The play of animals*. E. Baldwin (Tr.) New York: Appleton, 1898.

———. *The play of man*. E. Baldwin (Tr.). New York: Appleton, 1901.

Hall, G. S. *Youth* New York: Appleton, 1920.

Parten, M. Social play among preschool children. *Journal of Abnormal and Social Psychology*, 1933, 28, 136–147.

Patrick, G. T. W., *The psychology of relaxation*. Boston: Houghton Mifflin, 1916.

Piaget, J. *Play, dreams and imitation in childhood*. New York: W. W. Norton, 1962.

———. *Six psychological studies*. New York: Random House, 1967.

Rubin, K. H., Fein, G. G., and Vandenberg, B. *Play*. In P. H. Mussen (Ed.), *Handbook of child psychology*. Fourth Ed. (Vol. 4). New York: John Wiley, 1983.

Spencer, H. *The principles of psychology*. New York: Appleton, 1897.

Smith, P. K. and Dutton, S. Play and training in direct and innovative problem solving, *Child Development*, 1979, 50, 830–36.

Sutton-Smith, B. Novel responses to toys. *Merrill-Palmer Quarterly*, 1968, 14, 151–58.

Sylva, K. Play and learning. In B. Tizard and D. Harvey (Eds.), *The biology of play*. London: Heinemann, 1977.

SECTION TWO

Children and Relationships

Chapter 4

INFANCY AND INDIVIDUALITY: THE ORIGINS OF SOCIAL INTERACTIONS

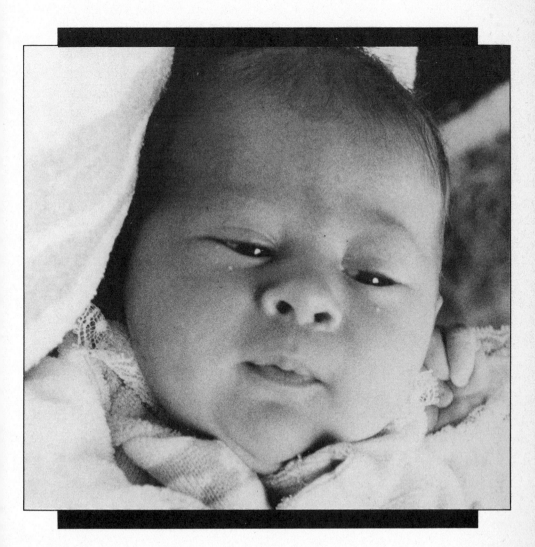

Objectives

After reading this chapter the student should be able to:

1. Describe physical and neurological characteristics of the newborn.
2. Write a summary of two research studies cited in this chapter that support the concept of social competence in infants.
3. Explain the roles that the smile plays in infant-caregiver interactions and the sequence of development of the smile.
4. List the nine characteristics of temperament and provide behavioral illustrations of temperament at two age levels.
5. Discuss the three temperamental types postulated by Thomas and Chess with special attention given to the potential problems of the "difficult child."
6. Prepare a table that shows the three types of infant-caregiver relationships described in this chapter and offer a description of infant and caregiver characteristics for each.
7. Discuss the behaviors of caregivers that reflect their attitudes toward children and parenting and state examples of potential child responses to different caretaking attitudes and behaviors.

The period of infancy refers to the first 18 months of life. During this period we observe dramatic and wondrous changes in the child's growth and development. And, of comparable importance, infancy forms the beginning of much of what is to come. By the end of infancy the baby will have undergone vast changes in his ability to interact with his human and nonhuman environment. He has become sociable and skilled in his relations with others and has begun to use language as a communicative device. The infant has attained object permanence (that is, memory of events) and has started to cognitively order his environment into classes through the use and aid of symbols. Physical maturation has enabled the infant to walk unassisted and her interactions with her surroundings have begun in earnest.

In this chapter we will examine and explore several important aspects of this period of development. Our focus will reflect the considerable growth of interest and research in infancy, especially studies that have helped expand our awareness of social competence in infancy and evidence of infant individuality.

INFANCY—DESCRIPTIONS AND CHARACTERISTICS

The joy of birthing, the excitement of creating, the anticipation of bonding, each are tempered by the realities of child rearing. Underlying these issues are a series of questions that parents and other caregivers alike have raised with the advent of each new infant. Does she know who I am? Am I recognized? Will she look like me? Am I seen as different from others?

Concern for the child as a social being permeates many of our hopes and beliefs in ourselves as meaningful adults in the lives of children, especially in the very young. For here we seek assurance of being recognized and being of importance.

The Newborn—Description and Characteristics

The average newborn is approximately 20 inches in length and weighs 7½ pounds. As our observations will confirm, the relative size of its body parts are unequal. The newborn's head is quite large, representing about 20 to 25 percent of its overall body length. Her limbs, in contrast, are substantially smaller and appear uncoordinated, apart from elicited reflexes. Interestingly, aside from issues of proportion and size, the human infant is born complete, possessing all characteristic physical features of the adult, including fingernails and eyelashes.

Typically, the newborn has a large head with a disproportionately large forehead, widely spaced and large eyes, a small and rounded

YOU KNOW, I'M MORE THAN JUST ANOTHER PRETTY FACE!

nose, a round face, a small (or absent) chin, and a very short neck. The newborn has little control over its head or legs, although, if cradled, the baby can turn its head from side to side. The newborn usually possesses somewhat bowed legs, with the feet bent inward at the ankles so that the soles of the feet are almost parallel.

Newborns have six soft spots on the top of their heads called *fontanels.* These openings allow for cranial flexibility during birth and growth of the brain during the first years of life. They do not fully close until about 18 months.

At birth a complete assembly of nerve cells is evident in the brain, but the brain itself is underdeveloped. During the first year of life the infant's brain will double in size. Most of this growth is accounted for by *myelinization* (that is, the development of the protective sheath around the nerve pathways) and *dendritic amplification* (that is, an increase in the branch-like filaments that connect the nerve cells and transmit nerve impulses between the cells.)

WHAT IS THE INFANT LIKE?

The scientific study of *social competence* in infants has taken several pathways. These include research focusing on (1) the infant's recognition and response to others; (2) the infant's awareness of herself; and (3) research on how infants communicate awareness of others, particularly, through the development of the enigmatic smile.

Infant Recognition and Response to Others

In a series of experiments with very young infants (Meltzoff and Moore, 1977, 1983; Field, Woodson, Greenberg, and Cohen, 1982), researchers have raised a series of interrelated questions, asking how infants perceive and demonstrate recognition of others. Specifically, they have asked:

1. Do infants perceive different emotions (facial expressions) in humans?
2. Do infants engage in similar emotional (facial) expressiveness?
3. Can the infant "match" adult emotional (facial) expressions?
4. Is "matching" a function of simple imitation? Or is matching produced by some other mechanism?

In a study focusing on social competence in very young infants, Field and her associates (Field et al., 1982) examined the reactions of 74 neonates (in this study, infants with an average age of 36 hours at the time of this experiment) to different adult facial expressions. These consisted of happy, sad, and surprised faces exhibited in a random order by a live

TABLE 4.1.   A Taxonomy of Infant Reflexes

The Moro reflex	The *Moro* or startle reflex occurs if the infant's head is dropped suddenly. Behaviorally, the infant will extend its arms, appear to engage in abrupt convulsive shaking, and cry, usually until comforted.
Hand and feet reflexes	The *palmar* or grasping reflex occurs when the palms are stimulated. The *plantar* or placing reflex occurs when the infant's foot is stimulated at its instep. The reaction consists of inward toe curling. If the outer side of the infant's foot is gently stroked the toes will curl and spread outward. This reaction refers to the *Babinski* reflex.
Leg reflexes	The *standing* reflex refers to a primitive straightening of the limbs in response to the infant's own weight. The *walking* reflex occurs when the infant, under its own weight, appears to "step" one foot at a time, when gently moved across a solid surface.
Body reflexes	The infant will demonstrate a *crawling* reflex when pressure is applied to its feet. A *swimmer's* reflex may be observed if the infant's back, above the waist, is gently rubbed.
Arm reflexes	An inadvertent object placed in the mouth or nasal passages will elicit a *defensive reaction*. This reflex appears in the form of a pushing or swiping behavior directed toward the offending object. The *tonic neck reflex* appears when the infant's head is turned to one side, whereupon the infant will extend the arm nearest the object of its gaze and flex upward his alternative arm. This reflex, in appearance, resembles a fencer's pose.
Head and face reflexes	The infant will display an adaptive *head-turning* reflex, when placed face down. Other face reflexes consist of the *crying* and *sucking* or *rooting* reflex, the latter enabling the infant to search and suck in response to the placement of the nipple in her mouth.

human model. By using a *habituation* procedure (in which the same stimulus, in this study a facial expression, is repeated until the infant shows signs of fatigue or boredom, immediately followed by the introduction of a different stimulus), differences in the newborn's recognition and response to "new" stimuli were detected.

TABLE 4.2.   Milestones of Motor Development

Average Age (in months)	Attainment
1	Holds head erect for a few seconds
2	Holds head and chest up when lying on stomach
3	Reaches for and touches object at midline
4	Reaches for object in front of contralateral shoulder
	Sits with support
	Can clasp and hold object
5	Rolls over for the first time
6	Can pick up cube from table using palm (but not thumb or fingers)
7	Rolls over easily when prone
8	Is able to sit without support
	Crawls
	Can pass object from one hand to the other
9	Manipulates two objects simultaneously
	Is able to stand without help
10	Creeps on hands and knees
11	Pulls self up to standing position
12	"Walks" by holding onto furniture for support
13	Stands without support
	Walks without help
14	Grasps objects with thumb and forefingers
15	Climbs up stairs (crawling)
18	Can climb onto a chair
19	Can crawl up and down stairs
24	Walks up and down stairs

Motor control is not established over all muscle groups at the same time. Instead, the sequence follows three general developmental principles. First, development proceeds in a *cephalocaudal* (literally, "head-to-tail") fashion, with control over muscle groups in the upper body and limbs occurring before control over those lower in the body. Second, development proceeds in a *proximodistal* (that is, near to far) fashion from the center of the body. Thus, for example, control over shoulder muscles develops before control over lower arm and finger muscles. Third, development is characterized by *hierarchical integration*, that is, the simplest skills are developed first and then become elaborated and more complex through integration with other simple tendencies and skills.

The results obtained from this study offered some surprising answers to the questions raised above. It was found that these infants were consistently able to differentiate happy from sad from surprised adult facial expressions. Moreover, they were able to match adult facial expressions with remarkable competence. Specifically, upon being presented a surprised face, newborns exhibited opened eyes and mouths, the latter forming an oval shape. Upon viewing the sad face they responded

The sequence of motor development as investigated by Mary Shirley.

by exhibiting a tight mouth, protruded lips, and a furrowed brow. A happy facial expression was accompanied by partially opened eyes and an upturned smile extending the length of the infant's mouth. Interestingly, it was also found that the infant's matching of the adult facial display was most likely to approximate the adult emotional expression during the middle period of trials when adult facial stimuli were introduced, indicating that the infant's responses were likely neither a result of some immediate arousal mechanism associated with the introduction of new stimuli, nor a reflection of some already established inherent reflex.

In a related study, Meltzoff and Moore (1983) tested neonates for their ability to imitate two simple adult facial gestures (a mouth opening and a tongue protrusion response) in order to more clearly define the matching process described above. Their concerns were severalfold. One interest of this research study was to examine the possible causes of imitative processes in young infants. Piaget (1962), for example, among others, has viewed the ability to engage in facial imitation as a critical achievement of social competence. Yet, in facial imitation, the infant must match a gesture of another person that he can see, with a gesture of his own that he cannot see, a somewhat sophisticated achievement that Piaget believed was beyond the perceptual-cognitive competence of infants younger than 8–12 months of age.

The results of the Meltzoff and Moore study demonstrate that newborn infants, ranging in age from less than an hour to 71 hours of life are able to correctly imitate two simple adult facial expressions. How do they accomplish this task: In attempting to account for these results, Meltzoff and Moore examined several possible explanations for their findings. These included *postnatal learning, imprinting, and infant mediation.* Regarding the first hypothesis, namely postnatal learning, it would appear that an infant's capacity to imitate at birth, without previous experience or opportunity to interact with others, negates an explanation favoring the learning of simple imitative responses.

The second hypothesis, imprinting, appears to possess several difficulties as well. First, in contrast to comparative observations drawn from the animal research, the two gestures imitated in this research do not appear to possess significant survival (adaptive) value in and of themselves. Second, as Meltzoff and Moore noted, the imitative responses studied did not reflect the fixed, sterotypical adaptive properties typical of innate (that is, unlearned) reaction patterns observed elsewhere. The infants studied here did not demonstrate on first exposure, perfect matching responses to the adult gesture; rather they appeared to adjust and correct their responses over successive trials. This latter finding of behavioral adjustment suggests an infant mediation hypothesis. Specifically, as these data suggest, infants appear to engage in some form of active thought between what is seen and what is performed. As Meltzoff and Moore propose, infants may relate information produced by self-performed shifts in body movement to representations of the visually perceived model and create the match required. As the infant matures, imitation becomes a more deliberate process; the older infant consciously attempts to match her behavior with that of a model. As these data suggest, the younger infant demonstrates skills commensurate with this process, perhaps, earlier and with greater success than is generally assumed.

These studies indicate that early imitation exists, although they do not offer conclusive evidence that newborns think. Nevertheless, their value in ensuring the infant's survival is greater than might be readily apparent. They demonstrate that infants move, look, and act upon stimuli, which reflect an awareness and interest in others of their kind. These behaviors, in simple terms, demonstrate an affinity to be among humans and in so doing stimulate adult interest. As Fogel (1984) observes, "At the most basic level, human interaction is a sharing, and newborns are biologically equipped to give their caregivers just this kind of feeling" (p.114).

The Familiar Face—Recognition and Response

One of the central concerns of caregivers is the degree to which the newborn recognizes and identifies with familiar persons. In practical terms, caregivers frequently ask, "Does my child know who I am?"

Newborns show evidence of being able to discriminate features of the face from its total configuration. Specifically, the newborn can discriminate among eyes, mouth, tongue, and other facial attributes. Yet, we may wonder, can the infant connect these different features in some recognizable form? One attempt to study this problem was offered by Carpenter (1975). By employing a specially designed viewing apparatus, she was able to observe the reactions of a two week old infant to each of the following six stimuli:

1. The infant's mother's face presented silently.
2. A female stranger's face presented silently
3. The infant's mother's face talking to the infant
4. The female stranger's face talking to the infant
5. The infant's mother's face "talking" to the infant but with the stranger's voice presented and heard by the infant
6. The female stranger's face "talking" to the infant but with her mother's voice presented and heard by the infant

TABLE 4.3. Directed Expressions of Infant Social Competencies: The Origins of Reciprocity

1. Turning toward the sound of a human voice and active searching for its source.
2. Attending to the pitch of a female voice over other tonal variations.
3. Selective termination of activity (e.g., sucking) when the human voice is heard.
4. Visually following a picture of a completed human face.
5. Preferring milk smells over sugar-water smells and selectively responding to human milk over cow's milk.

The recorded data were most impressive. Carpenter was able to show that a two week old infant was capable of remarkably refined discriminations between her mother and a female stranger. As expected, the infant looked longest at her mother talking to her with her own voice. Moreover, the infant also looked frequently at her mother's face when it was presented silently. Clearly, these stimuli were the most attractive and were responded to most frequently, particularly, in comparison to the stimuli featuring the stranger's face and voice. What happens when face and voice are mismatched? What does the infant do when her mother's face is presented with the stranger's voice or when her mother's voice is paired with a stranger's face?

As might be expected, the experimental juxtaposition of conflicting stimuli presented an untenable problem for the neonate. In both situations the infant became upset. She averted direct gazing, showed furtive glances at the face, and, occasionally, signalled upset by bursting into tears. The distortion produced by "mixed matching," contrary to the infant's "expectations," appeared to create aversive reactions, most notably, behaviors similar to fear.

The Human Voice—Recognition and Response

The adult is a composite of many stimuli, each of which becomes evident in the course of human interactions. Consequently, we need to ask, Which of these many attributes does the young infant recognize and respond to? Facial recognition, as we have seen, is an important focus for the infant's establishment of environmental continuity and her organization of information. In addition, other sources of information may offer important components contributing to the rich fabric from which social relations emerge.

Vocal and verbal stimuli provide an important body of data from which infants appear to derive significant sources of information. Studies of infant reactions to distress in others, for example, constitute one such critical body of accumulated findings. Sagi and Hoffman (1976) in an earlier study observed the reactions of neonates to one of three forms of vocal stimuli: (1) the cry of other infants, (2) a synthetic cry produced by electronic simulation, and (3) silence. They found that newborn infants cry in response to the crying sounds of other newborns, particularly those produced by live infants, a finding subsequently replicated by Martin and Clarke (1982). These results suggest that the newborn can respond in kind to the distress of another human, a rudimentary form of empathic response observed in other species.

Other studies, such as a related inquiry reported by Zahn-Waxler, Radke-Yarrow, and King (1979) suggest that the infant's initial capacity for empathic reaction to the distress of others increases in complexity and scope, forming a foundation for prosocial behavior. They found that children between the ages of one and a half and two and a half are not only aware of the meaning of distress in others, but are concerned enough to attempt reparation for distress they may have caused. Children in this age range also show willingness to help a distressed person even when they have not caused such distress.

The capacity of the human newborn to regulate his behavior to the sounds of his environment is significantly more sophisticated than is often assumed. In one remarkable study Condon and Sandor (1974) recorded several hours of newborn behavior on film and videotape. Included among these recordings were tapes of infants taken during both awake and sleeping periods. During awake times, when the infants appeared responsive and engaged, these investigators introduced prerecorded voice patterns of human sound, including English, Chinese, and nonsense speech. Using the technology of audiovisual and film mechanics, which allow for frequent playback, slow down, freezing, and framing of minute behavioral sequences, Condon and Sandor were able to perform a microanalysis of the infant's behavioral reactions relative to the prerecorded messages. Indeed, the responses that they observed and recorded in their infant subjects were small units of behavior; they included such acts as the lifting of a chin, the raising of a finger, the extension of a limb, and even the arching of an eyebrow. Through their careful matching of each infant's behavioral sequence, via an analytical breakdown of its behavior in correspondence with the rythmic flow and sounds of normal speech, Condon and Sandor found that their newborn subjects were, in fact, actively responding through *body language* to spoken language. Referring to this ability to coordinate body with sound as a form of *interactional synchrony*, Condon and Sandor observed that newborn infants could sustain a sequence of coordinated behavioral-verbal interactions for as long as a 125-word period of vocal communication. Of special interest is that whereas the infants obviously did not know the meaning of the prerecorded speech played, they were capable of sustaining this relationship to both English and Chinese verbal communications. (It might be noted that these newborns were United States born.) In contrast to these observations, neither nonsense speech nor random sound were capable of producing sustained or coordinated patterns of interactional synchrony.

Self-Awareness

At what age does an infant show awareness of himself? Is this recognition a spontaneous discovery? Or, does it follow a developmental process? These questions have been examined in several promising studies, each of which suggests some tentative answers, as well as future research directions.

In an initial study of self-awareness, Lewis and Brooks-Gunn (1979) utilized a somewhat unusual technique for studying infants' recognition of themselves. They instructed each infant's mother to surreptitiously apply a small dab of red rouge (hence, the term "red nose" experiments) to the infant's nose in an apparent preexperimental nose-wiping caretaking act. They then observed the infant's reactions when each was placed in front of floor-length mirror. The infants in this study ranged in age from 9 to 24 months of age.

Using responses such as smiling at the mirror, touching the mirror, touching her body, pointing at the mirror, acting "silly," and touching the mark on the end of her nose as measures of awareness, Lewis and Brooks-Gunn found that all of their infants showed some form of "recognition." That is, visual recognition of themselves under an altered "red nose" state was evident across infants. However, only among infants 15 months or older was this difference specifically identified; infants at 15 months of age and older clearly touched the ends of their noses, demonstrating accurate identification of altered differences in appearance. Apparently, infants as young as nine months of age show the beginnings of visual recognition of themselves. Thereafter, there appears a progressive, more extensive, and greater refinement of the infant's concept of personal awareness.

What determines when and how an infant shows awareness of himself? In part, this appears related to the requirements of the task posed for the infant and the circumstances surrounding its solution. Each appear to affect judgments of infant self-recognition.

Bertenthal and Fischer (1978) found that self-recognition in infants develops in accord with a predictable sequence of emergence. Moreover, this process follows a path in which an infant's capacity to solve more abstract (that is, difficult) tasks (for example, "Who's that?" in a mirror image matching task) of self-recognition parallels the infant's chronological age and, presumably, its experiential history. In their study of infants ranging in age from 6 to 24 months, they found that infants as young as six months of age look at themselves in mirrors. Yet, if an object is suspended above her head (and is visible through a mirror image), only somewhat older infants will look up in order to locate it. Apparently, when an infant is not required to locate a specific spot of difference in appearance (as in the previously cited research), ease in self-recognition is facilitated. In addition, what appears to aid in self-recognition tasks in infants is the availability of additional cues (that is, other images to compare herself with), particularly, those that move, are active, or contingent (for example, adults who play "mirror games" with the infant) upon activity.

The Enigmatic Smile

Perhaps no single feature of the human personality serves to create greater reactions and expectations in others than the human smile. While the smile has been observed in other species, it has achieved a special status in humans. In infancy, as well as adulthood, the smile is a complex and multifaceted expression of our self-status. It is a statement of personal being (that is, condition of satisfaction) as well as a sign of our emotional status (that is, degree of fulfillment). And the smile is an important tool of social communications and interaction, as well.

The study of the smile follows an extensive history of inquiry. Because of the important social value placed on the smile by adults, it has been studied across a variety of settings, as well as across different species (Bower, 1977, 1982).

Although its exact significance in an infant's social development is still far from being precisely established (Lamb and Campos, 1982), the smile appears to play many roles. One important feature of the smile is its status and use by the infant as a *sign* of emotional well-being and satisfaction. In this context, we are all familiar with the smile of a contented infant. A second use of the smile is its value as a *signal*, usually of recognition, of an important person or relationship. Here, an infant may smile at the approach of a familiar caregiver or favorite toy. And, finally, the smile may be observed as a *symbol* of some achievement. We may observe an infant smile when she has successfully reproduced some cause-effect relationship (for example, inadvertently kicking a ball, carefully noting what happened, and then, consciously reproducing this action).

The Development of the Smile

The first social or *full-smile* appears at approximately six weeks of age. While other forms of smiling may appear earlier, it is the social smile that serves most clearly as a portent of events to come. In this context, we need also note that age refers to conceptual, rather than chronological, age. By conceptual age scientists refer to age as measured from time of conception, usually *46 weeks* of life, or roughly 6 weeks of chronological age (that is, time since birth). Babies smile at their conceptual age of 46 weeks, regardless of their chronological age. Hence, we may anticipate that infants born prematurely will smile somewhat later, in chronological terms, while those born beyond term will smile earlier. The importance of a biologically-controlled timetable determining the advent of the full-smile remains to be established. Suffice it to note here, in terms of its adaptive value, this socially significant behavior is neither left to chance, nor accidental opportunity.

While the adaptive-survival value of the smile requires further study,

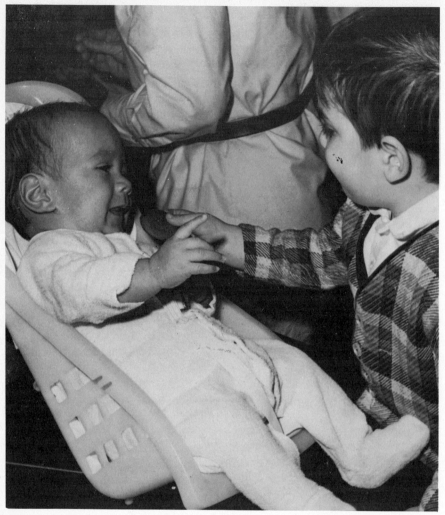

Children communicate with each other in many ways.

the social significance of the smile has been documented. To illustrate, the amount of time that caregivers choose to spend with their infants, as opposed to the amount of time they have to spend with him, rises appreciably once smiling becomes well established (Newson and Newson, 1976). Clearly, the socially-responsive, smiling infant will elicit more social responses from his caregivers than his less responsive counterpart. Moreover, young infants, as Brackbill (1958) found in her classic study, quickly learn the contingency or ping-pong (that is, cause-effect) relation between their behavior, in this instance smiling, and the behavior of others. In her experiment, when the infant smiled, the experimenter smiled back, uttered a "tsk-tsk" sound, and gently touched the infant on its stomach. Smiling dramatically increased as the adult introduced and maintained these behaviors, but was reduced as adult interest was withdrawn. Yet smiling reappeared as the maintaining behavior described was reintroduced.

While smiling, in any form, is often interpreted as a social act, "false-smiles" (that is, nonsocial smiles) appear earlier than the full-smile. During the *first week* of life a partial smile may be elicited by the gentle stroking of the infant's skin, by moderate changes in visual stimuli, or by the introduction of low-intensity sounds. During the *second week* of life, the partial smile appears responsive to the human voice, which appears as a more effective stimulus than a sound produced by a bell, whistle, or rattle. During the *third week* the smile itself changes, as well as the relative effectiveness of stimuli capable of generating smiling. *For the first time the full-smile appears.* This real smile is shorter in duration than the social smile, but involves the whole face and possesses all of the character of the social smile. Moreover, the most effective stimulus for its appearance is the human voice, particularly the female voice. By the fifth week we see another shift in stimulus control over the infant's smile. The human voice alone no longer elicits a smile; now visual stimuli, especially the human face, and particularly, the eyes, become the dominant eliciting stimulus. (Interestingly, perceptual experiments indicate that high contrast stimuli, particularly pairs of stimuli such as two dots on a white background, are capable of eliciting the smile at this time.) Research evidence suggests that the human face is the most effective eliciting stimulus since the average face contains two dark areas (that is, the irises of the eyes) surrounded by two white areas (that is, the sclera of the eyes) and it is this pair of high contrast stimuli that elicits the smile.

Emotional-Cognitive Interchange

As we have seen, the smile possesses considerable emotional significance for the infant. Yet, emotions also appear to serve intellectual-cognitive ends, as well.

Campos and Stenberg (1981) suggest that adult emotional input creates a *social-referencing* system for the infant, enabling her to more systematically organize her environment in the absence of direct experiential learning. Social referencing relies upon cues and information provided through adult emotional signals. The infant is sent "signals" that enable action within situations that may be characterized by uncertainty, ambiguity, or lack of experience. The cognitive value of adult-infant emotional interchange is illustrated by a number of research studies.

In a representative study, where researchers employed a modified visual cliff (an apparatus designed to create an illusion of height through a suspended-glass enclosed compartment that the infant is asked to cross), Sorce, Emde, Campos and Klinnert (1981) investigated how infants responded to differing levels of uncertainty created by the illusion of falling. Typically, when one year old infants are faced with an apparent four-foot dropoff, they avoid crossing the glass-enclosed compartment to reach their mother. Alternatively, when there is no apparent dropoff on a modified deep side of the compartment they cross the cliff without incident. Yet when the illusion is set midway at an intermediate level infants characteristically: (1) look to their mother and (2) use the specific facial affective information that the mother provides to determine whether to cross or not to cross. In terms of the latter, the mother's specific facial expressions significantly influenced her infant's decision to act. When the infant's mother expressed a fearful face, none of the infants tested crossed the deep side of the illusion. Yet, when the mother expressed a happy face, 15 out of 19 infants tested crossed. Of additional interest, similar findings were obtained to emotional expressions of anger (evidence of infant avoidance) and adult interest (evidence of infant crossing). Yet, when the adult emotion expressed was nonrelational to the task at hand (for example, a mother's expression of sadness) there was no clear preference toward crossing, or for that matter, avoidance of the crossing among the infants tested, but rather, considerable vacillation by the infant over whether to cross or not.

Infants have also been found to use other (namely, familiar) adult emotional expressions as sources of information (Klinnert, Emde, Butterfield and Campos, 1983). When a novel toy was introduced into a room where the baby, her mother, and a familiar woman were stationed, the familiar adult's facial expressions significantly influenced the infant's behavior. Among one year olds, with mothers instructed to remain expressionless, when the familiar adult smiled, the infant approached and touched the toy significantly more often than when the same adult exhibited a fearful facial expression.

Related inquiries (Svejda and Campos, 1982) demonstrate that infants less than one year of age (namely, eight and a half months of age) are capable of deciphering and responding to adult emotional cues. In this study, where vocal, rather than facial, expressions of fear, anger, and joy were introduced, infant behavior was significantly altered by adult vocal expressions introduced as infants approached an unfamiliar toy. Specifically, joyful vocalizations led to closer examination and more rapid approaches to an unfamiliar object, while angry and fearful vocalizations were accompanied by restricted exploration. As Lamb and Campos (1982) speculate, "Social referencing may be developmentally important to the extent it facilitates vicarious learning (that is, learning through indirect experience)." As they note further, "It would be dangerous for infants to learn to avoid electric outlets, noxious chemicals, poisonous plants, etc., only by direct experience. Learning mediated by social affective communication seems to be a biologically sensible alternative" (p.218).

When does social referencing begin? What cues, facial, vocal, or other, appear to facilitate cognitive organization of infant experiences? Is the process spontaneous or developmentally achieved? These and other related questions remain to be answered. However, some tentative answers may be suggested.

It appears, according to Campos and Stenberg (1981), that infants may use visual cues expressed by adults to order and organize their experience of uncertainty as early as five or six months of age. Clearly, by nine months of age the infant can and does utilize visual information. Moreover, there is some evidence that infants use vocal information apparently earlier than visual information as organizers of experience.

In germinal research in this area, Charlotte Buhler (1930) reported that by five months of age, some of the infants she studied were capable of responding appropriately to angry adult facial expressions, while at seven months of age, all of her subjects did. In her construction of a scale of developmental norms of emotional recognition and use, she found that at five months of age infants responded with appropriate emotional or behavioral expressions to combinations of adult vocal and facial information; at six months they responded to vocal emotional information presented alone; and at seven months they responded to facial emotional information presented alone.

The use of emotional cues clearly originates with familiar adults, most notably, the infant's primary caregivers. The primary caregiver, in turn, may facilitate her or his infant's reliance upon other adults by his or her reactions to an unknown adult stranger. For practitioners the implications for extended caregiving to include other adults through this process is clearly evident from the findings of a study conducted by Boccia and Campos (1983). In this study they asked mothers of eight-and-a-half-month-old infants to greet an adult stranger by either (1) a curt unfriendly hello and slight frown or (2) a happy hello and smile to the baby and the stranger. In the first condition infants engaged in rapid heart acceleration, less smiling and greater distress, while, in contrast, demonstrating heart deceleration and less distress under the latter condition. Clearly, primary caregivers may facilitate infant acceptance and positive approach to new caregivers through emotional-cognitive interchange.

INFANCY AND INDIVIDUAL DIFFERENCES

Individual difference play a prominent role in human affairs. In childhood, as in adulthood, we each seek to be perceived and treated by others as unique and different. And, in fact, we are different from one another. Consequently, we need ask, Where do these differences originate, when do they become evident, and, finally, what role do they play in individual development?

The existence of individual differences, particularly of biogenetic origin, have been well documented over the past 25 years (Korner, 1973; Scarr and Kidd, 1983). Young infants, in their initial perceptions and vocalizations, as well as in a host of other behaviors, demonstrate both diversity and uniqueness in their approach toward external persons and events and in their reactions to ostensibly similar environmental events. Moreover, and of significant developmental interest, these early identifiable differences appear to remain relatively stable over time. In this section we will describe some behaviorally important findings on individual differences and examine their potential consequences for early social relations.

In a germinal study in which early parent-child affiliations were investigated, Schaffer and Emerson (1964) observed two distinct sets/patterns of infant behavior. One group of infants studied displayed a behavioral style which led Schaffer and Emerson to refer to these infants as cuddlers, while a second group that they observed exhibited behaviors that led to their being depicted as noncuddlers. The cuddlers, as indicated by the term, were children who sought physical, bodily comfort from adults and engaged in frequent touching and hugging interactions. In contrast, the noncuddlers were more active, sought fewer adult restraints placed upon their behavior and were significantly less oriented toward touching and holding. Moreover, these infants tended to resist physical contact during periods of stress and fatigue. Different babies, as these investigators found, also elicited different responses from their respective adult caregivers. Cuddlers sought and received warmer and more affectionate treatment from adults. Noncuddlers, on the other hand, appeared to provoke different reactions from their caregivers. These infants sought fewer contacts and, in turn, elicited less frequent adult interactions. These contacts were also less affectionate or sustained. The long-range consequences of these differences in approach and reaction by infants to their caregivers were not studied. Nor could the etiology of these early social exchanges be established, viz., whether cuddliness or noncuddliness produced more or less positive parental reactions to their infants or whether the reverse was the case, that initial parental handling produced more or less responsive infants. Nevertheless, this study and others subsequently undertaken provide us with important evidence that infant behavior styles, critical to child-adult social transactions, appear early in life and, perhaps, form the basis for events and interactions to come.

TEMPERAMENT AND INDIVIDUAL DIFFERENCES

Temperament refers to patterns of individual variation that become evident relatively early in life. By their use of this term scientists have suggested that the evidence for differences in behavioral style originates at birth, rather than as a consequence of learning opportunities that follow. Early appearance, however, does not imply that initial behavior styles are permanent or nonchanging, but, rather, that evidence of distinct behavior styles as defined at birth does not follow periods of intense learning or socialization. In this context, temperament has become a useful concept for recognizing and describing a set of distinguishing characteristics that differ among infants and young children.

Contempory use of the concept of temperament is derived from, and follows, the longitudinal studies of Thomas and Chess (1968, 1977, 1980). Their research and that of contemporaries have both modernized and systematized the use of descriptive formulas in the categorization of children's behavior. The key to understanding their approach, as well as the significance of this work, was the shift, introduced by Thomas and Chess, from the study of *what* children do, to their emphasis on *how* behavior is performed. That is, Thomas and Chess suggested that social behaviors are marked by *formal* characteristics (e.g., amplitude, intensity, rhythm) as well as *content* characteristics (e.g., presence of attachment behaviors, display of specific dependency behaviors, evidence of aggression). This shift in emphasis enabled Thomas and Chess to study what children do across different situations and, in part, exclusive of setting, by observing how a given behavior becomes characteristic or stylistic. For example, by shifting focus from an isolated observation, such as the cry of a child to an unfamiliar person or event, to the relative frequency of approach or withdrawal behaviors to novel stimuli across different settings and in the presence of unanticipated events, they were able to define a characteristic mode of reaction that cuts across situational and temporal restrictions. In this case, knowledge of how a given child responds to a new or novel stimulus may be predictive of his reaction to the first bath, a first haircut, or the first day at school. Similarly, the cry, across multiple settings and interactions, may symbolize, as does the frown and other related avoidance behaviors, a characteristic of temperament that, in this case, is indicative of a negative quality of mood. Some children approach life with a fearful, tentative, almost negative, clearly apprehensive orientation, while others are spontaneous, on occasion, impulsive, frequently and character-istically zestful and vigorous.

A variety of research findings, possessing important implications for our understanding of human growth and development, as well as per-taining to parenting, teaching, and caregiving, have emerged from the study of temperament.

As shown in Table 4.4 nine dimensions of temperament have been identified. These categories, referred to as *primary reaction patterns*, to indicate their relatively early appearance in life, span a variety of psy-chophysiological reactions/adjustments, which may be applied to dif-ferent behaviors, settings, and temporal phases of the life cycle. To illus-trate, *rhythmicity*, which refers to the regularity of biological patterns, has initial application for our understanding of an infant's sleep/awake cycle both at home, as well as in novel settings, which may be applied to assessing relative adjustment to attending overnight camp at 10 years of age, or on going away to college at 18 years of age.

The degree to which early identified temperamental patterns are predictive of later adjustment through the life span has yet to be deter-mined. However, Thomas and Chess provide data that argue for the relative stability of their nine reaction patterns over the first decade of life. Moreover, it appears that these patterns are relatively enduring in the face of situational variations in experience and opportunity.

Another finding to emerge from the Thomas and Chess studies is that among the nine independent primary reaction patterns identified there is clustering and patterning of the separate attributes. Specifically, var-ied attributes may occur together, across different situations. This ten-dency toward clustering has lead Thomas and Chess to posit, based on their available data, the existence of three temperamentally-defined types of children. These temperamental constellations include the easy child, the difficult child, and the slow-to-warm-up child. As illustrated in Table 4.5 these three patterns of children may be characterized by different temperamental attributes, as well as different behavior reactions.

Among the children studied by Thomas and Chess, approximately 40 percent were defined as easy. In contrast, difficult children represented 10 percent of those studied, while slow-to-warm-up children were found to represent 15 percent of the children. As the cautious reader will note, only 65 percent of the children who participated in this research were readily categorized into one of these 3 groups. As Thomas and Chess report, not all children fit into a specific or inclusive temperamental category. Moreover, "among those children who do fit one of these three patterns, there is a wide range in degree of manifes-tation. Some are extremely easy children in practically all situations; others are relatively easy but not always so. A few children are

TABLE 4.4   Categories of Temperament, Their Definition and Scoring

1. *Activity level:* the motor component in a child's functioning and the diurnal proportion of active and inactive periods. Protocol data on mobility during bathing, eating, playing, dressing, and handling, as well as information concerning the sleep-awake cycle, reaching, crawling, and walking, are used in scoring this category.
2. *Rhythmicity (Regularity):* the predictability and/or unpredictability of time of any function. Data analyzed in relation to the sleep-wake cycle, hunger, feeding pattern, and elimination schedule.
3. *Approach or withdrawal:* the nature of an initial response to a new stimulus, whether new food, new toy, or new person. Approach responses are positive, usually evident in mood expression (smiling, verbalizations, etc.) or motor activity (eating a new food, reaching for a new toy, active play with a new person, etc.). Withdrawal reactions are negative, whether displayed by mood expression (crying, fussing, grimacing, verbalizations, etc.) or motor activity (moving away from, spitting new food out, pushing a new toy away, etc.).
4. *Adaptability:* responses to new or altered situations. Interest shifts from concern with the nature of an initial response to the ease with which the child is able to adjust or modify her behavior in a desired direction.
5. *Threshold of responsiveness:* the intensity (amount) of stimulation that is necessary to evoke a discernible response, irrespective of the specific form that the response may take or the sensory modality affected. The behaviors utilized are those concerning reactions to sensory stimuli, environmental objects, and social contacts.
6. *Intensity of reaction:* the energy level of a response, irrespective of its quality or direction (e.g., amplitude of crying, zest displayed upon encountering familiar object)
7. *Quality of mood:* the amount of pleasant, joyful, and friendly behavior, as contrasted with unpleasant, crying, and unfriendly behavior.
8. *Distractibility:* the effectiveness of extraneous environmental stimuli in interfering with or in altering the direction of an ongoing behavior sequence.
9. *Attention span and persistence:* two categories that are related. Attention span concerns the length of time a particular activity is pursued by the child. Persistence refers to the continuation of an activity in the face of obstacles.

Each category is scored on a three-point scale, as follows:

1. Activity Level—High, Medium, Low
2. Rhythmicity—Regular, Variable, Irregular
3. Approach-Withdrawal—Approach, Variable, Withdrawal
4. Adaptability—Adaptive, Variable, Nonadaptive
5. Threshold of Responsiveness—High, Medium, Low
6. Intensity of Reaction—Positive, Variable, Negative
7. Quality of Mood—Positive, Variable, Negative
8. Distractibility—Yes (Distractible), Variable, No (Nondistractible)
9. Attention Span and Persistence—Yes (Persistent), Variable, No (Nonpersistent)

Adapted from: Thomas A. and Chess S., *Temperament and development.* New York: Brunner/Mazel, 1977.

TABLE 4.5.   Temperamental Constellations: Typology, Patterning, and Behavioral Characteristics of Three Groups of Children

Type	Temperamental Pattern	Behavioral Characteristics
Easy Child	Regular rhythm, positive approach to new stimuli, high adaptability to change, mild/moderate intensity of reaction, positive quality of mood	Quick to develop regular sleep and feeding schedules, ready acceptance of new foods, smiles at strangers, adapts easily to a new school, accepts most frustration with little fuss, accepts rules of new games with no trouble
Difficult Child	Irregular in biological functions, negative withdrawal responses to new stimuli, non-adaptability or slow adaptability to change, high intensity or reaction, negative quality of mood	Irregular sleep and feeding schedules, slow acceptance of new foods, prolonged adjustment periods to new routines, people, or situations, relatively frequent and loud periods of crying, loud laughter, frustration produces violent tantrums
Slow-To-Warm-Up Child	Negative response of mild intensity to new stimuli, slow adaptability after repeated contact, mild intensity of reaction, moderate rhythmicity of biological functions	Negative mild responses to new stimuli such as first encounter with a bath, a new food, a stranger, a new place, or a new school situation. With reintroduction of new situations over time and without pressure, quiet and positive interest and involvement evident

extremely difficult with all new situations and demands; others show only some of these characteristics and relatively mildly.'' Finally, they note that, ''for some children it is highly predictable that they will warm up slowly in any new situation; others warm up slowly with certain types of new stimuli or demands, but warm up quickly in others'' (Thomas and Chess, 1977, pp.23–4).

The implications of different temperamental types are multiple. Different types of children will approach and respond to the challenges of development differently. From their data, Thomas and Chess identified 42 clinical cases of behavior disorder over the first 5 years of life (39 percent of the total sample of 136 children). Of these, difficult children comprised the most significant proportion of children likely to develop clinically-related behaviors. Such children, they indicate, are often children at risk. This appears especially so when environmental demands and expectations are in conflict with a child's behavioral style. They note, for example, that the difficult child is particularly prone to symptom development when parents are inconsistent, impatient, or pressuring in their approach to their child. Yet, they also caution that deviant development "was always the result of the interaction between a child's individual makeup and significant features of the environment" (Thomas and Chess, 1977 p.38). Specifically, temperament, as one component of personality, acted in conjunction with ability and motive in determining any specific behavior pattern that may have evolved in the course of the child's development.

The effects of differing temperament upon parents, teachers, and caregivers suggest another kind of implication to which these findings may be directed. For the *difficult child*, the demands of socialization, particularly, as initially expressed by parents, may constitute a source of considerable stress and conflict. Likewise, for parents, particularly the new parent, the especially young parent, the single parent, or parents under stress, the demands or perceived inflexibility of a difficult child may create erratic, resentful, and/or abusive behavior. Yet, other parents will see the difficult child as posing a problem to be resolved, an intriguing puzzle to be approached with care and wisdom, or as a challenge to their anticipations and expectations. They will refer to this child as "energetic," "lusty," or "spontaneous," and actively approach the task of effective parenting.

The *easy child*, by virtue of his temperament, will also create parental reactions, but of a different kind. The parents of an easy child may be pleased to have a child who requires little effort, time, or attention. To them parenting will be a delight. Yet, because of his temperament, the easy child may easily be overlooked, usually in favor of a more demanding sibling. Or his easy adaptability may be viewed by parents or school mates as indicative of his "softness" or lack of leadership character.

The parents and teachers of *slow-to-warm-up* children face another kind of task. Here there exists the danger of adults who too quickly engage in unwarranted categorization or typecasting of the slow-to-warm-up as being too timid, too cautious, or too slow. Or a teacher may view this student, without regard to temperament, as being too lazy. Vacillation between two adult reaction patterns may emerge, ranging from pressuring the child to adapt too quickly to new situations or new

challenges, to a reverse pattern, in which adults engage in overprotec-
tiveness. In the face of the former adult reactions, the child may withdraw from further activity, while the latter reaction, in shielding the
child from new situations, may deny opportunity for wider adaptation,
as well as restrict the child's range of activities, interests, and competencies. For the slow-to-warm-up child, the necessity for patience and
the importance of timing becomes crucial. The old cliché which suggests that the wise teacher learns from her students, tempering her
practice with an understanding of the learner, is a most apt expression
of an appropriate adult reaction to a child of slow-to-warm-up
temperament.

PATTERNS OF ATTACHMENT

> Whatever periodicities of behavior an infant is endowed with at birth, they
> do not continue unchanged but soon become linked to the regularities of
> the external environment of which he is now a part. Just as plants that
> open and close according to the amount of light available will adopt a reg-
> ular day-night pattern, so the infant's rhythms will come to function in
> response to the patterning of the environmental events he encounters
> (Schaffer, 1977, p.64).

The growth and development of each child follows, as Schaffer suggests, a process of intermeshing of inherent capacities, such as temperament, and external opportunities provided by her environment. In
this section we will explore ways in which early caregiving contributes
to development via the varieties of caregiving (that is, patterns of environmental events) that each child will encounter.

Early interactions between parents, usually mothers, and their children have been carefully studied and, in part, documented. Some of
these findings are summarized for the reader in Table 4.6.

As the reader will note, the issue of what is the best care for a young
infant remains to be answered. Clearly, any suggested response to this
question will, of necessity, vary for each child. Moreover, as we have
become increasingly more sensitive to this issue, scientists and educators alike have begun to recognize that the relationship between caregiving and caretaker is both more intricate and exquisite than has been
generally assumed. As Clark-Stewart (1973) has observed, "It appears
that the most significant dimensions of maternal influence are more
complex than gross caretaking patterns or measures of quantity alone"
(p.2).

The caretaking relationship is reciprocal, involving both an infant
and its caregiver alike. How a caregiver perceives the infant, as well as
her role as caregiver, will affect the quality and nature of the act of care-

TABLE 4.6 Early Interactions: Some Conclusions

1. Physical handling that is gentle, firm, close, and relatively frequent has a beneficial effect on the infant's early cognitive and motor development and on his attachment and responsiveness to his mother.
2. Distinctive and frequent verbal stimulation from the mother, by reading or talking to the infant, is related to the child's vocal expressiveness and language facility.
3. Adults serve as direct sources of stimulation for infants, as well as mediators of stimulation from the environment.
4. Children who are provided with adequate play materials and variety in materials and activities demonstrate mature cognitive growth.
5. Deliberate and playful adult stimulation (that is, sensitive and responsive interaction) is an important dimension of maternal influence.
6. An adult's immediate response to an infant's behavior has a significant effect on later occurrences of that behavior.
7. Social responses from an adult, which are made in response to an infant's smiling or vocalizing, increase the frequency of these behaviors.
8. A parent's prompt, contingent, and consistent response to an infant's signals promotes learning in which the infant recognizes that her behavior has consequences and that her actions can control her environment.
9. The ease with which a caregiver *reads* an infant's communications depends on the caregivers' skills, as well as how clearly the baby makes his needs evident.

From: Clark-Stewart, A.K. Interactions between mothers and their young children: Characteristics and consequences. *Monographs of the Society for Research in Child Development,* 1973, 38, Serial No. 153 and Clark-Stewart, A.K. *Daycare.* Cambridge, MA: Harvard University Press, 1982.

giving (Bugental and Shennum, 1984). As researchers have increasingly begun to recognize, the caregiving act represents a transactional process, that is, a series of interactional exchanges in which both adult and infant influence each other's behavior. Adults are important partners in this model. The caregiver who enters the adult-infant relationship, especially with little previous experience, nevertheless, possesses one of several images of infancy. An adult holding a media image of infants will see the young infant as cute and cuddly. Correspondingly, he is likely to exhibit behaviors designed to provoke behavior supporting this impression. The caregiver who holds a tabula rasa view of childhood, derived from Locke, in which she believes that children are to be shaped, molded, or formed into responsible adults, is likely to control and to monitor the child. The adult who "senses" himself as possessing "good rapport with children," largely irrespective of experience or training, is likely to focus on affective relations exclusively and to encounter (largely through trial and error) both good and poor interactions with infants. Each of us also brings to caretaking a special, usually unique, history of opportunities and experiences, some good and others bad. Some adults will conclude, from their own observations and experiences, that development is principally a function of unpredictable factors such as chance or luck. Other adults will derive additional insight from similar experiences and perceive themselves as agents of change. Finally, all adults bring to caregiving a perspective of parenting derived from their own experiences with their parents. Our parents serve as models for our behavior. We also may have had surrogate parenting experiences with younger siblings. As Bugental and Shennum (1984) note, "Child behavior cannot be thought of as producing some kind of automatic, unilateral response from all parents. Conversely, identical parental behavior cannot be expected to have the same kind or amount of impact on all children or on the same child at different ages" (p.2).

As we have seen, interest in describing and defining the index of quality care (see Table 4.6) has been of concern to researchers and practioners alike. In response, a variety of studies have attempted to address the dimension of infant-mother attachment as one critical variable contributing to quality of care. (For the practioner in the field a more specific and detailed consideration of caregiving and related issues will be considered in Chapter 9—Infant/Toddler Environments).

Studies of infant-mother attachment have generally focused on one of three contributing elements to infant-adult interactions:

1. infant disposition, temperament, or character
2. maternal attitudes, beliefs, and values
3. interactive behaviors occurring, usually, within a specific time frame

More recently, Egeland and Farber (1984) have attempted to expand this perspective by the introduction of a transactional model incorporating all three factors. By assessing neonatal, maternal, and interactive factors over time (viz., 12 and 18 months of the infant's life) they were able to describe the development of 3 different attachment relationships characteristic of infant-maternal relations.

The conclusions reported by Egeland and Farber (1984) are most germane to our interests. Among their observations it was found that neither infant characteristics alone nor maternal attributes considered separately were predictive of the form/quality of initial attachments, nor of their stability/change over time. Rather, as we would expect from our review of infant development, each participant contributes to the formation and success of the infant-caregiver relationship.

A second finding to emerge from this study pertains to qualities that appear to be important in assisting the establishment of the attachment

TABLE 4.7.   Three Patterns of Infant-Caregiver Attachment

Type of Caregiver	Infant Characteristics	Caretaker Characteristics
Securely Attached	Robust, explores the environment with zest and vigor, active; socially engaging	Sensitive, cooperative, accepting, accessible, encourages reciprocity; skillful in caregiving
Anxious/ Avoidant	Demonstrates little emotionality in infant-mother interaction; restricted, affectless exploration	Lacking in confidence, tense and irritable, rejecting; shows aversion to physical contact; avoids reciprocity, poor caretaking skills; mechanical in caretaking and resentful
Anxious/Resistant	Developmentally delayed, lower birth weight, lower Apgar ratings; impoverished exploration; difficulty being comforted; less socially engaging	Initially younger, insecure, and negative in reaction to their pregnancy; possesses poor understanding and lack of knowledge of infants' needs; level of competence increased over time and with experience

Adapted from: Egeland, B. and Farber, E.A. Infant-mother attachment: Factors related to its development and changes over time. *Child Development*, 1984, 55, 753–71.

bond. Apparently, a secure attachment is most often facilitated by caregivers who possess good caretaking skills, that is, the ability to enlist caring skills that are well paced, temporally-ordered, and sensitively applied to current needs. From these data, it was found that the mother who is sensitive to and perceptive of her infant's needs and exhibits appropriate responses in feeding and playing with her infant will engender a secure attachment.

Finally, it was found that initial attachments (that is, attachments occurring over the first year) may change over time. More specifically, the qualities and conditions of caregiving that initially contribute to differing patterns of attachment (as described) appear to shift over time and, as such, allow opportunity for more extensive or restrictive bonding. As Egeland and Farber note, "It appears that specific caretaking skills such as appropriate pacing and timing are important for the formation of a secure attachment during the first year." Yet, they continue, "Mothers' affective behaviors are important for maintaining the secure attachment once it is formed" (p.769). These data support the interplay of skillful caregiving provided within the context of demonstrative adult affection as central components in the formation of attachment.

SUMMARY

The period that we call infancy, roughly the first 18 months of life, is a rich and varied tapestry. During the process from the awkward appearing neonate with his large head and random movements to the sophisticated, interactive, mobile child, we witness enormous change. As we have seen, the basic program for growth unfolds from birth. The infant matches facial expressions and body movements and has certain measurable temperament characteristics from his first few days of life. He can quickly produce smiles and respond to human voices. All of these abilities suggest a competence far beyond what we once attributed to the infant state.

Awareness of self and awareness of others, especially in terms of maternal bonding, follow a developmental sequence of growing sophistication. The infant is clearly a social being and uses her skills to facilitate human interactions. However, as studies of temperament show, individual differences are as vital to infant-adult interaction as they are to adult-adult interaction. The concept of "easy child," "difficult child," and "slow-to-warm-up child" has special significance for adult caregivers. Appropriate responses to infants and toddlers require sensitive adults who can adapt their approach according to the needs and styles of the child.

Explorations

Do one or two explorations in each category to extend and enrich your understanding of this chapter.

PERSONAL EXPLORATIONS

These exercises are designed to help you look at your own life, specifically, your attitudes, dreams, myths, and realities.

1. Ask an adult member of your family what you were "like" as an infant (during the first 18 months of life). Summarize these descriptions in a one-page report and relate your descriptive data to three concepts or ideas of infancy discussed in this chapter. How have you changed? How are you the same?

2. If your family has a picture album look at the pictures of yourself and your siblings (if pictures are available), particularly, photos depicting interactions with other persons, both adults and children. What interactions can you observe from these photos that illustrate ideas presented in Table 4.6—Early Interactions? Write a brief summary of the interaction patterns which stand out. (If you don't have access to a family photos album, try to borrow one from a friend.)
3. Think about a particular infant you know well (sibling, relative, a child you recently babysat for, your own child). How would you rate this infant on each of the nine categories of temperament defined by Thomas and Chess?
4. Read and think about the data presented on caregivers and early interactions described in Tables 4.6 and 4.7. Then spend some time viewing, as objectively as possible, your own personality. Make a list of the ways you believe that you would do a "good" job as a caregiver. Make a second list of your personal characteristics that might be a problem. Write a summary paragraph of your potential strengths and weaknesses as an infant caregiver.

INTELLECTUAL EXPLORATIONS

These exercises are designed to increase your depth of knowledge in some of the areas discussed in this chapter.

1. Infant research has increased significantly in the last 10 years. Pick a subject not discussed in depth in this chapter, read two research articles that discuss this area and write a summary of the papers you read. Examples of potential topics include bonding, auditory/perceptual development in infants, learning, and memory.
2. Some recent writers have argued that even babies can learn to read. Find a book or article discussing this idea and examine its major thesis and support for its acceptance. What approaches are advocated? How do the author(s) justify their claims? Write a one page critique that includes your reasons for agreeing or disagreeing with the position you have examined.
3. Parenting is not an instinctual skill. We find many experts offering varying opinions on caregiving. Find two examples of caregiving advice to parents of infants and write a brief report comparing the two approaches.
4. Infants "at risk," including those with physical or mental handicaps, such as, blindness, Down's Syndrome, etc., as well as those subject to development delays or different individual temperaments, are receiving increased attention among researchers and popular journalists. Find one article in this area of interest in each of these two types of publication. Write a one-page summary of each article and another page comparing and contrasting the approach, style, and content of the two articles.

FIELD EXPLORATIONS

These exercises are designed to take you out into the world to find real examples that will illustrate and elucidate the material in this chapter.

1. Visit a toy store and look at the various toys that are recommended for infants up to 18 months of age. (If no such stores are easily accessible, look at catalogues that show children's toys.) Write a brief description of a dozen toys, including their recommended age levels. Then, using Table 4.2 as a reference point, decide which of these toys are appropriate for the ages specified by their manufacturer and give at least two reasons why you might purchase them for an infant in your care.
2. Looking at the same toys selected above, or others of interest, decide which toys may appeal to some temperamental types more than others. Categorize your selections and offer reasons for your decisions.
3. Visit a well-baby clinic, pediatrician's office, or other environment in which infants can be observed with their caregivers. Pick out two infants who seem to be responding very differently to what is happening. Notice the caregivers responses and interactions and write a clinical (factual) description of two or three interactions for each caregiver-infant pair. Bring your descriptions to class for discussion.
4. View some television commercials that use very young children (up to two years of age) in their advertisements. Write a brief description of each commercial and then write a summary of the different competencies you observed in the children depicted/employed.

References

Bertenthal, B. I. and Fisher, K. W. Development of self-recognition in the infant. *Developmental Psychology*, 1978, 14, 44–50.

Boccia, M. and Campos, J. Maternal emotional significance: Its effect on infants' reaction to strangers. Paper presented at the meeting of the Society for Research in Child Development, Detroit, April, 1983.

Bower, T. G. R. *A primer of infant development*, San Francisco, W.H. Freeman, 1977.

———*Development in infancy*. Second Ed. San Francisco, W. H. Freeman, 1982.

Brackbill, Y. Extinction of the smiling response in infants as a function of reinforcement schedule. *Child Development*, 1958, 29, 115–24.

Bugental, D. B. and Shennum, W. A. "Difficult" children as elicitors and targets of adult communication patterns: An attributional-behavioral transactional analysis. *Monographs of the Society for Research in Child Development*, 1984, Serial No. 205.

Buhler, C. *The first year of life*. New York: John Day, 1930.

Campos, J. J. and Stenberg, C. Perception, appraisal and emotion: The onset of social referencing. In M. E. Lamb and L. R. Sherrod (Eds.), *Infant social cognition: Empirical and theoretical considerations*. Hillsdale, NJ: Erlbaum, 1981.

Carpenter, G. Mother's face and the newborn. In R. Lewin (Ed.), *Child alive*. London: Temple Smith, 1975.

Clark-Stewart, A. K. Interactions between mothers and their young children: Characteristics and consequences. *Monographs of the Society for Research in Child Development*, 1973, 38, Serial No. 153.

————*Daycare*. Cambridge, MA: Harvard University Press, 1982.

Condon, W. S. and Sandor, L. Neonate movement is synchronized with adult speech: Interactional participation and language acquisition. *Science*, 1974, 183, 99–101.

Egeland, B. and Farber, E. A. Infant-mother attachment: Factors related to its development and changes over time. *Child Development*, 1984, 55, 753–71.

Field, T. M., Woodson, R., Greenberg, R. and Cohen, D. Discrimination and imitation of facial expressions by neonates. Paper presented at the International Conference on Infant Studies, Austin, Texas, 1982. (Also see *Science*, 1982, 218, 179–81.

Fogel, A. *Infancy: Infant, family and society*. St. Paul, MN: West, 1984.

Klinnert, M. Emde, R. N., Butterfield, P. and Campos, J. J. Emotional communication from familiarized adults influences infants behavior. Paper presented at the meeting of the Society for Research in Child Development, Detroit, April, 1983.

Korner, A. F. Early stimulation and maternal care as related to infant capacities and individual differences. *Early Child Development and Care*, 1973, 2, 307–27.

Lamb, M. E. and Campos, J. J. *Development in infancy*. New York: Random House, 1982.

Lewis, M. and Brooks-Gunn, J. *Social cognition and the acquisition of self*. New York: Plenum, 1979.

Martin, G. and Clarke, E. Distress crying in neonates: Species and peer specificity. *Developmental Psychology*, 1982, 18, 3–10.

Meltzoff, A. N. and Moore, M. K. Imitation of facial and manual gestures by human neonates. *Science*, 1977, 198, 75–8.

————.Newborn infants imitate adult facial gestures. *Child Development*, 1983, 54, 702–09.

Newson, J. and Newson, E. *Seven years old in the home environment*. London: Allen & Unwin, 1976.

Piaget, J. *Play, dreams and imitation in childhood*. New York: Norton, 1962.

Sagi, A. and Hoffman, M. Empathic distress in the newborn. *Developmental Psychology*, 1976, 12, 175–76.

Scarr, S. and Kidd, K. K. Developmental behavior genetics. In P.H. Mussen (Ed.), *Handbook of child psychology*. Fourth Ed., Vol. 11, New York: John Wiley & Sons, 1983.

Schaffer, H. R. and Emerson, P. Patterns of response to physical contact in early human development. *Journal of Child Psychiatry and Psychology*, 1964, 5, 1–13.

Schaffer, H. R. *Mothering*. Cambridge, MA: Harvard University Press, 1977.

Sorce, J., Emde, R. N., Campos, J. J. and Klinnert, M. Maternal emotional signaling: Its effect on the visual cliff behavior of one-year-olds. Paper presented at the meeting of the Society for Research in Child Development, Boston, April, 1981.

Svejda, M. and Campos, J. J. The mother's voice as a regulator of the infant's behavior. Paper presented at the meeting of the International Conference on Infant Studies. Austin, Tx, March, 1982.

Thomas, A., Chess, S., and Birch, H. G. *Temperament and behavior disorders in children*. New York: New York University Press, 1968.

Thomas, A. and Chess, S. *Temperament and development*. New York: Brunner/ Mazel, 1977.

———.*The dynamics of psychological development*. Brunner/Mazel, 1980.

Zahn-Waxler, C., Radke-Yarrow, M. and King, R. A. Child rearing and children's prosocial initiations toward victims of distress. *Child Development*, 1979, 50, 319–30.

Chapter 5

FAMILY PATTERNS

Objectives

After reading this chapter the student should be able to:

1. Define a system and give an example of potential stressors that can affect the family system.
2. List different communication behaviors and give examples of congruent and incongruent messages that can be communicated in the family.
3. List several dimensions in which families differ and be able to define a minimum of four.
4. Discuss the evolution of the nuclear family in Western culture and compare and contrast it with the extended family.
5. Discuss one of four family variations in depth, including its subtypes and strengths and difficulties.
6. List examples of child behaviors which may indicate problems in the family that require outside intervention.
7. List factors that contribute to coping behaviors in families dealing with illness or death of a family member.

The most profound set of relationships we experience in our lifetime are those that occur within our family of origin. This statement may seem self-evident. However, it was not until the 1950s that real attention was paid to family research and therapy. Today, in the "enlightened eighties" the family, viewed as a system, is still a new idea in contrast to the more traditional approach of individual growth and development. Carter and McGoldrick (1980) define the family as "a basic unit of emotional development, the phases and course of which can be identified and predicted" (p. 4).

MAJOR FUNCTIONS OF THE FAMILY

It is generally accepted that the major purpose of the family is to enhance the physical survival and personal growth of its individual members. This is done within an intergenerational context, which includes family attitudes, expectations, rules, taboos, and roles played over three generations (grandparents, parents, and children). The merging of these factors shapes the individual's view of the world. The attachments, interactions, and perceptions fostered in the family are life long, and coupled with the individual's personal temperament, they form her unique view of the world.

The U.S. model of parents and children living together (that is, the *nuclear family*) is still the dominant ideal "family" in our society. However, events within present society do not completely support past perspectives. The 1980 census showed us that less than 20 percent of U.S. families were composed of two parents and nonadult children living in one domicile. Divorce, single parenting, longer life spans for couples whose children have grown and left home, and the variety of different cultural groups who have shared arrangements, are part of a wide diversity in family living patterns. All of these differences in turn create different life styles and different worlds of experience for the child. It is important to understand these worlds through some of the major concepts of *family systems theory* if we are to understand and facilitate children's growth and learning.

Systems Theory

One way of understanding the family is through systems theory. We use the term system in a wide variety of ways. We talk about a heating system, a school system, a system of ideas, a family system. All of these have some similarities as well as differences. The term "theory" can be understood as a unified way of looking at and talking about a body of information. If we have a theory in common we can talk about relationships between various elements or events and attempt to explain and/or predict happenings in some consistent way. Thus family systems theory provides us with a set of concepts to use in discussion and a method of prediction that allows us to test our beliefs about families. As such, it is a useful tool for objective analysis of any particular phenomena we wish to follow. See Table 5.1 for some specific systems definitions.

TABLE 5.1.   Some Definitions of Family Systems Theory

Term	Definition	Example
System	A set of interrelated/interconnected subsystems that operate together for some purpose or goal.	Any family
Subsystem	A smaller unit of objects, items, members, etc., which interact separately and affect the working of the larger system.	Parents, siblings, twins
Operations	Actions that are performed to set elements in motion.	Behaviors, communications, events
Functional	An action or pattern that promotes movement toward the system's purpose.	A family picnic
Dysfunctional	An action or pattern that disrupts the movement toward the system's purpose.	A family argument

For example, a heating system consists of a variety of subsystems such as the thermostat, the furnace, and perhaps a fuel gauge. Its purpose is to provide heat for a particular area. Each subsystem has its own components such as wires, temperature sensors, and so on. An operation such as turning up the thermostat will generate a current in the thermostat which will then send signals to the furnace, which will in turn release fuel to produce heat. The system becomes dysfunctional if it runs out of fuel or if the thermostat stops working.

In a mechanical system it is relatively easy to trace the interactions within each subsystem and to understand and predict how they act upon the other subsystems to produce the desired goal(s). The more complex the system and the more varied the choices of operations, the more difficult it becomes to understand and predict outcomes. Also, the more possible outcomes there are, the more likely it is that there will be break downs or occasional dysfunctions in the system. Human systems are the most complex of all types of systems we attempt to analyze and, therefore, the most variable. As we look at family systems theories, we will use the terms and concepts just discussed as an aid to understanding.

Because different theories concerning family systems describe different aspects of the wide range of possible human behavior, we find there are a variety of family theories available. We will look at two system theories that discuss some of the different aspects of human development in the family. We hope these approaches will aid your attempt to better understand and appreciate the influences and interactions that shape the growth of children.

Developmental Family Theory—The Family Life Cycle

Developmental family theory looks at the family life cycle through time and sees changes and transitions as normal aspects of all family life. All change, both positive and negative, creates stress. The family's ability to cope with stress and with the day to day process of living constitutes the patterns, that is, the rules and roles, that influence the interactions of the family members.

Over time the family must be able to adapt to new changes and to develop alternate ways of interacting in order to remain functional. Dysfunctional family patterns create various problems for the system ranging from minor difficulties in meeting member needs, to behavior that is extremely destructive and can destroy the family. For example, a family with the tradition and accompanying expectations of high academic success might be more stressed with the birth of a retarded child than a family in which school drop out is an accepted pattern. Another family, with lower expectations, might find it equally stressful to have a child genius in their midst.

When an infant is born into a family she receives a biological and psychological inheritance. The degree to which the parents of this child are ready and able to take on their roles as parents is determined in large degree by how well they have completed the tasks of the previous stages. If they have succeeded in their occupational and marital choice and have sufficiently separated from their own original family (that is, have created a sense of "coupleness" and separateness) they will feel ready to welcome this new family member. In turn, the child will learn what her role in the family is and what is expected through her interactions with her parents and, later, others.

Each infant's personality, receptiveness, and responses will help to shape the total family process. *Mutuality* is an important, positive aspect of family interaction. Both child and parents have needs which must be met and need attainment is a necessary condition for further development. The "good-enough" family is one that meets the needs of its members; the "good-enough child . . . is able to engage with parenting figures in a mutual and reciprocal fashion, learning behavioral sequences that simultaneously promote attainment of its own and its parenting figure's developmental needs" (Terkelsen, 1980, p.33).

As the family moves through time and the infant becomes a toddler, and later, goes off to school, she will become "socialized," that is, learn patterns of behavior acceptable to the family and that segment of society to which they belong.

Looking at these developmental concepts it should become evident that some children will come to school with emotional as well as physical needs that are being inadequately met and that this will affect the child/teacher/school experience.

The child with a teen-age parent or the child being raised by much older parents, the family in the process of separation or divorce, the father who hates his present job or is moonlighting because of money pressures, the mother who is still overly attached to her original family are all *potentially* facing extra stresses in meeting present family needs. We will discuss some of these issues at a later point in this chapter. It is sufficient at this point to appreciate the profound impact of the family life cycle on the child and the potential for family stressors to influence the child's reactions and interactions in conjunction with the school experience.

Communication Systems Theory

In the theoretical orientation of communication systems theory, as discussed by Virginia Satir, for the child, "Communication is the largest single factor determining what kinds of relationships he makes with others and what happens to him in the world about him" (Satir, 1972, p.30).

Communication is not only verbal interactions. All behavior can be seen as a form of communication. Facial expressions, "body language," that is, movements and positions of the body, are commonly under-stood as nonverbal communications. Other behavior also communi-cates; being late to a meeting may communicate lack of concern or car-ing; bringing home flowers or helping carry packages can be understood as a loving message, and so on. Patterns and styles of com-munication are learned and are used by individual family members first for survival and then for growth and success.

Another basic concept in this orientation is the person's need for self-esteem, that is, the belief that she or he is worthwhile and valuable and can learn. The sense of self-esteem develops within the family context and is directly related to the messages received from parents and other family members.

Satir sees the primary task of the family as overcoming alienation and aloneness by creating a group of persons who know and care for each other. Self-esteem, self-worth, and self-image are all interrelated con-cepts that indicate a *learned* sense of self as a competent, lovable person.

Each family has rules that govern communication behavior and each individual plays a variety of roles in the family, which determine her interactions with others. The patterns of communication in the family can be functional or dysfunctional. Two types of communication are particularly important in this respect:

Incongruent messages—communication in which different aspects of the message do not match.
Congruent messages—communication and responses that are complemen-tary and matched.

Some common examples of incongruent messages include: incompati-ble words and voice tone—"I love you" is said in an angry or bored tone; when facial expression and message do not match; "I am sad" when a person is smiling; when a person agrees to do a task and then "forgets" because he didn't really want to do it; when a parent says "uh huh" and "that's nice" type responses to a child's message but is not really listening.

Incongruent messages tend to impede communication and create dysfunctional behaviors. Congruent messages, on the other hand, are those in which different aspects of communication match or which

TABLE 5.2. Communication Patterns

Type of Communication	Style of Communication	Recognized by	Overt Statement	Covert Statement
Congruent message	Leveling	Signals match	"I feel good about myself."	none
Incongruent message	Blaming	Tells others they are bad.	"You are wrong."	I feel guilty and unsure.
Incongruent message	Computing	Logical but nonemotional	"This is the right way."	"I am afraid of my feelings."
Incongruent message	Placating	Others are more important	"I want what you want."	"I fear you'll go away unless I please you."
Incongruent message	Distracting	Off the topic and confusing	"Let me entertain."	"I'm afraid to talk about that."

Adapted from: Satir V. *Peoplemaking.* (Palo Alto, CA: Science and Behavior Books, 1972).

tend to facilitate communicaton and help individuals and families function smoothly. See Table 5.2.

Naturally there are wide differences in operating style among families. Some of the ways families differ include:

1. family rules
2. family values
3. leadership patterns
4. clarity of communications
5. family productivity or efficiency
6. expression of conflict
7. how "open" or "closed" the family is to outside ideas, people, changes.

Family differences affect the child's view of the world and her view of self. None of these differences are functional or dysfunctional in themselves, they merely represent the myriad possibilities in family patterns which exist in any culture.

The Child's Experience within the Family

Our discussion of the functions of the family should make it evident that the child brings a complex set of internal beliefs and behaviors with

TABLE 5.3.   Some Definitions of Terms in Family Theory

Role—A set of *expected* behaviors that are associated with a defined status, i.e., wife, husband, sister, grandmother, etc.

Role Behavior—The actual behaviors a particular person performs in their role, e.g., if the family defines the role of big brother as protector of younger siblings, the extent to which this child actually does or does not protect will be his role behavior. Note the roles and role behaviors do not necessarily match. More stress will be experienced, however, by individual and family if the role and role behaviors are widely discrepant.

Rules—Spoken (explicit rules) and unspoken (implicit rules) requirements for behavior. "Children should not talk back to adults;" "Fathers work and bring home money for living;" "Mother and children go to church on Sunday, but Father doesn't have to go;" "Nobody in the family is supposed to talk about Aunt Martha;" etc.

Values—A belief held in common concerning the way people *should* behave and interact (e.g., religious practice, educational attainment).

Communication Pattern—A manner of communicating that is repeated in the family in a regular way. "Child asks permission to leave the table at the end of dinner;" "Father slams the door and leaves house whenever he is angry."

him as he begins school. Absence of this awareness or lack of understanding on the teacher's part can create additional stresses for the child and his family. Certainly by preschool age, the child has learned many family values, rules, and communication patterns and has achieved a sense of his own self-worth.

The school also has a set of values to impart: there are rules to follow and communication patterns to learn. The child will develop a new set of roles in school, that is, class clown, teacher's pet, little professor, and his sense of self-esteem will be enhanced or undermined by teacher and peer interactions and his feelings of being a successful learner. To the extent that the school and home provide noninterfering, that is, congruent communications, the child's world is enriched and he adds to his storehouse of knowledge; if the communications interfere with each other, however, the child may experience conflicts with potential long-range implications. For most children the primary attachments of the home are the central force in their development. Teachers *must* be able to accommodate their roles to the basic realities that shape the child's world.

Since there are many different types of families, we need to look at family patterns, both traditional and nontraditional, that make up our present social fabric.

TYPES OF FAMILIES

The Nuclear Family

The two-parent family with nonadult children at home has become a minority pattern in our present society. This is not as ominous as it may sound, however, since the nuclear family is an unusual pattern, both historically and culturally. The tribe, the extended family, and the multigenerational family have always been a more prevalent cultural pattern.

Cross-cultural studies show that most families consist of several generations living together. Very few societies have had the material luxury of an older, grandparent generation living separately or of young couples who move off on their own. In agricultural and other nonindustrial countries at different historical periods, survival alone dictated the sharing of work and resources. All related kin were often grouped together to allow for survival. Limited age span and high mortality rates kept the numbers of a family or kinship group to a reasonable size but rarely did any but unattached males go off on their own pursuits. Wars, diseases, and the difficulties of living made all members of a family valuable and productive members of the group.

In the last 50 years the nuclear family has become a prevalent form of family life in Western European society. In this country, the industrial revolution and a prosperous corporate society have created an even more unique model of the nuclear family, namely, parents and children living alone in distant geographical areas. Correspondingly, the kinship network has become scattered and often unavailable to the family.

Thus the nuclear family may present certain unique stresses as a family pattern. Expenses of maintaining a separate residence may mean that father works long hours and is away from home most of the child's waking hours. Social isolation may be a problem for a young mother with preschool or young school age children. Fewer children may mean elevated expectations for children's attainments as well. Each increases the stress within the family setting. Certainly, the world is far different for the only child, the younger of two, or the middle of three.

Economic conditions and the desire for an enhanced standard of living have created a newer variation of the nuclear family—the two-paycheck family (Rappaport and Rappaport, 1976).

Slightly over half of U.S. mothers with preschool children are now in the work force (Berns, 1985). This phenomenon has had a large impact on family living. Absence of kin to care for the children of these families increases the need for family and group day care, after school facilities, and other child supervision programs. The latch-key child has now become a common phenomenon of contemporary U.S. culture.

The family with both parents working offers a different life style from other nuclear families. Parents who are happy and comfortable with their choice still find themselves coping with child care, home maintenance, and personal power issues, which have varied ramifications for the child. How they are addressed within the family form part of the child's experience.

Family Variations

Single-Parent Families

Single parents are another increasingly large phenomenon of contemporary society. There are three categories of single parents, each with distinct characteristics:

DIVORCED AND SEPARATED FAMILIES. Probably the most noted pattern variation is the divorced family. Divorce rates climbed alarmingly in the seventies and early eighties until predictions of disaster and the demise of the family were voiced in thousands of newspaper, magazine, and journal articles. Statistics compiled in 1982 indicated that over five million children lived in either divorced or separated homes. It is now estimated that by the end of the decade 70 percent of all children will spend two or more years in a single parent home (Glick, 1984).

Irrespective of the transition from a two parent to a divorced or separated family, the child faces a major disruption of her world. Each child has only one set of parents and, except in extreme cases, the division of one's home is an irreparable tearing. Adults will usually rebuild their lives, find new partners, and create a new world. But never again will the child's world be the same. It is rare to find a child that does not harbor at least a secret wish that his family will be reunited.

In cases of divorce both adults and children go through a period of mourning similar to the grieving over a death. Moreover, it takes one to two years for the divorce process to be completed, and for the family to feel less stressed. During this time a child's school work and peer and adult relations may be affected markedly. Teachers need to be especially sensitive to the difficulties of this transition for the child and make sure that they provide support and encouragement. An unthinking teacher who insists that all children make father's day cards or that everybody's mommy come down to school and help the PTA may suddenly have a tearful or sullen youngster on his hands. Expectations of a "normal" family may color a teacher's choices in books read to the children or requests for parental involvement, and creates a potentially hurtful situation. Even teachers who feel they are knowledgeable and accepting may find themselves startled when a custodial father appears at a "mothers'" tea. Old stereotypes are difficult to escape. Articles, books, and workshops have recently begun to appear and are increasing teachers' awareness. Changing some of the previous "standard" curriculum practices, which ignored family variations, has begun. Films and television are also aiding public awareness.

TABLE 5.4   Factors Influencing Impact of Divorce on Children

Factor	Influence
Age of child	Much younger (0–2) and much older (18 and above) less affected
Income of family	Families who experience a severe downward economic shift are more heavily affected
Stability of custodial parent	The child caring parent who manages to cope well with marital disruption helps child's adjustment
Continued involvement of noncustodial parent or joint custody arrangements	Where both parents maintain contact and continued positive involvement children adjust better
Extended family and social network	The more help and support available from kin or friends the better the adjustment to the separation process
School support and understanding	Teacher attitude and school's ability to provide a stable environment and adapt curriculum to reflect alternative family lifestyles can help children cope with adjustment

SINGLE PARENT FAMILIES THROUGH DEATH.   The death of a parent also has a profound effect on the child. Yet, it is easier for a child to cope with death than separation or divorce. Rarely will the death of a parent have the same stigma and sense of failure that accompanies the early stages of separation. Moreover, community sympathy and support are given without the dual loyalties and confusions that often cause a child pain. (Except for involvement of both parents in leave taking, all the other factors indicated in Table 5.4 are relevant.)

The young child from approximately three to six or seven may find the idea of death hard to understand, and the explanations given may cause anxiety. If told that death is somehow equivalent to "sleeping" or "going away on a trip" the child may become fearful of falling asleep at night or of his remaining parent leaving the house. Sometimes young children also feel responsible or guilty. The egocentric nature of the young child and her limitations in cognitive understanding may lead her to believe that some anger or personal wish "killed" the parent. Since most children experience anger at their parents, usually in the process of being disciplined or thwarted in some desire, this is an easy association for them to make. Reassurance and clear, simple explanations are most helpful during the first period after a parental death. There are a number of excellent books for children, which can be shared, to help the child gradually acquire an understanding of what has happened. Teachers can be of immeasurable assistance when they provide support and conceptual understanding for children during such a loss. (Death of a parent is discussed further in this chapter under families with special problems.)

UNMARRIED PARENTS.   The idea of a never married parent is still a difficult issue in our culture. There are varied ways of becoming an unmarried parent. Adoption, foster parenting, and birth, planned or unplanned, are all current family patterns. Historically, only unplanned birth was a usual, if not necessarily acceptable, road to being an unmarried parent. Our society has taken a very negative view of illegitimacy in the past, but this has begun to change. Current trends seem to be less judgmental of the unmarried parent who elects to raise her own child. It is extremely important that teachers be aware of their own value system and of the values of the subculture in which their school is embedded. Negative messages concerning the worth of a child or her parents' lifestyle choices can cause deep rifts between the school and the surrounding community.

Until recently adoption and foster parenting by an unmarried person was an exception. In the last 10 years, however, there has been a large increase in the number of single people wanting to adopt or foster a child.

Fostering is defined as the care of a child who is not related by kinship and is not legally adopted. In many cases the care of the child is financially assisted by the state welfare system. State assisted foster care situations, unfortunately, are often highly variable. In most states the usual philosophy is to encourage the return of children to the natural parent(s) as quickly as possible. This goal, while certainly worthwhile, can mean that a child moves in and out of foster care situations a number of times as the circumstances of the family change.

Seems like every time I got settled in a new foster home and started to like it, my mother would be off the bottle and I'd get sent home again. I'd always hope it was going to work and for a while things would be okay. Then she'd start drinking again and pretty soon she'd be in the hospital and I'd be back in a new home. It'd always be a new one 'cause the one where I was before would have other kids by then. By the time I was 12 I'd been in 5 different homes and I didn't hope any more and once I was 15 I just started running away. It's still hard for me to believe I belong anywhere" (Author interview with a 25 year old).

Unmarried parents face all the trials and difficulties of any single parent. They have made an important and far-reaching choice in raising a child without the assistance of another parent. Again, the attitude of teacher and school personnel can assist or undermine this choice.

ADOLESCENT PARENTING. The number of teen-age mothers who keep their children has increased enormously in the last 10 years. Over one-half million children are born to teenagers (girls between 13 and 19) each year. This trend has caused a wide increase in support services in the last few years. Child care centers attached to high schools, parenting classes, and increased outreach at local health centers are being offered in many areas. There is much evidence to show that adolescence is a difficult time to give birth. Infant mortality rates are higher, mothers are less likely to finish school, are more likely to be on welfare, and more likely to have more children without a continuing male partner (Schultz and Jones, 1983). Many young girls give their children up for adoption at a point where they become harder to place (around school age) and this, unfortunately, can lead to a life in and out of foster care for the child. It seems likely that helping these families and widening their avenues of choice will be an ongoing problem.

Blended Families

Increases in divorce and remarriage have led to growing numbers of stepfamilies. A stepfamily is one in which at least one of the partners has a child living at home when the new family is formed.

Historically, with higher mortality rates, stepparenting has been a frequent occurrence since it has been unusual for single parents to raise children alone. However, the increase in divorce has created a unique family system that often includes multiple ties to the non-custodial parent and his or her family. Because of the complex and multiple connections and adjustments necessary, blended families are not as stable as remarriages without children. This means that some children face more than one divorce or separation in their lifetime. While the ties in the second family may not be as strong as to the original parents, a disruption is still stressful. Moreover, even children who have openly fought the remarriage have guilt and disappointment if the second marriage is not successful.

Extended Families

The extended family is still the most typical family pattern worldwide and is once more on the rise in the United States. For economic reasons the grandparent generation has most often resided with adult children in their domicile. However, many extended families include aunts or uncles, several adult children with spouses and offspring, or unmarried daughters with their child or children. Job loss, divorce, or death may bring an adult child back into the family home with or without offspring.

Some families, who have separate residences, may share an apartment house or several homes on the same or adjoining property, often with open access for the children. While viewed as a small town phenomenon, even in large cities a single neighborhood may house grandparents, sisters, brothers, aunts, uncles, in-laws, cousins, and their spouses and children all within comfortable reach.

The extended family has been a prevalent form of family life because it offers a number of advantages, especially for the young family. Resources including child care, transportation, and equipment as well as other material goods and services can be shared. Psychological support allowing for persons to talk with and share experiences and to serve as models in approaching common family problems helps relieve feelings of isolation and uncertainty which can plague a young couple in a nuclear family. Extended families also provide children with additional adults and children, both as potential models and as resources for interaction. In many subcultures in our society children may spend large amounts of time or even live with relatives other than their biological parents. This can be especially helpful during high stress periods such as illness, birth of a new sibling, or a job loss. Familiar and loving alternatives to the natural parents can provide a safe haven during life's storms without threatening the child's allegiance or self-concept.

Like any family pattern, the extended family also has potential stressors. Some individuals may find it difficult to leave the family of origin or to differentiate themselves from a family and discover their own identity. Forming alliances outside the family or with another of a different family orientation (from religion to life style) may be opposed. Also, overly dependent patterns may be perpetuated. The degree of "health" in the family network, both mental and physical, will be seen as the norm and emulated, while patterns of communication may be passed from generation to generation without periodic reevaluation or external input. The classic feuding families of the southern hills (Ozarks and Appalachia) are extreme examples of destructive family patterns which can be "passed down." Moreover, in some isolated communities negative genetic patterns have been prevalent because of extensive intermarriage. (These examples are obviously extremes.)

It seems likely that the extended family will continue to be an important and viable family pattern. Indeed, increased economic pressures appear to be causing an increase in the percentage of multi-generational families who share one domicile (Glick, 1984).

Non-families

At various historical points, non-family groups have joined together to provide mutual safety and resources. The most common cause for an aggregate way of life has been religious conviction. Historically, many groups have created separate communities based on their beliefs. The Amish and Menonites are two such groups, which still exist within our society today.

Utopian communities, based on nonreligious belief systems have also been formed where the children in these communities participate in their home environment and, often through the school, with other groups as well. The nineteen sixties and early seventies saw the creation of many "communes," which brought together nonrelated and often noncoupled individuals who brought children with them or produced them after joining. While communes appear to be less popular in the eighties, cooperative living of entire families or of single-parent families has become more common. The economic pressures of today's society are especially acute for newly formed couples and single parents. These cooperative enterprises provide many of the same benefits and stressors of the extended family model without kinship ties.

Homosexual couples, both male and female, who sometimes bring children from previous marriages or relationships into a new family pattern are now beginning to be acknowledged in our society. Until recently, the admission of homosexuality was sufficient grounds for the family court to remove children from a natural parent living with a same-sex partner. Automatic removal is now being tempered with objective reports on the quality of the home and the adjustment of the children.

Since families formed without kinship ties (by birth or adoption) have no legal status in our society they face a variety of difficulties not experienced by other family groups. Absence of social acceptance, limited legal recourse (common-law marriage can be used for inheritance purposes in some states), and limited access to some of the economic advantages of family living (for example, lower tax rates, family medical plans, and inheritance safeguards) produce unique stresses which may have an impact on the child's world. These create many potentially difficult encounters with nonfamily individuals and institutions. To some extent young children may be oblivious to the attitudes of the larger society, particularly since their egocentric view may lead them to assume that all families are like their own. Older children, however, are often very sensitive to potential rejection by peers and may show some difficulties with adjustment in other environments such as the school. Since the school must accept and encourage all children, regardless of their family background, sensitivity and understanding are essential attributes in teachers and staff. (We will discuss some guidelines for exercising teacher awareness later in this chapter.)

Parents foster children's communication.

FAMILIES WITH SPECIAL PROBLEMS

In addition to the need to understand family patterns and types, schools need to acknowledge families with special problems. Children may come to school bearing the burden of various traumas, including neglect, physical and sexual abuse including incest, alcoholic or drug addicted parents or other family members, problems with poor adjustment or mental illness within the family, struggles with severely ill or handicapped family members, and problems of poverty and prejudice, especially in relation to ethnicity.

According to an article by Walter J. Junewicz (1983), poor home conditions affect a substantial percentage of children. Citing several studies, he lists five types of vulnerable family environments:

Certain home conditions increase children's vulnerability to parental emotional neglect or abuse. Westman (1979) states "the only practical solution is to think in terms of children in life situations that engender vulnerability." Sameroff (1976) viewed 'parent-child unit vulnerability' as a useful concept because of the interacting stressful conditions that occur during the caretaking experience. The home environments of emotionally neglected or abused children fall along a continuum reflecting the kind and degree of parental stimulation offered the children. These family environments do not meet the children's basic emotional needs for nurturance, security, and stability. Westman (1979) concludes that "37 percent of all children in the United States live in vulnerable caretaking units and are at risk for childhood or adulthood maladaptations." Other researchers (Booz, Allen and Hamilton, Inc., 1974) point out that 28 million children live with an alcoholic person, 5% of all children live with one or more mentally ill parents (Westman, 1979) and 10% of all children are involved in clinically significant strained relations with their parents (Thomas and Chess, 1977). Yet, emotional neglect and abuse are grossly underreported because of the difficulty in diagnosing subtle and complex interactions of parent-child relationships and because of the difficulty in legally establishing a charge of emotional abuse/neglect.

In 1982 a study was made of a sample of protective service cases handled within the past three years by a county child welfare agency. One hundred children, representing 66 families, were documented as having "serious mental injury" as defined under Pennsylvania Act 124. Protective intervention and psychiatric treatment were neccessary for each child and/or parents. Five types of vulnerable family environments were identified, in which parents were: (1) suffering from mental illness; (2) abusing drugs and/or alcohol; (3) enmeshed in serious interactional stress; (4) projecting inadequate life adjustments; (5) displacing serious personal conflicts. (pp. 246–47).

Some illustrative examples follow:

Neglect

Karen

Karen is a pale, quiet six year old. She speaks with a slight lisp and is often observed sitting at a table with her chin resting in her hands staring out the window instead of attending to the work sheet in front of her. Her teacher has noticed that she lacks self-confidence and often says "I can't do it" when a new project is undertaken in the classroom.

Today she seems even more withdrawn than usual and Mrs. Sullivan is experiencing some frustration with her inattentiveness to her work. The teacher's voice reflects her feelings in its sharp tone "Karen, come to my desk. I want to talk to you about your work." Karen gives a small jump as her attention is brought abruptly back to the room. Her eyes fill with tears as she stands up and walks toward the desk. By the time she reaches the teacher Karen's head is dropped to stare at the floor and her tears fall quickly though she does not make a sound. Her thin body is visibly shaking. Mrs. Sullivan stares at her with a helpless feeling. She had not expected such a severe reaction. Her annoyance stems from concern and now she feels uncertain as to what to say to Karen's severe emotional distress. The rest of the class has stopped their work to watch the proceedings. Then Mrs. Sullivan has an idea. She writes a quick note to the school nurse briefly stating Karen's daydreaming and her reaction to being called to the desk. She puts it in an envelope and seals it. "Melissa, please walk Karen to the nurse's office and give her this note. Karen, I am not upset with you and I think Mrs. Taylor will help you feel a little better." The two children leave and Mrs. Sullivan turns back to her class. "Karen is having a bad day today and needs some time out. Let's all go back to work now."

Mrs. Sullivan has handled a difficult situation with common sense. She will find when she goes to the nurse's office at lunch that Karen is sleeping on a cot in the next room. The nurse's questions elicited a tale of her mother's drinking, a loud and noisy argument lasting a good part of the night between Karen's mother and her current boyfriend, and Karen and her two younger sisters huddling together in Karen's bed until the house was finally quiet.

The adults were "sleeping it off" this morning and Karen had dressed herself and come to school without breakfast, leaving her two sisters behind. She had been sitting at school but her thoughts were at home as she worried about her sisters and her mother. She had no energy left to attend to the task the class was involved with yet she had felt guilty and upset when she heard the teacher's annoyance. Feelings of help-lessness and inadequacy were chronic for Karen and contribute to low self-esteem and depression that impede both her school progress and her social interactions.

A social-case worker for the school system will be called in to "investigate" Karen's home life and this referral may lead to some concrete help for Karen's family. Her mother's alcohol problem needs to be addressed and Karen and her sisters need some intervention or their adjustment and school problems will become life-long difficulties.

In the 1983 study previously cited, Junewicz states:

> Some parents in this category were so consumed by their dependence upon drugs or alcohol that little time or effort remained for parenting tasks; others, while under the influence of these substances, exhibited behavior that threatened the children's psychological well-being. A dangerous by-product of parental substance abuse is the children's exposure to the 'drug culture' and contact with a variety of violent and disturbed individuals. . . . In protective service investigations in which parental drug usage or trafficking is alleged, the parents are often so totally resistant to the protective worker's intervention in their lives that law enforcement personnel are neccessary. Alcohol-involved parents, if visited regularly, usually reveal themselves by appearing intoxicated to the protective worker. If they cannot be engaged in treatment, careful observations and facts about their drinking pattern and the resultant child condition may have to be presented to the court (pp.247–248).

Children like Karen are present in many class rooms and their very future may depend on the school's ability to be aware and sensitive to behavioral signals from the child indicating stress. In the same article Junewicz discusses the need for early detection of emotional abuse and neglect.

> Case management of emotionally abused and neglected children requires coordination and close cooperation among helping professionals in the community and protective service staff. Early detection of emotional neglect and abuse and help for all family members are imperative. Many of the families do not become known to child protective service agencies. They are sometimes seen by private physicians, psychologists, and psychiatrists. The study indicated that emotional neglect and abuse occur at all income levels; they are not limited, as is sometimes assumed, to "lower" socioeconomic classes. Children's stress generated by success-oriented, high-achievement parents who are overzealous in their demands to succeed can be as injurious as the environment in which the child is affected by other stresses. Professionals are often reluctant to intervene in such cases (1983, p.250).

Physical Abuse

Stevie

At four years old Stevie's small wiry body is seldom still. He wanders around his Head Start classroom moving from activity to activity with little peer interaction. Now he goes to the block corner and begins pulling blocks from one of the shelves so they clatter onto the floor.

"Hey, you're knockin' my building!" Jimmy yells. Jimmy stands up to confront Stevie and suddenly Stevie erupts. The block in his hand swings and catches Jimmy on the shoulder.

"Yeow! Stop it!" Jimmy's voice, while still angry, sounds frightened as well. This child with the block is more violent than Jimmy can face. He ducks and runs.

Stevie is swinging the block as he chases Jimmy yelling, "I'll get ya, I'll show ya!"

Stevie's teacher runs quickly and grabs him as he passes. She pulls the block from his hand. Stevie, totally out of control, hits at the teacher screaming, "Damn you, damn you." The teacher's arms enfold Stevie so he can not hit out and she calmly speaks to him.

"It's all right, Stevie. I know you're angry but you can't hit with a block. It's all right, Stevie. Mrs. Baker is helping you so you can feel angry but not hit." Her calm quiet voice continues for another minute before Stevie recognizes the calm, even tone. Suddenly the tension in his body dissipates and he begins to cry. Mrs. Baker sits down on the floor and moves Stevie into her lap so he can cry and be held.

Mrs. Baker has seen children like Stevie before. His hyperactivity, hostility, and violence mask a frightened little boy's attempt to cope with a hostile world.

In an article reporting on a study of mother-child interactional style, Bousha and Twentyman (1984) found that abused children had significant rates of physical and verbal aggression as compared with controls who were not abused.

Child abuse and neglect have received increased attention. Hot lines, state mandated reporting, and educational and supportive programs for abusive and neglecting parents are beginning to become more common. Currently, 43 states have made the reporting of child abuse mandatory among teachers.

The circumstances and reasons for child abuse and neglect are varied but there appear to be patterns that can be identified. In an analysis of over 2900 child maltreatment cases over a 10-year period in eastern Pennsylvania it was found that physical abuse tended to occur in response to some behavior of the child that was rarely unusual in the course of normal child rearing (from fighting or jealousy to refusal to eat or wetting themselves.)

Emotional cruelty, on the other hand, was related to adult problems. Most notable was conflict between adults. In addition poor parenting skills and an "apathy-futility" syndrome were noted as precipitating factors (Herrenkohl, Herrenkohl, and Egolf, 1983). Because of the difference in causative factors, they suggest that different modes of intervention and treatment are appropriate. They state: "For physical abuse the focus could most efectively be directed to improving the parent-child interaction. In the case of emotional cruelty, the focus could most effectively be directed toward improving adult interactions and to reducing conflict between adults. With neglect . . . as in the apathy-futility syndrome, . . . long-term support" may be recommended (p. 431).

Junewicz, (1983) also points out that not all parents are able or willing to modify their behavior toward their children. This is especially true of those parents whose own psychological dysfunction or mental illness hampers their ability to parent. He offers the following advice to protective agency personnel.

> If parents are unwilling or unable to work toward modifying the home environment and their destructive attitudes, the special skill of protective agency personnel is nessessary. The following suggestions can help in the management of such cases:
>
> > Observe and document in writing the child's behavior and actions that suggest that the child is living in a stressful home environment. Keep dates and times of incidents that cause concern. Look for patterns.
> >
> > Consult with other professionals as to the validity of your diagnostic conclusions and interpretations.
> >
> > Set up lines of communication with physicians, public health nurses, and other community professionals to identify "at risk" children as early as possible.
> >
> > Reach out to the child to determine if he or she expreses distress about living at home. Is the child revealing a problem at home to others?
> >
> > Approach the parents about your concern in an effort to appeal to them to look at what is affecting their child and how they may be contributing to the problem. Ask them to seek help with your assistance.
> >
> > Although many families can be directed to help, others are not so agreeable. Court intervention may be neccesary after assessment by the protective agency.
> >
> > Protective agency personnel should not hesitate to intervene with families who refuse help, and should consider court intervention.

> Court dispositions of emotional neglect and abuse cases depend upon the testimony presented. A protective service order directing the family to treatment may be sufficient to bring about constructive change along with periodic review of the case by the court to assess progress or lack of it. In more serious cases, emergency removal of the children from the family unit is necessary. (pp. 250–251).

Although not all of these items are applicable to the school environment, it is clear that awareness and a willingnes to be alert to the signals of abuse and neglect are critical in documenting possible problems.

Sexual Abuse

Tanya

Tanya is almost five and is generally active and cheerful. When she arrived at her nursery school today, however, she was unusually quiet and had gone to the housekeeping corner and sat in the rocking chair with her doll. She rocked her baby and sang softly to it while the other children played about the room. Occasionally, she interacted with a child when he spoke to her but otherwise she maintained her involvement with the doll.

Miss Brown, the head teacher, had noticed Tanya's behavior and assumed she was feeling a little "under the weather." Just before snack the chord on the piano signalled clean up and bathroom time. Tanya did not join the other children, however, and Miss Brown went over to her and held out her hand. "Come on, Tanya, let's clean up for snack." Tanya got up, placed the baby on the rocker, and took Miss Brown's hand. At the bathroom, Tanya went to the sink and Miss Brown said, "Do you need to go to the toilet, Tanya?" An expression Miss Brown couldn't identify crossed Tanya's face but she did not respond. Then she turned and went to the farthest cubicle and Miss Brown heard her unzipping her jeans. On impulse, Miss Brown walked over to the cubicle saying "Do you need some help honey?" Suddenly she stopped short. The child on the toilet had a pained expression on her face and tears in her eyes though she made no noise. The inside of her legs were mottled with black and blue marks. As she urinated some blood appeared in the toilet. Miss Brown knelt down beside the child and put one arm around her shoulders. "Tanya, how did you get hurt, honey?" she asked in a soft voice. Tanya looked at her for a moment and then hung her head down. Miss Brown took some paper and patted the child dry. She helped her stand and put her pants back up and then helped her wash and return to the snack group, all the while chatting in a warm, pleasant tone about snack, the class guinea pig, and the story

Miss Jean was going to read after snack. Tanya held Miss Brown's hand until they returned to the snack table and then joined the other children.

Miss Brown is now faced with a dilemma. Clearly Tanya has been abused in some way and it seems quite likely that the abuse has been of a sexual nature. Tanya's behavior and her inability to tell what has occurred may be because of fear or through a lack of verbal concepts to discuss her experience. Miss Brown knows she must report what she has seen and she also suspects that she and Tanya, as well as Tanya's family are about to begin a very difficult and potentially damaging social and legal process.

Levin, (1983) reports:

Recent literature indicates that school personnel, generally, seriously underreport and often mishandle suspected child abuse and neglect because of failure to recognize the signs of abuse and failure to report suspected abuse to the proper authorities. Lynch (1975, p. 141) estimated that reports covered only 1–10% of the actual occurrences. Others estimate that only 1 of 20 cases gets reported (Zgliczynski and Rodolfa, 1980, p. 41). Broadhurst (1978, p. 22) reports that even where educators are mandated by law to report, schools accounted for less than one-third of the reports of child abuse.

Why do educators fail to report child abuse and neglect? The research completed to date shows that schools are on the whole not prepared to deal adequately with the child abuse problem. Collucci (1977, p. 99) indicates that less than 5% of the nations's schools have working policies and procedures for reporting child abuse and neglect. Manley-Casimar and Newman (1976, p. 17–19) showed that many teachers do not know the symptoms of child abuse. Furthermore, those who suspect child abuse often do not want to get involved for fear of meddling with parents' right to discipline their children as they see fit. Eighty-four percent of American parents use corporal punishment to discipline their children (Richey, 1980, p. 332). (Levin, 1983, p. 15).

Miss Brown will call the social service agency closest to her center to report the suspected abuse and a social service professional from that agency will be at the school within an hour. Since Tanya's mother usually picks her up, she will be taken into a private office to talk about what Miss Brown has seen and the child and parent will be escorted to a local hospital for the child to be examined. The social service person will also have informed the police should their help be necessary. If the offender is a family member, the agencies involved may be able to work with the family in a therapeutic mileu, which approaches such abuse as a signal of a dysfunctional family unit. Whether or not this occurs there will be legal ramifications, and Miss Brown may well find herself testifying in court at some point in the future. If the sexual abuse involves incest, the very process and outcome of intervention may be damaging to the child. Orday (1983) advocates the reforming of judicial procedures, in such cases.

Current procedures for handling incest cases have three major shortcomings. First, they are harmful to the victim. When parent-child incest is reported to the authorities, the victim often is removed from her home and is subjected to repeated pretrial interviews in busy offices by people who do not normally deal with children. After suffering the probes of investigators, prosecutors, and others, the victim faces the ordeal of testifying in court, where she may be accused of seductive behavior, lying, or wanting to hurt her family or father. Because of the combination of the incest taboo, the victim's youth, and the victim's close relationship with the accused, the present pretrial interview process and testifying in court may cause the child severe emotional distress, confusion, and feelings of guilt. A second problem with the legal response to parent-child incest is that it ignores the involvement of the family, which must be taken into account if treatment is to be successful. Incest arises from a constellation of family problems, including an unsatisfactory relationship between the parents, social isolation, and overcrowding of the family.

Practice in incest cases has a third distinct failing: The evidence it provides at trial is not reliable. Unfortunately, proof in court depends upon the testimony of the child victim and, thus, is subject to their weaknesses as witnesses. The problems caused by young children's subjective sense of time, inaccurate memory, and limited ability to communicate can be exacerbated by especially poor recall of the repeated incestuous experiences and by the tendency to withdraw or regress when under emotional stress. Furthermore, the triers of fact—judges and jurors—have a limited ability to evaluate the testimony of the parent-child incest victim. Even an expert would not want the task of assessing the credibility of the child based solely on the flawed, emotional testimony available in court (pp. 69–70).

Levin recommends specially trained individuals to interview children out of court and to testify on their behalf to help avoid trauma for the child. Such a process could also help therapeutic intervention with the family, by decreasing the accused-accusor relationship and stressing helping the whole family by addressing the issues which are causing the family to be dysfunctional. Correction, rather than punishment, is clearly a more humane and appropriate approach to any family problem. Schultz and Jones (1983), in an article addressed to social service professionals, give some objectives for the sociomedical management of child sexual abuse.

Objectives of sociomedical management of child sexual abuse include the following:

1. Protect the child victim from further unwanted sexual acts from adults. Professionals should report the sexual offense to the proper

authority in their community, who, in turn decides on intervention or nonintervention. Some physicians may choose to intervene
or treat the victim themselves, particularly if dissatisfied with
social welfare services.

2. The professional should allow parents to ventilate [sic] anger and/
    or guilt about the child's sexual experience and to reassure them,
    when appropriate, that they acted correctly in bringing the child
    in, that they are "good" parents and not necessarily responsible for
    what happened. The normalization of both parent and child
    response to the sexual event may be required of professionals.

3. The professional should reassure the parents that the effects of
    many types of sexual acts, particularly one-time events, need not
    be long lasting. Childhood innocence should be protected as long
    as it proves functionally healthy.

4. The professional should encourage the parents of the abused child
    to take a matter of fact approach in discussing the incident with
    the child. Discussion with professionals is essential to child protec-
    tion and to clear the air. Sex education lectures by professionals or
    parents should be avoided at this point. Parents need professional
    assurance that both the mentioning of the sexual incident and its
    after effects, if any, will probably decrease in frequency. If normal
    age-appropriate coping does not ensue, the professional may
    choose to refer the case to a family agency or a social service
    agency in the child's community, or to a pediatrician. Some treat-
    ment costs may be paid through various State Victim Compensa-
    tion Acts.

5. Sensitive medical examination should be done, although physical
    evidence of abuse may be minimal in view of the types of sexual
    activities reported by our sample, vaginal exams should not be rou-
    tine. In incest cases, overwhelming medical documentation can be
    a powerful weapon in persuading the disturbed family to accept
    social service intervention through the state welfare department.
    Woodling and Kossoris (1981) have found that childhood rape of
    female children differs substantially from molestation in terms of
    physical effects'' (pp. 105–6).

Sexual abuse of children is usually the most shocking and difficult
type of abuse for school personnel. Many teachers feel inadequate in
terms of their knowledge in detecting symptoms or signs of child abuse.
In a sample of 285 elementary and high school teachers in the Midwest
Levin (1983) found only 34.2 percent of the teachers had ever reported
a case of physical abuse and most of these reported only 1 case. Only
21.2 percent of the teachers had ever reported a case of physical neglect
and most of these reported only one case. Only 8.1 percent had ever
reported a case of emotional abuse and the same number had reported
a case of emotional neglect. Finally, only 5 percent of the teachers had

ever reported a case of sexual abuse. These findings strongly suggest the need for more adults to become knowledgeable concerning potential symptoms of child abuse. Table 5.5 lists some indications of molestation.

Other Family Stressors

Even the most loving and mature parents may face stress that can disrupt and damage family life. Temporary stressors such as job loss, moves from one house to another, accidents, or temporary illness may cause a brief period of family dysfunction. Other problems may be of a more enduring or catastrophic nature and require long-term support and attention.

Special Needs Family Members

Care of a special needs child or adult, as defined and discussed in Chapter 12, is one such major stressor. Chronic and catastrophic illnesses of either parent or child as well as the death of parent or sibling can create

---

TABLE 5.5.   Social Indicators of Acute and Chronic Molestation

Single indicators listed below do not establish a diagnosis of sexual abuse, but several symptoms displayed by children warrant serious consideration and concern:

1. Nightmares, or night terrors, usually with violent or sexual components
2. Arriving early for school and/or leaving late (if sex partner or offender is not related to school setting)
3. Recent history of running away from home
4. Recent disruptive or aggressive behavior toward adults or older adolescents
5. Poor peer relationships or absence of friends, accompanied by gender role confusion
6. Recent inappropriate sexual self-consciousness, vulnerability to sexual approaches, or pseudoseductive behavior
7. Recent sexual promiscuity or frequent masturbation
8. Allegations by siblings of sexual mistreatment
9. Victim (female) assumes maternal responsibilities inappropriate for her age and family circumstances
10. Father, stepfather, or paramour who denies sexual involvement with abused child but has "blackout spells" due to alcoholic intake, or says that girls should be prepared for later sexual experiences, or who says "all fathers are like that" (i.e., are sexually involved with their daughters), or who says "she's promiscuous anyway," or who is abnormally concerned about child's dating behavior or who keeps track of girl's menstruation calendar

From: Schultz, I. G. and Jones, P. J., Sexual abuse of children: Issues for social service and health professionals. *Child Welfare*, 1983, 62: 98–107. Reprinted by permission.

life-long symptomology in the remaining family members. A literature review by McKeever (1983) concerning the siblings of chronically ill children, points out that the research at that time strongly suggests that siblings of chronically ill children are themselves a population at risk. Their survey of life events as etiological factors in childhood disease found that sibling illness ranked among the most stressful. Because of the demands of the illness, siblings tend to get less parental attention and affection. Another study, reviewed by McKeever, reached a similar conclusion about the siblings of children with cancer. Siblings' scores on age-independent measures indicated that they were less well-adjusted and were in greater need of support than were other family members. Apparently siblings often live through the experience with the same intensity as the patient and then live with life-long disease-related memories and concerns.

McKeever also cites studies pinpointing problems in adjustment, behavior problems, and academic problems. Negative self-image and high anxiety levels are noted among siblings of both handicapped children and cancer victims. Somatic problems such as sleep disturbances, enuresis, appetite problems, headaches, recurrent abdominal pain, and a preoccupation with their own health are commonly noted.

McKeever (1983) states, "It is imperative that siblings are equipped with explanations suitable for peers and outsiders, given their frequent role as family informer. It is also crucial that siblings are kept updated with age-appropriate disease-related information. (p. 210).

A parent's ability to cope with the stressors of chronic illness seems to be a key to the continued functioning of the family. McCubbin et al. (1983) have analyzed parental coping patterns in families with a child with cystic fibrosis. They discuss three positive parental coping patterns "(a) maintaining family integration, cooperation, and an optimistic definition of the situation; (b) maintaining social support, self-esteem, and psychological stability; and (c) understanding the medical situation through communication with other parents and consultation with the medical staff" (pp. 367–368).

McCubbin et al., (1983) further note that:

1. Parental coping is a viable target for primary prevention, that is to say, intervention in family life before a problem is manifest. . . .
2. Some families may be considered at greater risk than others by virtue of the influence of family structure, income and age of the chronically ill child upon parental coping. "Three family 'at risk' situations are suggested by the sociodemographic data: a. Single-parent families, b. Families with an older CF member, c. Families with limited income (pp. 367–368).

Death of a Parent

Death of a parent is another major stressor for a family. In an article discussing helping the children of fatally ill parents, Adams-Greenly and Moynihan(1983) found that five basic needs must be faced. These include: "(1) the need for information that is clear and comprehensible; (2) the need to feel involved and important; (3) the need for reassurance about the grief of adults around them; (4) the need for their own thoughts and feelings; and (5) the need to maintain their own age-appropriate interests and activities" (p. 223).

Furman (cited in Adams-Greeley and Moynihan, 1983) identified three major factors that contribute to a child's ability to cope with parental death: (1) the child's maturation level and cognitive ability to comprehend death; (2) the child's previous experiences with loss and longing; and (3) the educational and supportive help given by the surviving parent, especially in terms of the recognition, expression, and tolerance of feelings.

The preschool child is often alarmed to find that death can be so powerful and may feel directly and personally threatened. Because of animistic thought, preoperational children in this age group attribute life process and consciousness to the dead; they see death as "a living on under changed circumstances" (Adams-Greeley and Moynihan, 1983).

The school-age child is more intellectually aware and is greatly involved in understanding and mastering the world outside the home. This applies to perceptions of illness and death. It is often reported that younger children in this group personify death, identify with the dead, and try to keep death at a distance to allow time to escape. Death to them is external, frightening, and dangerous and may take the form of the devil, a monster, a skeleton, or an angel. As children grow older and enter Piaget's stage of concrete operations, their ability to focus on the real consequences of dying increases.

As part of the "educational and emotional support" of the child, teachers need to be able to understand and respond appropriately to the crisis of death in a child's life and to be an on-going resource in the child's later adjustment.

Minority Families

U.S. society is composed of a wide variety of ethnic and religious minorities, some of which come from the family types discussed. Yet there are also special stresses endemic to being a member of a minority group. Throughout our history children of immigrant families, who spoke a language other than English and attended an English speaking school, have found it necessary to shed much of their cultural heritage. Black families have carried the additional stress of prejudice of color, and, in some areas, prohibitive laws and social practices. Many of these families have banded together in "ghetto" neighborhoods, which have served a function similar to the extended family network, frequently providing a safe common "ground" for understanding and mutual survival.

The negative attitudes of the dominant culture have meant struggles in forming adequate self-images and maintaining ethnic identity for many individuals and families. Limited access to education and status occupations, which has often accompanied minority status, also has created economic hardships. Prejudice and poverty have long been partners among minorities.

Since the middle 1960s the United States, through the intervention of the federal courts, has taken steps to integrate and increase educational

---

TABLE 5.6.   Teacher Awareness

Environment of Neighborhood
Knowledge of ethnic groups in school population
Knowledge of cultural aspects of school population
Knowledge of socioeconomic groups in school population
Knowledge of resources and problem areas within local community
Knowledge of the procedure for reporting abuse/neglect in your school/state
Family Awareness
Knowledge of family composition of students
Knowledge of particular family stressors
Knowledge of chronic or endemic difficulties of families
Knowledge of traditional family patterns of students
Providing a "listening" ear for parents and encouraging their sharing of
   potential stressors for the child
Child Awareness
Watch for indicators of stress in children
Provide a stable, comfortable, psychologically "safe" environment in the
   classroom
Be calm and matter-of-fact in cases of active stress behaviors
Use children's literature and activities that show a variety of cultural and fam-
   ily patterns
Be aware of potential stereotypic responses in children and steer activities
   toward diversity
Self Awareness
Be aware of your own attitudes toward divergent family patterns.
Avoid sterotyped messages to children and families—i.e., mother's tea at
   school
Know your own vulnerabilities concerning types of family stress
Increase your knowledge base concerning developmental levels and appro-
   priate strategies for helping children with special problems

---

and occupational opportunities for minority individuals. Bilingual education, especially in the Southwest portion of the United States, is more available and schools more visibly attuned to cultural pluralism. (See chapter 8.)

Nonetheless, teachers must be aware of their own feelings, attitudes, and prejudices and endeavor to educate themselves concerning the culturally distinct groups within their school community.

THE FAMILY AND THE SCHOOL

In a pluralistic society all individuals must be afforded respect and dignity. It also becomes increasingly clear that individuals come from and exist within a multitude of family styles and patterns. This diversity must become a recognized reality with the societal institutions which serve families. The school has an especially important role as the major institution sharing responsibility for the welfare of children. Teachers, administrators, and staff personnel cannot provide a viable learning environment without adequate understanding and sensitivity to family dynamics and the impact of environmental and situational stresses. Assumptions and stereotyped expectations have no place in the classroom.

The ability of children to cope with the complex, confusing, and the sometimes painful realities of their lives can be dramatically improved if teachers are willing to be alert, informed, and if necessary, vocal advocates for the child.

Guidelines for Signs of Stress

The following are some guidelines for signs of stress in young children:

Active Signs
excessive activity
explosive anger
frequent fighting with others
crying, whining, or clinging to adults
enuresis
frequent upset stomach, or headaches
frequent absences
bruises or evidence of pain

Passive Signs
extreme quiet or withdrawn behavior
sudden change in emotional affect

daydreaming
excessive nail biting, scratching, thumbsucking
frequent masturbation
fixation on one activity or object
frequent rocking or stroking of self

SUMMARY

Family systems concepts give us a set of terms and ideas that allow us to observe, discuss, and hopefully predict functional and dysfunctional family patterns. It is important for us to recognize the variety and complexity of families and the potential stressors that affect the growth and health of family members. We must have an appreciation for the child's world and be willing to act as caring, observant adults in the school and other institutions that care for children. Children are truly society's most valuable and most vulnerable asset.

Explorations

PERSONAL EXPLORATIONS

These exercises are designed to help you look at your own life—attitudes, experiences, dreams, myths, and realities.

1. Family rules are either explicit, clearly stated, or implicit, understood but not talked about. Some implicit rules are so hidden that they are difficult to uncover. For example, the explicit rule might be, "You should work hard at school"; the implicit rule might be, "Our family members are smart enough to excel and you are expected to reflect positively on the family"; the unconscious rule may be, "You should be perfect." Make a list of several rules in each of the first two categories, then see if you can uncover the unconscious rule as well. Once you have your rules, analyze their impact on your life.

2. Think about the communication patterns in your family. What kind of messages did you receive? Were they different for different members of the family? List some of the messages that different members sent, analyze whether they were congruent (leveling) or incongruent (blaming, distracting, placating, or computer-like). Are there any patterns you can see? What about your own style of communication? Bring your findings to class for discussion.

INTELLECTUAL EXPLORATIONS

These exercises are designed to increase your depth of knowledge in some of the areas discussed in this chapter.

1. Review several issues of a journal in the family field. *The Journal of Marriage and the Family, Family Process, The Journal of Divorce,* and *The Journal of Family Relations* are all candidates. What type of articles are published in this journal? For what kind of audience? Do they show a pattern or trend? Do they have special theme issues? How easy or difficult are they to understand? Write an outline of what you discover about this journal.
2. Choose one of the family types discussed in this chapter that is different from the nuclear family. Do a library search to see how many fairly recent books (since 1980) have been published that touch on this type of family. (Naturally, you are limited to what your college has acquired.) Write down the full bibliographic reference for each book and bring your list to class to compare with what other students have found on this family type.
3. Child abuse and neglect have become topics of national concern. Clip out the articles you find in the newspaper for one week on this topic and bring them to class for discussion.

FIELD EXPLORATIONS

These exercises are designed to take you out into the world to find real examples that will illustrate and elucidate the material in this chapter.

1. Visit an Alcoholics Anonymous meeting (this can include Alanon, Alateen, or Adult Children of Alcoholics). After the meeting write a brief summary of the actual happenings and another paragraph on your feelings and learnings.
2. Spend an hour or so in a local supermarket on a weekend. Unobtrusively observe two or more families (use nuclear family model of male + female + children). What kind of rules and roles can you observe? What communication styles do they use? Are their patterns functional or dysfunctional? Why? Write a one-page summary of what you learned.
3. Do an open ended interview of someone you know (or someone referred to you) who has experienced one of the family traumas discussed in this chapter, that is, divorce, death, illness of a member, abuse, and so on. Just let them talk and share with you the effect of the experience. Take no notes but come to class ready to discuss your reactions and what you learned.

References

Adams-Greenly, M. and Moynihan, Sr., T. Helping the Children of Fatally Ill Parents. *American Journal of Orthopsychiatry* 1983, 53, 210–29.

Berns, R. M. *Child, Family, Community.* New York: Holt, Rinehart and Winston, 1985.

Booz, Allen and Hamilton, Inc. An assessment of needs of and resources for children of alcoholic parents. Final Report to the National Institute on Alcohol Abuse and Alcoholism. National Technical Information Services General Publication P.B. 241119, 1974.

Bousha, D. M. and Twentyman, C. T. Mother-child interactional style in abuse, neglect, and control groups: Naturalistic observations in the home. *Journal of Abnormal Psychology*, 1984, 93, 106–114.

Broadhurst, D. D. Update: What schools are doing about child abuse and neglect. *Children Today*, 1978, 21–33.

Carter, E. A. and McGoldrick, M. *The Family Life Cycle.* New York: Gardner Press, 1980.

Colucci, N. D. The schools and the problem of child abuse and neglect. *Contemporary Education*, 1977, 48, 97–101.

Furman, E. *A Child's Parent Dies.* New Haven: Yale University Press, 1974.

Glick, P. C. How American families are changing. *American Demographics*, January, 1984, 6, 20–5.

Herrenkohl, R. C., Herrenkohl, E. C. and Egolf, B. P. Circumstances surrounding the occurrence of child maltreatment. *Journal of Consulting and Clinical Psychology*, 1983, 51, 424–31.

Junewicz, W. J. A protective posture toward emotional neglect and abuse. *Child Welfare*, 1983, 62, 243–252.

Levin, P. G. Teachers' perceptions, attitudes, and reporting of child abuse/neglect. *Child Welfare*, 1983, 62, 14–20.

Lynch, A. Child abuse in the school age population. *Journal of School Health*, 1975, 35, 140–144.

Manley-Casimar, M. E. and Newman, B. Child abuse and the school. *Canadian Welfare*, 1976, 52, 17–19.

McCubbin, H. I., McCubbin, M. A., Patterson, J. M., Cauble, A. E., Wilson, L. R., and Warwick, W. CHIP-Coping health inventory for parents; An assesment of parental coping in the care of the chronically ill child. *Journal of Marriage and the Family*, 1983, 359–69.

McKeever, P. Siblings of chronically ill children: A literature review with implications for research and practice. *American Journal of Orthopsychiatry*, 1983, 53, 209–18.

Ordway, D. P. Reforming judicial procedures for handling parent-child incest. *Child Welfare*, 1983, 62, 68–75.

Piaget, J. *The Child's Conception of the World.* Patterson, NJ: Littlefield, Adams, and Co., 1960.

Rappaport, R. and Rappaport, R. I. *Dual-Career Families Re-examined.* New York: Harper & Row, 1976.

Richey, D. D. Educators and the primary prevention of child abuse. *Educational Forum*, 1980, 44, 330–334.

Sameroff, A. *Annual progress in child psychiatry and child development.* New York: Brunner/Mazel, 1976.

Satir, V. *Peoplemaking.* Palo Alto: Science and Behavior Books, 1972.

Schultz, L. G. and Jones, P. J. Sexual abuse of children: Issues for social service and health professionals. *Child Welfare*, 1983, 62, 99–107.

Terkelsen, K. G. Toward a theory of the family life cycle. In E. A. Carter and M. McGoldrick, (Eds.), *The family life cycle.* New York: Gardner Press, 1980.

Thomas, A. and Chess, S. *Temperament and Development.* New York: Brunner Mazel, 1977.

Werner, E. E. Alternate caregivers for children: A perspective. *Children Today.* 1983, 12, 22–7.

Westman, J. *Child Advocacy.* New York: The Free Press, 1979.

Woodling, B., and Kossoris, P. Sexual misuse, rape, molestation and incest. *Pediatric Clinics of North America*, 1981, 28, 2, 481–99.

Zgliczynski, S. M. and Rudolfa, E. Preservice curriculum: The teacher's responsibility to the abused child. *Journal of Teacher Education*, 1980, 31, 36–44.

Chapter 6

PERSONALITY DYNAMICS

Objectives

After reading this chapter the student should be able to:

1. Discuss ego development and compare and contrast two theories in this area.
2. Define the terms ego control and ego resiliency and explain their predictive relationship to child behaviors from three to seven years of age.
3. Draw and explain the helix of self-other relatedness as postulated in the cognitive-developmental theory of ego development.
4. Compare and contrast the concepts of attachment and dependency.
5. Give three examples of affiliative and prosocial behaviors in infants and young children.
6. List differences in aggressive behavior between male and female children and give possible explanations for the development of these behaviors.
7. Review the findings of cross-cultural research in relation to prosocial development.

All humans act upon, respond to, and interact with others. And these dynamics occur within myriad social interactions. As we saw in Chapter 4, the capacity for social adaptations is not only evident in early childhood, but appears characteristic of our species from the very first moments of life. Moreover, social interchange appears a necessary ingredient of caregiving, serving, in part, to ensure the survival of the young. In this chapter we will explore how young children organize and initiate social experiences which facilitate their early developmental learnings.

EGO DEVELOPMENT

The concept of ego or "self," as suggested in Chapter 4, refers to the attitudes, characteristics, and behaviors that each of us use as means of defining ourselves. (Our sense of "I"ness.) These features of personhood, as we have noted, are ever-changing, representing the child's encounters with and responses to new experiences throughout the course of her development.

The notion of ego has held distinct meanings and varied importance among different theorists. Sigmund Freud viewed the ego as a separate component of personality, serving to monitor and, above all, modulate between the demands of the id (that is, biological mandate) and superego (that is, moral imperative). However, Freud also viewed the ego as serving to assist the child in adapting to the realities of his social and physical world.

Freud's work became the underpinnings of two separate lineages: U.S. ego psychology (through discussion of the adaptive functions of the ego and superego), including Erik Erikson; and British object-relations theory (through the nature of early identification with parents) as represented by Klein and others. Both of these approaches expanded Freud's orientation by focusing on the environment and its interplay with the development of the person. Between these two theories there is a shared conviction that personality development occurs in the process of interactions between the organism and the environment, rather than through the internal processes of maturation alone.

Erikson

Erikson's contributions to the refinement and understanding of the ego follow several major extensions of Freud's work; these include Erikson's emphasis on development as a life-long, continual process of adaptation, his emphasis on the healthy personality, and his then unique view of development as a task-challenge process. As Erikson (1980) has observed, the developmental process is a dynamic, ever-evolving one whereby,

> Each successive step, then, is a potential crisis because of a radical *change in perspective*. There is, at the beginning of life, the most radical change of all: from intrauterine to extrauterine life. But in postnatal existence, too, such radical adjustments of perspective as lying relaxed, sitting firmly, and running fast must all be accomplished in their own good time. With them, the interpersonal perspective, too, changes rapidly and often radically, as is testified by the proximity in time of such opposites as "not letting mother out of sight" and wanting to be independent. Thus, *different capacities use different opportunities* to become full-grown components of the ever-new configuration that is the growing personality (p. 55).

The idea of growth as occurring over the life-span forms an important cornerstone of Erikson's view of development. For him, the human organisim is a dynamic, ever-changing, and, correspondingly, potentially growing entity. In part, growth is internally motivated and internally regulated. However, the opportunity for growth is also created through external crises (that is, challenges) which, according to Erikson, approximate different periods of the life cycle. For Erikson, this process encompasses eight periods extending from early infancy through old age.

The Early Years

During the first years of life the young child encounters three crises or challenges to development. These include the crisis of trust vs. mistrust (infancy), the crisis of autonomy vs. shame and doubt (toddlerhood), and the crisis of achieving initiative vs. guilt (preschool).

TRUST VERSUS MISTRUST.   By *trust* versus *mistrust* Erikson refers to "an attitude toward oneself and the world derived from the experiences of the first year of life" (1980, p. 57). As the infant participates in its first encounters with caregivers, it forms an attitude toward the world and of persons as being reliable, dependable, and accessible, or alternatively, as being capricious, haphazard, and thoughtless. This attitude, derived from its caretaking experiences, provides the infant a basic orientation that either fosters trust in others or, conversely, mistrust of others. Moreover, the experiences and attitudes formed at this time become a part of the infant's self-perceptions. A child who experiences its caregivers as responsive will emerge from this stage with a sense of buoyancy and hope. This child will perceive the world as safe and trust

TABLE 6.1.   **Epigenetic Sequence of Psychological Development**

Stage	Period	Social Achievement	Consequence of Failure
Trust versus mistrust	Infancy	Mutality of interests, attachment	Withdrawal, depression
Autonomy versus shame, doubt	Early childhood	Self-control, personal esteem	Failure, dependence
Initiative versus guilt	Middle childhood	Adventure, participation	Seclusiveness
Industry versus inferiority	Late childhood	Skill development, technological mastery	Inadequacy, mediocrity
Identity versus role confusion	Adolescence	Integration of psychological roles	Psychosocial dissonance
Intimacy versus isolation	Young adulthood	Commitment to others, affiliation and partnership	Fear of others, self-absorption
Generativity versus stagnation	Middle adulthood	Productivity, reproduction	Pseudointimacy, impoverishment
Ego integrity versus despair	Maturity	Wisdom, acceptance of past labors	Despair, regret

From: Cohen, S. *Social and personality development in childhood.* New York: Macmillan, 1976.

in his or her capacity to explore and discover its intricacies and wonders. In contrast, the child who is neglected or abused will emerge from the first year of life with a sense of despair, in part, directed toward others, and incorporating her self, as well. This child is likely to possess little optimism and adopt an attitude of guardedness and vigilance.

AUTONOMY VERSUS SHAME AND DOUBT.   A second crisis that faces the developing child involves the task of achieving *autonomy* as opposed to the experience of *shame* and *doubt*. According to Erikson (1980), a baby will display autonomy from his earliest moments of life, for example, in the special way in which he angrily tries to wiggle his hand free when tightly held. However, under normal conditions, it is not until the second year of life, with the increased capacity for independent movement and action, that he begins to experience a new challenge: becoming an autonomous "doer" or, alternatively, maintaining a dependent

INSET 6.1

The classic study reported by Anna Freud and Sophie Dann (1951) of orphaned children who were subjected to the brutalities of Nazi racism over the first years of their lives, attests to the consequences of severe mistrust. These six German-Jewish infants, orphaned shortly after birth, spent their first years together in a concentration camp. As the war ended, they were liberated (at approximately three years of age) and flown to England to be placed under the care of Sister Sophie Dann. Since the children had spent most of their time together (without consistent adult care, as well as under impoverished circumstances) they had formed deep attachments to one another. Initially, upon placement, these attachments excluded adults and other children beyond their own group. Yet, over time, and in the care of a consistent and trusting environment, they were able to establish positive relations with others, including adults.

role status. At two years of age he is ready for a decisive encounter with his environment, an environment which, in turn, feels called upon to convey to the child "its particular ideas and concepts of autonomy and coercion in ways decisively contributing to the character, the efficiency, and the health of his personality in his culture" (Erikson, 1980, p. 56). The choice then, for the toddler, is in making her will known, in exerting herself as a "doer" in control of herself and her environment. In contrast, the adult community must decide what limits or boundaries need be applied in helping the child to focus her energies toward constructive and acceptable channels of expression. As Erikson indicates, this period is a time for the exercise of wills, both that of the child and those of her parents. If parents effectively guide the child's energies she will grow in her sense of autonomy. If they restrain or hinder the child consistently, she will learn to be more compliant and dependent. These negative experiences will cast doubt in the child's mind concerning her capacity for effective self-direction and lead to feelings of shame through her inability to meet parental expectations. Here, the challenge to caregivers is to set realistic expectations and reasonable standards.

INITIATIVE VERSUS GUILT.   The quest toward achieving identity continues into the preschool years in the form of maintaining and extending *initiative* while postponing and avoiding *guilt*. At this stage the child is in transition, moving between his immediate family and the wider community. Peers and play experiences become increasingly more important both for the extension of learnings and for the testing and rehearsal of roles yet to come. Moreover, the child, during this period, comes to experience himself as a learning and knowing person. Patterns of learning, which focus upon the learning process (for example, how to approach a new task or a willingness to experiment with art materials) assume as great a significance as the products of learning (for example, knowing the letters of the alphabet).

The child's inquiries at this point need to be encouraged, rather than restricted. Curiosity and creativity must be enhanced and facilitated. Yet the freedom of an inquiring mind may be easily discouraged.

The child who innocently asks difficult, personal, or potentially "embarrassing" questions, may quickly experience guilt at the hands of an insensitive or thoughtless adult. Similarly, the child whose inventions or ideas are misunderstood and condemned by the suspicious or unknowing adult may experience an intense feeling of guilt and confusion. Thus, inquiry becomes forbidden, and many topics become fraught with danger and secrecy. Natural inquiries that focus on sexuality, birth, death, bodily functions, and related concerns often cause adults undue concern and are avoided rather than responded to easily and honestly. All of these negative reactions on the part of adults give the child the message that he should *not* ask, *not* wonder, *not* be curious, and when he is all of these things he feels he must be wrong or bad. Adult understanding and acceptance of natural curiosity is crucial to the child's future ability to use her or his inquiring mind.

INSET 6.2

"Teacher, look at my rainbow, Ain't it pretty?" Tommy asks.

"Now, Tommy, we don't say 'ain't', and didn't I tell you to follow the picture of the rainbow on the wall. You have the colors all mixed up. Which one belongs on the top?"

What has Tommy learned from this exchange? Perhaps to copy rather than to be creative. Or, perhaps to avoid words the teacher doesn't like. And, perhaps, not to do anything until you are sure you are doing it 'right.'

In the classroom, the child who experiments and tries a variety of approaches to a task may find himself being reprimanded. The negative message given by the teacher can cause uncertainty, fear, and guilt. Such experiences hinder future learning and creativity.

Self and Interpersonal Development

The theory of ego development proposed by Erikson has led to a variety of changes in our views of the developmental process, most particularly, in our understanding of the acquisition of selfhood. In addition, the conceptual framework offered by his writings has led to recent research that has attempted to clarify and detail this process for greater understanding and practice.

Ego-Control and Ego-Resiliency— Children in Process and Children at Risk

One important series of studies in this area has been reported by Jeanne and Jack Block (1980) in terms of ego-control and ego-resiliency. Their work, which studies personality development within a longitudinal context, has significant implications for our understanding of self-development in children between three and seven years of age.

Drawing upon the psychoanalytic concept of ego, as originally defined by Freud (namely, as a regulator of id-superego demands), the Blocks set out to examine the emergence of children's ego resources. Specifically, they sought to *chart* and then *map* the various strategies that children devise in constructing a balance between gratification of personal (that is, id) needs and the boundaries imposed upon their behavior by others (that is, superego constraints).

In approaching this task, the Blocks rephrased and divided the psychoanalytic concept of ego into two central components: *ego-control* and *ego-resiliency*. The notion of ego-control used here refers to the degree to which a child actively manages her impulses and needs. Correspondingly, as a personality dimension, ego-control may be viewed on a continuum ranging from overcontrol at one extreme, to undercontrol at the other. (In this model the midpoints of this continuum are seen as comprising an individual's area of greatest adaptation.) Ego-resiliency enlarges upon this concept, providing allowance for modifications in ego-control in response to new or changing situations. That is, ego-resiliency calls attention to the child's capacity for modification of established levels of control, for example, in his postponement of immediate needs or in the redirection of a goal. Like the notion of ego-control, ego-resiliency may be viewed on a contiuum of values ranging from high resilient to low resilient. (In contrast to ego-control, however, the ends of the continuum, rather than the middle, constitute areas of resourceful (that is, high) adaptation on one extreme, to poor (that is, low) adaptation on the other.) Figures 6.1 and 6.2 offer the reader some behavioral descriptions of each of these dimensions of ego functioning.

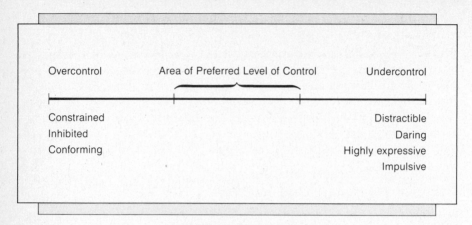

FIGURE 6.1   Ego-control
Adapted from: Block, J. H. and Block, J. The role of ego-control and ego-resiliency in the organization of behavior. In W. A. Collins (Ed.), *Development of cognition, affect and social relations.* (Minnesota Symposium on Child Psychology, Vol.13, Hillsdale, N.J.: Erlbaum, 1980).

Utilizing an extensive battery of psychological test and assessment procedures, the Blocks gathered data on 130 three year old children. By maintaining continous contact and later retesting a significant proportion of their initial sample, they were able to obtain longitudinal data on these dimensions of ego development during the children's preschool and early school-aged years (that is, from ages 3 to 7).

The Blocks (1980) report findings that confirm and extend our under-

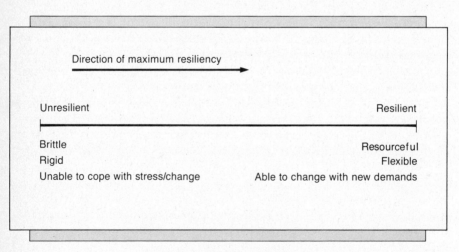

FIGURE 6.2   Ego-resilience
Adapted from: Block, J. H. and Block, J. The role of ego-control and ego-resiliency in the organization of behavior. In W. A. Collins (Ed.), *Development of cognition, affect and social relations.* (Minnesota Symposium on Child Psychology, Vol.13, Hillsdale, N.J.: Erlbaum, 1980).

standing of early personality dynamics and its implications for later social functioning and adaptation. Confirming (although through different procedures) the work of Thomas and Chess on temperament reported earlier (see Chapter 4), they found that ego-control and ego-resiliency may be reliabily measured as early as three years of age. Moreover, early identified ego patterns were predictive of personal and social adaption at age seven.

Children identified as highly active at age three subsequently manifested a variety of derivative personal attributes (for example, aggressive, assertive, domineering, less inhibited, and less compliant behaviors) at age seven. These same children, first identified as undercontrollers at age three, also exhibited less focused social behaviors (for example, energetic, restless, impulsive interactions with others) at age seven. Early ego-undercontrol, consequently, was found to be affiliated with later negative interpersonal behaviors. In contrast, early ego-controlled children (that is, shy, aloof, uninvolved, solitary) were observed in later social interactions to be withdrawn and to exhibit few involvements.

Early ego-resiliency was found to be associated with later positive interpersonal transactions (for example, empathy, social responsiveness and protectiveness). In *combination* with high ego-control, high ego resiliency at age three was found to be most predictive of positive personal and adaptive social interactions at age seven; these children exhibited well-socialized patterns of adaptation in their interactions with others, which appeared to be based upon strong personal acceptance and a well-defined self-concept. In contrast, high ego-control, combined with low ego-resiliency was predictive of poor personal and social adaptation at age seven; these children were ineffective, in part, being overcome by feelings of personal inadequacy in social interactions and often being victimized or stigmatized by others. For these children the world appeared threatening and overwhelming, taxing their perceptions of themselves as achievers and creating anxiety leading to immobility.

How are these patterns formed? The Blocks suggest that these early personality mosaics are likely created through a combination of temperament and early family interactions. Overcontrol, for example, appeared in response to family patterns characterized by excessive structure and order. Conversely, undercontrol appears most evident among children where family involvement is limited or nonexistent.

In looking at the dimensions of ego-resilience, the Blocks found that low resilience appears among children of families characterized by conflict or uncertainty as well as lack of clear focus. High ego-resilience appears most clearly among children with families that are well-integrated in their moral and philosophical beliefs, where parents, in addi-

Peer relationships are critical to each child's development.

tion, appear sensitive and loving, as well as closely involved with their children.

Social Cognition—Children Getting to Know Others

More recently, other attempts to explain personal and social development have been made by social-cognitive theorists who base their work on Piaget. Kohlberg's research (1969, 1971, 1976) on moral judgment, for example, addresses the development of the individual's understanding of the social world and what constitutes moral behavior. (See pro-social/affective development later in this chapter). Moreover, his work has led to important theories and investigations of subdomains of the ego. For example, the role-taking stages described by Selman (1976, 1980, 1982) have expanded the social perspective that underlies each of Kohlberg's moral stages.

Selman's Theory of Social Cognition

According to Robert Selman, social cognition emerges via stages of increasingly complex understanding of one's self in relations to others. These understandings consist of a series of transitions that parallel the child's emerging cognitive competence, reflecting both the limits and breadth of his intellectual understandings of his social environment, just as the child's cognitive maturity is reflected in his general intellectual understandings and processing of his nonsocial environment.

Selman's theory views the dynamics of becoming aware of one's behavior as a constructive process, one which, of necessity, leads to a reflective understanding of social interactions incorporating the behaviors of others. As children become aware of their own social behaviors and their consequences they are led to construct models of interaction that meaningfully include the behavior of others. This idea may be illustrated in a rudimentary social behavior where the action or means toward achieving a goal is incorporated in the activity itself (that is, what adults might call intentionality), rather than being seen as a separate component. For example, as Stone and Selman (1982) suggest in the following illustration:

> Imagine a kindergartener in an arts and crafts program who wants the tape when another child is using it. Her automatic, unexamined means toward this goal might be physical force. If she is successful in getting the tape, she could assimilate this action scheme (i.e., grabbing) to her logical structure. If she is unsuccessful, she might have to accommodate the scheme by noticing that people get mad when she grabs, but they don't when she asks. By repeated observation of the goal and her actions, the child comes to differentiate her actions from her goals (p. 165).

One value of this theory, as made evident by this illustration, is that it provides us with a useful framework for exploring and understanding the limitations in children's social reasoning and negotiating skills, which characterize their social interactions. Moreover, this theory holds predictive value in forecasting specific behaviors and strategies characteristic of the individual child's social interactions at different ages. For example, between the ages of three and six, Selman suggests that children will employ impulsive strategies such as grabbing and hitting in social interactions, while between the ages of six and eight, one-way strategies such as commanding and directing will become most evident. Between eight and ten, two-way strategies, which are based on acknowledged reciprocity between the child and another's point of view, will appear. Hence, social interactions might include the use of such strategies as persuasion, suggestion, and voting. Only later, between the ages of ten and twelve, do collaborative strategies, such as time sharing and pooling of resources, designed to incorporate the needs of all participants, begin to emerge.

Clinical-Developmental Theory: The Harvard Model

Another view of social cognition attempts to bridge psychoanalytic and Piagetian assumptions (Noan and Kegan, 1981; Kegan, 1982). This perspective, called *clinical-developmental psychology*, uses the ideas of Piaget, Kohlberg, and Selman as a framework for the study of personality development across the life-span. As a new approach, it introduces the notion of an evolving "psychologic" or *self-other differentiation* attempting to show how each individual's growing understanding of differences between himself, including his feelings, needs, and ideas, and those of other people, including their feelings, needs, and ideas, evolves. Concepts proposed by Erickson are also shown as paralleling this theory. (See Table 6.2.)

Clinical-developmental theory postulates that the fundamental motive (or motion) to personality development is the setting and resetting of boundaries between the self and others. Beginning with the infant's initial "undifferentiated" self, which assumes that all of the world is a part of the self and that her wishes and needs control all—a state of no boundaries or *Includedness* (called Stage 0)—a gradual change in the ability to recognize and understand the differences between self and "other" develops. This growing understanding is first visible when the infant protests separation from her primary caretaker. "Separation and anxiety," this well-known phenomenon which occurs between six and nine months and ends around two years of age, is coupled with the cognitive ability to hold an object in memory. Thus object permanence and separation anxiety are the cognitive and affective expressions of a single "motion" in personality development, the process by which "self" and "subject" in the underlying logic become "other" or "object" in a new logic.

Between the ages of about two and five a new psychological organization becomes the "psycho-logic" of the child. Termed the *Impulsive Period* (Stage 1) the child's behavior is embedded in his perceptions and impulses; there is no differentiation of self and feelings. Thus the child *is* his impulses rather than a person who experiences impulses. If we

TABLE 6.2. Balances of Self and Other as the Common Ground of Several Developmental Theories

Underlying Structure	Stage 0: Incorporative	Stage 1: Impulsive	Stage 2: Imperial	Stage 3: Interpersonal	Stage 4: Institutional	Stage 5: Interindividual
Self versus other	S-Reflexes (sensing, moving) O-None	S-Impulses, perceptions O-Reflexes (sensing, moving)	S-Needs, interests, wishes O-Impulses, perceptions	S-The interpersonal mutuality O-Needs, interests, wishes	S-Authorship, identity, psychic administration O-The interpersonal mutuality	S-Interindividuality, interpenetrability of self systems O-Authorship, identity, psychic administration ideology
Piaget	Sensorimotor	Pre-operational	Concrete operational	Early formal operational	Full formal operational	
Kohlberg		Punishment & obedience orientation	Instrumental orientation	Interpersonal concordance orientation	Social orientation	Principled orientation
Erikson	Trust versus mistrust	Initiative versus guilt	Industry versus inferiority	Affiliation versus abandonment	Identity versus identity diffusion	

Adapted from: Noam, G. and R. Kegan, *Social cognition and psychodynamics: Towards a clinical-developmental psychodynamics.* Cambridge, MA: Harvard University Press, 1981.

INSET 6.3   Stage 0—Inclusive:

Anna is 15 months old and attends an infant-toddler center in the mornings while her mother attends a local job training program. She has been there for two months but each day she cries when her mother drops her off at the center.

"I just don't understand," her mother says to the head teacher. "I've always been able to leave her when I work or go to school, but lately she fusses whenever I leave. I thought she would stop after a day or two here, but she still cries every morning and I just don't know what to do."

"What time do you bring her in, Mrs. Shay?" the teacher asks.

"About a quarter to nine."

"That means you have to rush in and rush out, doesn't it? You know, Anna is at the age when she can remember things now. It's not uncommon for little ones to go through what we call separation anxiety. I don't think it's anything you're doing, just that she is getting old enough to notice when you are gone and be afraid. Do you think it would be possible to come about a half an hour earlier? Maybe if you stayed a while until she was playing quietly, that would help. We can also make sure that she is with the same teacher's aide every morning so she has a familiar person to come to when you do leave. She will outgrow the fear, but we might be able to make it easier on her and you. It tends to be real rushed here at 8:45, too. Lots of kids getting dropped off; that makes it even more confusing. What do you think?" the teacher stops to give Mrs. Shay a chance to think about the ideas just presented.

"Well, it would be kinda hard, but it would be worth it if Anna stopped fussing so much," Mrs. Shay responds.

"Let's try it for a couple of weeks and see how it goes, then we can decide if it's helping and what we want to do from there. Let me know when you come in and I'll have talked to one of the aides to set things up."

Anna is fortunate that both her mother and the center are aware of her distress and willing to take the time and effort to problem solve ways to help her with this transition period. Many parents are unaware of this reaction in toddlers and may react negatively when a child who has been willing and compliant previously begins to protest separation. Other parents become overly concerned and curtail activities rather than separate from the child. Either reaction is inappropriate and will tend to prolong the period of fear and excessive dependency. Having familiar others available, allowing time for the separation process, and being patient are the main ingredients to easing the process.

Teachers need to be aware of the developmental aspects of the child's behavior as well as the strategies for helping. The stage 0 child is gradually acquiring the cognitive understanding that permits this separation behavior to occur and then to pass. Teachers and parents who are able to keep this perspective see the positive aspects of the child's growth as well as the difficulties of the adjustment.

watch the young child we may see that he often "is" his feelings at a given moment. When he is angry or upset, *all* of him is angry and upset. He cannot talk about events objectively—he is. This state is in part a reflection of the child's inability to perceive two ideas at the same time. (One important consequence of this confusion in early childhood is the child's inability to take the role of another person cognitively, which is tied to the Piagetian concept of *reversibility*.) Another example in the affective area is the child's inability to experience ambivalence. While the child is differentiated enough to recognize that the world is not an extension of herself, she still confuses her perceptions and impulses with others'. The preschooler does not see others as having a point of view of their own, feelings of their own, even a mind separate from her own. And, since she is embedded in her impulses and perceptions, she expects the world to react to events from her point of view. To illustrate, when the three year old interrupts a conversation being held by adults, it is based on the expectation that it is anticipated, that the adults will expect and want to hear as much as the child wishes to communicate. It does not occur to the child that the adults are separate and busy and will not wish what the child does. This same child may begin a conversation with another child in the "middle," that is, she will have thought the first part of the conversation in her "head" and begin talking at whatever point she approaches her peer. Her conversation starts where she is thinking, with the absolute assumption that the other "knows" what is in her mind. These types of behavior are described by the Piagetian concept of egocentrism and by Freud's romantic picture of the Oedipal child who believes that another can be perfectly attuned to her feelings.

A transition period occurs between five and seven, which leads the child toward Stage 2, the *Imperial Stage.* During this period the child becomes more organized and is able to attend for longer periods of time and gradually begins to separate his impulses from others'. To previous fantasy activity, such as being Spiderman or Cinderella, the child adds the dimension of reality, such as being a doctor or teacher. This marks a greater ability to differentiate "reality" from fantasy. Moreover, this separation includes the beginnings of recognition that appearances can differ from reality (for example, "It looks good in the commercial on television but it ain't so hot when you get it home," confides one child to a friend); the recognition of subterfuge (for example, "She tells you 'maybe' but that mostly means no."); stereotyping in her drawings and in the affective domain.

From approximately seven to the early teens the child grows in his sense of self-sufficiency. The essence of this next "psycho-logic" (the Imperial Stage, Stage 2) is a kind of independence and autonomy, which is manifested psychologically and interpersonally. There is a self-con-

INSET 6.4 Stage 1—Impulsive:

"Bad, bad Mommy!" Liza screams, hitting her mother on the hip and arm with balled fists. "You bad!"

Liza's mother catches the child's arms so that she can not continue to hit. "I hear you are mad at me Liza, but you can not hit me. It hurts and I don't like it. You can be mad but you can't hit." The voice is calm and even and Liza then begins to cry.

Sitting on the floor, Liza's mother takes the child in her lap and cuddles her as she cries. "What is making you feel so bad, honey?"

"You took my Teddy," comes the quavering answer.

"He is in the washing machine taking a bath Liza; he'll be clean and good as new pretty soon. Would you like a cookie while you are waiting for him?"

They both get up and head for the kitchen, and Liza begins to chatter about her dolls waiting for Teddy. The storm has passed.

Liza's mother was able to handle her daughter's upset and anger without becoming angry or threatened by the child's bad feelings. She knows that Liza's feelings come and go quickly as she struggles with the many frustrations of being small and three years old. The world is often a confusing and scarey place, and a missing Teddy bear is a major tragedy, for the moment. Her mother accepts her bad feelings without allowing her to continue to strike out and hurt another person. The limits that are set are realistic and nonjudgemental, and so the situation soon passes. Liza's mother also realizes that while she can not always anticipate Liza's every want and need, Liza really believes that her mother can "read" her mind and expects her needs to be filled automatically.

Teachers of two to five year old children find themselves needing patience and understanding as they deal with the impulsive reactions of the preschool child. Multiply these reactions by the 8 to 10 children in a group and it is not surprising that those who work with this age child are very tired at the end of the day. Providing the right balance of freedom and limits within a group setting is a challenge; not providing it can produce chaos.

tainment that was not there before. The child now has a private world which he knows his parents cannot enter. He can control his impulses, he "has" feelings and can therefore tell someone else, "I am mad at you right now but I was madder yesterday." With impulses as "object" he can coordinate an impulse at one moment with an impulse at another. Thus the child begins to see himself as having an "enduring disposition" and the important process of building the self-image is in full swing. Piaget's observations of "conservation," the child's ability to hold in mind the enduring quality of a substance and not be fooled by appearance, also apply to the "self." The child develops "classes" to which the self belongs and sees himself as one of the smart kids, one of the dumb kids, a Catholic, a poor kid, a kid whose parents are divorced, and so on. The limit of this logic, however, is that it is embedded in the "class." The child cannot coordinate "classes"; she cannot coordinate two points of view; she cannot take the system of enduring dispositions ("needs") as an object or element of a bigger system. Thus at this stage the child *is* its classes, needs, and wants rather than "having" them. Just as she was embedded in others at Stage 0, and embedded in impulses and perceptions at Stage 1, she is now embedded in these needs and wants and classes. The importance for parents and teachers in understanding these limitations is profound. The parent who teases the child with "Boy, are you dumb" is telling him what class he belongs to. If this is reinforced at school, because the child is in the "low" reading group, or is "dumb" at math, he will soon decide that *is* who he is and his "dumbness" becomes that oft-mentioned *self-fulfilling prophecy* (Rosenthal and Jacobson, 1968).

The social experience brings many opportunities to "know the inherent contradictions of one's underlying psychologic" (Noam and Kegan, 1981, p. 12). Just as Piaget hypothesizes that we experience disequilibrium (the confusion from exposure to information that doesn't fit with our present schemata) and then change our schema (the process of equilibration), so our social milieu gives us "opportunities" to experience conflict with the appropriate psychosocial supports to deal with its demands that we "see" the world in new and different ways. However, as we move further along in the life-span the nature of our opportunities become less uniform and the psychosocial supports (parents, teachers, peers, siblings, significant others) become more variable. As we discussed previously, the child with alcoholic or abusing parents has a far different environment than one who is raised by parents who can be loving, supportive, and aware. And even these more stable homes will vary depending on whether they are two-parent, one-parent, extended family, or ethnic minority. The implications of these differences are many; some children will move through transitions and on to the next stages with ease, while others will be delayed or suffer from a more intense struggle in their attempts to move forward toward more mature levels of awareness of self and other.

The transition between Stages 2 and 3 usually takes place during the teen years. The adolescent begins to emerge from an embeddedness in his "needs" and "wants" to a dawning ability to coordinate independent points of view and take another person's independent purposes into account at the same time she is considering her own concerns. The new "psychologic" leads to the capacity for mutuality, empathy, and reciprocal obligation but the acquiring of these capacities is not without pain and confusion as the subjective view within her "self" becomes

INSET 6.5   Stage 2—Imperial:

"I used to be good at everything before I came to school and now I'm only smart on Saturday and Sunday. The rest of the time I'm one of the 'dumb' kids."

Between 5 and 10 years of age the child is beginning to define himself according to the new categories in which he finds himself involved. School attendance is the single biggest event of these years, and even for the child who attended nursery and day care, the 'regular' school holds a kind of magic. By now the child knows she has feelings and understands that adults and others want certain behaviors from her. At the same time there are still limits in her ability to meet adult expectations, especially, if her own needs and wants conflict with those of adults. Playing by the rules becomes increasingly important (though the rules may change, the child feels a 'need' to win). One way to order the world and feel more control is to categorize and classify. If I know the rules of the class I can avoid conflict and confusion. That makes good sense until we realize that some of the 'classes' the child constructs can become negative, self-fulfilling prophecies, like being one of the 'dumb' ones. Rules for dumb kids may include acting the class clown or withdrawing and daydreaming or whatever other behaviors the children who fit into this class learn to perform. What they do will vary more than the fact that being in that class means being not quite OK, and this feeling and the accompanying behaviors can stay with the affected individual into adulthood. "Once I learn who I am supposed to be, I am likely to continue to act that way because you treat me like a person who acts that way."

Teachers must meet the challenge of providing a learning environment that parents and supervisors will approve (for example, grouping children by 'ability'), but they must also try to avoid the creation of rigid expectations for children concerning who and what they are supposed to be. Again, finding a balance is the important thing, in this case between efficient teaching and individual needs. This requires careful planning and sensitivity on the part of all the adults who work with this age child. Too many children finish elementary school already defeated because they have found themselves in categories that stifle their ability and belief in their own capabilities.

---

perplexingly complex. This transition has its most common expression in adolescent "moodiness" and alternating periods of mature, independent, reciprocal behavior, with periods of more immature "demands" to meet the needs and wants she has always taken for granted. Adults often find this alternation of behavior and moodiness exasperating. After all, that child seemed cooperative and understanding yesterday, why not today? Patience and an expectation of vascillation during this struggle can help the parent and child "weather the storm."

The sequence of self-other relations can be represented by a helix, in which personality circles back and forth around an enduring developmental tension. (See Figure 6.3.) The developmental tension of "self" and "other" provides an appropriate context for a better understanding of the interrelationships between individual stage and social interaction. The helix makes the process of movement and growth a lifelong shifting with neither individuation and separation nor inclusion and intimacy as ultimate goals, but rather each having its appropriate part to play in each evolution within the life-span to a point where both are integral facets of our interactions.

One of the values of this model is its ability to utilize concepts from a

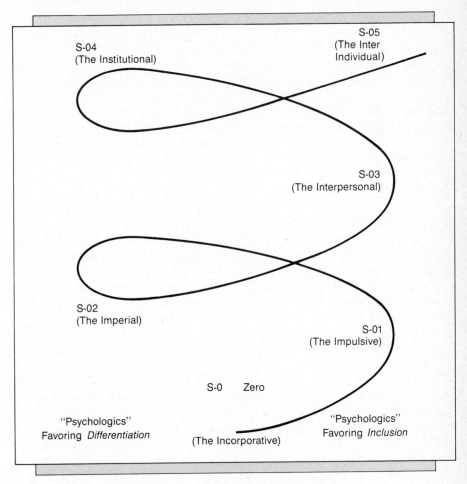

FIGURE 6.3:   A helix of self-other relations
From: Noam, G. and Kegan, R. *Social Cognition and Psychodynamics: Towards a clinical-developmental psychology.* Cambridge, MA: Harvard University Press, 1981.

variety of theorists (see Table 6.2) showing the parallel nature of many of these concepts and creating a bridge between cognitive and affective paradigms.

The view of social cognition has been challenged on both theoretical and practical grounds (Damon, 1977, 1983). Specifically, two questions have emerged in the examination of models of social cognition: (1) Is the concept of stage the best means of characterizing the child's emerging recognition of others? and (2) Is the child's level of social cognition at any specific period so cognitively fixed that specific events and happenings cannot contribute to some advanced levels of understanding. The first question asks whether the child's knowledge of others is stage-determined, that is, qualitatively different at specific periods or ages in early childhood or whether the child's level of understanding is a continuous process where differences emerge among children, not as a function of age but of degree of experience with others. The second question asks whether at any given period (within a stage) one should view each situation as possessing different learnings with specialized requirements for solution and, hence, dependent upon individual experience and personal competencies. This alternative view of social cognition as cumulative, rather than as segmented by stage, and as specialized rather than generalized, has been suggested by Hoffman (1976) and others.

A Continuous Model of Social Cognition

The position advocated by Hoffman is based on empirical and naturalistic observations of very young children (some of which were cited in Chapter 4), which demonstrate early recognition and social competence occurring among infants. These and other data, particularly studies reflecting the child's emergence of moral understandings, have led Hoffman to propose that the process of social cognition begins earlier than Selman has indicated, and that it proceeds in a more rapid and nonstage-like fashion. This process, according to Hoffman, roughly approximates a gradual series of changes in the child's growing awareness of others.

As do other theorists, Hoffman finds that early life is characterized by an initial fusion of self with others with few distinct external references. Between one and two years of age the infant shows evidence of awareness of being separate from others. While this capacity is not fully developed, many infants demonstrate appropriate empathic responses to the distress of others, suggesting recognition of differences in emotional status by the young child as well as the capacity for enacting an appropriate reaction to such recognition. One illustration of this event, cited by Hoffman, involves the case of an infant who brought his own mother to comfort another child in distress. At about the age of two this capacity appears to broaden, specifically, becoming evident by the child's capacity for both sensing distress in others and being able to respond by herself to such distress. At this time, for example, we find that children are able to share their blanket or prized toy with a child under stress. According to Hoffman, during this period the child is able to sense and act appropriately to its observation of distress in others. Between the ages of six and nine another phase of empathic understanding appears. Now, accompanied by the development of abstract reasoning, the child is able to respond to events beyond her immediate circumstances. Specifically, the child is able to use a guiding principle to determine responses, (for example, it is our obligation to care for the needy and less fortunate), as an antecedent to action.

While the work of Hoffman contradicts Selman's concepts, some of his questions and underlying assumptions contest Noam and Kagan's work as well. Even though the clinical-developmental approach rests more squarely on individual experience, as suggested by Hoffman, it is still a stage-related and generalized theoretical position.

Both the structural-development views of Selman and Noam and Kagan and the continuous approach of Hoffman on the nature of social cognition share common attributes, as well as having individual and distinct perspectives. In terms of common properties, each recognizes that social cognition is a developmental attainment, that is, a process that occurs over time. Each view, moreover, acknowledges that the emergence of social cognition begins with the child and his or her need to relate to other persons. Both positions also find that this transition is first initiated through concrete experiences characterized by active involvement, which broaden to include concepts that are more abstract and principled. It is also acknowledged across approaches that social cognition reflects intellectual, as well as affective (that is, emotional) components. And finally, each recognizes the role of others, including

INSET 6.6

It may be noted, as Sagi and Hoffman (1976) have found, that infants as young as one day old become upset and cry when exposed to real cries of distress in other babies, or to cries produced by electronic simulation. Hoffman contends that this evidence suggests the existence of empathic capacities in young organisms that enables them to respond correctly to distress signals of others, which, in turn, serves as the basis for prosocial behaviors that follow.

institutionalized experiences such as those offered through family inter-actions, school encounters, and other broad cultural opportunities, as well as persons, including parents, teachers, siblings, and peers, in the transition from self to social interest.

Another set of criticisms, from Carol Gilligan (1982), is aimed specifi-cally at Noam and Kagan and Kohlberg's work on moral development. While Gilligan is also a part of the Harvard group, she points out in *In a Different Voice* (1982) that the stages as proposed by these theorists are primarily male-oriented and that girls and women are more other-oriented at all stages of development.

ATTACHMENT/DEPENDENCY/AFFILIATION/FRIENDSHIP—THE EMERGENCE OF SOCIAL RELATIONS

Personal development, as we have seen, is neither an independent, nor self-attained accomplishment. People, from the earliest moments of life, interact with others. And from these interactions bonds of interrelat-edness are formed. In this section we will look at four facets of early social interaction, namely, attachment, dependency, affiliation, and friendship.

Attachment

The first social relationship typically revolves around one exclusive, caregiving other, most often, our maternal caregiver. This arrange-ment, in part, reflects species-specific behavior patterns among pri-mates. However, it also reflects cultural, historical, and traditional roles in U.S. society. During the first half of this century, it was assumed that women would engage in early caregiving and child rearing. More recently, under changing economic and family patterns, egalitarian child care, with joint parental participation, as well as multiple care arrangements involving nonparental others, has become more com-mon (Ainsworth, Blehar, Waters, and Wall, 1978).

The importance of early attachments has been widely discussed (Ains-worth, 1973; Bretherton and Waters, 1985; Schaffer, 1977). It has been noted, for example, that the child-parent bond formed through attach-ment represents the first affectional bond, thereby serving as a *proto-type* (that is, model) for future affectional (that is, love) relations. It has also been observed that attachments enable the infant to experience emerging emotional states within a safe and familiar context. Finally, early attachments appear critical in the infant's learning of behaviors that are basic to social interchange. As we noted in the preceding sec-tion, a child's awareness and acquisition of adaptive coping mechanisms in response to the demands of her environment are formed within the context of personal-social relations. As Schaffer (1977) observed,

> Whatever periodicities of behavior an infant is endowed with at birth, they do not continue unchanged but soon become linked to the regularities of the external environment of which he is now a part. Just as plants that open and close according to the amount of light available will adopt a regular day-night pattern, so the infant's rhythms will come to function in response to the patterning of the environmental events he encounters (p.64).

Attachment refers to a process of *proximity-seeking* of young animals to members of their own species. This process, as zoologists have noted, occurs among different primate groups ranging from humans to baboons. In each species, proximity-seeking initially appears to serve a comparable, adaptive function, namely, the survival of its young. Yet through fulfillment of this primary function, a secondary consequence has been observed; as the young organism interacts with his primary caregiving adult, affectional ties are established, which transcend the original caretaking function. This development, which, of necessity, occurs over time (over the first year of life in humans), not only insures the survival of the young, but also creates enduring bonds of friendship, love, and affiliation among species members.

As Mary Ainsworth (1964, 1969) reported in several original inquiries in this field, attachments are both complex and multidimensional in both composition and appearance. She observed, for example, that attachments are based on *affection* rather than primary needs. That is, the young organism does not form an enduring bond with caretakers because they feed or minister to its physiological needs, but rather because they are social objects who *amuse, entertain, play with, initiate, direct, stimulate,* or otherwise create sustaining social events that enliven personal contacts (Carew, Chan and Halfar, 1977).

Ainsworth also noted that attachments appear, at least initially, to be *restricted* to specific others. That is, the infant directs her initial behavioral repertoire (that is, crying, smiling, clinging, following, sucking) to familiar, known, or established persons in her environment. This intensity and continuity of involvement enables the infant to focus her affections, and these will, over time, generalize to others. In part, the narrowing of social interactions allows for concentration and rapid learning and appears characteristic of human social-emotional involvements. (By analogy we might note that children acquire "best" friends, while adults "fall" in love, in each case appearing to direct all of their energies, for some brief interval, to some specific other.)

Another important facet of the attachment process is that it constitutes a series of *actions,* involving identifiable behaviors. From its initial
repertoire of behaviors (sucking, smiling, clinging, following, and
crying), to later appearing behaviors (selective vocalization, burying his
face in his caregiver's lap, lifting his arms in greeting, using his caregiver as a base for environmental explorations), the infant engages in
observable actions that are focused on and directed at specific others.

It is also important to note that attachment is an *active-participatory
process.* The infant in establishing proximity-seeking transactions utilizes her entire (that is, known and emerging) behavioral repertoire.
Her visual, auditory, and other sensory modalities are intially employed
in this process, which quickly extends to include emerging behaviors,
as well. For example, even during the first months of life the infant
"learns" to anticipate interactions with familiar caregivers; a three
month old will engage in body posturing that eases being picked up and
held by a familiar figure. In this illustration, a pliable and conforming/
malleable body posture usually indicates recognition and acceptance,
while a rigid or stiff pose may reflect unfamiliarity, strangeness, and an
attempt to maintain distance.

Finally, as Ainsworth notes, attachments are *interactive* in character
and direction. The establishment of enduring affectional ties is not one-
sided. In practice, both infant and caregiver play complimentary roles
in the formation of attachment bonds. Each participant initiates and
each responds to interactions created by the other. Moreover, each
member contributes to the quality and tempo of established behaviors,
using familiar patterns of interaction to create new opportunities for
interaction (for example, the use of play in feeding transactions). Above
all, attachments, as other enduring affectional bonds, are mutual in
their inception and continuance. As we noted earlier (see Chapter 4),
early social bonds are clearly *orchestrated* through the joint activities
of infant and caregiver. The ensuing relationship is, in consequence,
"an ever-changing one, in that the behavior of each partner gives rise
to an increasingly complex response in organization in the other partner; the mutual entwining of interaction sequences thus takes place at
progressively high levels" (Schaffer, 1977, pp. 172–173). Moreover,
attachments generalize to include others, serving as a primary pattern
for our expanding network of social contacts and ties.

Dependency

Around two years of age an alternative system of social behaviors
appears in the emerging behaviorial repertoire of the young child.
These behaviors, which include positive attention-seeking actions (that
is, the seeking of attention through acceptable channels of expression),

negative attention-seeking (that is, deriving attention through disruptive activity), reassurance seeking (that is, seeking comfort or protection), touching and holding (that is, deriving assurance through close physical contact), and being near (that is, keeping in close contact or avoiding separation from others) are typically referred to as dependency. These behaviors are characteristic of all children and appear in greater or lesser degree in response to situational or environmental stress.

While dependency behaviors may appear as a natural extension of the attachment phenomena, in reality, attachment and dependency are distinct forms of social expression and interaction. Each differ in terms of their behavioral character, in their emotional significance, and in terms of our current understanding, in origin and developmental importance, as well.

Attachments, as we have seen, appear as natural outcomes of behaviors directed toward an exclusive caregiver (at least initially) and are created and sustained over an extended period of time. This relationship, moreover, is mutual in nature, person-oriented, and reciprocal in inception and maintenance. Attachments also appear early in the child's life, changing as a function of the infant's emerging behavioral repertoire and in concert with the growing affectional bond shared by the infant and caregiver. Dependency relations do not share these characteristics.

Dependency occurs in the form of *learned behaviors*, generally ini-

TABLE 6.3.   Comparison of Attachment and Dependency

Attachment	Dependency
Behavioral Contrasts	
Egalitarian orientation	Divided by status
Dyadic initiation	Child-initiated interaction
Reciprocal relationship	Egocentric orientation
Person-specific focus	Indiscriminate in application
Response integration	Response segregation
Emotional Contrasts	
Intense emotional commitment	Emotional involvement limited
Love-oriented relationship	Help-oriented relationship
Person-oriented focus	Need-oriented focus
Sustained relations	Brief encounter
Conceptual Contrasts	
Innate origin	Social learning etiology
Goal—love relationship	Goal—helping relationship
Developmental orientation	Situational orientation
Affective focus	Affective-task association

From: Cohen, S. *Social and personality development in childhood.* (New York: Macmillan, 1976).

tiated by the chid and supported through parental or caregiver responses. Both positive and negative attention-seeking behaviors (that is, "Watch me jump!"; "No! I won't. . . . ") represent responses that the child has learned will elicit attention from adults. Support for this observation comes from a variety of sources. Male children generally engage in more negative attention-seeking behaviors (usually physical, action-oriented responses), whereas female children tend to exhibit more positive attention-seeking behaviors (usually verbal, status-maintaining responses). These observed differences in behavior, at all ages, are likely derived from differential reinforcement patterns applied to early gender distinctions.

A second source in learning dependency behaviors is that males and females are usually reinforced differently for exhibiting "task" versus "emotional" forms of dependency. In traditional caregiving among parents, boys are encouraged to ask for help or to seek assistance and are discouraged from crying or leaving a task unfinished. Girls, in contrast, are permitted to cry under stress and are less frequently encouraged to complete challenging tasks. This initial acceptance of *task-oriented* dependency in boys, coupled with permission to engage in *person-oriented* dependency among girls, has been hypothesized to be one of several correlates of the greater achievement of males in "tasks" and related accomplishments, in contrast to female concerns for people and "person-oriented" causes. Dependent behaviors are also subject to different reactions from others, which will affect the frequency or nature of their appearance. For example, a child at work at the painting easel may spot an adult passing by and engage in a low intensive positive attention-seeking dependency response (for example, "Look at my picture."). Eliciting no reaction, our child may intensify his or her attempt to draw the attention of this same adult by offering a middle-level intensity bid for attention (for example, "Mr. Jim, come look at my picture."). If again the child receives no response and if he feels somewhat exasperated, he may engage in a high amplitude bid for attention (for example, *"Look at my picture!"*)—literally a scream for attention. In similar fashion, another child might confront a caregiver in her bids for attention with a behavior that she has viewed as being successful elsewhere (for example, "I'm going to hold my breath until . . . ").

These and related observations support the idea that dependency represents a series of learned behaviors subject to adult-peer attention and control. As we may note, dependency transactions are, in contrast to attachment, child-initiated, egocentric rather than sociocentric (that is, personally-focused rather than other-oriented), and frequently indiscriminate in application. Unlike affiliation, the child under stress will often seek emotional support from any adult who is generally available, rather than a specific caregiver.

The emotional character of dependency also differs from our observations on attachment. While attachment is characterized by an intense emotional commitment, is love-oriented, and possesses a clear, sustained affiliative basis, dependency is usually situationally limited in terms of emotional involvement, is help-oriented, and is most often characterized by a brief socio-emotional interchange, that is, dependency transactions are limited in duration and, in general, do not measureably enhance or contribute, in a developmental fashion, to an ongoing or continous relationship.

The origins of dependency appear to reside in social learning opportunities. The more dependent behaviors that are supported, the greater the levels of dependency. Moreover, excessive adult responsiveness to dependent behaviors appears to lead to fewer self-initiated, independent or self-sustained competency strivings in children. While affiliative social transactions tend to encourage development, in cases of adult-inspired dependency, such transactions are not developmentally enhancing for children.

Affiliation

As we have seen, the young infant offers us clear evidence of social participation and affiliative interests in others. This orientation toward others, moreover, is present from the first moments of life. While initial infant concern appears to center on adults, serving a protective-adaptive function, interest in others is not confined to adults. Within the first year of life, and certainly into toddlerhood and beyond, the young child will make active attempts to incorporate peers and others into her or his social environment (Rubin and Ross, 1982). In this section we will explore some of these early social transactions, noting the expanding of these relations as they come to include age-mates, as well as the changing nature of the child's social affiliations over time.

The study of emerging affiliative interactions represents a relatively new area of inquiry. Yet some important findings have already begun to appear. In general, these data comprise three sets of inquiries and related findings: (1) caregiver-infant versus infant-infant interactions, (2) infant versus toddler peer affiliations, and (3) children's early versus later peer interactions. In part, as the reader will note, these distinctions are clearly age-related, reflecting a growing concern among researchers in viewing emerging social affiliations within a developmental framework.

Two sets of data on caregiver-infant versus infant-infant social transactions have been reported in the literature. One set of these studies focuses on differences in form and level of sophistication across pairings. Other studies, by contrast, have sought to discover linkages between these separate interpersonal experiences. From these different approaches some interesting findings have emerged.

During the first six months of life infants apparently show little interest in peers. For example, when placed beside one another, infants between two and three months of age will look at, reach out, or even touch each other but in a cursory manner, the way they explore any new object. Between six and nine months of life infants begin to demonstrate closer, and somewhat specialized, interest in peers. At this time smiling, differential vocalizations, and following become more prominent. However, these are transitory and still sporadic in nature. At about nine months of life peer interactions become truly social, that is, individual transactions become coordinated, demonstrating true recognition of peers by integrated efforts at social interchange. Behaviorally, for example, infants may be observed engaging in object exchanges, including offering and taking objects from one another. Shortly thereafter, rudimentary social games appear, for example, run and chase, peek-a-boo, and so on. As the infant enters his second year of life these activities enlarge to include games which involve taking turns. Infants now may be observed engaging in intentional imitation and brief "conversation." Moreover, as the infant widens his social

TABLE 6.4.   Early Affiliative Behaviors Directed toward Peers and Age Mates

The First Year
  Birth to six months
  a.   Reaching directed toward others
  b.   Touching directed toward others
  c.   Smiling at others
  d.   Vocalization toward others
  Six months to one year
  a.   Coordinated acts (including two or more acts performed together)
  b.   One-way social acts (unreciprocated social behaviors)
  c.   Semisocial acts (minimally reciprocated social behaviors)
The Second Year
  a.   Increase in simple, coordinated, and reciprocated interactions
  b.   Appearance of emotionally toned behaviors (behaviors given positive or negative affective status)
  c.   Sustained social exchanges appear
The Third Year
  a.   Positive and negative social interactions increase
  b.   Verbal exchanges become prominent
  c.   Increase in use of more sophisticated social skills and modes of interaction

Adapted from: Hartup, W.W. Peer relations. In P.H. Mussen (Ed.), *Handbook of child psychology.* Fourth Ed. (Vol.4) (New York: John Wiley and Sons, 1983).

sphere to include peers, he does so with exceptional enthusiasm. During the second year the infant still shows sustained interest in his caregiver but now also shows an increasing regard for the activities of peers.

Peer-oriented affiliations differ from infant-caregiver transactions. Specifically, peer-initiated social transactions occur somewhat later in infancy than adult-infant interactions, are simpler in behavioral style, and are significantly more transitory than adult-infant interactions. Certainly, infant-infant transactions are, at least, initially less sophisticated and more rudimentary in scope and consequence. How may these differences be explained?

A number of contrasts appear to underlie differences in infant-caregiver versus infant-infant transactions. In infant-caregiver interactions, for example, the average transaction is significantly longer than that observed among peer pairings. Adults, obviously, are better able to initiate, as well as to sustain infant behaviors through their sensitivity to and capacity for allowing and encouraging them to interact. Moreover, adults possess the sophisticated ability to assume complementary roles and behaviors to those responses initiated by infants. "Peek-a-boo" play, for example, is more readily facilitated through the ability of the adult to "take on" role reversal. Finally, it is important to note that adult-infant play is more frequently multidimensional (that is, complex), focusing on persons as well as objects. Infant-infant play appears to center on objects of mutual interest, rather than to involve direct communication or play with one another.

How do infant-infant affiliations differ from toddler-toddler peer transactions? While infant-infant transactions are transitory, incidental, and nonspecific, during toddlerhood, peer interactions become longer, nonincidental, and more object-oriented. These object-oriented contacts usually involve, at least, initially common interest in the same toy or object. However, as inevitably each child becomes aware of the other child's interest in the same toy or object, she is forced into alternative, new responses, namely, turn-taking behaviors. By this rudimentary, unplanned need to exchange objects, a new pattern of social contact is initiated which, subsequently, sustains extended social transactions; common interest in the same object starts the process, which transforms the activity and generates interest in turn taking itself. Turn taking then becomes a rudimentary form of social interaction, which sustains continued interest in social behavior. Shortly thereafter, turn taking assumes another dimension, that of role reversals. The child observes and then seeks to perpetuate a reciprocated social interchange with another child as a variation on a play theme. Thus the infant learns how to be influenced by the actions of another and, in turn, how she may influence her peer at play.

As these observations suggest, "Toddlers are able both to initiate and maintain encounters with peers. In addition, they are able to combine social acts into complex social messages and to coordinate those messages with a partner into fairly sophisticated games" (Vandell and Wilson, 1982, p.187).

Friendship

As we have seen, social behaviors make their initial appearance through infant-caregiver transactions. These early learnings, over time, are then extended and reapplied, principally toward peers. Moreover, such learnings, through different applications, come to possess different meanings, as well as contrasting purposes. While the infant-caregiver transaction is based upon the child's need for protection, care, and instruction, peer affiliations are created to serve different goals, among them, recognition, acceptance, and companionship. As Hartup (1983) observes,

> Child relations, in general, are based on the child's dependency and the adult's need to control the child. Children's actions toward adults consist mainly of appeals and submission; the adult's actions toward the child consist of dominance and nurturance. On the other hand, the most common actions of children toward children are sociability, dominance, and resistance. . . . From babyhood to adolescence, then, the adult-child and child-child social systems are differentiated both cognitively and socially" (p.108).

As children enter the preschool years, the quantity and quality of peer affiliations change. Specifically, the children tend to abandon immature or inefficient social actions with increasing age, maintain and amplify attained modes of interaction, and acquire more mature ones. Interactions become increasingly language-based, and begin to approximate communications that more closely resemble adult forms of expression. Observations confirm the increasing use of better language forms and accompanying signals such as the employment of visual attention (that is, eye contact), body posture (that is, interactional synchrony), and referential communication (that is, speaker-listener accommodations). In social activity, coordinated interactions become especially prominent. Play activity shifts from unoccupied and solitary status to more collaborations in social problem solving. More importantly, the child is now not only more responsive to people in general, but shows increasing evidence of social differentiation. Hartup (1983) cites evidence indicating that bids for attention become more frequently directed toward peers and less commonly focused upon teachers and adults. In one such study, involving naturalistic settings where nursery school and kindergarten children could be observed, Stith and Conner (1962) compared dependency and helpfulness directed toward peers and adults. Interestingly, helpful behavior was significantly more frequently directed toward peers than adults. Moreover, in interaction with adults, children were more likely to seek help than to offer help, whereas, in peer-peer transactions children were as likely to help as to seek help from age mates.

During the preschool years, immature social actions begin to fade, being replaced by more direct, peer-coordinated activity. Strayer, Wareing, and Rushton (1979) found among nursery school children significant differences in the proportion of prosocial behaviors; that is,

INSET 6.7   A Study of Early Friendship Patterns

John Gottman and Jennifer Parkhurst (1980) observed young children between the ages of three and six years in natural settings in interactions either composed of established personal pairings (that is, friendships) or among new aquaintances. The settings were informal and involved unplanned play activities in familiar surroundings. From this vantage point Gottman and Parkhurst were able to note and distinguish between the differing quality of friendship patterns among children at these two important periods of social development.

Among the younger children they found that social interactions were characteristically founded upon fantasy, commonly agreed upon imaginative activity, and the enactment of dramatic themes created through make-believe roles. In contrast, among the older children social transactions were more reality-based, demonstrated more organization, were more frequently of serious intent, and possessed greater literal meaning; interactions among these children were more task-oriented, involved differentiation of activity among participants, and allowed for somewhat more diverse role performance.

Underlying these observations, the author found that the patterns of communication employed by these two groups and the *intent* of their verbal transactions significantly differed; the younger children, in behavior and communication, adopted a "climate of agreement," which relied upon harmonious interaction, including common agreement/consent and the avoidance of disagreement/conflict. Similarities and commonalities were stressed and communications among the children (for example, offering explanations, being responsive to requests for information, and so on) supported this focus. In contrast, the older children, in behavior and communication, adopted an interactive climate, wherein allowance of differences, disagreement, and conflict were more permissible; for the older children, the realities of individual differences was acknowledged, allowed for, and more readily accepted.

sharing, helping, cooperation, and comforting, directed toward peer age-mates (60 percent) versus adult teachers (40 percent).

While the relational meaning of friendship is not fully appreciated until the end of childhood, the beginnings of friendship are becoming apparent.

INTERPERSONAL DYNAMICS

As the sphere of children's interactions grow, shifts from personal to social interactions increase. In this sense development moves from an intrapersonal (that is, within self) framework to include interpersonal dynamics (that is, between persons). In this section we shall examine this process in terms of some selected interpersonal facets of social development, namely, children's aggression, prosocial development, and sex-role development.

Aggression

Both the development and perpetuation of aggression are serious concerns for adults who rear and teach children. As children grow and learn to express themselves, there are inevitably times when their behavior may cause injury to others. Caregivers find themselves at odds in finding solutions to the effective management and curtailment of such activities. On the one hand, caregivers may wish to support the child's need to develop effective, assertive coping mechanisms. On the other hand, there is the necessity of imposing restrictions on behaviors capable of causing injury to others. Clearly, aggression in children poses difficult issues for adults invested in child care and management. In this section we will examine some causes and influences of aggressive behavior in children.

The acquisition (that is, learning) of an aggressive response is closely associated with observational learning principles. By viewing *models* performing aggressive actions, the child readily acquires similar behavioral responses. This finding may be offered as suggestive in explaining the relative ease and speed with which aggressive responses are acquired across different age groups, particularly among young children with restricted experiential backgrounds and limited conceptual capacities. For the young child, observational learning appears to be a particularly effective mechanism for the acquisition of aggressive response patterns, especially since the child learns how to be aggressive at a developmental period when perceptual learning is favored over conceptual learning.

While observational learning principles may account for the acquisition of aggressive behavior, there are differences in the performance of aggression across varied age groups, as well as among boys and girls that may be most easily explained in terms of experienced reinforcement and situational sanctions surrounding the child's aggressive responses. Performance is dependent upon the child's cognitive awareness of the consequences of behaving aggressively, as well as the child's exercise of deliberate choice in the display of such behavior. For the young child the consequences of behaving aggressively are often not clearly defined by others or may be inconsistently applied. This confusion can lead to the child's misuse of aggression. Added to these difficulties, the young child is also restricted in his command of behavioral alternatives to aggression; the relative absence of alternatives to aggression may prohibit the adoption of more conciliatory behavior patterns.

Among boys and girls differences in the frequency of performed aggression, as well as its structural expression (that is, physical versus verbal aggression), appear to reflect disparate cultural sanctions surrounding the performance of aggression. Among boys, cultural sanctions in support of physical aggression are quite prominent. On a behavioral level, aggressive responses are generally supported or encouraged. For girls, however, cultural expectations for the performance of aggressive acts and reinforcement surrounding such activity are more circumspect. While girls are discouraged from exhibiting various forms of physical aggression, they are permitted to display verbal or indirect forms of aggression (that is, gossip, tattling).

Differences in the frequency and style of aggression displayed by boys and girls are of particular interest since they highlight the role and importance of cultural conditioning and social sanctions in the performance and control of such behaviors. These factors, traditionally, have received less attention as explanatory concepts than the available evidence warrants. Socio-cultural conditions have assumed less importance than biological factors that emphasize sex differences in general activity level and endocrine functioning as causative elements in the development of aggression. However, there is increasing evidence that suggests the need to revise our assessment of these conditions in the development and control of aggression.

From anthropological studies, such as Mead's historical account of *Sex and Temperament in Three Primitive Societies* (1969), we have learned that culture, rather than gender, determines which behaviors will be acquired and performed by men and women, respectively. From these studies of geographically isolated tribal units it was found that either sex can be aggressive. Among the *Arapesh* Mead found that both sexes exhibit behavior that resembles our concept of femininity, while among the *Mundugamor* both men and women demonstrate behavior patterns, including the extensive employment of aggressive, competitive, and hostile-related actions, that approximate our concept of the masculine image. In contrast, the *Tchambuli* exhibit a form of role reversal, relative to our sex-role standards, in which the females display "masculine" and the males exhibit "feminine" behavior patterns.

Biological explanations of aggression founded upon endocrinological origins also require revision. Traditionally, it had been argued that differences in the secretion of androgen (the hormone responsible for the production of testosterone in males) and estrogen (the hormone associated with the production of progesterone in females) are responsible for the occurence of aggression and sexuality in male and females. However, available evidence now indicates that both boys and girls secrete androgen and estrogen prior to puberty. Moreover, in both sexes the secretion of these hormones, previous to the onset of adolescence, appears too negligible to account for alleged differences in aggression, particularly since behavioral differences in aggression among the sexes become prominent long before the child reaches puberty (Rossi, 1974). Correspondingly, it appears reasonable to conclude that cultural conditioning and applied social sanctions form two critical dimensions in the development of aggression.

Children's exposure to aggressive models has also been associated with the learning of new response patterns. Earlier research in this area (Bandura and Walters, 1963), subsequently supported by more recent studies, suggested that a child's observation of aggressive models may be closely tied to several important outcomes. One such consequence is the creation of inhibitions *or*, the release of inhibitions surrounding the display of aggression. Here, previously observed (and learned) aggressive responses are either suppressed *or* released upon the child's viewing of aggression in others. Indeed, the model's performance may function as either a positive or negative sanction for the child's imitation of observed behavior. In essence, watching others serves an eliciting effect, in part, similar to a "monkey see-monkey do" behavior sequence. Another illustration especially evident in young children is the "Three Stooges" effect. Here, children's exposure to highly aggressive film content is often accompanied or followed by comparable slapstick behavior of an aggressive nature. In sum, as reported by Bandura (1973), modeling influences can function as teachers, instigators, inhibitors, disinhibitors (that is, releasers), stimulus enhancers, and emotion arousers of aggression. These eliciting conditions, combined with external sanctions or reinforcement, foster the enactment of aggressive behavior in both children and adults.

TABLE 6.5.   Television: Some Characteristics and Conclusions of TV Viewing as It Affects Children

1. Almost every home in the United States has a television set (98 percent). Many households have at least one extra television set (52 percent).
2. U.S. children spend a great deal of time viewing television. Children between the ages of 2 and 18 years watch an average of over 3 hours of television a day. By adding weekend, holiday, and school vacation hours to these figures, children spend more time watching television than they spend engaging in any other single waking activity, including attending school, interacting with family members, or playing with other children.
3. Over 70 percent of prime time dramatic fiction programs sampled between 1967 and 1979 were found to contain violence; children's cartoon and weekend morning programs consistently contained the highest levels of violence among all categories of programming.
4. Parents generally report that they place few or no restrictions on their children's television viewing; children report even fewer parental controls than their parents report.

Adapted from: Parke, R. and Slaby, R.G. The development of aggression. In P.H. Mussen (Ed.), *Handbook of child psychology.* Fourth ed. (Vol.4) (New York: John Wiley and Sons, 1983).

Prosocial-Affective Development

As we have seen there is growing evidence of social competencies (that is, social awareness) in infants and young children. Moreover, as we reported earlier in this chapter there is accumulating evidence that children's behavior is also conceptually linked in intimate association with others from the very beginnings of life. This evidence appears, as we reported, in early affiliative behavior displayed by infants and toddlers in interactions with adults and children alike. In this section on prosocial-affective development we turn our attention to some representative behaviors that define, shape, and extend social bonding throughout childhood. Specifically, we will examine the origins of responses which are considered synonymous with prosocial activity (namely, sharing and caring, helping and cooperation, generosity and altruism).

Historical/Theoretical Studies

In an extensive review of the literature on prosocial behavior, Radke-Yarrow, Zahn-Waxler and Chapman (1983) cite early historical interest and keen recognition among earlier investigators of the behavior of young children. To illustrate, over 50 years ago Stern (1924) wrote of the young child:

> Even the two year old child has the power of feeling another's sorrow, not
> only in the sense that, infected by the other's feelings, he grows sad and
> anxious with him and cries in response to the other's tears ... but in the
> higher sense of putting himself in the other's place, identifying himself
> with his sorrow, pain, or fear, and trying to comfort, help, or even avenge
> him (p.521).

Other considerations of the development of prosocial behavior can
most clearly be found in the early writings of Freud and Piaget. Each
of these theorists, as well as proponents of their ideas, have suggested
explanations pertaining to the origins and development of social awareness and the acquisition of behaviors representing the rights and interests of others.

Orthodox psychoanalytic theory, as proposed by Freud, views prosocial behavior development as being mediated primarily through
affective-emotional mechanisms, namely, feelings generated in
response to the plight or distress of others. For psychoanalytic theory,
guilt represents a critical component in the development of all forms of
morality. Bad feelings (namely, guilt) are abstracted from specific situations (both in a cognitive and internal sense) and become attached to
present and future behavioral transactions. As the child broadens her
social interactions, she transfers acquired guilt in response to observed
events to anticipated events, whereby anticipatory guilt serves as an
early internal warning signal of forthcoming emotional reactions that
may be triggered by the imagined enactment of further misbehaviors.

Several problems are associated with the psychoanalytic explanation
of early moral development. While this theory offers some account of
why children may refrain from committing transgressions, as well as
how they may feel upon engaging in a negative act, it does not adequately account for the development of alternative, prosocial behaviors. That is, how prosocial behaviors (namely, sharing and caring,
helping and cooperation, generosity and altruism) develop, what feelings accompany these behaviors, how such emotions are generated
and what role cognitive-intellectual factors may play in such behaviors
are not explained.

An alternative account of moral development, based upon the child's
acquisition of moral judgment (that is, the capacity for decision making
involving others) has been offered by Piaget (1932) and expanded by
Kohlberg (1969). According to this view, morality consists of the child's
understanding and application of rules that govern social relations.
These rules flow from early hedonistic concerns to a gradual consideration of abstract principles of justice and equality.

For Piaget, rules come from two sources: from the child's parents, including other important adults in her or his life and from the child's own, naturally occuring experiences with and among peers. From adults, the child is exposed to a system of formal decrees, each subject to adult elaboration and classification. Rules, as derived from this context, achieve their significance through the child's reverence for external and empowered authority. Complimenting this source of rules, the child, in her role as a peer comes to experience and view her behavior, as well as that of her peers, as subject to autonomous initiation and execution through principles derived from egalitarian interactions, that is, social contract. That is, through the creation, participation, and revision of activities, established and conducted by increasingly democratic principles, the child learns an alternative means of rule formation and purpose. She discovers that rules can be initiated by individual members of the group and that they achieve their acceptance through social (that is, group) consensus.

The process of rule formation, its growth and elaboration, has been noted by Piaget and others to occur, most notably, in such realms of children's activity as peer-initiated games and play (see Chapter 3). In the game, the manner in which rules are formulated and practiced, as well as revised, is taken by Piaget as evidence of a developmental progression in which rules shift from being obligatory and sacred (as with parental and adult decrees) to being subject to choice and mutual accord (evidence of social contract) among participants.

Kohlberg (1969, 1976), building on Piaget's concepts, developed a more elaborate and extensive model of moral development, which articulates six stages of gradually more sophisticated and independent judgment concerning appropriate behavior in a "moral dilemma." Moral dilemmas are situations in which the solution creates a conflict of interest (for example, stealing a drug to save a life). (See Table 6.6 for an outline of Kohlberg's stages.)

Piaget's views of moral development are based upon his belief in the importance of informal teaching and nonguided peer exchanges as the principal vehicles/framework for ethical decision making and moral growth. This perspective is segmented and holistic rather than integrated and specific; the Piagetian view emphasizes discontinuous (that is, stage-determined) changes, rather than continuous (that is, cumulative-incremental) orderings of experience. As discussed earlier in this chapter critics of social-cognitive developmental theory see a variety of limitations in this perspective. Piaget's approach offers us a global outline/diagram of moral development, but provides us with little information on the role of specific training experiences/opportunities or references to modeling factors, including suggestions of how social sanctions or reinforcement principles operate in the acquisition or

TABLE 6.6. Classification of Moral Judgment into Levels and Stages of Development

Basis of Moral Judgment Levels	Stages of Development
I. Moral value resides in external, quasi-physical happenings, in bad acts, or in quasi-physical needs rather than in persons and standards.	Stage 1: Obedience and punishment orientation. Egocentric deference to superior power or prestige or a trouble-avoiding set. Objective responsibility.
	Stage 2: Naively egoistic orientation. Right action is that instrumentally satisfying the self's needs and occasionally others'. Awareness of relativism of value to each actor's needs and perspective. Naive egalitarianism and orientation to exchange and reciprocity.
II. Moral value resides in forming good or right roles, in maintaining the conventional order and the expectancies of others.	Stage 3: Good boy orientation. Orientation to approval and to pleasing and helping others. Conformity to sterotypical images of majority of natural role behavior, and judgment by intentions.
	Stage 4: Authority and social order-maintaining orientation. Orientation to "doing duty" and to showing respect for authority and maintaining the given social order for its own sake. Regard for earned expectations of others.
III. Moral value resides in conformity by the self to shared or sharable standards, rights, or ideals.	Stage 5: Contractual legalistic orientation. Recognition of an arbitrary element or starting point in rules or expectations for the sake of agreement. Duty defined in terms of contract, general avoidance of violation of the will or rights of others, and majority will and welfare.
	Stage 6: Conscience or principle orientation. Orientation to conscience as a directing agent and to mutual respect and trust.

From: Kohlberg, L. Stage and sequence: The cognitive-developmental approach to socialization. In D.A. Goslin(Ed.), *Handbook of socialization theory and research* (Chicago: Rand McNally, 1969).

maintenance of specific prosocial behaviors. Moreover, the cognitive-developmental view does not effectively reconcile affective-emotional growth in conjunction with intellectual-cognitive development as cocomponents in the rule formation process; while children's rules may, in fact, be derived from direct experiential encounters, the roles of emotional and behavioral principles that define the settings and quality of interaction therein require further elaboration.

Culture and Prosocial Development

While knowledge of the origins and concern of the specific processes responsible for the development of prosocial behavior await further study, research conducted on cultural diversity has provided some interesting clues and directions for future inquiries. Two projects stemming from this tradition appear to offer some special insights.

In a major anthropological study, Whiting and Whiting (1975) observed children's behaviors within the context of cultural differences among six historically distinct and geographically dispersed cultures (namely, Indian, Kenyan, Mexican, Okinawan, Phillippino, and U.S.). In each of these cultures, 6 boys and 6 girls between the ages of 3 and 6 years and an equal number of males and females between ages 7 and 11 years (creating a total sample of 134 subjects) were observed in their natural settings over periods ranging from several months to 1 year. Specifically, each child was observed for an average of seventeen 5-minute periods in a variety of social interactions, including in courtyards near their homes, in the fields, on school grounds, with adults present and absent, during group work, as well as in play and during casual social activities. Using factor analysis (that is, a procedure for statistical categorizing of data) several dimensions of behavior were isolated for further review, including the presence of *altruistic* versus *egoistic* *behavior.*

INSET 6.8

Altruism consists of behaviors where the child offers "help" (including food, toys, and information), or "support" which suggests "responsibility" to or for another. In each interaction another person is the primary recipient or beneficiary of the child's "concern." By contrast, *egoistic* behavior includes seeking control, attention, or help from others, which benefits the individual child, rather than another.

From extensive analysis of the data it was found that a majority of the children in the Kenyan, Mexican, and Phillippino cultures were high above the median (that is, 50 percent level) of the total sample in altruism, while most of the children in the other three cultures (Okinawan, Indian, and U.S.) scored low in altruism. Specifically, 100 percent of the children in Kenya were above the median, 73 percent of the Mexican children, 63 percent of the Phillippino children, 29 percent of the Okinawan, 25 percent of the Indian, and 8 percent of the U.S. children. These differences were evident at the level of group and individual analysis within a given culture and were observed in the younger and older children, as well. Further analysis of the data also revealed some significant differences pertaining to probable etiological (that is, causative) factors associated with altruism compared with the egoism-producing cultures. In the altruistic cultures, females played major roles in the subsistence of the family unit: women in these societies contributed substantially to the economy and the food supply. In addition, the family unit in these cultures consisted of extended family groupings, with multiple ties and obligations, in most cases, established across generational boundaries. In this context, the most critical cultural factor associated with the development of altruism appeared to be the extent to which children were given defined roles within the family unit and assigned tasks, including assumed responsibility for other, usually younger, members of the family. Cultures in which children had high responsibilities in service to others were cultures in which the children also demonstrated significantly higher altruism scores.

Another series of cross-cultural studies, conducted by Madsen and his associates (1967, 1970, 1975) offers us several insights into the development of cooperation in young children. For this research Madsen (1970) developed a specially constructed game board (referred to as the cooperation board) in which children utilizing a string-pulling strategy compete for prizes. The unique feature of this piece of apparatus is that children must cooperate with each other in order to win prizes; competition on this task is clearly maladaptive, while cooperation is self-serving, as well as helpful to others. From his studies of children from different cultural communities all over the world, a consistent pattern of findings has emerged: children reared in traditional rural settings and subcultures, including small, semiagricultural communal settlements, cooperate more readily than children reared in modern urban communities. These trends, moreover, are international, rather than simply cross-national, being evident in children from Mexican villages versus Mexican urban settings, children from Israeli kibbutzim and Arab villages versus Israeli and Arab urban centers, rural Colombian children versus their urban counterparts, and children from rural New Zealand Maori communities versus New Zealand, European, or urban

Maori children. As these findings suggest, communities encouraging shared responsibilities in childhood, integration of group efforts, and intergenerational ties, promote less competition, and in turn, higher levels of cooperative effort.

These studies, along with other work such as Gilligan's (1982), also give rise to questions of sex role identity and the part that development of one's concepts and understandings about gender play in social development.

Sex Role Development

Research evidence suggests that the learning of gender identifications is an important facet of personal growth and development in U.S. society. A child's feelings about herself, her interactions with others, and the skills and abilities she will develop, as well as excel in, each will be influenced through her affiliated gender identification.

When does such learning occur and what forms does it take? While difficult to assess directly, it appears that sex-typed learning occurs during the child's first 18 months of life (Power, 1985) and intensifies subsequently. Studies of parental responses to their infants, in terms of the sex of the child, indicate that daughters are viewed as being smaller, possessing finer features, being softer, and being less alert than sons. These perceptions appear among parents despite the absence of real (that is, objectively verifiable) physical differences. Interestingly, fathers tend to perceive their sons as being stronger and hardier than their daughters, while girls are stereotypically viewed as being more fragile than boys. Perhaps a function of these perceptions, one of the most consistent findings on early differences in the treatment of male and female children is that more physical stimulation and gross motor play is directed toward male infants than female infants. Fathers, especially, play with male infants differently than with their female offspring, and

INSET 6.9

As the reader should note, our interest in this issue reflects a concern for how we, as important adults in the lives of children, view and treat children. Currently, as this discussion will indicate, boys and girls, contrary to our best wishes, are, in fact, perceived and accorded different treatment among parents and teachers alike, these differing behavior reflecting the child's gender identity, rather than her or his ability or needs.

differently than mothers appear to play with each gender. In particular, when fathers play with their sons they are physically rougher, emphasize more gross motor activities, and, relative to mothers, use fewer toys.

From toddlerhood to three years of age, sex-role learnings become most evident as children initiate pronounced sex typing in their play activities and interests. According to Huston (1983) during this period children

> Select sex-typed activities in spontaneous play; they classify themselves and others according to gender; and they classify many of the concrete objects and activities around them according to culturally defined sex-appropriateness. By age three, all of these trends are consistently evident, though children's knowledge of cultural stereotypes and their adherence to them continue to increase with age (p. 407).

The differential roles parents play, relative to their sons and daughters, during this period clearly focus their children's attention upon these gender distinctions and related expectations. In several studies of preschool children, where the teaching behaviors of parents in interaction with their children were directly observed, it was found that parents communicate higher expectations and greater demands for independent task performance to their sons, while, among their daughters, parents are more likely to provide help at signs of distress and to focus their attention more on the interpersonal dynamics of the teaching situation than on its task demands.

Early observed patterns of differential treatment by parents toward their sons and daughters, respectively, continues into middle childhood. At this time parents allow boys more freedom to pursue activites away from the home and without adult supervision than they do girls. Paradoxically, girls are expected to be more responsible than boys, but are provided fewer opportunities to engage in independent behavior.

INSET 6.10

As Huston notes, there is a subtle, although clear message associated with such distinction. She writes, "When parents respond quickly to a girl's request for help, they may communicate their low evaluation of the child's competence; when they demand independent effort from a boy, they may signify confidence in the child's ability" (1983. p.431).

TABLE 6.7.   A Parental Agenda for Egalitarian Development between Boys and Girls

1. Each parent will engage in and encourage comparable amounts of gross motor play with their children.
2. Parents will encourage the use of similar toys and games in their children.
3. Parents will demand comparable amounts of effort in tasks assigned to or required of their children.
4. Parents will provide equal amounts of help to their children.
5. Each parent will encourage comparable amounts of independence in their children.
6. Each parent will allow similar degrees of freedom from adult supervision of their children.
7. Each parent will encourage comparable levels and forms of dependency in their children.
8. Each parent will play a significant and equally responsible role in the development of their children.

Sex Stereotyping in the School

The school, next to the child's family, represents the second most important institutional/instructional source of socialization. How, then, do teachers influence sex-role development? Interestingly, in spite of educational opportunity and training, teachers exhibit considerable sex-role stereotyping, but of a different variety than that recorded among parents. Studies based on classroom observations of teacher behavior in both preschool and elementary school report, for both sexes, that the school experience often reflects a "feminine bias"; behaviorally, boys receive greater disapproval and other forms of negative attention from teachers than do girls (Fagot, Hagan, Leinbach, and Kronsberg, 1985). In addition, several studies report that teachers perceive females and feminine personality attributes more positively than males and masculine personality attributes. Other evidence extends these findings by suggesting that teachers may express greater disapproval of boys than their actual behavior may support, primarily as a result of generalized expectations among teachers that boys will misbehave more frequently than girls.

Peer Contacts and Sex-Typing

Within the context of home, school, and media exposure, children are offered ample opportunity to acquire "masculine" or "feminine" sex-role behaviors. These learnings, moreover, are vigorously practiced and rigidly reinforced among peers. As noted earlier, by the time the

TABLE 6.8.   A Teacher's Agenda for Avoiding Sexual Stereotyping in Boys and Girls

1. Children will be encouraged to use all toys, materials, and equipment, irrespective of gender identity.
2. Teachers will attend and respond to each child's behavior, irrespective of her gender identity.
3. An attitude of "can do" will be advocated in each classroom for each child.
4. Exemplary male and female models will be cited, discussed, and held in esteem.
5. Children's and adult's roles will not be identified by gender identity.
6. Children will be encouraged to engage in cross-sex activities.
7. All children will be encouraged to engage in independent responsible activities.
8. Each child will be valued for her or his personal and individual qualities.

child is two years of age she or he actively engages in anticipated sex-delineated behavior patterns. Observations confirm that children at this age generally engage in more frequent interaction among same-sex peers than opposite-sex peers. In cross-sex pairings of children at this age, it has been observed that girls appear more passive and withdrawn when they interact with a male counterpart than with a female peer while, in contrast, males are less responsive to interchanges initiated by females, as opposed to those of male peers.

In one study conducted among two year olds, it was found that male, as well as female children, were more responsive to same-sex peers than to opposite-sex peers, irrespective of the quality of the interaction; both boys and girls tended to be more attentive to positive as well as negative interchanges initiated by same-sex, that is, male and female peers, respectively (Fagot, 1981).

Peer support for same-sex activities, and correspondingly, negative response to cross-sex behaviors, appear in earnest by the time the child is three. Boys and girls who engage in "sex-appropriate" behavior/activities are positively supported by their peers of both sexes; children who display preference for cross-sex activities are frequently criticized and/or socially isolated. Adherence to sex-appropriate behaviors appears to be maintained, in most instances, across the school years (LaFreniere, Strayer and Gautheir, 1984).

There appears to be no ready explanation to account for the rigidity of early sex-role learning, its practice or its maintenance. Most likely a combination of parental, teacher, and media influences combine to produce sets of expectations for and support of those behaviors which have come to be traditionally associated with gender identity.

SUMMARY

The discussion of social development in this chapter shows the diversity and breadth of theoretical orientations in this area and gives us some orientation to the complexities of the interaction between the child and his environment regarding the process of becoming a social being. Whether we look at ego development in a broad context or at the component areas of positive and negative social relationships, we see an emerging picture of the child embedded in a series of interactions which help her learn and define who she is. From the attachment/ dependency issues of the primary caregiver-infant pair to the sophisticated moral decisions of self-other interests, each of us develops an image of ourselves in relation to others. We are friend or foe, compliant or aggressive, feminine or masculine, intimate or isolated, as a result of our culture, our parenting, our peers, and ourselves. In other words, we become the sum of those social influences filtered through the sieve of our own temperament and emerging personality. We can not know who we are outside of the realm of social interaction, and because of the profound influence of these relationships, it becomes extremely important that the adults who live with and care for children understand and facilitate social growth and awareness. For those of us who work with young children our roles become especially important. A positive sense of "I-ness," a trust in the care and kindness of others, a sense of unlimited opportunity regardless of gender do not come about by accident but through design. The challenge of making that design a positive force in the life of the child is up to us.

Explorations

PERSONAL EXPLORATIONS

These exercises are designed to help you look at your own life—attitudes, experiences, dreams, myths, and realities.

1. Think back to your earliest memories of being a "boy" or a "girl." When did you learn that you could or could not do something based on your sex identity? How did these learnings affect what you thought about yourself? How did they affect what you believed you could do? Were your beliefs and your family's teachings the same as those of the other children in your neighborhood? Write a page describing your development in this area.
2. What friendship patterns were common in your home, your neighborhood, and the school where you grew up? What is your own per-

sonal history of friendships? Draw a picture of your "best" childhood friend and write three reasons why she or he was your friend.

3. Kohlberg's most often cited moral dilemma concerns Heinz, a man whose wife is dying of a disease that can only be cured by a very expensive drug that only one druggist in town possesses. Heinz does not have the money to pay for the drug and the druggist has refused his offer to pay for the drug over time. Should Heinz steal the drug or let his wife die? Write your answer to this dilemma and then see if you can decide what "stage"of moral development your answer fits. Go to class prepared to discuss your thoughts and feelings about this dilemma.

4. Carol Gilligan has challenged Kohlberg's stages of moral development as being male oriented; she says that females are more other oriented at all stages of development. From your own experiences offer a reaction to this contention.

INTELLECTUAL EXPLORATIONS

These exercises are designed to increase your depth of knowledge in some of the areas discussed in this chapter.

1. In a contemporary journal, such as *Child Development*, survey the number of articles in one or two issues that relate to attachment, dependency, or affiliative behavior in children before the middle childhood years. Write a paragraph on each of two articles that take different theoretical positions.

2. What do contemporary teaching journals say about sex-role sterotyping in the classroom? What recommendations are made concerning classroom practices? Bring a list of several recommendations to class for discussion.

3. Find a recent book or journal of cross-cultural studies. What findings are discussed concerning the development of the child and her social relationships? Write a brief synopsis of this information and compare the children in the study with what you know of U.S. children of the same ages.

4. "Affective" or "humanistic" education (that is, education that attends to the emotional and personal development of the child) has had varying degrees of acceptance in the public schools over the last two decades. Find a book or two articles that discuss approaches to this kind of education and write your reaction to the place of affective education in the schools.

FIELD EXPLORATIONS

These exercises are designed to take you out into the world to find real examples that will illustrate and elucidate the material in this chapter.

1. Visit an infant-toddler center or some other environment in which you can observe youngsters below the age of one year. How do they respond to adults, to peers? How do they initiate, facilitate, or discourage others from interacting with them? Write a factual description of your observations.
2. Observe a group of preschool children at a local center or playground. Make two columns on a sheet of paper and list affiliative behaviors in one column and aggressive behaviors in the other column. Which are more prevalent? Are there any patterns you can identify by age or by sex? Bring your data to class for discussion.
3. Watch a series of children's programs on television (Saturday morning is the best time). Tabulate the incidence of cartoon and "live" violence. Tabulate the incidence of prosocial behaviors. How do "children's" programs compare in violence with some of the prime time television you watch? Using the modeling concepts presented in this chapter, what types of behaviors would you expect to occur among children who watch a great deal of television? Write a paragraph concerning your informed opinion of the potential effects of television on children.
4. Interview a child psychologist, school psychologist, therapist, or counselor who deals with children's emotional problems. What are this person's views on child development and the major causes of emotional difficulty in children before the age of 10. Plan to report on this interview in class.

References

Ainsworth, M. D. S. Patterns of attachment behavior shown by the infant in interaction with his mother. *Merrill-Palmer Quarterly*, 1964, 10, 51–8.

———. Object relations, dependency and attachment: A theoretical review of the infant-mother relationship. *Child Development*, 1969, 40, 965–1025.

———. The development of the infant-mother attachment. In B.M. Caldwell and H.N. Ricciuti (Eds.), *Review of Child Research* (Vol.3), Chicago: University of Chicago Press, 1973.

Ainsworth, M. D. S., Blehar, M. C., Waters, E., and Wall, S. *Patterns of attachment*, Hillsdale, NJ: Erlbaum, 1978.

Bandura, A. *Aggression:* A social learning analysis. New York: Holt, Rinehart and Winston, 1973.

Bandura, A., and Walters, R. H. *Social learning and personality theory*. New York: Holt, Rinehart and Winston, 1963.

Block, J. H. and Block, J. The role of ego-control and ego-resiliency in the organization of behavior. In W.A. Collins (Ed.), *Development of cognition, affect and social relations.* (Minnesota Symposium on Child Psychology, Vol.13). Hillsdale, NJ: Erlbaum, 1980.

Bretherton, I. and Waters, E. (Eds.), Growing points of attachment theory and research. *Monographs of the Society for Research in Child Development*, 1985, 50, 1–2.

Carew, J. V., Chan, I., and Halfar, C. *Observing intelligence in young children: Eight case studies.* Englewood Cliffs, NJ: Prentice-Hall, 1977.

Cohen, S. *Social and personality development in childhood*. New York: Macmillan, 1976.

Erikson, E. *Identity and the life cycle*. New York: Norton, 1980.

Fagot, B. I. Sterotypes versus behavioral judgments of sex differences in young children. *Sex Roles*, 1981, 7, 1093–96.

Fagot, B. I., Hagan, R., Leinbach, M. D., and Kronsberg, S. Differential reactions to assertive and communicative acts of toddler boys and girls. *Child Development*, 1985, 56, 1499–1505.

Freud, A. and Dann, S. An experiment in group upbringing. *Psychoanalytic study of the child*, 1951, 6, 127–68.

Gilligan, C. *In a different voice: Psychological theory and women's development*. Cambridge, MA: Harvard University Press, 1982.

Gottman, J. and Parkhurst, J. A. A developmental theory of friendship and acquaintance processes. In a W. A. Collins (Ed.), *Development of cognition, affect and social relations* (Minnesota Symposium on Child Psychology, Vol.13). Hillsdale, NJ: Erlbaum, 1980.

Hartup, W. W. Peer relations. In P. H. Mussen (Ed.), *Handbook of child psychology*. Fourth Ed. (Vol.4) New York: John Wiley and Sons, 1983.

Hoffman, M. Empathy, role-taking, guilt and the development of altruistic motives. In T. Lickona (Ed.), *Moral development and behavior*. New York: Holt, Rinehart and Winston, 1976.

Huston, A. C. Sex-tying. In P. H. Mussen (Ed.), *Handbook of child psychology*. Fourth Ed. (Vol.4) New York: John Wiley and Sons, 1983.

Kegan, R. *The evolving self*. Cambridge, MA: Harvard University Press, 1982.

Kohlberg, L. Stage and sequence: The cognitive-developmental approach to socialization. In D. A. Goslin (Ed.), *Handbook of socialization theory and research*. Chicago: Rand McNally, 1969.

———. From is to ought: How to commit the naturalistic fallacy and get away with it in the study of moral development. In T. Mischel (Ed.), *Cognitive development and epistemology*. New York: Academic Press, 1971.

———. Moral stages and moralization: The cognitive-developmental approach. In T. Likona (Ed.) *Moral development and behavior*. New York: Holt, Rinehart and Winston, 1976.

LaFreniere, P., Strayer, F. F., and Gauthier, R. The emergence of same-sex affiliative preferences among preschool peers: A developmental/ethological perspective. *Child Development*, 1984, 55, 1958–65.

Madsen, M. C. Development and cross-cultural differences in the cooperative and competitive behavior of young children. *Psychological Reports*, 1967, 20, 1307–20.

Madsen, M. C. and Shapira, A. Cooperative and competitive behavior of urban Afro-American, Anglo-American, Mexican-American, and Mexican village children, *Developmental Psychology*, 1970, 3, 16–20.

Madsen, M. C., and Yi, S. Cooperation and competition of urban and rural children in the Republic of South Korea. *International Journal of Psychology*, 1975, 10, 269–74.

Mead, M. *Sex and temperament in three primitive societies*. New York: Dell, 1969.

Noam, G. and Kegan, R. *Social cognition and psychodynamics: Towards a clin-*

ical-developmental psychology. Cambridge, MA: Harvard University Press, 1981.

Parke, R. and Slaby, R. G. The development of aggression. In P.H. Mussen (Ed.), *Handbook of child psychology.* Fourth Ed. (Vol.4), New York: John Wiley and Sons, 1983.

Piaget, J. *The moral judgement of the child.* Glencoe, IL: Free Press, 1965 (Originally published, 1932).

Power, T. G. Mother- and father-infant play: A developmental analysis. *Child Development,* 1985, 56, 1514–24.

Radke-Yarrow, M. Zahn-Waxler, C., and Chapman, M. Children's prosocial dispositions and behavior. In P.H. Mussen (Ed.), *Handbook of child psychology.* Fourth Ed. (Vol.4) New York: John Wiley and Sons, 1983.

Rosenthal, R. and Jacobson, L. *Pygmalion in the classroom.* New York: Holt, Rinehart and Winston, 1968.

Rossi, A. S. The missing body in sociology: Closing the gap between physiology and sociology. Paper presented at the Eastern Sociological Society Meetings. Philadelphia, PA: 1974.

Rubin, K. H. and Ross, H. S. *Peer relationships and social skills in childhood.* New York: Springer-Verlag, 1982.

Sagi, A., and Hoffman, M. L. Empathic distress in the newborn. *Developmental Psychology,* 1976, 12, 175–6.

Schaffer, H. R. (Ed.), *Studies in mother-infant interaction.* New York: Academic Press, 1977.

Selman, R. L. Social-cognitive understanding. In T. Lickona (Ed.), *Moral development and behavior: Theory, research, and social issues.* New York: Holt, Rinehart and Winston, 1976.

———. *The growth of interpersonal understanding.* New York: Academic Press, 1980.

Stern, W. *Psychology of early childhood.* New York: Holt, 1924.

Stith, M. and Conner, R. Dependency and helpfulness in young children. *Child Development,* 1962, 33, 15–20.

Stone, C. R. an Selman, R. L. A structural approach to research on the development of interpersonal behavior among grade school children. In K.H. Rubin and H.S. Ross (Eds.), *Peer relationships and social skills in childhood.* New York: Springer-Verlag, 1982.

Strayer, F. F., Wareing, S., and Rushton, J. P. Social constraints on naturally occurring preschool altruism. *Ethology and Sociobiology,* 1979, 1, 3–11.

Vandell, D. L. and Wilson, K. S. Social interaction in the first year: Infants' social skills with peer versus mother. In K. H. Rubin and H. S. Ross (Eds.), *Peer relationships and social skills in childhood.* New York: Springer-Verlag, 1982.

Whiting, B. B. and Whiting, J. W. M. *Children of six cultures.* Cambridge, MA: Harvard University Press, 1975.

SECTION THREE

The Child in School

Chapter 7

OBSERVING AND GUIDING CHILDREN

Objectives

After reading this chapter the student should be able to:

1. List one long-range and one short-range goal and one long- and short-range specific behavioral objective for a public school setting at the levels of district, school, classroom, and group.
2. Name the three purposes of evaluation and explain them.
3. Write an analysis of three different types of testing/assessment methods.
4. Discuss important qualities and values of adults who work with children and explain the relationship of these values to decision making in the classroom.
5. List the five modes of involvement with children and describe several techniques in each mode.
6. Outline the areas of classroom routines.
7. Discuss different ways of involving parents in the schools.

GETTING TO KNOW THE CHILD—THE TEACHER AS DECISION MAKER

"Getting to know you, Getting to know all about you." These words from a song in *The King and I* are the starting point of any new relationship. We take this concept for granted in most settings and yet in the school it is easy to lose sight of this fundamental need. Faced with a group of young children it may seem an almost impossible task to really "know" each child. It is often easier and more expedient to assume that these children will be like most children their age and to rely on our knowledge of child development and age norms when interacting with or planning for them.

Unfortunately, generalizing is a dangerous practice and may, in the long run, do as much harm as good. There are a variety of potential differences between children and within the individual child, which must be understood and utilized if we are to provide a meaningful and appropriate learning environment for him. To ignore these differences is to put some children at serious risk. Expectations that seriously exceed or underestimate the abilities of the child can establish life-long attitudes of failure or underachievement. Rosenthal's work on the power of the self-fulfilling prophecy, that is, the tendency for each of us to perform as we believe others see us, speaks to the need for genuine understanding of the abilities and limitations of each child (Rosenthal and Jacobson, 1968).

But how do we get to "know" the child, especially in a group setting

TABLE 7.1.   Factors in Child Differences

Specific Child Factors:

Developmental Age—The child's level of functioning as compared with developmental norms. Usually assessed under different areas of development such as psychomotor, social and affective development, and language and cognitive norms.

Mental Age—A composite score on a standardized intelligence test. Calculated as mental age (score on test designated in years and months)/chronological age (actual age in years and months since birth) × 100.

Stage—In Piagetian terms the cognitive functioning of the child according to particular thinking processes. Sensorimotor, preoperational, concrete operations, and formal operations are the stages in his theory. Other uses of the concept of stage as a separate set of characteristics include Freudian psychosexual stages and Kohlberg's stages of moral development.

Special Skills and Interests—All children differ in their abilities and skills from one area of development to another. Some children also show particular skills or talents that should be recognized and encouraged. Artistic or musical abilities are the easiest areas to use as examples but attention to particular strengths, such as mathematical logic, or interests, such as dinosaurs or rocks, aids in planning curriculum or merely sparking the interest of individual children.

Special Needs—Some children also have limitations or particular problems that require attention. Obvious examples are handicaps of various kinds, but, again, needs may manifest themselves in a variety of ways from shyness to specific learning problems.

Environmental Factors:

Family Background—As previously discussed in our chapter on families there are many differences the child brings to the school environment, which rest within the influence of the family. Divorce and separation are obvious examples. Attitude toward school, number of children in the family, work of parents, are a few of the other kinds of factors which can influence the child's response to school and what he will learn there.

Ethnic Background—While this is also a familial factor, ethnic information can be a broader class of characteristics, which go beyond the confines of the family. Mexican-American children would be thought rude if they looked an adult directly in the eyes when they spoke to her. Teachers with an Anglo-Saxon background believe a child is lying or hiding something if she is not willing to look them in the eye. Such differences in response and expectation can lead to major misunderstandings.

Social/Geographical Information—Different parts of the country and different stratas of society can also have characteristic ways of behaving, which will influence their interaction. Even the language pattern of an area can be a problem if an unknowing teacher demands pronunciation different from what the child can speak or understand. Such differences can be broad or subtle, but they must be understood if the teacher is not to make serious errors in his interaction wtih particular children.

where the demands of teaching and caregiving require so much of our energy and attention? This is where the role of observation, assessment, and testing become critical. The concept of diagnostic/prescriptive teaching is a relatively new approach in teaching especially in the normal classroom. However, the increasing demands for early academic skills make it critical that the teacher be able to accurately assess the child's level of functioning in order to avoid inappropriate curriculum decisions. It has become necessary more often to be able to defend curriculum positions, especially if a particular child's skills are markedly different from the norms demanded by a set learning sequence. For example, administrators and parents must sometimes be convinced that a child is just not ready for a particular set of tasks. Such a stand requires that the teacher have documentation, that is, the "facts," and these facts can only be acquired through a willingness to diagnose, that is, test, the child and thoroughly understand her learning profile.

Curriculum Planning

Planning is an integral part of every teacher's job and yet it is a segment of her work that often goes unnoticed. Neither the parent nor casual observer is aware of the time and energy that has gone into deciding the sequence of events for a particular day, the preparation of materials and centers, or the goals a teacher has set for a learning activity. All of that work has been done before school starts.

Goals and Objectives

Teachers are basically decision makers: they must decide on specific educational goals and objectives—what to do, when, and with whom, over and over, both before teaching begins and while they are actually "in action." "Is Mary having trouble with this concept? She appears to be confused. Who should I call on to answer this question? Is Marie ready to try this learning center?" On and on the questions reverberate in the mind of the teacher as he moves through his day.

Educational goals and objectives take place at a number of levels. Some goals are long range and sweeping, whereas others will be quite specific, limited to a particular lesson or the learning of a specific skill for one child. Table 7.2 presents a summary of these levels.

Appropriate planning includes both *specific and general behavioral objectives*. In each case, objectives enable us to determine whether or not learning has taken place and to state in clear form desired learning outcomes. Without goals and objectives it is difficult to show the sequence and scope of learning that is desired and/or achieved. Yet objectives that are age-inappropriate are equally meaningless. Ongoing

TABLE 7.2. Levels of Curriculum Planning

Definitions:
Goal or General Objective:
An overall and general statement concerning a desired learning outcome; for
  example, each child will learn to appreciate the contribution of various
  ethnic groups to the society as a whole.
Specific or Behavioral Objective:
The actual behavior, which can be recognized and demonstrated, which
  shows that learning has taken place; for example, after a visit to the Indian
  Council, each child will make one statement concerning the contribution of
  Indians to the state, which the teacher will print on a group chart.
Levels of goals and objectives:
Long-range goals—These can be district or school wide as well as for a
  particular classroom or individual.
Long-range goals:
1. *District level*—Each child in the district will be able to read and write at a
    level sufficient for full participation in society.
2. *School level*—All of the children in X school will have the opportunity to
    participate in extracurricular activities.
3. *Classroom level*—Each child will learn to read musical notes during the
    course of the semester.
4. *Group level*—The advanced math group will learn to read and plot
    graphs during January.
5. *Individual child*—Jose will learn to speak in complete English sentences
    during the kindergarten year.

Long range objectives (parallel to above goals):
1. Each individual will pass an eighth grade literacy examination before
    graduating from high school unless he or she is part of an exempt
    population, i.e., mentally retarded young adults.
2. Eighty percent of the school population will participate in at least one
    extracurricular activity during the school year.
3. Each child will be able to identify the names of the notes when given a
    simple song with 75 percent accuracy.
4. Each child in the advance math group will be able to explain one graph to
    his group and plot one graph by the end of the month.
5. Jose will be able to share an object with the class during show and tell
    using at least five complete English sentences of his own devising.

Short-range and limited goals and objectives—At each level it is also possible
  to devise short-range goals and objectives for a particular event or lesson.
General Objective: Children will learn to sing and appreciate a children's
  folksong, "I Know an Old Lady Who Swallowed a Fly."
Behavioral Objective: Each child will participate in singing, "I Know an Old
  Lady . . . " and will be able to hold up the picture of the animal swallowed
  at the appropriate time in the song.

evaluation is therefore necessary to ensure that learning goals are met or modified when neccessary.

Evaluation

Evaluation serves *three* distinct *purposes* in the planning of goals and objectives. These are *diagnostic, formative,* and *summative.* The first purpose is diagnostic: What is the child's present level? How do his abilities relate to the particular areas we wish to teach? Diagnosis takes place prior to instruction. We use the overall goals of the program to determine which areas of the child's abilities we need to examine. Formative evaluation takes place during actual teaching. Its purpose is to assess the student's progress during a particular lesson or unit of study. It requires periodic checking of objectives and the child's learnings at a current point in time. Formative evaluation is a continual process since it must be used to form new objectives as the program moves along. "If I have taught a lesson and three of the children did not learn what I expected, then I must replan and reteach for those particular children." Summative evaluation is an overall assessment that occurs at the end of a year, a semester, or an area of study. It evaluates to what extent the long-range objectives have been met.

All three forms of evaluation require assessing and monitoring the learning process in an ongoing way, as well as prior to planning of lessons and units of study. In turn, each of these steps requires the teacher's knowledge and understanding of each child. There are other purposes for the planning and evaluation process, however, which should not be ignored. Different programs and approaches to teaching must be planned and evaluated in similar fashion. Does one approach to teaching reading or music prove more efficient, more interesting, or more effective than another? Does a particular school's methods of organizing the classrooms provide a better learning environment, for example, as evidenced by a higher level of proficiency in some learning areas? These kinds of questions are also important and go beyond the specific learning of the individual child. They are the process by which the field of education tries to improve and learn.

Another purpose of evaluation is, of course, reporting to parents and others the progress of individual children. Parents and teachers need to form a partnership dedicated to the learning of the individual. As a parent I want to know how *my child* is doing, what he needs to learn, and how I can help. A report card is a superficial reporting system and is much less effective than the parent-teacher conference in offering specific examples of children's work and information particular to that child.

The accuracy and relevance of the teacher's diagnostic and evaluative information can be a great aid in gaining the cooperation of parents in whatever ongoing decisions are appropriate for the child. At times a child may need special help or an outside referral. The teacher and the school personnel involved must be able to show parents real evidence of the child's level of performance. Whenever a teacher is unsure of her competency in gaining accurate information concerning an area of the child's development or learning, the child should be referred to an appropriate source. Most schools have a variety of specialists either directly available or on call. These include psychologists, speech therapists, and medical personnel, who can follow up on the classroom teacher's diagnostic or formative information. Specialists are available even within the school. Parents, however, must be consulted and approval for additional testing acquired before testing is begun. Once more, the teacher's ability to diagnose and assess becomes a valuable tool in securing parental understanding and support.

It should be obvious by now that assessment plays a major role in teaching whether we are planning curriculum, reporting to parents, referring for additional testing, or evaluating goals and objectives for our own program, an experimental program, or an entire school district's program. We need to know how to do our evaluations with some degree of accuracy and efficiency. Therefore, let us look at the different approaches to testing and assessment.

Methods of Assessment

Definition

Assessment is a broad term referring to the acquisition of information about the performance by an individual or group of some particular behavior or behaviors. A wide variety of methods are available for obtaining this information.

Methods of Assessment

Observing is watching behavior and recording what is actually happening during a specified interval.

TYPES OF OBSERVATION.   *Anecdotal records*—brief descriptions of behavior as it is observed without interpretation, also called *event sampling*. *Running record*—similar to an anecdotal record but for a longer span of time. *Developmental checklist*—list of specific observable behaviors: Observer watches an individual in a setting and checks off those behaviors that are seen, for example, "Can jump with both feet; can catch an eight-inch ball with two hands; can throw a bean bag into a three-foot circle from a distance of five feet." Items on such a checksheet are usually derived from observing and testing large numbers of children and establishing "norms," that is, behaviors that most individuals of a particular age will be able to perform.

FREQUENCY CHECKLISTS OR TIME-SAMPLING RECORDS. A particular behavior, which is preselected, is observed and a tally kept of the number of times it is performed within a given period. For example, a list of aggressive behaviors such as hitting, biting, or grabbing toys could be observed for 10-minute segments at hourly intervals. Such information could be gathered for an entire nursery school population, for an individual child, or for a given area within the school setting.

Interviews and Self-Reports

Getting information directly from the individual is another method of gathering data. Information gained directly has the advantage of authenticity. However, it is also limited and shaped by the perceptions of the reporter and may lose objectivity.

SELF-REPORTS. Individual accounts of events that occur to the child in either the outside world or in the internal intrapsychic world.

INFORMAL INTERVIEWS. Verbal interactions usually conducted by asking a few questions which encourage an open-ended response. Each interview is recorded in some way so that the information retrieved can be referred to and analyzed later.

CLINICAL INTERVIEWS. A specified set of questions and actions are solicited from the person interviewed. Questions may vary slightly, but the overall plan of the event is followed carefully. Piagetian tasks such as having a child seriate a set of sticks and questioning her to determine the kind of logic used in solving the problem is one example of a clinical interview.

Standardized Tests

Stardardized tests include a set of tasks or questions that have been devised and tested on a large sample of individuals (who become the norming population) and then statistically analyzed to determine some score. The score then represents the level of performance expected in the future for a different group of persons. Standardized refers to the process of administering the test in exactly the same manner each time. The way directions are given, the questions asked, and the behavior of the person being tested are expected to be the same so that comparison with the original group of persons and their scores can be considered accurate. In a mathematics achievement test, for example, a child with a particular score could be said to be at the third grade-second month level in mathematics because that is the norm (that is, average score) that the original population at that level received. The child's real level in school would not affect his score; therefore, a second grade child would be considered functioning above his level in mathematics while a fourth grade child would be below his level.

INTELLIGENCE TESTS. One of the earliest types of standarized tests developed, these tests are given individually by people who are trained in their administration. A series of tasks and questions, which are progressively more difficult, are given and the individual's I.Q. is determined by his score or mental age (as compared to original or "norming" group) divided by his chronological age times 100. For example, a mental age of six years for a five year old would yield an I.Q. of 120.

PROJECTIVE TESTS. Also given by trained testers, often psychologists, these tests are meant to determine the individual's level of intrapsychic functioning. They are usually used for individuals who have various psychological disturbances.

ACHIEVEMENT TESTS. These are usually paper and pencil tests in which questions are related to areas already studied. Frequently given at the end of a school year or when applying to college, they assess the acquired knowledge of the individual.

DIAGNOSTIC TESTS. These are given to determine areas of weakness in a specific subject-matter area such as reading or mathematics. They usually look at sets of subskills in an attempt to pinpoint where remediation could be helpful.

Informal Assessment Tools

These are methods of acquiring information about an individual's level of functioning without using specific or formal standardized instruments. They are sometimes referred to as *criterion reference testing* because the specific behaviors measured are linked to the goals of the teaching environment. In preparing to teach a child to read, for example, the teacher will want to know what letters of the alphabet the child can name. The criterion is naming the letters, and the child either can or cannot name them. If the child does not know certain names the teacher can proceed to teach them. The importance of informal assess-

ment is the direct relationship between what is being tested and what
will be taught in the classroom.

DEVELOPMENTAL CHECKLISTS.   These are items that the child is asked to perform (as opposed to mere observation), which will assess her readiness
for particular teaching. Age norm lists are used, but there is no need for
specific rigidity in directions and methods. To determine if a child is
ready to begin printing, for example, teachers can check several skills
that develop prior to printing, such as drawing with large crayons, cutting with scissors, and placing small pegs in holes. If the child has sufficient fine-motor control to do these well, she will most likely be ready
to start learning to print.

INTEREST INVENTORIES AND SURVEYS.   Knowing what an individual enjoys
and is interested in can help in choosing materials and activities for
teaching purposes. Interest inventories can be given in written or oral
form, but results must be recorded in some fashion for easy use. A
check sheet with areas of interest at the top of each column and children's names along the side is one simple recording method (see Figures 7.1 to 7.3). The teacher puts a mark under each appropriate area
and can then quickly see what are the main interests of the group or
individual.

SAMPLES OF CHILD'S WORK.   One of the best indicators of a child's level of
performance is, of course, his own work. Stories and creative writing
are especially helpful because of the variety of information they reveal.
Obviously, such skills as penmanship, spelling, and punctuation will be
displayed, but also evidence of the level of the child's vocabulary, his
thought processes, and his creativity can be uncovered. However, anal-
yses of a child's work must be interpreted with some degree of caution.
A limited number of examples can be misleading since a particular
topic may not have sparked the interest or creativity of the child or may
have been done on a "bad" day. Examples of more formal work such
as workbook pages or tests are limited by many unknowns, including
the child's level of anxiety when doing the work, the child's understanding of the particular topic, and the writing ability of the individuals who developed the materials.

TEACHER-MADE TESTS.   Teachers vary in their ability and training in writing tests as well as other instructional materials. These classroom oriented tests can be especially helpful since they usually relate closely to
the teacher's learning goals and objectives. However, teachers need to
check their materials carefully. If a majority of the children miss a particular item on a test or worksheet, it is a good idea to drop that exam-

Has sufficient discrimination at this level
Needs additional work

Group Check Sheet — Levels

CHILD'S NAME	LEVEL	LEVEL	LEVEL

FIGURE 7.1 Group check sheet

From: Rae, G. and Potter, T. C. *Informal reading diagnosis: A practical guide for the classroom teacher,* Second Ed. Englewood Cliffs, N.J.: Prentice-Hall, 1981.

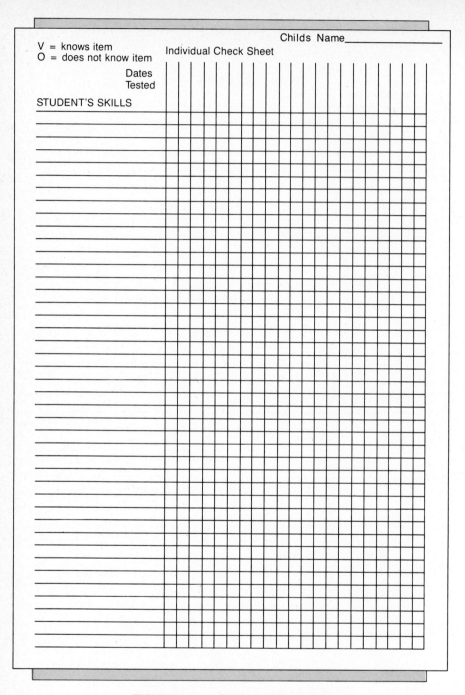

FIGURE 7.2 Individual check sheet

From: Rae, G. and Potter, T. C. *Informal reading diagnosis: A practical guide for the classroom teacher,* Second Ed. Englewood Cliffs, N.J.: Prentice-Hall, 1981.

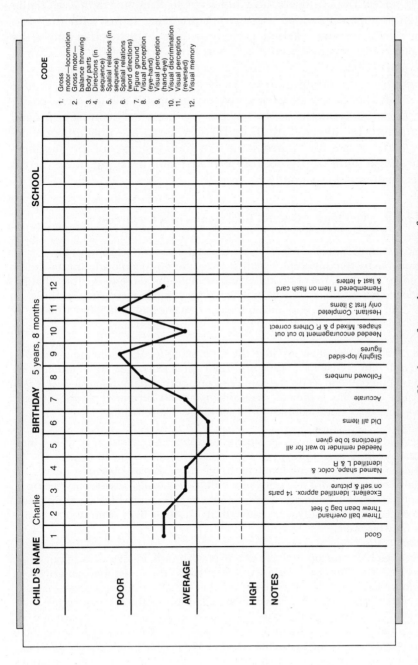

FIGURE 7.3   Profile sheet of psychomotor performance

From: Rae, G. and Potter, T. C. *Informal reading diagnosis: A practical guide for the classroom teacher,* Second Ed. Englewood Cliffs, N.J.: Prentice-Hall, 1981.

ple. Whether the children have not learned the item or it was badly written is very difficult to ascertain. Going over items with the class either during or after correcting them can show the teacher where the material was misinterpreted or was misleading. Children cannot always articulate what is confusing them and it is better to give them the benefit of the doubt than to create confusion or feelings of unfairness. Professional test writers know how difficult it is to write really clear, accurate test items, so the teacher need not feel he must be judged incompetent or "wrong" if all of his test items are not appropriate. Table 7.3 discusses four ingredients of a good test; except for standardization these items apply both to teacher-made tests and those instruments written professionally.

TABLE 7.3.   The Four Essential Ingredients of a Good Test

Objectivity

A good test must be objective. This means that the same score must be obtainable by two different testers. If two different people administer the same test on the same child and come up with the same score, then that is evidence for the objectivity of that test. If two people test a singer for her ability to hit a high C, and one concludes that she can, while the other concludes that she cannot, then that test is not objective.

Reliability

To be reliable, a test must produce the same score for the same individual on two different occasions. For example, if a child scores 125 on an intelligence test on one day and 83 on the same test on another day, then that test is not reliable. Reliability is difficult to establish, but measurement psychologists have devised several techniques for assessing test reliability.

Validity

To be valid a test must measure what it is supposed to measure. This is a most important, and most difficult quality to establish. If we try to measure intelligence by measuring foot-length, we may have an objective and a reliable measure—but it is not valid. Validity is usually assessed by seeing if a test will *predict* behavior. Thus, if persons who score high on a proposed test of creativity actually do creative things in their lives, then we say that test may be valid.

Standardization

Suppose we have a proposed test of anxiety. An individual scores 14 out of a possible 60 on this test. Does a score of 14 mean the individual is highly anxious or not very anxious at all? We don't know until we standardize the test. What this means is that we need to administer the test to a large number of individuals. Once we have their scores, we can compare our individual's score with them. It might turn out that most people score above 20 on the test, in which case the score of 14 might imply low anxiety. On the other hand, most people might score below 10, in which case 14 would indicate high anxiety.

CONFERENCES. As with interviews, a conference is a first hand encounter and permits interaction and observation simultaneously. Unlike an interview, though, a conference, whether with a child or with parents, is a two-way process. Answering and asking questions, sharing class work, and discussing goals, desires, and educational plans are all present in a model conference. Good communication skills and a desire to learn about the other person are the most valuable assets a teacher can have in a conference. Notes written after the conference is over can help one remember important information and insights. Conferences can be a useful tool in diagnostic, formative, and summative evaluation.

The Case Study—Putting It All Together

Full case studies are not frequently compiled by the classroom teacher. There are a variety of reasons for this, including the length of time full case studies take to compile and the level of expertise that is often needed to insure accuracy and validity. Given the variety of tasks the regular teacher normally performs, it is not surprising that most teachers do not maintain case studies. (A complete case study is included in this chapter as an example.) Yet, occasionally, a full case study is needed, and familiarity with the components of one is important both in compiling such reports and in reviewing the case studies of school psychologists or other referral persons. Items in a case study include:

1. Identifying information, that is, child's name, birth date, grade in school, sex, address, phone number, parents' names, and date of the record.
2. Background information, which includes data from school records, home information, health and early developmental data, testing information, and, possibly, notes on social and emotional development, parental interviews or conferences, and child reports.
3. Anecdotal records, which are observations of the child's behavior.
4. Analysis of anecdotal records, that is, categorizing behaviors according to areas of development, such as affective, language, cognitive, and psychomotor and/or according to social relationships, and peer interactions, as indicated by what has been selected for observation. A discussion of trends and indications from this analysis follows. Objective, not interpretive, reporting is the important ingredient in this section.
5. Summary, which brings information together to show relationships and overall patterns across the separate areas analyzed. Basically this is a picture of the child, her strengths and weaknesses, and her educational prognosis.
6. Educational plan. (With special-needs children this is referred to as the Individual Education Program or I.E.P. See Chapter 12.) Not all case studies include this section, but certainly one which is attached to class-

INSET 7.1   Assessment Report

Child: Charlie
Sex: Male
Age: 5 yrs., 8 mos.
Tested: 7/11 through 8/1
Summary of Results

Charlie was given a series of nonstandardized tests in the psychomotor, language, cognitive, social, and academic areas during the time from July 11 to August 1. Through this assessment a general picture of Charlie's functioning in these areas was obtained.

Overall, Charlie appears to be functioning at a normal level for his age (5 years, 8 months). He seems especially skilled in the psychomotor areas, particularly in gross motor skills and in carrying out physical actions involving the use of his body. He appears to comprehend well (he scored exceptionally high, in the 7-year range, in auditory comprehension on the language inventory) and to be able to mentally think through situations and problems (he scored high on following word directions in spatial relations items and was able to mentally carry out the addition and substraction items on the academic skills inventory).

The areas in which Charlie appears to be somewhat less skilled at this time are the areas of fine motor control and visual perception. He had difficulty controlling the crayon to draw shapes and difficulty seeing differences in letters and words on the visual perception items (he refused to complete the letter-and word-related items, although he was able to correctly identify alphabet letters). These difficulties may have influenced his slightly below average rating on cognitive skills involving fine motor control and visual perception (he classified by only one dimension; he put together only the 3- and 6-piece puzzles). He also demonstrated a need to have physical contact (that is touching) with the pictures used to assess motor encoding and number concepts.

Charlie rated average in visual memory and the ability to use his body in following a sequence of directions. However, he rated below average in auditory memory. When he was asked to perform a number of actions using objects he could only remember one object and one action. He seemed to have difficulty remembering the order of items, the items named, and the directions given to wait until he was told to begin. He also rated slightly below average (about 1 year) in auditory discrimination, verbal problem solving, and generative language. These characteristics may have influenced his need throughout the entire testing experience to have directions repeated several times even after beginning items.

Throughout the testing experience, Charlie was cooperative. However, he seemed to enjoy the more active tasks and to be somewhat doubtful, and correspondingly less cooperative, in completing tasks involving visual perception and auditory memory. He left the testing situation 2–4 times each time (excluding breaks) but could be directed back. By the end of each session he was eager to be finished.

Charlie's generally cooperative attitude and his strenghts in auditory comprehension, gross motor skills, and knowledge of alphabet letters and numbers/

numerals are strengths upon which to build in increasing his skills in areas where lacks are evident.

In all activities it is important to provide Charlie with tasks he feels he can do, which are of interest to him, and in which he has active involvement. Specific activities to increase motor encoding skills could include going on imaginary walks and performing action songs. In classification, having experiences grouping items in various ways (such as blocks, tools, toys, or pictures, etc.) may be appealing and helpful. Carrying out actions, directions, sound patterns, rhythms, etc., are ways to increase auditory memory. To increase visual perception and fine motor skills, working with keys and locks, mazes, nail boards, tools, and other manipulative materials of his choosing may be helpful. Exposing Charlie to an environment rich in language and encouraging him in speaking about various experiences he has will contribute to building his language skills.

I found Charlie to be an enjoyable child to know and test. I feel that he has definite areas of strength. By building on these areas he can work toward strengthening the areas that are not as strong at this time. Time, growth, and experience will all help to contribute to his development.

---

room goals needs to address this area of concern. Here specific suggestions or prescriptions for activities or methods of teaching are recommended for a particular child. Both classroom, individual tutor, and parent/home activities can be designated.

Other Reports and Data Management Systems

If a teacher does diagnostic-prescriptive teaching, one task will be gathering information, which must be systematically organized. Since full written studies on each child are prohibitive other methods for keeping data available and useable must be devised. Using the business concept of data management, we need to keep records that summarize information obtained from various sources and then file that information in a way that provides for rapid access. Although computers are an ideal way to record and access information, not many classrooms have these tools readily available and even fewer teachers know how to use them. Therefore, individual and group checksheets, student file folders, and profile sheets of test item levels are more realistic data banks for most classroom teachers.

It should be clear by now that assessment is an involved process. One might wonder if the value is proportionate to the outlay of time and energy. The importance of timely and accurate appraisal of the educational needs and potentials of students is paramount. We can, after all, build a house without architectural plans, but the risk of collapse is great unless we are very knowledgeable and experienced. When dealing with the educational future of a real, live child, we cannot justify the risk of failure. Yet how many of us know of friends or loved ones who have suffered from school difficulties. Such problems are too prevalent and the repercussions too severe to allow us to avoid our responsibilities as classroom teachers in the name of time requirements or dislike for "busy work." No one teacher can solve all the problems or stave off all the difficulties that a child can face within the school system. But neither can any one teacher afford to be a catalyst for failure and loss of self-esteem. Appropriate decision making rests on the shoulders of the individual teacher. Meeting the challenge will continue to be an exciting, and sometimes wearying process. (We will discuss the importance and relevance of this responsibility in Chapter 14.)

WORKING WITH CHILDREN

When we begin to work with children, it can seem like an overwhelming task to do the "right" thing. Everyone wants to feel effective and

valuable, and helping to shape the lives of young children can seem like an enormous responsibility. Probably the best place to start is with the recognition that there is no *one* way that is correct or fool-proof. Personality, values, and training all combine to become the "style" of any particular teacher. Developing one's own style of teaching is a life-long process and the initial steps may provide some discomfort and uncertainty. Hopefully, the learning is also exciting and stimulating, so that the difficulties are outweighed by the enjoyment and the challenge.

Good teachers come in all stripes, from bouncy and enthusiastic to quiet and calm. Certain qualities do contribute to positive interactions with young children, and these can be learned and consciously enhanced. They can be key to becoming a significant adult in the lives of children.

Qualities and Values of the Teacher

Qualities of a Significant Adult

1. Being a nurturing person.
2. Being a positive role model.
3. Being a careful listener.
4. Being a nonjudgmental observer.
5. Being self-confident.
6. Being conscientious.
7. Being enthusiastic.
8. Being a responsible decision maker.
9. Being knowledgeable about children's levels of development.
10. Being careful to use appropriate techniques of guiding, teaching, and disciplining.

The above list may seem like a large undertaking, but these qualities foster our growth toward maturity and self-esteem. As we work to become better teachers, we also become more like the ideal adult we would like to be. Our ability to grow and develop will, hopefully, keep pace with the growth of the children with whom we work. *Growing Up with Children* was chosen for the title of this text because of our firm conviction that our own growing and learning are integrally linked to the children we share our lives with.

Another area of adult development that has importance in working with children is that of values. Each teacher will have values that are important to her and will be reflected in her decisions both in day-to-day incidents and in her philosophy of education. A teacher who values spontaneity will differ in response from a teacher who values order and structure. Neither value is right or wrong, per se, but each can have markedly different effects on her choices within a particular event.

Research on values in early childhood education offers eleven beliefs which are central in working with young children.

Teacher Values in Early Childhood Programs

1. Valuing the individuality of the child.
2. Valuing aesthetics.
3. Valuing creativity.
4. Valuing the emotional development of the child.
5. Valuing the intellectual development of the child.
6. Valuing the physical development of the child.
7. Valuing the social development of the child.
8. Valuing the development of school skills.
9. Valuing the health and safety of the child.
10. Valuing the involvement of the parent in the preschool.
11. Valuing confidentiality and ethics.

Giving these values priority in our work with children will help ensure the *quality* of the decisions made in planning and interacting with them. For example, if I value individuality as well as the acquisition of school skills, I will make curriculum decisions that are appropriate to each child's level of functioning. If I value the emotional development, as well as the intellectual development of the child, I will provide a balance of activities and promote growth in both. It should be easy to see how values are integral to the decision-making process. And since our values inevitably shape these decisions, conscious and careful attention to the values we all hold and to those appropriate to working with young children is of tremendous importance.

Modes of Involvement

In addition to personality and values we also need to be trained in techniques for working with children. There are a variety of modes of involvement, which can be viewed along a continuum from casual and informal to highly structured and directive. All modes are equally viable depending on the goals and demands of the particular situation. Let us look at these more closely.

Modes of involvement

Informal . . . . Directive
Interacting . . . . . Facilitating . . . . . Guiding . . . . . Teaching . . . . Disciplining

Defining Terms

Interacting—Casual involvement characterized by spontaneous involvements of two or more individuals. Adult-child interactions are usually conversational in nature and avoid directive statements.

Facilitating—An involvement in which one individual (usually the adult) provides opportunities for experimentation and problem solving through provision of materials, arrangement of space, or verbal ideas or questions.

Guiding—The shaping of involvement through active questions, suggestions, and planned activity centers. Guiding does not limit the child's creativity or choices but does operate to meet certain values and goals in a more planned manner.

Teaching—A directed involvement to meet some specifically stated goals and objectives. Although all of our involvements with children can be considered teaching, this term is used to apply to those activities that are planned and executed as teaching sequences.

Disciplining—Those involvements that require direct restructuring of the child's behavior either verbally or physically. These are the most directive of our involvements because they often arise from the need to avoid or stop behavior that is disruptive or destructive. While disciplining should be done in a positive manner, it still uses the most restrictive and specific sets of demands that adults place upon children.

This differentiation of the five modes of involvement can help us in working with children. A closer examination of each type demonstrates different techniques, goals, and values.

Interacting

VALUE—enhancing the development of the child and positive involvements with others.

GOALS—giving children the opportunity to spontaneously engage in events with others.

TECHNIQUES:

1. Operate at the child's eye level. For an adult this will mean sitting on the floor or in a child-sized chair.
2. Respond to the child and initiate conversation based on current activity.
3. Give the child your full attention.
4. Use language the child understands.
5. Avoid didactic comments aimed at a particular response.
6. Be positive and genuine.

EXAMPLE.   Teacher is sitting on a child-sized chair at the snack table. Several children are eating jello and drinking milk. One child is poking at jello with a spoon so that it wiggles. T. says, "Are you having fun making the jello wiggle, Veronica?"

V. says, "I like the way it bumps and jumps. It tastes good, too."

T. says, "That's a really big bite you just took. I like the way the jello tastes too. My favorite jello is grape."

Veronica responds with, "Mine is raspberry."

"Mine is grape, too," Eric adds.

"I like lime," Tammy says.

"Grape." "Lemon." Each child chimes in with his or her favorite.

"We like lots of different kinds," T. says.

In this conversation the teacher's comments are oriented to the event of the moment. Although learning is certainly going on, the teacher's role is to model spontaneous interaction, not to shape the events. Through this kind of interaction the children have the opportunity to be on a level with the adult and to enjoy his or her immediate experience without undue restriction.

Facilitating

VALUES—Creativity, individuality, and the development of the child.

GOALS—Encouragement of exploration and problem solving through providing materials and events within the environment.

TECHNIQUES:

1. Daily schedule is planned with alternating periods of quiet and activity and at a pace to suit the level of the children.
2. Space and equipment are arranged to provide for comfortable use with clues as to appropriate behavior. For example, cubbies are accessible and outfitted to encourage children to hang up their coats independently.
3. Curriculum is varied and materials are appropriate to the ages and experience of the children.
4. New materials are introduced and explained before placing them out for exploration.
5. Toys and supplies are located near where they will be used and with appropriate space for work and equipment for cleanup.
6. Materials that are not to be used are stored out of sight.
7. Centers with limited space are marked by the appropriate number of chairs, easels, aprons, and so on.
8. Teachers ask open-ended questions, which stimulate exploration and problem solving without suggesting choices.
9. A large percentage of materials and activities are provided which promote creativity. For example, crayons, paint, and paper are used rather than coloring books.

10. The teacher's comments on the children's work are nonjudgmental and encourage diversity.

EXAMPLE. Three children are finger painting at a center near the sink. The teacher approaches the center and pulls up a small chair to watch. "How do you like my picture, teacher?" one boy asks. "You are using those new colors in a very interesting way, Jerome. Tell me about your picture."

The teacher's response acknowledges the child's use of the "new" colors in an encouraging way and promotes verbalization about his creation with an open-ended question. Finger painting is an activity that encourages exploration and creativity and its location near the sink will promote clean-up by the children in a natural manner with very limited teacher prompting.

Guiding

VALUE—Prompting the development of the child through experiences and involvements that actively engage her.
GOALS—Increase in verbal, social, intellectual, physical, and emotionally appropriate behavior.
TECHNIQUES:

1. Directions are given as needed without being overly directive or bossy.
2. Directions are short and positive, telling the child what to do instead of what not do so.
3. Directions are given in direct proximity to the time and place they are needed.
4. It is made clear whether the child has a choice or not.
5. Teacher asks questions in activities that encourage the children's ideas and elicit from the children a variety of possible approaches to a problem.
6. Some activities challenge the children to hypothesize, predict, and explain without getting a "right" answer from the teacher.
7. Discussion of activities with the children encourages planning before an event, for example, children say what equipment they plan to use on the playground today.
8. Children who solicit attention in negative ways, for example, whining, calling out, interrupting and so on, are ignored, and positive attention is directed toward those children who are exhibiting cooperative behavior.
9. Competition is discouraged in favor of cooperation and personal goals for achievement.
10. Children are given opportunities to evaluate activities, request and suggest changes, and introduce topics of interest to themselves with teacher support and encouragement.

EXAMPLE. Two boys are experimenting at a center that contains a variety of differently shaped magnets, a box of objects, and two open box halves one of which has "yes" and the other "no" printed on the bottom. The teacher joins them and, kneeling at their level, asks, "What have you boys found out about these magnets so far?"

"This one pushes this one like this," responds one child.

"Do they all do the same thing?" the teacher asks next.

"Nope, this one pulls it the other way," states the other boy.

"What do you think would happen if you used this horseshoe magnet with those other two bar magnets? Will they attract, pull them toward it, or repel, push them away?"

"I think it will pull it."

"I think it will repel," says the other.

"Well, when you discover which happens, maybe you can figure out what makes them work that way."

The teacher's involvement in the boys' work with the magnets has guided them to experiment in a more purposeful way, provided them with more accurate terminology, and expanded their thinking to the level of hypothesizing and potential rule formation. All of this was done in just a few moments without overtly telling them what to do or what kind of an answer they should give. The activity itself is set up to encourage a variety of possible explorations, including the sorting of types of magnets, the classification of objects by their interaction with the magnets, and experimentation with the actions of one magnet on another. The boys' interaction with the materials would have been valuable to them whether or not the teacher had involved herself in their experimenting. Her guidance, however, markedly increases the learning potential of the encounter.

Teaching

VALUE—Promoting the development of the child, especially in the area of school skills and intellectual development.

GOALS—Increasing attentional and focusing behaviors and providing experience in specific school-related learning tasks.

TECHNIQUES:

1. Goals and behavioral objectives for the prescribed lesson are clearly worked out in advance by the teacher.
2. Materials and equipment for the lesson are prepared and conveniently located.
3. The attention of the children is engaged before the lesson begins.
4. Length of teaching sequence is geared to the developmental level of the child.
5. Learning activity is interesting and required responses are designed for a maximum of involvement and success.

6. Specific learning is reviewed at the end of the lesson so that children have a clear message concerning expected learning outcomes.
7. Products of learning sequences are given value by the teacher's acknowledgement and by giving equal attention to each child's work.
8. Children are allowed maximum participation in the teaching sequence congruent with the nature of the lesson.

EXAMPLE. Six children are sitting around a table working with clay. Pieces of the clay are being rolled between their hands to make long, thin, sausage-like strips. As they form a strip they take it and form it into various alphabet letters. Each child has several letters on the oil-cloth in front of her. The teacher comes to join them and pulls up a small chair.

"It will be time to clean up in just a few minutes. I see many different letters in front of each of you. Joyce, what letters did you make?" the teacher asks.

"I made a "J" like in my name and the "B" like we talked about," Joyce responds. Each child takes a turn telling about his letters.

"And who can tell us how you formed the capital "B" letter?" the teacher asks.

The teacher is spending a few minutes at the end of a work period reviewing. The letter "B" had been introduced in the teaching sequence that occurred before the work period. Making the letter "B" in clay plus any other letters they wished to make has absorbed these 5 year olds for the last 15 minutes. The teacher's directed lesson on the "B" is being reinforced by several activities including these clay letters. Her few moments of review allow the children to show their accomplishments and also indicate her interest and acknowledgement of their efforts. Each child needs his moment of recognition and acceptance. This particular group of children is not ready to print the letter the class is learning but their activity is meaningful and appropriate for their developmental level. By planning for these different levels the teacher makes sure that each child feels successful.

The entire teaching sequence included the teacher's introduction of the letter, her instructions to each group concerning the activity they would do to "practice" their "Bs," the work period with its brief review for each group, and the clean-up time. The entire lesson took just 30 minutes but its implications for the children in terms of "school" learning are enormous. Each child must feel she *can* learn or her school future will be bleak.

Discipline

VALUE—Promoting health and safety and the social and emotional development of the child; respecting the individuality of the child.

GOALS—Movement from egocentric to sociocentric behavior and the internalization of empathy, emotional connectedness, and school standards of behavior appropriate to the developmental level of the child.
TECHNIQUES:

1. Make limits and rules clear and appropriate to the level of the children.
2. Follow through on consequences for inappropriate behavior.
3. Model desired behavior and give recognition to children who are exhibiting desired behaviors.
4. Whenever possible ignore disruptive behavior to avoid reinforcing it.
5. Give directions, reassurance, and assistance before reprimands.
6. Talk to children at eye level, especially when they are upset or showing out-of-bounds behavior.
7. Restrain the child if necessary to protect him or others.
8. Remove the child as an aid to regaining composure, not as a punishment.
9. Avoid verbal ridicule, sarcasm, or punishment, which humiliates the child; especially be sensitive in front of other children.
10. Help the children learn to recognize emotions and verbally express concerns instead of acting them out.
11. Anticipate potential problems such as limited equipment or materials, over-tired states, and shift plans to avoid conflicts.
12. Have a repetoire of songs, stories, poems, and games that aid transitions and other difficult periods.
13. Have a signal such as a special bell or piano chord which means stop.
14. Give praise and attention frequently rather than have the child seek notice with undesirable behaviors.
15. Get to know the lovable part of every child to avoid singling out any in a too negative or too positive way.

EXAMPLE. During outdoor play two four-year-old boys begin to argue over use of a tricycle. The larger child pushes the smaller, who sits abruptly from the push and begins crying.

"My goodness, sitting like that really hurt, didn't it?" The teacher helps the crying child up and with her arm around his shoulder speaks to the other child. "Come on Peter, let's go sit under that tree together and talk over what happened."

The teacher's voice tone is calm and her manner friendly and empathetic. Neither child is ignored or reprimanded at this point. Under the tree they can sit and discuss what happened, with each child telling how he feels and what he wants. The teacher will help each child hear the feelings of the other and then try to help them find another way of settling their problem. If they are not able to find an amicable alternative the teacher will impose one, and she will also make clear the inappropriateness of pushing or arguing as a way of solving problems. However, she also knows that four year olds have limited control over their feelings and are not yet able to "walk in the other's shoes." Her aim is toward empathy and problem solving rather than control or punishment. Self-control is acquired slowly through maturation and learning, and the teacher's recognition of this promotes an approach of warmth, understanding, and limit setting.

Teacher behaviors consistent with the modes of involvement we have discussed help children grow and learn because they value and respect the child for who she is at this moment in time. Too often we are overly concerned with how the child will "grow up" without the awareness that she will "grow herself up" quite naturally if we give appropriate attention to her learning today. Each of us has a lifetime of growing to do but we can only accomplish it one day at a time. Planning is a vital and necessary part of a teacher's job, and we have already discussed the importance of short- and long-range goals and objectives. However, the quality of the child's life and his ultimate learning and knowledge rest on the day to day encounters of home, school, and community. It is up to the significant adults in children's lives to make learning a pleasure and life an exciting and rewarding challenge.

Classroom Management

Moving away from direct involvement and planning, there are a variety of routines in the school that must be managed efficiently, both to provide a safe and comfortable environment and to maximize the ease of the school day. Attention to five areas of routine can greatly enhance the comfort of all. These areas are: (1) beginning and ending of the day, (2) toileting, (3) mealtimes, (4) rest times, (5) transitions between activities.

Beginning and Ending of the Day

1. Children should be greeted by a teacher or other familiar figure when entering the school and be bade farewell at the end of the day.
2. Activities that allow free choice and adapt to the pace of the individual permit easier transition from home to school.
3. Quiet activities at the end of the day are particularly important in full day programs to avoid fatigue and cranky behavior as the child leaves.
4. Children who are tearful or fearful on entering need individual attention and calm acceptance of their feelings until they can "settle in."
5. The opportunity to take home art papers and other projects is important for the children as a transition between home and school. A tote bag with handles helps papers arrive in viewable condition.

Girls build sandcastles too.

Toileting

1. Have regular times for routine toileting as well as open access.
2. Accept accidents without blaming or shaming the child.
3. Have children use the toilet after an accident and then change to dry clothes.
4. Show a positive attitude when the child uses the toilet successfully.
5. Train to good health habits by monitoring washing hands after toileting and before meals without didactic statements.

6. Encourage independence without unrealistic demands for success in early toilet training.
7. In infant programs pay attention to changes in infant's bowel movements and report to health supervisor.
8. Communicate with parents about child's toileting behaviors and coordinate home and school efforts as much as possible.

Mealtimes

1. Have a quiet activity before mealtimes.
2. Smaller portions with seconds are preferable to full plates that cannot be finished.
3. Food needs vary from child to child and within one child from one time to another so forcing is never advisable.
4. A "one bite" rule is usually effective in getting children to taste new foods.
5. Introduce only one new food at a time.
6. A relaxed, pleasant mealtime is an important focal point of the day and sufficient time should be alloted.
7. Independence in serving, eating, and cleaning up should be fostered.
8. Cooking experiences for children, which contribute to meals or snacks, are valuable and should be planned as often as feasible.

Rest times

1. A daily rest time (usually after meals) is necessary in every full day program.
2. A regular place for a mat or cot encourages a feeling of safety and promotes easier resting.
3. Soft instrumental music can be beneficial to resting and relaxing.
4. Not every child should be expected to sleep but all children need a resting space.
5. Rubbing backs or shoulders can relieve tension if a child is anxious and it aids resting.
6. "Warm fuzzies" in the form of special blankets, special soft toys, or thumbsucking are expected with young children.
7. Careful attention to voice tone and pitch by a teacher can aid sleep by soothing and comforting the child.
8. No child should be left unsupervised in a naproom or other isolated space because some young children wake in an agitated state and need prompt reassurance and attention.

Transitions between activities

1. Warn children at least twice, at 15 and 5 minutes, for example, before a long activity period will end so they may wind up their project and get ready to leave.

2. Have places and routines for storing unfinished work so a child may return to it at a later time.
3. After the "stop" signal have *all* children participate in clean up.
4. Monitor the clean up process so that materials are handled and returned properly. If necessary, stop the group again and ask for their evaluation of the clean up time. Let them tell each other what needs to happen to finish.
5. With very young children let them perform one simple clean up chore such as putting the dolls back in the cradle and then stop.
6. Give positive feedback for children's efforts and teach specific skills as necessary, such as, matching block size on front of storage container to put correct size in right spaces.
7. At the gathering place (for example, the large rug area) have one teacher doing action songs and fingerplays with children as they arrive. This diversion helps keep children occupied and speeds others to come and join the fun.
8. In transitions that involve putting on or removing outdoor clothing, let older or more capable children help younger or less capable ones to encourage peer modeling and to provide extra hands in speeding the process.

These routines if handled consistently, calmly, and cheerfully become an integral part of the child's learning and provide a backdrop for the other activities of the school. Handled inefficiently they can turn the program into a "daymare" for all concerned. It is useful to observe routines in any new setting for young children. The manner in which they are handled gives valuable insights into the quality of the overall program.

Working with Parents

Parenting in today's world is a far different task from that faced by previous generations. The nuclear family with one or two parents and children living under a separate roof from kin places an enormous burden on adults. Providing full time continuous care with little or no relief is, in itself, a large task. In addition, in a large percentage of families both parents work and time given over to parenting tasks is often reduced. Single-parent families suffer even more from overload.

In previous generations children were seen as an economic asset either in terms of providing labor, such as on a farm, or bringing home wages. They were also seen as someone to take care of the parents as they grew older and could no longer support themselves. In few families do these types of benefits still prevail. Rather, parents support children through a more prolonged period, especially, if they go on to advanced schooling, with no real expectation of any return except the emotional ties of parent and child. However, in our complex society where a variety of negative influences abound, from drugs and street gangs to religious cults and continuing warfare, parents often worry about their ability to safeguard their children and bring them to maturity unscathed.

With all of the myriad problems of contemporary Western civilization and its increased demand for highly educated, technologically aware workers, it is not surprising that parents are very concerned with their child's schooling and take great pride in the youngster who is showing precocious ability, especially in literacy skills. Most parents see education as the best avenue for their children to become productive, happy adults, and research shows that this goal is what parents express as their most important hope for their children.

However, there are few places in our society today to learn about parenting before one actually becomes a parent. In earlier times we learned about parenting from our own parents and other kin. If I liked the way Aunt Bessie treated my cousins, I might model my parenting on her, as well as, or in opposition to my own parent. In extended families it was not unusual for children to gravitate toward homes where they felt more comfortable or better accepted. A current concern centers on the question of where does a young person learn how to care for children? In the 1960s and 1970s some high school home economics programs included courses in child development. Some added laboratory based nursery schools as part of this experience. Few of these nursery schools are still funded. Child development coures are still available in some high schools and affiliation with a local nursery school or day care program allows some "hands on" experience. These courses are open to both male and female students, of course, but few male students choose this option.

Research shows that the younger mother is more likely to have unrealistic expectations concerning her child's development. There are no data concerning young fathers' expectations. Yet, even parents in their twenties often feel unprepared and unsure of themselves concerning their ability to care for young children. Child birth classes are important but what happens when that infant is brought home? Reading books by experts is not a guarantee of success. Nor do all experts agree, or, as we have seen, do all children fit neatly into developmental guidelines.

Teachers of young children are expected to understand child development and have both knowledge and experience in dealing with the many facets of the young child's experience. We also need to understand the psychological and economic stresses on their parents and be a resource and partner in the job of helping children grow in appropriate ways. Home and school can cooperate or compete depending on the ways in which they see their roles and goals. It is the teacher's job, as an educated professional, to build the bridge for cooperation.

By the time the child has reached the school, be it an infant center, a nursery school or daycare program, or the public or private school graded system, the parents have already made the first step of entrusting their child to the system. The next step must come from the teachers and administrators of the school. The more parental involvement and cooperation that can be attained, the better job the school is likely to do for the individual child. What are the various ways to involve parents? They range from simple to complex but a few of the important ones are:

1. Initial interviews
2. Parent visits to the classroom
3. Parent conferences
4. Home visits
5. Group meetings such as PTA
6. Open house programs
7. Classes and informational meetings
8. Policy setting committees

Initial Interviews

1. Always have a meeting with parent(s) before the child enters the school.
2. Get all necessary forms with background history and health information, including emergency numbers.
3. Inform the parent(s) of all school policies, rules, and schedules.
4. Allow time to answer all questions.
5. Having printed sheets of common questions and answers and child development information pertinent to their age child is helpful.
6. If possible, have parents meet the teacher and visit the classroom where the child will be placed. (A must in infancy programs.)
7. Let parents know policies for future visits.

Parent Visits to the Classroom

1. Have specific times when parents are encouraged to sign up for visits.
2. Have an open policy to set up other times with notice. (A day we will be watching films should be avoided.)
3. Issue a set of guidelines for parents in advance.
4. Request that parents observe in an unobtrusive way so they can see the interactions of their child and other children without the child being overly distracted.
5. Expect the child to do some acting out or exhibit attention-getting behavior.

6. Talk to the class about appropriate behavior when visitors come to observe.
7. Have a parent conference as soon after an observation as possible.

Parent Conferences

1. Plan conference times as much as possible in slots convenient for parents.
2. Be prepared with specific information and examples of children's work and behavior.
3. Always give information in a positive way stressing the strengths as well as difficulties a child may be facing.
4. Show parents your respect by soliciting their input concerning the child's behavior at home, their reactions to observations, and their concerns about school work.
5. Do not attempt to change or teach parents about their child or what you feel they "ought" to know.
6. Explain exactly what objectives you have for the child in the school setting and give parents specific activities that could be done at home if they appear interested or desire them.
7. If there is a difference of opinion concerning some aspect of the child's work or potential, additional resources and help should be sought. Tests or documenting evidence should be gathered and a larger team meeting with parents arranged to present material and discover solutions.

Home Visits

1. Make home visits only when directly invited by the parent.
2. If the school or program includes home visits, parents must be informed before they enter their child in the program.
3. If the purpose of the visit is to observe the child, have checksheets and other recording material available for the parent to see.
4. If the purpose of the visit is contact with the family, use care that you give no judgmental signals verbally or with body language.
5. Do not discuss the visit or your reactions to any one not directly authorized to receive them. For example, inform school administrator or give a written report for a specified team conference; do not tell fellow teachers or friends. Confidentiality is an important concern and reports for all school files are official documents which can be brought into courts and other legal proceedings.

Group Meetings

1. Some type of parent organization is always desirable for a school and should be encouraged and supported.
2. Where a parent-teacher organization is formed, parents should have

use of school facilities and take charge of administrative functions in conjunction with those teachers who want to participate.

3. Membership in such groups should be voluntary and no one should be pressured to be a member. It is to the teacher's advantage, however, to be a member since it strengthens the link between home and school.

4. Goals for such an organization should be set by the members and discussed with the administration, not for approval, but for input and suggestions.

5. Meetings of such an organization will usually attract more attendance if children's work or performances are included.

6. Groups who choose to raise funds for the school or provide other concrete help should have maximum assistance from school personnel as long as this is obtained without coercion.

7. Social activities in which school and parent groups plan and participate are usually useful morale builders for all concerned.

Open House

1. Functions that allow visiting, such as open houses, should be planned carefully in advance by teachers and administrators.

2. An open house is best set in evening or weekend times to maximize parents' attendance. One night and one day period can encourage those with unusual schedules to attend as well.

3. One open house near the beginning of the school year is a good ice breaker and establishes early contact with parents.

4. In a year round program a set schedule for open house visits, two to four times a year, allows everyone to plan their schedules effectively.

5. During open house the teachers and aides should greet and talk to parents in general terms. There should be no parent conferencing.

6. A sign-up sheet for parent conferences should be available for parents who would like more information on their individual child.

7. Every child should be equally represented in displayed work or other child products.

Classes and Informational Meetings

1. It is important to be sensitive to parent concerns and make note of information parents request.

2. A survey done periodically to find out what kind of informational meetings parents would like to have is a valuable approach.

3. Bring outside experts of various kinds to make presentations to parents. Many universities and agencies have personnel who will give free presentations to school groups.

4. If parents desire class meetings, which will run over several weeks, make sure that insurance, janitorial fees, and other costs are clearly spelled out in advance.

5. As much as feasible, the school should be open to other nonprofit

groups who want to use the facilities. The more the school is the center of community activities, the more it will have their support and cooperation.

Policy Setting Committees

1. Whether or not there is a parent-teacher association, it is important to have parent representation on school policy setting committees.
2. Equal input to policies insures better cooperation and understanding.
3. If parents, teachers, and administrators disagree concerning some policy, such as early reading programs, for example, then an outside expert or series of experts should be brought in to provide different viewpoints and considerations.
4. Parents always have the right to take their child elsewhere if they disagree with the policies of a particular school, and such decisions should be respected without unfavorable comment or defensiveness.
5. All policies agreed upon by committees or other governing bodies, such as a board of directors, or set by administrators, should be written clearly and simply for parents to understand (without undue "pedagese"). They should then be circulated and made available in a regular, accessible place.

If parents are involved in the various ways we have been discussing, they are more likely to feel themselves a part of the school team. Teachers cannot be a resource for parents unless they can respect their own needs and the needs of parents simultaneously. To be available as a resource to parents without taking on roles inappropriate to the training and purpose of the school, such as counselor or mentor, requires maturity and careful boundary setting. To say, "I'm not qualified to give you advice in that area," is not a statement of defeat but one appropriate to certain circumstances. Schools do well to have a good referral list of community resources available for parents when necessary.

Just as the school can be a resource for parents, so parents can and often are a resource for the school. We have mentioned PTAs, fund raising committees, and the like, but in many schools parents also volunteer time in the classroom or serve in other expert capacities. From the father who is a fireman and comes to class to talk, to the parent who each week runs off needed material on a mimeograph machine or tutors a child, or the parents who go along on the school trips so there will be enough hands to hold and eyes to see, parents are a valuable resource. Parents often need to be told what is needed or what would be useful and asked if they are willing to help. Many parents will not see themselves as having anything to offer the school, and it is important for teachers to let parents know of the many ways they can make contributions.

Our remarks are especially true for working parents and single parents who may have limited time and energy to pitch in on a regular basis. The bilingual parent who can translate for a new set of parents in a late day or evening slot or the parent who knows where to call to get some needed material at discount is equally valuable. Every parent is willing to do something on an occasional basis. Help beyond the classroom should not be ignored when tapping parents as resources. Again, the more involvement the parent has in the school the more likely we are to make a good team.

Community Resources

Asking parents to help seems a fairly natural response for a teacher, but most of us are more timid about approaching others in the community to perform services for us. One of the most common uses of community resources are for field trips. The local grocer, fire stations, and post office are obvious targets, but what about the woman who has started her own floral business or a local manufacturing firm? These contacts teach children many things about how the real world works and about options and divergent thinking. Learning what is available in the neighborhood from walking trips or bus excursions is another way of tapping resources for the classroom.

And what happens when you need extra hands in the classroom? When parents are working, who is available? A relatively recent innovation has been the use of older, retired citizens as foster grandparents and helpers of often extraordinary merit. They have many life experiences to share and are usually more patient and resourceful than many younger and more stressed individuals. Sometimes a senior citizen's center will "adopt" a school and come to help and enjoy the children. If the school or a particular teacher is interested in such a program, they need to contact local groups and possibly do a community awareness campaign to assure all that participation could be a worthwhile project. Some work is necessary to get it all together, but the rewards can be great indeed.

The local high school is often another resource. Young people interested in a potential career working with young children or who are taking a child development course and want some direct experience are good candidates. Even middle school and upper elementary children can be helpful if they are near enough and do not need extensive supervision. With young people this age, however, adults need to be patient and remember that youngsters vary greatly in maturity, so do not be too surprised or disappointed if their involvement varies in commitment or quality. Coming to help provides a good model for younger children and no elaborate requirements should be made.

You can begin to get a glimmer of the vast possibilities of reaching out to a variety of people and institutions in your community. Although none of them are "answers" to tight budgets and inadequate staffing, the willingness to break out of narrow definitions of "school" and "resources" can provide exciting possibilities.

Explorations

Do one or two of the explorations in each section to enrich and extend your learning from this chapter.

PERSONAL EXPLORATIONS

These exercises are designed to help you look at your own life—attitudes, experiences, dreams, myths, and realities.

1. A value is a belief we have about what is right and proper or moral. However, Simon, Howe, and Kirschenbaum point out that beliefs are not really values unless we act on them (1972). Spend some time writing down your values concerning education. Look at teacher behaviors and student behaviors. When you finish, analyze how many of these values you believe are held in common by the teaching profession. Then ask yourself which of these you act on in your life? Which ones did your teachers and schools foster actively? Be prepared to discuss your analysis in class.
2. Think about several children you know personally. Using Table 7.1 list the ways each of these children are the same or different on the dimensions discussed. How many of the differences are child-related? Environmentally-related? What does this tell you about the children you might encounter in the nursery/day care/school setting? Write a paragraph of your reactions.
3. Which of the five modes of involvement discussed in this chapter feels right for you? Why? Which feels uncomfortable? Do they all feel equally valid in the school setting? Why or why not? Come to class prepared to discuss your findings.

INTELLECTUAL EXPLORATIONS

These exercises are designed to increase your depth of knowledge in some areas discussed in this chapter.

1. Pick a subject you are interested in that is taught in the lower elementary grades. (Keep it simple, like animals, gardening, airplanes and pilots.) In the children's library find several books about this topic and

after a brief review of them write two goals and two specific objectives for both short- and long-range learning.

2. Review one standardized test, including the test itself and the test manual. What kind of information does it give you about the way the test was designed, the original group who took it (the norming population), the manner of presentation of the test, what the scores mean? How useful would the information from this test be for the classroom teacher? Be prepared to discuss your findings in class. (You can find such tests at colleges and universities in the following places: counseling centers, psychology departments or clinics, education departments or similar teacher training programs.)

3. Specific teaching sequences are included in teaching manuals for reading and mathematics programs for young children as well as other subject areas for older children. Review one teaching manual and bring the manual and your review to class for group discussion.

FIELD EXPLORATIONS

These exercises are designed to take you into the world to find real examples that will illustrate and elucidate the material in this chapter.

1. Attend a local PTA/PTO meeting and observe the interactions at a "business" and a personal level. List the actual events of the evening and then think about the following items for class discussion. Who is in charge? How involved are teachers, administrators? What are the goals of the organization? Can you tell? How well attended was the meeting? How do these various factors seem to fit together?

2. If your local school district has a school psychologist or other testing specialist see if you can arrange an interview. Ask: What standardized tests are administered and when? How are the results used? How valid are the results? What other kinds of testing are done? What other kinds of assessment does this person feel is appropriate in the schools? Bring the results of your interview to class. If no such person exists in the school, ask a teacher the same questions.

3. Visit a center for young children. Observe and list the modes of involvement and the management techniques by one teacher in a 30-minute period. Write a brief paragraph of your reactions to this list.

References

Rae, G. and Potter, T. C. *Informal reading diagnosis: A practical guide for the classroom teacher*, Second Ed. Englewood Cliffs, N.J.: Prentice-Hall, 1981.

Rosenthal, R. and Jacobson, L. *Pygmalion in the classroom.* New York: Holt, Rinehart and Winston, 1968.

Simon, S. B., Howe, L. W. and Kirschenbaum, S. *Values clarification.* New York: Hart, 1972.

Chapter 8

MULTICULTURAL EDUCATION

Objectives

After reading this chapter the student should be able to:

1. Trace the historical roots of our dual legacy of human rights and racism/discrimination in this country.
2. Discuss highlights of the civil rights period from 1954 to 1975.
3. List three of the "ism's" of our society and discuss the ways they are harmful to children.
4. Define multicultural education and list several reasons why it is important for all children.
5. List and discuss the areas of learning necessary to be a competent teacher of multicultural education.
6. Discuss items and activities that can be observed in a multicultural classroom.
7. Describe several approaches to working with dialect-divergent and second-language children along with some of the problems a child will have in transferring from one language system to another.

The United States is a mosaic of many people. Since its inception, with the arrival of the earliest colonists, culturally diverse individuals and families have sought to settle in this land as an escape from religious persecution, wars, and poverty. From these people many variations within U.S. society were created including multiple languages, customs, traditions, beliefs, religions, and crafts. These people have different political persuasions, racial identities, ethnic heritages, sexes, ages, socioeconomic memberships, and national origins. From this diversity, multicultural education in the United States has become a necessary and fundamental concern of the schools. As education seeks to become relevant, it must meet the needs of all of its people. For only through active acknowledgement of and attention to the multicultural nature of its student population can U.S. education hope to truly educate all of its youth.

HISTORICAL CONTEXT OF CULTURAL PLURALISM

The Beginnings of Cultural Discrimination

The earliest colonization of the United States was achieved by people who were fleeing from repressive governments in which basic freedoms were limited or absent. They passed on, in their search, a belief in human rights as universal and basic—something one is born with rather than something learned or dispensed. Unfortunately, this basic ideal was soon tempered by other forces that laid a foundation for discrimination and denial of human rights to certain groups. These two counter forces still exert their influence in contemporary society.

The first census of the United States, taken around 1790, showed that more than half the population consisted of non-English inhabitants. Those listed were primarily of African, Scotch-Irish, Welsh, German, Dutch, Swedish, and French descent (Kopan, 1974). In addition to a black slave population, the Irish Catholics were one of the first groups openly attacked when their establishment of church schools was viewed as a menace to national security. This led to the burning of schools and convents in Boston, Philadelphia, and New York. By 1853 open discrimination became organized politically in the form of the Know-Nothing Party.

Shifts in immigration patterns beginning in the 1880s, which brought people from Southern and Eastern Europe and the Far East, led to organized discrimination. Groups of various persuasion were formed to restrict so-called inferior people in the United States. In 1882 the *Chinese Exclusion Act* was passed, shortly thereafter being applied to all immigrants. In 1907 Congress appointed the Dillingham Commission which published the infamous Dillingham Report. This report sought to prove that these later, new immigrants were "inferior" to earlier immigrants, primarily as a function of national origin; the report laid the foundation for cultural stereotyping in this country (Dillingham Report, 1911).

In 1890 immigration quotas were first set, and then in 1917 legislation restricting immigration on the basis of ethnic origin, particularly from Southern Europe and Southwestern Asia, was passed.

The Melting Pot Concept

The idea of acculturation was put forth in a play by Israel Zangwill called *The Melting Pot*, which was first performed on Broadway in September 1909. This theatrical performance set forth the concept of America as a new country in which, " . . . all the races of Europe are melting and reforming" (Zangwill, 1909, p.37).

By the turn of the century the idea of a distinctly U.S. culture, a U.S. self-image, and a U.S. nativism took hold. After World War I this U.S. idealism flourished in terms of the broad acceptance of *assimiliation*, the giving up of one's initial ethnic or cultural identity to become "American." Yet, for some groups, particularly those of different color, assimilation was impossible. Interestingly, in many states it was unlawful to teach a foreign language in the public schools.

In 1924 the *National Origins Act* reduced annual immigration quotas by ratio, to the number of previously immigrated nationals in the country as of 1890. This act also excluded all Asiatics from citizenship. By

1943, the Chinese Exclusion Act was replaced and other quotas were set. In 1952 the *Immigration and Nationality Act* (the McCarran-Walter Act) set forth additional national and ethnic restrictions. These laws remained in effect until 1965 when President Lyndon Johnson signed the *Reform Immigration Act* (Koppan, 1974).

World War II led to a continuation of multicultural discrimination. In addition, the results of physical and mental tests of soldiers and various other minority group members were given questionable and discriminatory meaning. Conclusions drawn from this data led to additional discriminatory practices which became more pronounced against all races and were evident in such areas as housing, education, employment, health care, and justice under the law.

> Migrations throughout the United States by Puerto-Ricans, Mexican Americans, Black Americans, and Native Americans brought on second-generation discrimination and the outright practice of open and legalized segregation. The Italians, Slavs, Greeks, and Jews who were looked down on by the Irish, Germans, and Scandinavians, who were in turn looked down on by the English or others of Anglo-Saxon origin—all looked down on, discriminated against, and segregated the color-visible groups—particularly Blacks (who had been recently subject to slavery), Chicanos, Native Americans, and Puerto Ricans (Hunter, 1974, p.14).

A second legacy of World War II involved the desegregation of the armed services and multicultural exchanges among soldiers and citizens of different national affiliation. Stereotypes were often hard to maintain when personal knowledge and friendships developed. Greater awareness of the diversity and integrity of other cultures was acquired by numerous young U.S. citizens. Nonetheless, the melting pot concept had failed. Since no active, national effort to understand and accommodate different cultural groups was forged, ethnic communities and "ghettos" remained.

The Other Side of the Coin—Civil Rights Gains

During the turn of the century there were, of course, voices for tolerance and for a more balanced U.S. consciousness. In 1916 John Dewey introduced the concept of "cultural pluralism" in an address before the National Education Association (Dewey, 1916), and in 1924 Horace Kallen unsuccessfully sought to show how cultural pluralism made U.S. life richer (Kallen, 1924).

Gradually a more tolerant view toward religion was developed through several U.S. Supreme Court decisions. In 1919 the right of a private religious school to teach a subject in a foreign language had been prohibited by law, but by 1923 the Court ruled against this restriction. The right to attend a religious school, as well as the right for such schools to exist, was upheld by the Court in 1925.

A variety of factors contributed to a recognition of the need for greater multicultural understanding. Natural population growth, the participation of the United States in two World Wars, and the growing agitation and frustration with the disparities between priviliged and discriminated-against groups finally gave rise to the civil rights movement. The Supreme Court decision in 1954 in *Brown vs. Board of Education of Topeka* was the beginning of a series of antidiscriminatory legislative acts (see Table 8.1). The Court's statement concerning the importance of equal education led to an active desegregation of separate schools in the South, and elsewhere.

This historic ruling read, in part:

> Today, education is perhaps the most important function of state and local governments. In these days, it is doubtful that any child may reasonably be expected to succeed in life if he is denied the opportunity of an education. Such an opportunity, where the state has undertaken to provide it, is a right which must be made available to all on equal terms (*Brown vs. Board of Education*, 1954).

Table 8.1 shows the numerous antidiscriminatory changes that occured over the next 21 years. The concepts of cultural pluralism and multicultural education achieved increasing prominence.

Teachers at various levels were also involved in the movement toward increasing multicultural education in the schools. The American Association of Colleges of Teacher Education formed a Multicultural Education Commission in 1970 and in 1972 published a statement, "No One Model American," with the caution that multicultural was not a euphemism for disadvantaged. Their statement remains a model for the field in defining multicultural education. It states, in part:

> Multicultural education is education which values cultural pluralism. Multicultural education rejects the view that schools should seek to melt away cultural differences or the view that schools should merely tolerate cultural pluralism. Instead, multicultural education affirms that schools should be oriented toward the cultural enrichment of all children and youth through programs rooted in the preservation and extension of cultural diversity as a fact of life in American society, and it affirms that this cultural diversity is a valuable resource that should be preserved and extended. It affirms that major education institutions should strive to preserve and enhance cultural pluralism.
>
> To endorse cultural pluralism is to endorse the principle that there is no one model American. To endorse cultural pluralism is to understand and

TABLE 8.1.   Civil Rights Gains from 1954 to 1975

1954	*Brown v. Board of Education of Topeka* requiring education to be available to all on equal terms
1957	Civil Rights Commission established by Congress to investigate complaints alleging that citizens are being deprived of their right to vote by reason of their race, color, religion, or national origin, or by reason of fraudulent practices
1961–62	Lawsuits to eliminate discrimination in public schools instituted in large cities and small communities in the North and West, covering gerrymandered school boundaries, transfer policies, and discriminatory federal patterns
1963	Voting Rights Act (Congressional action)
1964	Civil Rights Act (Congressional action)
1966	James S. Coleman (Johns Hopkins University) survey concerning lack of availability of equal educational opportunities for individuals by reason of race, color, religion, or national origin in public institutions at all levels
1971	School busing for equal quality education
1972	Proposed Consitutional amendment on equal rights for women, passed by Congress, awaiting ratification by a total of 38 states.
1972	Court orders allowance of bilingual program (Spanish): *Serna v. Portales Municipal Schools*
1972	Instructors' rights—such as *Board of Regents v. Perry*—dealt with refusal to rehire college instructors without explanation or hearing
1973	Litigation by Native Americans for adequate compensation for lands of South Dakota Black Hills to Native Americans and their gold, silver, and timber taken by abrogation of 1866–68 treaty
1973	Student rights—Court actions sustaining student rights to due process, *Board of Regents v. Roth*
1968–74	The six-year study of educational practices affecting Mexican-Americans in the Southwest by the U.S. Commission on Civil Rights
1974	Job discrimination in employment practices challenged
1974	*Lau v. Nichols* right of child to instruction in his own language
1975	PL94-142 Education for all handicapped children mandated for children ages 3 to 21

Adapted from: William A. Hunter, (Ed.), *Multicultural education through competency-based teacher education.* Washington, D.C.: AACTE, 1974, p.17.

appreciate the differences that exist among the nation's citizens. It is to see these differences as a positive force in the continuing development of a society which professes a wholesome respect for the intrinsic worth of every individual. Cultural pluralism is more than a temporary accommodation to placate racial and ethnic minorities. It is a concept that aims toward a heightened sense of being and of wholeness of the entire society based on the unique strengths of each of its parts (AACTE, 1973).

Groups in education began talking about "difference" as opposed to early concepts of "disadvantaged" or the more derogatory term "deviant," which previously had been used to describe children from poor or ethnically different backgrounds. Bilingual and bicultural programs were supported in various areas of the country, especially in the Southwest and Florida, where Spanish-speaking populations were large. Colleges developed ethnic study programs, and elementary and secondary schools followed suit. Those portions of the country with diverse ethnic populations found that involving parents in the schools and in decision making could provide valuable insights into teaching their "different" children. So a period of growth and increased sensitivity to multicultural issues flourished.

By the late 1970s new economic crises, characterized by rampant inflation and cutbacks in production leading to job losses, defused concern for multiculturalism. An increased demand for jobs and productivity turned the attention of the nation's people to their pocketbooks, detracting from more idealistic pursuits. Between 1980 and 1982 funds for education and other social welfare programs were greatly curtailed. Not all gains were lost, certainly, but a step backward in the progress toward "equal education" was experienced throughout the educational community. These cutbacks were also felt by others involved with a variety of health and welfare agencies. The era of civil rights reforms had apparently come to its end.

The United States Today

We need to ask, what is our present reality? The legacy of the past is still clearly with us. People of color (predominantly African-American, Asian-American, Native American, and Latino/Hispanic) are still underrepresented in the legislative and corporate power centers of the United States. Yet, as reported in the 1980 census, for the first time in this century, the combined percentages of "minorities" exceeded the white Anglo-Saxon "majority."

A white "backlash," as it has been termed, has surfaced in the United States, in part in protest against previous civil rights decisions. For example, recent Supreme Court decisions have tended to favor white protests against reserved spots among the nation's medical schools for minority candidates. Native Americans and Hispanic students (those who speak Spanish as a primary language) currently have the highest drop-out rate among high school students. And, although some black Americans have made significant economic gains, for others poor housing, ghetto life, and high unemployment, especially among males, is still too frequent an occurrence. Recently, we have experienced new waves of immigrants. Many flee political strife, particularly third world refugees such as Cubans, Mung, Vietnamese, and Arab groups. Many of these people arrive with few financial assets and widely differing cultural backgrounds and languages. These different needs will continue to burden the welfare and educational institutions, which have the primary responsibility of helping them settle and become oriented to this new land. The tradition of providing opportunity and human dignity coexists with a legacy of racism and discrimination. Only in some of the more insulated areas of our country are cultural struggles less often a common part of the immigrant's political and economic reality. Federal support for assimilation has been reduced, and it has become the task of the states and local institutions, including the schools, to act. Cultural plurism is reality. Whether it will be accepted and used as a creative force or a destructive one remains to be seen.

MULTICULTURAL EDUCATION FOR THE YOUNG CHILD

The Council for Interracial Books for Children publishes a variety of informative materials concerning the "ism's" of our society. In particular, they refer to racism, sexism, and ageism as pervasive and detrimental forces in books and other media to which children are exposed. In their bulletin, "Racism: Related Problems, Research, and Strategies," they state:

Research has shown that between the ages of three and four, children are aware of the status assigned by race and sex. Their perceptions are shaped by their experience with significant adults and by the messages they receive from the environment.... All three—home, community, and larger society—contribute to children's sense of self, provide role models, and pass on values. It is simpler for children to grow up in an environment where family, community, and the larger society are in harmony—where all endorse similar cultural values and behaviors. But in the United States, the cultures and values of peoples of color are devalued and subordinated by the white population.... This means that children of color ... usually received supportive messages from their families and communities, but very different, negative messages form the institutions controlled by whites—and this includes educational institutions. This white environment—which reinforces only Euro-American cultural values, appearance, speech, beliefs, and behaviors—is generally hostile to the way that children of color, their families, and their communities look, speak, believe, and behave. At the same time, white children are encouraged to acquire an unrealistic belief that they are superior, a belief that is harmful to them and damaging to others in our pluralistic society (Interracial Books for Children, *Bulletin*, 1983).

This article points out how young children learn from our language and our behavior, and from movies, TV, books, toys, and advertising that white is the "norm" and the "rightness of whiteness." The English language itself reinforces this concept in subtle ways. There are varied positive meanings for whiteness while blackness contains many negative ones.

Numerous research studies over the years have found that in both black and white children racial awareness is strongly formed by age four. A 1966 Wisconsin study found that most white children under the age of five assigned positive roles and characteristics to white children and negative ones to black. When this study was replicated 13 years later in 1979, similar results were obtained. Black children, on the other hand, assigned both positive and negative roles or characteristics to both blacks and whites. Black children draw themselves less positively than white children, often making themselves smaller than whites, frequently drawing themselves as white, or incomplete, with limbs missing (Katz, 1978). Thus constructing a positive and knowledgeable racial/cultural self-concept becomes a major developmental task for minority children, especially those of color.

There is evidence to show that racism also dehumanizes white children and damages them intellectually. Judy Katz states: "Racism and ethnocentrism develops . . . so that they are unable to experience themselves and their culture as [they are]" (Katz, 1978, p.12). She goes on to say that further studies indicate that racial prejudice in white children limits their cognitive development, affecting their ability to reason, impairing their judgment, and distorting their perception of reality. Alice Miel says of white suburban children: "We observed that [they] learn to be hypocritical about differences at a very early age. The prejudices of their society were still very much with them, but they had had it drilled into them that it was 'not nice' to express such feelings" (Miel, 1976, p.13). The self-concept for white children can also be distorted. Katz writes:

> The superior attitude, "white is right," often leaves whites confused about their identity. . . . Because United States culture is centered around white norms, white people rarely have to come to terms with that part of their identity. White people do not see themselves as white. This is a way of denying responsibility for perpetuating the racist system and being part of the problem. By seeing oneself solely as an individual, one can disown one's racism. Lack of understanding of self owing to a poor sense of identity causes whites to develop a negative attitude toward minorities on both a conscious and an unconscious level (Katz, 1978, pp.13–14).

Teachers are also products of their culture. As with others, childhood educators have attitudes, create assumptions, and enact behaviors that

INSET 8.1   Black Children

Jack L. Daniel

"Black English" constitutes one of the most important, if perhaps the most controversial, cultural differences that Black children bring to the classroom. Children using the language forms valued in the Black community have been diagnosed improperly as learning disabled and, subsequently, placed in special classrooms. One study found that when Black and white children read the same composition aloud, the Black children received lower grades.

In the federal case of *Martin Luther King Junior Elementary School v. Ann Arbor School District Board*, it was found that misunderstandings of Black English led to Black children being placed improperly in speech pathology classes and being treated negatively in other ways. The court ruled that by failing to address Black children's language differences, the Ann Arbor School District violated the children's rights to equal educational opportunity. For a detailed discussion of this case and of Black English, consult Geneva Smitherman's *Talkin and Testifyin* (Houghton Mifflin, 1977) and *Black English and the Education of Black Children and Youth* (Wayne State University, 1981).

Many Black children do not communicate with authority figures in the same way that white children do. Many Black children, for example, are taught to avoid eye contact when talking with adult authority figures. Indeed, such eye contact would be viewed as a sign of defiance, disobedience, and anger. Such children might appear to be inattentive and nonparticipatory in the classroom, when in actuality they are merely adhering to their community norms regarding eye contact when listening to adults.

Janice E. Hale, in *Black Children: Their Roots, Culture and Learning Styles* (Brigham Young University Press, 1982) provides detailed information on the socialization of Black American boys and girls, Black children's cognitive styles, play behavior, and the African cultural influence on Black American culture. She notes, for example, the African and Black American emphasis on sound and movement as well as a preference for play involving people as opposed to objects.

Black American children's singing games are an excellent example of play employing many of the distinctive features of African and Black American culture. Linda F. Wharton's *Black American Children's Singing Games* (University Publishers, Inc., 1980) documents the use of blues styles, call and response, dance movements, and rhythm in these games. Many of these games can be very useful for elementary vocabulary development, self-expression, and teaching children appropriate aspects of social interaction.

Black body language, in general, reflects many cultural differences that are of major importance for teachers in desegregated school settings. At the Second International Conference on Nonverbal Behavior: An Intercultural Perspective, Judith Lynne Hanna of the University of Maryland presented a thorough

Council for Interracial Books for Children, 1983.

review of this literature. She and many others have discussed cultural differences in handshakes, eye movements, dancing, walking, interaction distances, and touching.

are shaped by societal racism. Research studies have shown that teachers, including those of color, expect less from minority children, with the exception of Asian-American children, paradoxically, who are often expected to excel. Teachers also more often ignore, correct, criticize, or interrupt children of color, while listening to their white classmates. Some even permit white children, or lighter skinned children of color, to sit closer to them. This behavior reinforces feelings of superiority in white children and lowers the self-esteem of minority children (Miller, 1968).

INSET 8.2   Racism in the Classroom

A study was conducted with 66 white female undergraduates and 264 seventh and eighth graders attending 3 junior high schools in a Midwestern community. White and black junior high schoolers were randomly assigned either a "gifted label" or "nongifted label." Each student teacher was then given this "information" and asked to perform a teaching task. Systematic recordings were taken during the teaching task, with observations focused on six variables:

1. Teacher *attention* to students' statements.
2. Teacher *encouragement* of students' statements.
3. Teacher *elaboration* of students' statements.
4. Teacher *ignoring* of students' statements.
5. Teacher *praise* of students' statements.
6. Teacher *criticism* of students' statements.

Comparisons of teacher interaction with black and white students were made; black students were given less attention, ignored more, praised less, and criticized more. Most startling, perhaps, was the interaction between race and label. It was suggested here that it is the gifted black who is given least attention, is the least praised, and is the most criticized, even when comparing him to his "nongifted" black counterpart.

Martin Maehr and Pamela Rubovitz, 1971 (Unpublished study).

INSET 8.3   Native American Children

The American Indian's culture is unique.... Although each tribe is different and has traditions that are specific to that population, there are some general attitudes that can be found in many Indian groups.

American Indians generally *do not believe in drawing attention to themselves* especially through competition and aggression. Since competitive and aggressive behavior are endemic to Anglo society and taught and perpetuated in the schools, it is obvious that an Indian child will feel conflict in this area. It is morally conflicting, for example, for a Cherokee child to be called upon and singled out in class. Only when he or she represents a group can the child feel comfortable in responding to the teacher's demands. Team or group competition is acceptable, but in single competition recognition of the "winner" implies a negative attitude toward the "loser" and is not acceptable.

Indian people of a relatively traditional background *do not look at time in the same way the dominant society does.* The Anglo culture is much more time oriented than the Indian culture. In Anglo schools children are punished if they are late for school, certain subjects are studied at certain times and at no other times, bells announce the time for recess, lunch, dismissal. School children are exhorted not to "waste time" (a Native American would feel time cannot be wasted if learning is a continuous experience), and that wasted time has to be "made up" (the past cannot be made into the present).

Schools are usually set up on an authoritarian basis, that is, the principal and the teachers have total authority over the pupils, and learning is teacher directed. *Authoritarianism is generally not acceptable* to Indian children; they have not been exposed to it as have their Anglo counterparts. Most Indian children who have been brought up traditionally are respected as thinking and feeling human beings capable of making choices.

The learning process is different in the two culture also. *Indian children tend to learn through observation and self-discovery.* They explore, set their own pace, and enjoy learning and experiencing. The Indian child may become bored with the noncreativity of the educational methods found in many classrooms and fail to participate in any manner acceptable to the teacher.

Very often *parents of Indian children are not comfortable in their dealing with schools.* This discomfort is especially acute when Indian parents are not fluent in English, and the staff does not find ways to bridge the gap. In addition, the culture of the particular nation should be integrated into the curriculum, as should accurate history and information on Indian people.

NOTE: Playing Indian is a common childhood activity in the United States, as well as in other countries. Children hop up and down, putting a hand against their mouths and yelling "woo-woo-woo" or raise one hand shoulder-high and say "how" or "ugh." Such nonauthentic behaviors, which reflect the influence of peer socialization, schooling, movies, and other media, mock Indian cultural practices and demean Indian people. So do well-intentioned programs spon-

Council for Interracial Books for Children, 1983.

sored by various organizations in which children take on "Indian" names, form themselves into "tribes" and meet every other week to "play Indian." There is nothing harmful in children dressing up to play clowns, witches, cowboys, pilots, etc. These are roles that can be taken on by people of any racial, religious, or national group, but being an Indian is not a role. Indian people are human beings with diverse cultures and distinctive national identities. Being Lakota (Sioux), Hopi, Navajo, etc., is an integral aspect of their human condition. To suggest that other people can become "Indian" by simply donning a feather is to trivialize Indian people's diversity and to assault their humanity.

Supplementing behavioral transgressions, teachers and parents often avoid discussing racism or other discriminatory "ism's." Often when race or positive cultural differences are omitted we reinforce negative cultural attitudes. Moreover, if no alternative learning is offered at home or school to correct the distorted concepts children may acquire, we are, in effect, giving our approval to such stereotypes.

According to the Council for Interracial Books for Children, if, in fact, events are hidden and,

> in the same vein, teachers claim to be "color blind" when they say, "I just see the child, not the color," by denying racial differences, those teachers are refusing to see the child's full humanity, which includes the child's membership in a racial and cultural group. By the same token, when adults speak of children of color as "culturally deprived," then they are really saying, "My culture is superior to theirs" (Interracial Bulletin, 1983, p.10).

Recognition of our own prejudices, many of which have been buried deeply in an effort to "love and care for" all children, may be a painful and difficult task for teachers. Learning to hear casual statements, like "That's white of you," "Don't be an Indian-giver," as signs of racism; learning to recognize the feeling of discomfort when one is the only white face in a crowded elevator with brown and black faces; noticing that one has chosen library books to read to a child which contain only white children are all important learning. They are subtle evidence of what we might call, "the white habit." While not usually accompanied with preconceived malice, or even conscious thought, they, nevertheless serve as a reflection of years of negative acculturation.

Sullivan (1974), in discussing effective teaching in a pluralistic society, issues a multicultural challenge to teachers and to the institutions which train them: "commitment is the first step, but it must be followed by competence, confidence, and content. That is, it is not enough to like the children; the challenge is to teach them effectively within a cultural context." (p.56)

Creating a Multicultural Classroom for Young Children

Self-Awareness

As we noted earlier the first step toward a multicultural classroom is an internal survey of one's own attitudes, beliefs, and prejudices. As the Interracial Bulletin points out, "Becoming anti-racist is an ongoing process. No magic kit exists. No one book, no single course can provide all the answers. . . . By anti-racist is meant the taking of conscious, delib-

Love is a necessary component for each child's development.

INSET 8.4   Chinese American Children

Itty Chan

Chinese-American children are taught to respect the teacher and the school and to cooperate with instructions for learning. Often their reverence for learning and their patient cooperativeness are mistaken for passivity and a lack of spontaneity. Sometimes when a child is quiet and/or appears not to participate actively, as in circle time, it may be because the child is waiting patiently for someone to finish talking before speaking. Chinese-American children are taught not to interrupt; being pressed to compete in order to be heard may make them uncomfortable.

In the Chinese culture, independence means "to stand on one's own feet" rather than "to stand alone." A young child might feel competent at, and confident in, undertaking many responsible jobs but shy away from standing up in front of a group to sing or speak because standing alone can bring a feeling of loneliness to a child from a group-oriented culture. Chinese-American children usually prefer to perform in small groups, and teachers should consider this when they encourage Chinese American children to get up at "show and tell" time or similar activities.

Chinese-American children are encouraged to be observant of details and relationships. They are not encouraged to engage in daydreaming or Western-style fantasy play. Often imagination is integrated with rational thinking and expresses itself in innovative ways of seeing things and putting things together.

From an early age Chinese-American children are taught to be aware of the people around them and to be observant of how people behave and relate to one another. They learn to pay more attention to deeds done than to words, so teaching by example and by being consistent with what one says is of crucial importance. For instance, when telling a noisy child to be quiet, it is often more effective to look directly into the child's eyes and speak in a soft but firm voice than to raise one's voice. Use of examples to illustrate, and use of demonstrations to instruct, are effective teaching methods.

Chinese parents have particular concerns regarding the health care of their children. Two are noted below.

On getting wet. Keeping their children dry and warm is important to Chinese parents. They are likely to object to water play and frown upon fingerpainting, easel painting, or clay modeling, which are "messy play" and require lots of water for washing up afterwards. Playing in snow and rain puddles might also cause them dismay. Understanding this concern, a teacher could substitute sand for water on the water play table and provide similar learning experiences in pouring, dumping, and measuring volumes, and so on. Likewise, a long waterproof smock may be used during "messy" play.

On keeping warm. Chinese parents often put many layers of clothing on their children in winter. Chinese parents appreciate having teachers be sure that

Council for Interracial Books for Children, 1983.

their children are covered with blankets during nap time, and that their children do not stay in drafty spots.

Like all other parents, Chinese parents appreciate a teacher's sincere and caring concern about the child's well-being. Some suggestions for reaching out to and working with Chinese American families follow.

1. Because Chinese parents may not know the English language, all school notices or memos for parents should be translated into Chinese.

2. If there are no bilingual staff members, a bilingual person should be available for communication with Chinese-speaking parents. (Note that it is traditional in U.S. schools for the teacher to talk only with "the parent." In the Chinese-American community the responsibility for child care is often shared by other family members, that is, a grandparent, older sibling, or other relative.)

3. School meetings, conferences, and home visits may best be carried out in an informal way as it is often difficult for Chinese parents to speak up in meetings, because they may feel it is impolite to say too much or to argue in public. The purpose of such meetings should be made clear in advance to Chinese parents. Also, it is important for them to know that a bilingual person will be available. Care should be given to the scheduling of meetings and home visits, because in most Chinese families, both parents work and their work schedules are often not nine to five.

4. Teachers must not tell a Chinese-American child that he or she should speak English and not Chinese "because this is America and not China." The indirect message is that being Chinese is not valued. Such statements also ask children to reject their cultural heritage and try to be what they cannot fully be, namely, European-American. This is most damaging to a child's self-concept as a unique individual and as a Chinese-American. Language is closely tied to self-esteem, and a child's "mother tongue" must not be undermined and never belittled.

---

erate steps to challenge injustice and promote fair treatment" (p.11). This position advocates the need to learn about racism and to learn about different cultures and cultural differences including the variations within each cultural group. Sometimes in learning about aspects of a culture it is assumed that all individuals from that culture will behave in the same way without thought to differences within the group itself. For example, Puerto Rican Blacks who speak Spanish have a totally different cultural and linguistic background from Southern Blacks and possess a totally different culture from Hispanics of the Southwest whose roots are in Mexico. Similarly, different tribes of Native Americans maintain different cultural-ethnic attitudes.

If programs of training do not possess the information or experiences that will benefit an aspiring teacher, it will prove helpful to seek resources and opportunities enabling self-learning. The Council for Interracial Books for Children, for example, publishes a free catalog of antiracist, antisexist, antiageist teaching materials. (Write to CIBC, 1841 Broadway, New York, NY 10023.)

TABLE 8.2.   Behaviors and Attitudes in a Multicultural Classroom

Environment

1. Displayed pictures such as community helpers and community resources include different ages, sexes, and ethnic backgrounds.
2. Books in the library corner show girls as heroines, old people in positive roles, multiracial groups, and possibly other languages such as ABC books in Spanish, as well as the more conventional fare.
3. If it is a holiday period, different holidays of the season are shown and different traditions for celebrating the same holiday. For example, pinatas are shown as well as Christmas trees, Channukah traditions as well as Christmas.
4. If children are present who speak a language other than English, either the teacher, an aide, or another child is used to help translate and assist these children so they can be a part of the group.
5. Signs and labels show languages other than English, especially, the primary languages of the children in the classroom.
6. Children are not corrected for dialect differences or mispronunciation. The teacher and aides role model correct language appropriate to the cultural environment and their own primary language (an Anglo-American teacher must not try to use a dialect or language she does not understand).
7. The teacher uses poems and stories, chants and songs, and different cultural styles of dramatic play, which reflect other cultures and ethnic groups as well as the standard Euro-American.
8. The teacher and all other adults in the classroom listen and interact with equal time and attention to all children regardless of ethnicity.
9. Toys such as puppets, dolls, and puzzles represent all races, in all white as well as multiracial classes.
10. Paint and crayons are available in colors that approximate accurate skin tones for a variety of ethnic groups.
11. Children are encouraged to share and participate in a manner consistent with their own cultural background. Native American children, for example, learn at home to dislike being singled out in public even for praise. Many children of color come from traditions that encourage cooperation rather than competition and prefer working in groups rather than alone.
12. Visitors, representing various ethnic groups, are invited to the classroom to share their cultural background, languages, and roles in the community with the children.

In the Classroom

In visiting an average preschool, daycare, or Headstart classroom what are some of the differences one is likely to encounter? Easily observable differences will reflect color, language, and sex. More subtle differences will consist of dialectic variations, religious or cultural traditions, or ethnic family patterns and attitudes. In a large urban area, all of these differences may be reflected in the diversity of the children attending the center and, one hopes, among its staff, as well.

There are a variety of easily observable classroom features which provide evidence that multicultural education is at work and of value in that setting. Table 8.2 gives a dozen items which offer a good starting list.

Table 8.2 offers some of the more obvious practices that can be easily observed. Less obvious, but equally important, items include the involvement of parents in school planning, the way in which conflicts which include racial statements are handled between children, and the overall staffing pattern of a center. The latter should reflect, not only the presence of different ethnic groups, but should also have sufficient representation by these groups of people in positions of responsibility and power.

Language Differences and the Early Childhood Program

It is important for the teacher of young children to have some basic understanding concerning language systems in general and language development of children, in particular. In Chapter 3, Table 3.4 gives an overview of typical stages in language development from birth to six years of age. In Table 8.3 you will find some basic concepts concerning language systems.

Language is the child's most important means of knowing. If the family's language differs from that of the school, both need to be encouraged to enhance learning. Otherwise, a signal is sent to the child, and to his family and community, that they are unacceptable to the school. It is this kind of message that often causes alienation from academic goals, which hampers a young person's future. Rae and Potter (1981) state:

> Whatever the child's primary language/dialect, he or she should acquire language habits through an ordered set of learning experiences that include these characteristics:
>
> 1. Intensive practice in listening and speaking in the primary language.

TABLE 8.3.   The Organization of Language Systems

1. Every language consists of phonemes, which constitute the sounds of the system.

2. Different languages will utilize different phonemes, some of which may conflict in transferring from one language to another. For example, there is no initial "ch" sound in Spanish equivalent to that of the English sound in "children," therefore Spanish speakers do not *hear* that initial sound and substitute "sh" which is the closest equivalent.

3. Groups of phonemes are organized into morphemes, which constitute the meaning and some grammatical elements of language. For example, the word "toys" consists of two morphemes, the object "toy" and the "s" which indicates plural in English.

4. The arrangement of morphemes into larger linguistic units of phrases and sentences follows a definite structural order, which constitutes the grammar of that language.

5. Different language systems may have different morpheme and structural components, some of which can conflict when transferring from one system to another. In Hindi, the language of India, verbs are placed at the end of a sentence which would produce an English translation like, "Hotel which direction is? Transferring from one system to the other requires both a vocabulary and a structural shift. Children whose primary language is not English will often make "errors" in order reflecting their own system.

6. Virtually every language has a variety of dialects all of which are equally correct linguistically even though one may be considered the "preferred" pattern of speech.

7. Dialects develop according to geography, social class, occupation, age, and ghetto occupation, as well as individual (idiolects) variations in language usage. Furthermore, native speakers in any dialect tend to abbreviate and slur words so that they can be difficult to understand. Is "I'm gonna go" equivalent to "I'm going to go"?

8. Adults and children learn to use a variety of dialects over time and with appropriate models learn to switch from one to another with ease. For example, an individual is likely to speak quite differently when socializing in a local pub with a group of friends than when attending an important professional meeting.

9. Language is an ever-changing entity with new words being added, and old ones being dropped or gaining new meanings. ("Cute" originally meant bow-legged in English.)

10. Words encompass both denotative and connotative meanings, which a native speaker is often unconsciously aware of but which a nonnative speaker may misunderstand or use incorrectly. What nondictionary definition do you associate with the word "gay" in our present U.S. culture?

11. Idioms, phrases which have derived meanings that do not fit with the literal translation of the words, are features of language that are particularly difficult for nonnative speakers and sometimes, for young children within the same system. What do you really mean when you tell someone to "go fly a kite."

12. Written language systems are incomplete representations of spoken language with many clues to meaning such as voice tone, emphasis, and facial expression missing. Therefore genuine learning of a language is achieved through the ear not the eye.

2. Development of oral fluency in this primary language prior to reading in this language.
3. Development of oral fluency in a secondary language or dialect prior to reading in the secondary language (p.24).

Because teachers of young children deal primarily in oral language, they are the ideal agents for promoting fluency and comfort in primary and secondary languages. This is also a developmentally sound approach since the period from two to seven years is the stage of maximum language development. A classroom that promotes oral fluency is providing a child with the best possible tools for success in later schooling. This is true both because of the self-confidence and self-esteem the child gains from having her own language or dialect treated with respect and because these tools are essential to later academic learning such as reading and writing.

There are some differences that should be noted between working with children with dialect variations and with children for whom English is a second (or possibly third) language. Table 8.4 gives some ideas in working with children with dialect differences in the classroom.

The suggestions in Table 8.4 also apply to bilingual children, yet there are other constraints which must also be considered in relation to language learning. As stated earlier in this chapter, the *Lau vs. Nichols* U.S. Supreme Court decision in 1974 stated that a child has the right to instruction in his primary language. Most school districts have interpreted this by instituting programs of bilingual instruction if 50 percent or more of the children speak a similar language, other than English. Multilingual classrooms usually use partial approaches.

Rae and Potter (1981) describe different approaches to instruction:

There are two basic approaches to bilingual instruction. The "dual approach" divides the day or week into English and alternate language segments. Thus the child learns concepts and subject matter in the primary language and spends part of the time learning English. The "concurrent" approach uses both languages in the classroom with instruction being given in each language simultaneously. The teacher presents a concept in one language and then in the other. Materials for the classroom are written in multiple languages.

The ideal goal of both of these methods is "full literacy" for both the English-speaking and the non-English-speaking child, an approach to language learning that includes culture and history as well as all regular skills in reading and writing (p.25).

Recently another approach has been developed and is being tested in the Spanish-speaking community of East Los Angeles, California (Hall,

TABLE 8.4.   Working with Dialect-Divergent Children

1. Each child's speech reflects his environment and should be treated with respect and acceptance.
2. Reading to children from good children's books, which use language in imaginative and creative ways, is one of the best sources for "hearing" the new language patterns.
3. Include reading some books that are written in dialect: those that match the children's and some that are also different. If this is too awkward, have an aide or parent who is comfortable with the dialect read to the children.
4. Provide many opportunities for dramatic play based on books. The child who responds "It is I" to the troll under the bridge is not only being one of the Billy Goat's Gruffs, he is learning a "formal" English speech pattern.
5. Play games in which responses are given in complete sentences. In a guessing game, "I have something round and red. Who can guess in a whole sentence what I have? I think you have . . . or I guess you have . . . ?" If a child responds with one word, for example, "apple," the teacher may respond, "Johnny thinks I have an apple? Who else wants to guess?" If a child responds with a complete sentence compliment him, "Jose, I like the way you guessed by using a whole sentence."
6. Use songs and chants that model a variety of sentence patterns including dialect patterns.
7. Rather than correct "errors" simply embed sentence fragments in your own speech (for example, a child's statement, "Don't want," is responded to with, "You don't want the spinach? What else do you want?") Modeling is important.
8. In using language-experience stories with children (stories that a child dictates for a teacher to print, perhaps below a painting or after a group experience) *always print exactly what the child says*. If the child says, "I ain't gonna get no dog."—print that! Often a teacher has "corrected" to "I'm not going to have a dog" only to find the child learning that "ain't" is spelled "not."
9. Our goal is to provide the child with alternate speech patterns from which he can gradually learn to choose according to the situation, not to eradicate or change her native dialect.
10. Learn as much as you can about the children's dialect, its jokes, stories, and idioms. Let the children and parents see you as a learner.

1985). This program is designed specifically for Limited English Proficiency (LEP) children who have acquired some skills in English but are still struggling with the academic language proficiency needed to master subject matter in English. The program teaches social studies in a "sheltered English" context in which multilanguage textbooks, artifacts, ethnic recordings, oral history records, and other "linguistic sup-

INSET 8.5   Bilingual Children

Children who enter a preschool program speaking only limited English or another language will experience severe difficulties. In the first place, the children bring experiences that are often culturally different from those of the teacher and the other children; their set of references is not the same. Second, the children are unable to talk with the teacher and understand instructions. As a result, they are unable to participate fully in activities that lead to self-concept building and other aspects of development.

Bilingual/bicultural children may find that some of their behavior patterns are ignored or discouraged in the preschool. Often teachers are unaware of the different socialization patterns among cultures, and they may expect or attempt to encourage behaviors unfamiliar to the children, leading students to feel frustrated or rejected.

Successful programs should:

1. *Provide an environment* that reflects the language and culture of the children they serve. This requires that staff members and program resources be representative of the group's racial and cultural mixture.
2. *Build on the strengths* that bilingual/bicultural children bring to a new learning situation. The children have a language, and with it a rich cultural background with values and expectations—a strong base for learning.
3. *Continue the development of the first language* and facilitate the acquisition of a second. Children should be made to feel that the language or dialect they use is both acceptable and welcome—the fact that they are *communicating* is most important. Show children the pleasure and necessity of communication in *both* languages.
4. *Be aware of the child's home values* and expectations; one way of acquiring this information is to involve parents in various aspects of the program.
5. *Integrate both languages* into all areas of the curriculum in an atmosphere of respect and appreciation for cultural diversity. If both languages are part of the regular classroom environment, children will help each other learn both languages. All children will benefit from understanding that there are many ways of speaking and different ways of behaving.

Researchers have found that bilingual children use language more precisely and accurately than nonbilingual children. Knowing two or more words for a given reality enables bilingual children to think more easily in the abstract. Learning a native language does not keep children from learning in a second

Council for Interracial Books for Children, 1983.

language. Research shows that children taught to read in their native language do as well reading in the majority culture language as children whose only instruction is in the majority culture language.

ports" are used to assist the transition between bilingual and English academic programs such as later elementary school and high school. This transition approach could well prove an effective model not only for bilingual programs but for the many multilingual classes where there is more than one alternate language spoken (a very common condition found in North Eastern areas of the United States) or where there is less than the required 50 percent of second language children to form a bilingual class.

Multilingual classrooms must often turn to other techniques since there are few teachers who can speak several languages. Many classrooms of young children often have just one or two children who speak another language or several children who speak different languages and know little or no English. These children present a unique problem for the teacher and one that cannot be ignored. One approach to this problem is the use of peer tutors. Frequently, there are children in the classroom or center who speak sufficient English, as well as the primary language of another student, to serve as interpreter and tutor. Children usually feel comfortable with another child and will speak more freely with her than with adults. The tutor also gains in his own feelings of confidence and self-esteem at this task. If a child is not available in the school, it is sometimes possible to "borrow" an older child from the elementary or secondary school, who can come several times a week to help teach the new child some basic English vocabulary and assist with language-experience projects.

Another possibility is to find a parent or community person who speaks both the child's primary language and English, who will tutor the child and make audio tapes of alphabet books and other basic vocabulary with pictures. Photographs of classroom objects and routines are another helpful set of materials to use with a tape. The tape with words and phrases spoken in each language, first in one language and then the other (a random pattern in switching from English to the second language and back actually works best) is an excellent teaching tool. It can be used with headsets by one or several children during class time or can be shared with a small group or the whole class for a short group lesson. It also helps the teacher learn some key vocabulary and can be kept as a resource to be used for other students. A library of

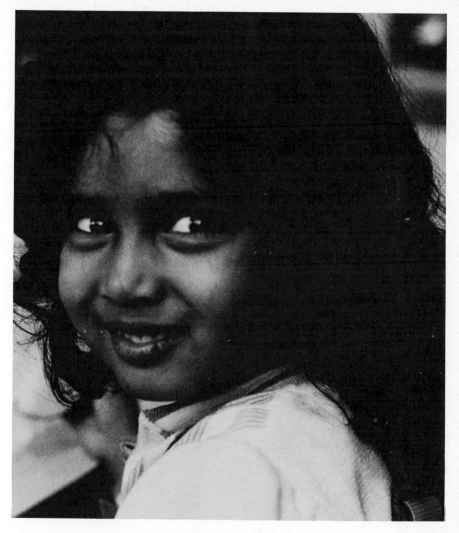

Childhood is a time for getting to know others.

these tapes can be shared throughout the school with children of different language groups.

The ideas and concepts discussed in this section are offered to help develop an awareness of the complexity and importance of multicultural education for all children in all classrooms. The number of techniques one uses will vary with the diversity of the class, but even in monolingual or monocultural classes exposure to the multiplicity and richness of our culturally pluralistic society should be a basic goal of education.

SUMMARY

We have attempted to highlight some of the history in this country that focuses attention on human rights and the practices of discrimination and racism. We follow a dual legacy which must be addressed again and again. The period from 1954 to 1975 saw enormous strides in the area of civil liberties and the awareness of the United States as a culturally pluralistic country. Multicultural and bilingual/bicultural education received much publicity and made some gains. However, teacher education has not always kept pace with the appropriate training needed for multicultural education and we are now in a period of reduced federal support for all human service programs. Therefore, it becomes the task of the local institutions and the individual teacher to learn about the detrimental effects of racism, sexism, and ageism and the techniques for countering such devastating prejudices. The multicultural classroom exists only when the individual teacher is convinced and dedicated to its implementation.

We end this chapter with a quote from Sullivan (1974):

> The challenges to educate minority youth are many but they must be accepted. There is no such thing as a neutral education process. Education either functions as an instrument which is used to facilitate the integration of the younger generation into the logic of the present system and bring about conformity to it or it becomes "the practice of freedom," the means by which men and women deal critically and creatively with reality and discover how to participate in the transformation of their world. In essence, we need teachers who are competent—confident in their ability to deliver quality education experiences in a pluralistic cultural milieu. We are asking for teachers with faith in what human beings can become, with a driving ethical imperative which requires them to accept responsibility for helping students achieve everything that is possible, and with the finest technical preparation for carrying out this obligation (p.69).

Explorations

Do one or two explorations in each category to extend and enrich your understanding of this chapter.

PERSONAL EXPLORATIONS

These exercises are designed to help you look at your own life—attitudes, experiences, dreams, myths, and realities.

1. Think about your first encounter with an ethnically different child. Try to remember what you felt and thought. What was the outcome of your meeting? Write a brief description of this experience.
2. Make a list of your ten best friends. Then write next to each what you know about their ethnic background, cultural traditions, and unique family patterns. How homogeneous or heterogeneous a group do you see? Is this pattern typical of the area in which you live? How will this pattern contribute, either positively or negatively, to being a teacher of multicultural education?

INTELLECTUAL EXPLORATIONS

These exercises are designed to increase your depth of knowledge in some of the areas discussed in this chapter.

1. Pick one of the civil rights gains listed in Table 8.1 and go to the library and do some research to learn more about it. What were the main issues being decided? Why were they so important? Write a synopsis of your findings and bring it to class. (If everyone takes different items, the synopses can be shared and discussed together.)
2. Check out a beginning text in a language you do not know. Spend some time studying the sound system and some beginning vocabulary. Put together several simple sentences and try to learn to say them. Bring the sentences to class and be ready to discuss this new language.
3. Find two or more articles in educational magazines (preferably those for young children) that discuss multicultural issues. List the main points from each and their full reference and bring it to class for discussion.

FIELD EXPLORATIONS

These exercises are designed to take you out into the world to find real examples that will illustrate and elucidate the material in this chapter.

1. Attend a film that is in a foreign language you do not know (and preferably without subtitles). After the show try to write a synopsis of the plot and what the experience was like for you.

2. If there is a day care program or Headstart class in your area with other ethnic groups besides your own, make a visit and observe the children and teachers. Using Table 8.2, see how many of the dozen items are evident in this environment. Write down your observations.
3. Attend a cultural event such as a religious ceremony, a holiday, a wedding, a folk dance festival, or some other practice of an ethnically different group. Observe the similarities and differences between this group and your own. Write a paragraph detailing what you learned from this experience.

References

AACTE Commission on Multicultural Education. "No one model American." *Journal of Teacher Education*, 1973, 264–65.

Arenas, S. "Bilingual/Bicultural programs for preschool children." *Children Today*, 1978, 7, 2–6.

Brown v. Board of Education of Topeka, Shawnee County, Kansas et al., 347 U.S./483 (1954).

Dewey, J. "Nationalizing education." *Addresses and Proceedings of the National Education Association*, 1916, 54: 84–85.

Dillingham Report, U.S. Senate, 61st Congress, 3rd session, Senate Document #747, Abstracts of the reports of the Immigration Commission, II, Washington, D.C.: Government Printing Office, 1911.

Friere, P. *Pedagogy of the oppressed.* New York: Herder and Herder, 1970.

Hale, J. E. *Black children: Their roots, culture and learning styles.* Salt Lake City, Utah: Brigham Young University Press, 1982.

Hall, N. (Ed.). "Limited English children can be taught in English." *UCLA Education*, 1985, 3, 1: 8–9.

Hunter, W. A. (Ed.). *Multicultural education through competency-based teacher education.* Washington, D.C.: American Association of Colleges for Teacher Education, 1974.

Interracial Books for Children. "Racism: Related problems, research and strategies." *Bulletin*, 1983, 13: 8–14.

Kallen, H. M. *Culture and democracy in the United States.* New York: Boni and Liveright, 1924.

Katz, J. *White awareness: Handbook for anti-racism training.* Norman, Okla.: University of Oklahoma Press, 1978.

Kopan, A. T. "Melting pot: Myth or reality." In E. G. Epps (Ed.), *Cultural pluralism.* Berkeley, Cal.: McCutchan, 1974.

Lau v. Nichols 414 U.S./563 (1974).

Miel, A. *The shortchanged children of suburbia.* New York: The Insitute of Human Relations Press, 1976.

Miller, D. K. "Socioeconomic class and teacher bias." *Psychological Reports*, 1968, 23: 806.

Rae, G. and Potter, T. C. *Informal reading diagnosis: A practical guide for the classroom teacher*, Second Ed. Englewood Cliffs, N.J.: Prentice-Hall, 1981.

Sullivan, A. R. "Cultural competence and confidence: A quest for effective teaching in a pluralistic society." In W. A. Hunter (Ed.), *Multicultural education through competency-based teacher education*. Washington, D.C.: American Association of Colleges for Teacher Education, 1974.

Wharton, L. F. *Black American children's singing games*. Baltimore: The University Press, 1980.

Zangwill, I. *The melting pot*. New York: Macmillan, 1909.

Chapter 9

INFANT/TODDLER ENVIRONMENTS

Objectives

After reading this chapter the student should be able to:

1. Discuss, with illustrations, the social, emotional, physical, sensory, and language development of early, middle, and late infancy and toddlerhood.
2. List the characteristics of competent infant caregivers.
3. Describe the differences and similarities between family day care and center-based day care.
4. Discuss the difference between developmental learning and contexual learning and give examples appropriate for infants and toddlers.
5. Describe several appropriate interest centers for infants and toddlers, which could be included in any program.
6. List characteristics of appropriate toys and give examples of toys for each period of infancy and for toddlers.
7. Compare and contrast two programs developed for infants and toddlers.

The human infant is a remarkable organism. As we have seen earlier (Chapter 4), the child from birth onward is both a sensitive and competent learner. As research studies have demonstrated, babies have the ability to experience and know their world through acute perceptual awareness, as well as active discrimination of sensory experiences using all five senses. Moreover, newborn infants also appear capable of integrating sensations using several senses simultaneously, thereby enabling them to form primitive images of persons, objects, and settings. These capabilities, evident at birth, become increasingly more complex and sophisticated over time. In this chapter we will explore the role of early environments and caregivers in fostering the growth and development of infants and toddlers.

INFANCY AND TODDLERHOOD

Infancy refers to the first 18 months of life. Yet, infancy does not form a homogeneous phase of development. Rather, it is marked by major developmental changes, as well as rapid alterations of function. As such infancy is usually divided into several chronological phases including early infancy (2 to 6 months of age), middle infancy (6 to 12 months), and late infancy (12 to 18 months).

Toddlerhood is generally viewed as a continuation of infancy, referring to the period of life between 18 months and two and a half years to three years of age.

TABLE 9.1.   Characteristics of Early, Middle, and Late Infancy

Social Development

  Early infancy

   The baby demonstrates emerging attachment behaviors and shows evidence of trust in others. Distress is alleviated by prompt adult attention. The infant shows positive reactions to adult attention including gazing, smiling, and wiggling her arms and legs. The infant likes face-to-face interactions including talking, singing, and adult smiling. Activities that include rocking and playing with her body usually promote active involvement. The infant seeks adult proximity and may enjoy watching children.

  Middle infancy

   The baby clearly separates caregivers from others. He will respond accordingly to facial and verbal expressions of disapproval, as well as approval. The child actively engages in greeting responses, as well as departure reactions. Enjoyable games include pattycake and peek-a-boo, as well as observation and imitation of others engaged in simple imitative behaviors (for example, waving bye-bye). There is active interest in other children, usually centered on toys or commonly desired objects.

  Late infancy

   Beginnings of autonomy can be seen in baby's behavior. The child wishes to explore his environment but with frequent returns to primary caregiver. He begins to assert himself in interactions with others but is still easily redirected. Active exploration and testing of limits is present. In addition, the child will engage in helping under supervision. Imitation of adults is prominent both in the adult's presence and absence. Preferred play and games include vocalizing to adults and pointing as substitute for words and actions. Also he will roll ball to adults, hand objects to adults; much solitary play with stacking, dropping, and nesting.

Physical Development

  Early infancy

   The infant will lift and turn his head to look at bright objects. Kicking, swiping, reaching, and rolling over are followed by holding and mouthing rattles, fingering toys, and pulling the body a few inches along a mat. Babies enjoy brief periods of sitting up with pillows for support and lap sitting while touching and picking up toys. Also, they enjoy being placed and picked up, which create "interesting sights," form visual, tactile, and kinesthetic variations in stimulation. Baths and floor play provide enjoyable exercises.

  Middle infancy

   During this period the baby will play with a wide assortment of objects including rattles, balls, soft animals, wooden or plastic teether, stack toys, take-aparts, and objects in containers. The baby likes to sit, crawl, and stand in an adult's lap or on the floor. Explorations involving standing, walking, and crawling begin in this period. There is greater activity, in general, and considerable fussing (usually during teething) and clutter. Opportunities for safe exploration are mandatory.

TABLE 9.1.   Characteristics of Early, Middle, and Late Infancy
(*Continued*)

Physical Development (cont.)

Late infancy

Greater activity and movement are characteristic. However, behavior is "organized." The child likes to sort objects, stack toys, arrange simple puzzles and boxes. Feeding of self is characteristic and engaged in with vigor and zest. Climbing, running, and pushing skills are most evident. Walks, stair climbing, and simple wheeled and push toys are enjoyed. Adult supervision of activities to insure health and safety is required.

Sensory Development

Early infancy

The infant reacts to motion and changes in lighting and is sensitive to temperature, olfatory (smell), and gustatory (taste) stimuli. The mouth is the most prominent organ for exploration. However, she also searches for sounds and follows objects as they appear and disappear. The baby enjoys music, mobiles, and rattles. Washing, snuggling, rocking, and diapering are stimulating.

Middle infancy

Busy-boxes stimulate sound and movement explorations. The baby will actively search for hidden and dropped toys. Touching and handling of objects become prominent in addition to continued mouthing of objects. Interest in details complements global explorations of toys and objects. Curiosity appears to dominate activity.

Late infancy

The baby shows continued interest in details with prominent interest in small objects. She uses simple shape-sorters, cups, and rings. Sand and water experiences provide active exploratory opportunities. Outings that allow for new sights and sounds are welcomed. Touching and mixing activities, including water painting and play dough, are enjoyed. She begins to scribble with a large crayon or pencil.

Emotional Development

Early infancy

Active and continuous stimulation involving others is sought. Baby likes to be touched, held close, rocked, and spoken to. He appears alert and highly responsive to being picked up and engaged. He enjoys play with adults and smiles in response to familiar figures.

Middle infancy

Schedules and routines, such as set eating and sleeping periods, appear to be preferred. Preference in toys and familiar adults also appears prominent. Recognition of facial features and emotional expressions in others is evident.

Late infancy

Both changing moods and strong preferences dominate emotional status. Sudden changes, particularly displays of anger, become evident. In addition, toys and food preferences are highly prominent. Structure and patient support from adults is required.

TABLE 9.1. **Characteristics of Early, Middle, and Late Infancy**
(*Continued*)

Language Development

Early infancy

The baby utters cries and soft sounds and vocalizes, babbles, coos, and gurgles. She may imitate mouth movements. She listens to voices and music and may repeat sounds and react to her own name. She is interested in the adult's use of sound and attends to and enjoys music and sound from a variety of sources.

Middle infancy

Vocalization becomes rhythmic and patterned. Sounds elicit attention. Imitation of animal sounds occurs. Word forms for familiar objects (for example, food and drink), events (sleep) and persons (Mama, Dah) appear. He responds to simple, clearly articulated and well-spaced adult conversation and language usage. Active vocabulary building becomes evident, particularly during the later phases of this period and shortly thereafter.

Late infancy

The infant begins to echo and repeat words spoken by others. Two-word phrases appear and labeling, especially, of body parts, objects, and pictures becomes prominent. There is intense interest in picture books and naming. Expressive vocabulary dramatically increases and active efforts at sentence construction become evident toward the end of this period.

Adapted from: Infant and Toddler Programs: A Guide to Very Early Childhood Education, by C. Z. Cataldo, Addison-Wesley, Reading, MA, 1983. Used by permission.

PROGRAMS

Early infant, extra-familial care arrangements are usually initiated by families sometime between the infant's third and sixth month of life. However, infants may be placed in the care of others, depending upon family needs, available caregivers, and state regulatory requirements occasionally at birth, or shortly thereafter. In the past infants were usually cared for by members of the extended family; however, present trends in the United States indicate greater use and earlier placement of children in alternative facilities and with extra-familial caregivers (Clarke-Stewart and Fein, 1983).

Currently this kind of extra-familial placement is most often done through small independent, entrepreneurial providers. These home caregivers, referred to as family day care (FDC) providers, offer flexible baby sitting and other child care arrangements as proprietary "centers" which operate from a private residence (a day care home or the child's own home) and usually include up to five other preschool or after school-aged children under the care of one provider. Family day care

TABLE 9.2.   Characteristics of Toddlerhood

Social Development

Greater differentiation of behavior becomes apparent; the child may be cooperative, resistant, assertive, and loving in turn. Exploration and sociability increase. Play becomes a dominant feature of activities. Decision making, sharing, and waiting in turn, taking turns, chasing, and copying appear in games and other forms of interaction. Separation from parents with increased interest in peers and other children is most evident. Special care needed to effectively manage small group situations; they are not yet able to particpate in group oriented play.

Physical Development

There is greater refinement of motor skills and competencies. The toddler can run, climb, and steer sit-on toys and cars. He enjoys building with blocks and playing with cars. Sand, water, and play-dough activities can be actively enjoyed. He can undress himself with some assistance. Independence in feeding is evident and toileting skills are increasing. Swings, climbers, and games with balls are among preferred activities. The toddler likes walks, drawing, painting, pasting, and cooking.

Sensory Development

Differentiation of objects, interest in details, and assemblages of things dominate his interest. The toddler enjoys collecting rocks, shells, cars, and leaves. Seriated toys are used, as well as objects that can be taken apart and reassembled, though too many pieces ensures frustration. Animals are distinguished from one another, as are shapes and sounds. The toddler, however, cannot perceive complex differences in numbers, alphabet letters, and games requiring memory or rules.

Emotional Development

The toddler demonstrates considerable social awareness and responsiveness; she seeks social praise and the pleasure of others. However, the toddler is also emerging as an individual, independent person. At this stage the child shows considerable pride and confidence in herself. Self-control is emerging and pride in bodily control is evident. Cooperation in group play is lacking, and the toddler shows considerable difficulty in remembering rules.

Language Development

Considerable language growth may be observed. The toddler is now both able to comprehend others, as well as articulate his own needs. The child can communicate in words and phrases and use concepts with greater consistency and clarity. Interest in songs and records is appreciable, and listening to stories is well established. Limitations in language include limited abstract ability and reasoning, grammatical errors, and egocentricism.

Adapted from: Infant and Toddler Programs: A Guide to Very Early Childhood Education by C. Z. Cataldo, Addison-Wesley, Reading, MA, 1983. Used by permission.

arrangements are characterized by flexibility in placements, negotiated hours, varying availability of space, informality in program offerings, and ready response to differing family needs.

A second, and increasingly prominent form of child care arrangement in the United States, is the center-based (CB) facility. Center-based programs usually operate out of larger facilities, particularly for three-

TABLE 9.3. Persons, Settings, and Groups Served by Day Care

Sponsor	*Funding Source*
Legislature	Government
Entrepreneur	Private enterprise
Parents	Nonprofit organization
Community group	(a) Church
Social service agency	(b) Hospital
Researcher	(c) College
Company	(d) Union
Scale	*Accountability*
National	Individual parents
Multiple	Licensers
Single	Sponsors
	Researchers
Director	*Staff Roles*
Clinician	Teacher
Adminstrator	Social worker
Educator	Researcher
Social worker	Caregiver
Researcher	Therapist
Caregiver	Nutritionist
	Nurse
	Assistant teacher
	Aide
	Custodian
Participants	*Services Offered*
Children	Health
Clients	Nutrition
Patients	Social work
Consumers	Babysitting
Students	Education
Constituents	Training
Parents	Facilitate development
	Diagnosis

Adapted from: "Early Childhood Programs," by A. Clarke-Stewart and G. G. Fein, in P. H. Mussen (Ed.), *Handbook of Child Psychology*, Fourth ed. (Vol. 2), John Wiley & Sons, New York, 1983. Used by permission.

to five-year-old preschoolers, some of which are franchised as private early childhood centers (for example, Kindercare, La Petite Academy), while others are publicly sponsored by colleges or universities or governmental agencies. Another trend is company day care, which serves the employee needs of large corporations or hospitals. While center-based child care facilities operate to accommodate the needs of families through sponsoring group-based programs for children, usually of preschool age, many centers have modified their facilities and have initiated programs designed to meet the growing needs for infant-based care arrangements. Table 9.3 suggests some of the diversity in these programs in organizational character, sponsorship, clientele served, and other dimensions of interest.

Although programs vary in form and content, Clarke-Stewart and Fein (1983) note that:

> Publicly funded centers have been observed to have, on the average, better adult-child ratios (1:6 vs. 1:8), more teachers with training in child development (66 percent versus 44 percent), teachers who have been in the center longer (three versus two years), more parent involvement, higher quality overall, and more comprehensive services. Similarly, licensed day care home providers are more likely than unlicensed individuals to talk, help, teach, and play with the children, to provide a stimulating physical environment, including music, dancing, books, and educational TV, and serve nutritious food (p.923).

CAREGIVING AND CAREGIVERS

Children spend time with other people and it is through these shared interactions that they thrive and grow. However, optimum development is not a spontaneous act, but rather a nurtured and guided experience. As Clarke-Stewart (1982) observes, "The need for responsiveness starts early in the infant's life. It is important for the baby to learn that the world is in many ways a predictable place and that he can anticipate and to some extent control the people and things in it" (p.99).

Whether infants acquire a sense of trust and a sense of control of their world is dependent on their adult caregivers.

Parents

The foremost vehicle of early infant learning occurs through the intense, personal relationship that infants share with their most significant others, usually their parents. As Clarke-Stewart (1982) notes regarding the importance of this relationship in providing a foundation for later development, "it is essential that parents interact with the infant not only frequently but in response to the specific signals and demands that the baby makes" (p.99).

Frequency of interaction, as we observe, is coupled with the idea of *quality of interaction*, which suggests that a parent's presence also must serve a specific, especially significant function. For the very young, the notion of quality of interaction means that, "The timing and content of the interaction should not be at the parent's whim, but should mesh with the infant's needs, desires, interest, and schedule" (p.99).

Effective caregiving involves being physically present and personally involved and responsive to the infant's signals. In practical terms, such caregiving requires responding to the infant when she cries, smiling when she smiles, helping her reach a toy beyond her grasp, and encouraging her to explore new situations and people. As women and couples with children have increasingly sought employment outside the home, they have had to rely on others in the sharing of custodial responsibility. A majority of these parents have asked in earnest, "Can surrogate parenting offer good care to my child?" and "How will surrogate parents affect my child's continuing relationship with me?"

Too Many Caregivers

The issue of how surrogate parenting affects young children, particularly their continuing affiliation with parents, cannot be answered simply. Yet there is good support for some reasonable answers to this question. First, as suggested earlier (see Chapter 6), young children form attachment bonds with primary caregivers over time, namely, the first year of life, and, consequently, affiliative bonding, as a developmental process, should not be treated as a temporary or quickly terminated attachment. Second, the attachment bond that the young child develops as an outcome of shared interactions is less dependent on physical caretaking or feeding than on playful engagements. This playful interaction is possible for all parents, even those whose schedules only allow for limited interactions with their children. Third, attachment does not appear to be founded upon exclusive interactions with a single caregiver. In fact, young infants form attachments to their fathers (and siblings) even though many fathers spend limited time with their very young children. Finally, as Clarke-Stewart and Fein (1983) observe, throughout the world it is the rule, rather than the exception, for children in all communities to be cared for by more than one caregiver and to form more than one attachment. Interestingly, referring to literature cited in their comprehensive review of 186 nonindustrialized societies, they found only 5 where the child's biological mother was also its "almost exclusive" caregiver. In industrialized countries too, this pattern of extended caregiving prevails. As these authors note, although it is true that having "too many" caregivers is a poor practice, to avoid having "too many" does not imply there should only be one.

Caregivers

Since the single most critical factor in the infant's and toddler's environment is his caregiver, we need to examine, in some detail, how caregivers affect the very young. In part, this exploration is multidimensional since caregiving is a dynamic and changing process, being highly dependent upon *meeting children's existing and emerging needs.* As Honig (1985) observes,

> Babies need a special person to tune in to their way of signaling distress— the vague, not too specialized fussiness that communicates need. The diagnostic skills of a quality infant caregiver must be very well-honed: first, to enhance accurate, perceptive interpretations of infant needs; and next, to provide prompt, tender, responsive care. Thus, the first critical issue for high quality infant/toddler care is the choice of a caregiver (p.40).

A variety of models have been proposed in viewing the tasks of early caregivers (Jacobson, 1978; Clarke-Stewart, 1982; Honig, 1981, 1983; 1985; Cataldo, 1983; Jorn, Persky and Huntington, 1984; Leavitt and Eheart, 1985). One representative model is reproduced in Table 9.4.

Who shall serve the infants we care for? As suggested in Table 9.4, the competent infant-toddler caregiver combines a variety of *personal attributes* with positive *attitudes* and *values* in a manner leading to predictable adult-infant *behavioral transactions.*

Personal Attributes

Not all people choose to interact with the very young. Some are too fearful, others are reticent, while others find infants too unpredictable or too messy or, simply, too much work. As Jacobson (1978) indicates, working with very young children demands that the adults who serve them possess personality characteristics that will sustain their efforts in meeting the necessary and changing needs of energetic infants, as well as enable the adult to enjoy the children they serve. Certainly, flexibility, patience, sensitivity, a positive self image, a focused orientation on caring for others, and a capacity for humor are necessary ingredients for effective caregiving.

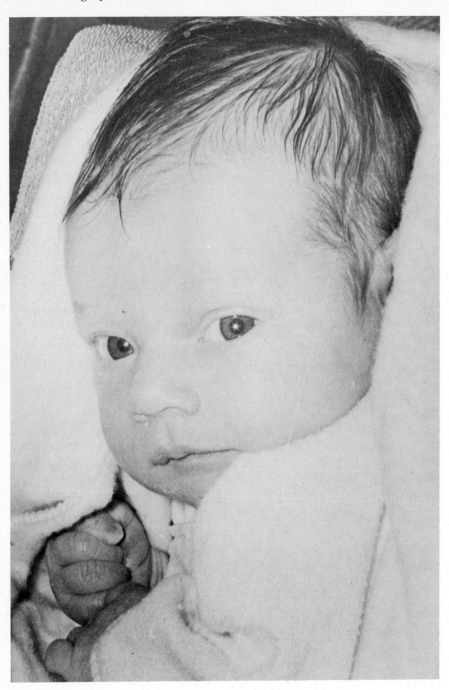

Infants need sensitive and attentive caregivers.

TABLE 9.4.   Characteristics of Competent Infant Caregivers

Desired Caregiver Characteristics	Cues to Desirable Caregiver Characteristics
I. Personality Factors	
A. Child-centered	1. Attentive and loving to infants
	2. Meets infants' needs before own
B. Self-confident	1. Relaxed and anxiety free
	2. Skilled in physical care of infants
	3. Individualistic caregiving style
C. Flexible	1. Uses different styles of caregiving to meet individual needs of infants
	2. Spontaneous and open behavior
	3. Permits increasing freedom of infant as development
D. Sensitive	1. Understands infants' cues readily
	2. Shows empathy for infants
	3. Acts purposefully in interactions with infants
II. Attitudes and Values	
A. Displays positive outlook on life	1. Expresses positive affect
	2. No evidence of anger, unhappiness, or depression
B. Enjoys infants	1. Affectionate to infants
	2. Shows obvious pleasure in involvement with infants
C. Values infants more than possessions or immaculate appearance	1. Dresses practically and appropriately
	2. Places items not for infants' use out of reach
	3. Reacts to infant destruction or messiness with equanimity
	4. Takes risks with property in order to enhance infant development
III. Behavior	
A. Interacts appropriately with infants	1. Frequent interactions with infants
	2. Balances interaction with leaving infants alone
	3. Optimum amounts of touching
	4. Responds consistently and without delay to infants, is always accessible
	5. Speaks in positive tone of voice
	6. Shows clearly that infants are loved and accepted

TABLE 9.4.   Characteristics of Competent Infant Caregivers (*Continued*)

III. Behavior (cont.)
  B. Facilitates development

1. Does not punish infants
2. Plays with infants
3. Provides stimulation with toys and objects
4. Permits freedom to explore, including floor freedom
5. Cooperates with infant-initiated activities and explorations
6. Provides activities that stimulate achievement or goal orientation
7. Acts purposefully in an educational role to teach and facilitate learning and development

From: Arminta Lee Jacobson, "Infant Day Care: Toward a More Human Environment," *Young Children 33*, no. 56 (July 1978): 20. Copyright 1978, National Association for the Education of Young Children, 1834 Connecticut Ave., N.W., Washington, D.C. 20009. Reprinted by permission.

Attitudes and Values

Clearly, the attitudes and values that we possess also influence our work with the very young. Here, interest in and attraction to infants, coupled with a capacity to enjoy and receive satisfaction through infant-caregiver interactions, are most important. Adults who choose to work with infants are able to show warmth and affection, to treat infants gently, rather than punitively, and are capable of accepting and respecting infants.

Behaviorial Transactions

Behaviorally, the adult who works with infants and toddlers must be able to translate his personal attributes and professed beliefs into concerted effort. The adult caregiver should enjoy interacting with infants and have a positive interest in infant/toddler learning. He needs to understand the importance and variety of learning to be accomplished by the infant or toddler, as well as his role in encouraging the child's learning. Here, clearly, is the heart of the matter. As Jorn, Persky, and Huntington (1984) note, the teacher of the very young must,

> show initiative and resourcefulness in working with the children and in adapting the program to meet their individual needs and preference. All activities must be carried out in a way that suits the babies and makes them interested in and curious about the world rather than bored by it (p.71).

INSET 9.1   Up Front with . . . Bob Mason

Jean Hartmann

Bob Mason loves children. You can see it in his face. Sitting in his East Side home with four-month-old Joel in his arms and the other babies asleep upstairs, he exudes serenity. "I am content," he says. "I enjoy what I am doing."

He is a big man, with clear blue eyes and a light brown beard. He wears black suspenders with the jeans and flannel shirts he favors; he fits the image of a truck driver, which in fact he used to be, more than a day care father.

Every day at three o'clock the babies go home. That's when Bob's wife, Jean, who teaches science at Martin Luther King School, and the couple's three children get home from school. Then Bob goes out and runs five or six miles along Blackstone Boulevard. It's his way of releasing tension and getting frustrations out, he says. By then, he admits with a chuckle, "I need it."

Seven years ago, Bob was working with kids at the Fox Point Boys' Club. He played basketball with them, supervised dances, operated the summer camp—in short, spent his days with them. His title was social recreation director. His own daughter was little then, and he took care of her in the mornings until he went to work at noon; she was in day care in the afternoons. But neither Bob nor Jean was particularly satisfied with the child care options available.

Then the director of the Boys' Club resigned, and Bob was asked to step in. He refused. "I want to work directly with kids," he says. "I don't want to be an administrator."

He decided to take a year off and start the process of getting a license to operate a day care center in his home.

His first two clients were his daughter and a neighbor's baby, and he's been going strong ever since. Bob has never advertised, relying on word of mouth alone for parents to find him. And they do.

A native of Cumberland [Rhode Island], Bob was an indifferent student in high school, primarily interested in sports. After graduation, uncertain about what he wanted to do with his life, he joined the Navy.

Near the end of his stint in the mid-sixties, Bob was stationed at Quonset Point. His brother, an Episcopal minister, was assigned to Settlement House, a South Providence community service house sponsored by the diocese. One weekend his brother invited Bob to come and meet the kids he worked with. That same weekend he brought Bob with him on a hospital visit and introduced him to a child dying of cancer. This was a turning point in Bob's life. He says he began to realize how sheltered his life had been and to feel a need to involve himself in community service. He began to spend every weekend at Settlement House, working with the kids and getting to know the families.

Jean was working at Settlement House on a college work-study program when they met. Drawn together by their love of children and commitment to serving the community, they were married 17 years ago. They tried unsuccessfully to have children, so they adopted three: Brooke, 12; Cesar, 9; and Gus, 6.

The Providence Sunday Journal, July 7, 1985. Reprinted by permission.

"Do you believe it?" he said. "They kept asking us, 'What kind of baby do you want?'"

"We want a baby," Bob told the adoption agency people. "We just want a healthy baby."

The couple insisted the baby's race was not important. Their three children are black.

Bob eventually got a bachelor's degree in business management from Bryant College, an unlikely course of study for him and one he admits he never really enjoyed. But he needed to prove to himself he could earn a college diploma, although he has never worked in a business-related field. It was his work with children at Settlement House that led in time to his job at the Boy's Club.

His license allows him to take up to six children at a time. He now insists in operating only from seven A.M. to three P.M. so he can spend more time with his family. When he has free time, after helping his own kids with their homework and attending to other family responsibilities, he runs or works out at a health club. He is also a photography buff.

But mostly he likes being with kids. "For the time the kid is here," he says, "he's my child. I spend a lot of time just playing with the kids. I won't let them just sit. I get down on the floor with them—kids need a lot of physical contact."

What happens when they all start crying at once?

"They learn patience."

The best part of the job is, "I can still play with little ones; I still have babies. But then," he adds with a twinkle in his eyes, "they go home."

Sitting on the floor of his living room, changing Joel's diaper, Bob looks up, grins and says, "Now this is the great part of the job."

He says that being a day care father has led him to greater appreciation of the difficulties women who are housewives and child-rearers encounter.

"Most guys," he says, "have no idea. . . . "

ACTIVITIES AND INTERACTIONS

The activities, namely, experiential and developmental learning opportunities, that adults provide for infants and toddlers comprise the second most important component of the infant/toddler environment. However, we need insert, in this context, that activities, as defined by planned program offerings are not the important events in the child's life. Rather, all interactions in infant/toddler programs involve the caregiver in close and continuous interactions with the child.

The significance of our clarification becomes most evident as we consider several expectations associated with infant/toddler programming. Most often these include: (1) recognition of the importance of personalized interactions; (2) the creation of developmental learning opportunities; (3) focus on the individual needs of each child; and (4) the necessity for providing safe spaces and activities for the very young. These factors surface as core elements around which infant/toddler programs are built.

Programs designed for the very young increasingly have come to recognize that *developmental learning*, as opposed to *contextual* (namely, school-based instructional) *learning*, is a basic foundation. Developmental learning is not formally taught but rather emerges from the needs and growing competency of the infant. Whereas later learning may be directly ordered and taught (arithmetic reasoning or phonetic recognition) or be designed to achieve correlated goals (being able to perform mathematical operations or to sound out words in order to read), developmental learning is less specific and extends throughout all experiential contexts. Developmental learning serves to accomplish certain functions, some of which are preparatory to later learnings—for example, stimulating interest; facilitating exploration; encouraging autonomy. This latter emphasis leads to the implementation of infant/toddler activities that are: (1) multiple in function and diversity, rather than those which suggest or lead to specific or singular outcomes (sand play with digging and pouring accessories rather than instructions on making a sand castle); (2) that stimulate multiple, rather than singular explorations (a variety of blocks to stack, push, build, and pretend with); and (3) that are, of necessity, integrated within a specific temporal and situational setting (banging a drum while a marching record plays). This contemporary perspective enhances *here and now* learning rather than distant applications.

Developmental learning opportunities during the first three years of life must be appropriate to the chronological ages of the children and appeal to the cognitive mechanisms that characterize their learning. Curricula for infants must consider the characteristics of each period of infancy and toddlerhood as outlined in Tables 9.1 and Table 9.2.

Naturally, programs need to recognize that the mental processes responsible for knowing and learning during the first three years of life undergo enormous changes. From a Piagetian perspective, children progress through differing cognitive phases that enable them to extend their understanding of the world and to employ different mechanisms for processing such learning. During the first two years of life Piaget, describes six different phases of sensorimotor learning, each of which enables newer learning opportunities through the child's emerging and reconstructed cognitive capacities.

An important aspect of caregiving in this period is the awareness of the difference between infants' and toddlers' themselves. While programs serving infants and toddlers may be housed in the same setting, and are often undifferentiated from one another they, in fact, serve two separate and distinct populations. Erickson's differentiation of pre-

INSET 9.2   How Object Play Begins

A composite picture of the changes that take place in a child's encounters with objects over the first three years of life can be drawn from the recent work of several psychologists. Although the procedures differed among the studies (for example, a child observed at home or a child seen in laboratory; limited sets of objects presented or a large group of objects presented), the trends toward more discriminating treatment of objects and greater complexity of object combinations are clear. In the following account, the ages are only approximate—individual children vary, some exhibiting a given type of behavior a bit earlier, some a bit later.

Several miniature objects—a cup, saucer, spoon, hairbrush, truck, trailer, doll—are placed before a child on a table. What is he likely to do? Following, in part, the work of Marianne Lowe, we can predict that:

At *nine months*, the child will grasp a nearer, brighter object and bring it to his mouth, grasp another and do the same. After mouthing the object, he might well wave it or bang it on the table, then inspect it, turn it around, and bang it again or return it to his mouth. He uses only a few action patterns.

At *twelve months*, the child is likely to investigate (look at, turn, finger) each object *before* doing anything else with it. He might then put the spoon in his mouth once or twice, place it in the cup, and perhaps place the cup on the saucer, but other objects are still treated at random (mouthed, banged, waved).

At *fifteen months*, inspecting and investigating clearly precede other behavior. More and more consistently objects are accorded appropriate or conventional uses. The child will place the cup on the saucer and sip from it, and the spoon will be used more deliberately as if he were feeding himself. He will pick up the brush and run it over his hair; next he may push the truck back and forth. He may make the doll stand up.

At *twenty-one months*, the child will search for an object to "go with" other things. After putting the cup on the saucer, he will look for the spoon, find it, stir the imaginary drink and then drink it. He will then give the doll a drink from the cup or perhaps offer the observer a drink. He might brush his hair very carefully. He might place the doll in the truck.

At *twenty-four months*, the child feeds the doll realistically and puts it down for a nap after lunch. He brushes its hair and takes it for a ride in the truck. The truck and trailer will be lined up as if the truck were pulling the trailer, and the child may search for something to lead into the trailer.

Between *thirty and thirty-six months*, the child will move the doll, making it pick up the cup and drink, then wash and dry the dishes, and put them away. The doll is made to brush its own hair. Thus the power to act purposefully is attributed to the doll. The truck and trailer are hooked together and moved with motor noises, and the doll may be made to drive the truck, perhaps to some specific location and back.

C. Garvey, *Play*, Cambridge, Mass.: Harvard University Press, 1982. Reprinted by permission.

Over the three-year period these important developments stand out:

1. The child increasingly differentiates between various action patterns compatible with each object, and he fits together action and object appropriately (for example, he moves from mouthing every graspable object to putting only the spoon in his mouth).
2. He comes to combine objects that go together into functional relationships (he assembles the cup, saucer, and spoon).
3. He puts action patterns in sequence to form larger, coherent wholes (he links cooking, eating, and washing up).
4. He applies action patterns to himself (brushes his own hair), then to others or replicas of others (he brushes his mother's or a doll's hair). Finally, he attributes to replicas the ability to act (as when he causes the doll to brush its own hair or moves a toy dog while making barking noises).
5. He invents absent but appropriate objects or substances to complete action patterns (he stirs imaginary coffee with a toy spoon).
6. He transforms objects for use in actions and action sequences (he stirs imaginary coffee with a toy rake, used as a spoon).

---

school stages surrounding infancy and toddlerhood and Piaget's recognition of intellectual distinctions among infants and toddlers suggest the importance of viewing developmental learning activities in infant and toddler programming as different.

Activity Centers for Very Young Children

Activity centers are special multifaceted areas designed to attract, stimulate, or interest children. Such centers usually contain activities which are organized by *theme* or specific *purpose* or *content*. For example, a center may be movement-oriented or characterized by a specific type or style of play (water or sand). Some suggested interest areas include:

1. *The Rattle Corner.* During the latter part of early infancy, through the first half of middle infancy, babies show great interest in objects that can be manipulated to move and make noise. Rattles are ideal multifaceted toys for encouraging fine-hand coordination, enhancing sensory awareness, and challenging emerging manipulative skills in very young children. Such instruments can be purchased at relatively small cost in a variety of sizes, shapes, and colors. They feature differing sounds and, in some cases, differing sights, as well. Common household objects can be used as alternative "noise" objects. These include bells, wooden spoons, plastic cups, beads in containers, or food in containers.

TABLE 9.5. Baby Interest Centers and Their Primary Focuses

	Social Interaction	Physical Mastery and Manipulation	Sensory Stimulation and Perception	Emotional Well-being and Personality	Communication and Language
1. Rattle corner		X	X		
2. Reaching center		X	X		
3. Sensory corner			X		X
4. Manipulative area		X	X		
5. Interaction game area	X		X	X	X
6. Touring cart	X		X	X	
7. Exercise mat	X	X		X	
8. Water table		X	X	X	
9. Feeding tables		X	X		X
10. Puppet and doll house	X			X	X
11. Creative corner		X	X	X	
12. Music area			X	X	X
13. Construction center	X	X	X		

14. Curiosity corner		X		X
15. Identity area	X		X	X
16. Social roles: life-sized materials	X		X	X
17. Social roles: miniature toys	X			X
18. Problem solving center		X		X
19. Sand table		X	X	
20. Gymnastics area	X	X	X	
21. Play-dough table	X	X	X	
22. Sink and bathroom area		X	X	
23. Comfort corner	X	X	X	
24. Language and book center	X	X		X
25. Specials space	X	X		X
26. Outdoor area		X	X	
27. Diapering center	X	X	X	X
28. Rest area		X	X	
29. Clothes cubbies	X	X		
30. Parent corner			X	

From: *Infant and Toddler Programs: A Guide to Very Early Childhood Education* by C. Z. Cataldo, Addison-Wesley, Reading, MA, 1983. Reprinted by permission.

TABLE 9.6. Examples of Activities for Infants and Toddlers: A Planning Guide*

	Social Interaction	Physical Mastery and Manipulation	Sensory Stimulation and Perception	Emotional Well-being and Personality	Communication and Language
Independent play	Baby observes and plays near others	Put busy boxes and blocks in cribs	Give water and play-dough to children	Have babies bring own cup and toy from home	Provide cardboard-backed pictures for play
Peer play	Use babies' names in greeting and play	Set up climber-slide for a small group	Play a textured-object guessing game with a small group	Use photos of all the children in a book	Play animal sounds game with a small group
Exploratory play	Examine worms or bugs with a small group	Help babies build with a small variety of blocks	Have a finger-food feast	Use a new set of family dolls	Provide a set of simple musical instruments
Cognitive activities	Play who's missing game with a small group	Teach word-action games using body	Use a texture mystery bag in a guessing game	Teach words for body parts	Use simple rhymes and songs

Playthings and equipment	Have dress-ups for role playing	Provide sit and ride toys and large pegs	Use puzzles and shape-sorters	Provide rubber family figures in block area	Play a simple lotto game
Simple games	Supervise a hide-and seek game with a small group	Count the adult's toes	Sort jars by smell or weight	Play a faces picture match-up game	Play what's missing with flannel board
Special activities	Take a small group for a walk and collect weeds	Create a walking path with taped steps	Use balloons or bubbles in an open area	Make a cardboard house with windows	Arrange a grocery foodbox match-up game

*Examples are for 18-month-olds.
From: Infant and Toddler Programs: A Guide to a Very Early Childhood Education by C. Z. Cataldo, Addison-Wesley, Reading, MA, 1983. Reprinted by permission.

321

In addition to offering babies manipulative experiences, the rattle corner provides opportunities for social interaction with adult caregivers and other infants.

2. *The Recognition Corner.* The recognition corner is a unique, special learning area, used to foster self-image and recognition of others in toddlers. Here, the child may find a variety of materials that allow him to practice short- and long-term personal memory skills, recognition of familiar objects, and identificaiton of self and familiar others. Materials might include mirrors and mounted photographs of the children and pictures of favorite toys, animal friends, siblings, pets, and parents. This interest area can be frequently changed or modified according to growing developmental recognition and new learning. For example, a caregiver may start with photographs that feature the child exclusively, then add small group portraits, and finally, add large group or class pictures.

3. *The Snack Area.* Even routine tasks, such as the feeding of infants, can be developmentally significant when caregivers view such events as opportunities for creating sensory, linguistic, and social interactions. At snack time, for example, as the babies are brought together, chairs can be arranged in a semicircle, with caregivers allowing a clear view of peers and the opportunity to participate in other-directed caregiver interactions. As foods are introduced to the children such arrangements allow for visual observations, the expression of auditory recognitions, and the sharing of vocalizations. Finger foods, which enhance fine-hand motor dexterity, self-control, and independence may be encouraged, as well as imitated, as one baby watches another infant's attempt at gaining greater autonomy. After clean-up caregivers may set the chairs back and create a visiting corner as a natural extension of snack time.

4. *The Miniature Toy Area.* Between 18 months and 3 years, young children show great enchantment with miniature, imitative toys such as small trucks, cars, buses, miniature household furniture, toy phones, and so on. These materials, in addition to being easily manipulated, offer numerous opportunities for toddler explorations and enactment of different occupational roles. With the gradual introduction of miniature people, another dimension is added to the activity. Lastly, with added components, such as buildings and roads, miniature toy play may provide opportunity for enlarged creative expression and new discoveries. Used apart, or within the context of peer play, they stimulate verbal interactions, language practice, and expanding communication skills. Table 9.5 provides a map for programming activity centers.

Table 9.6 offers a model for program planning, which integrates different programmatic transactions (left hand column) with some program goals (topical headings). This guide contains activities for older infants and early toddlers. The activities in the central area of the table can be listed to reflect the developmental ages and needs of younger and older infants and toddlers. For example, among early infants (two to six months of age) a "simple game" using smiling and funny faces can promote infant and adult social interactions. During later toddler-hood, where emphasis on social activities shifts to peers, social inter-action may be enhanced through the use of a simple game such as washing dolls in the water table, or taking turns on the slide.

Toys for Young Children

Activities involving children usually center about objects and toys. These may be simple or complex, homemade or store bought. Common household items can provide both a unique and less costly means for enhancing developmental learnings than manufactured products. Since very young children possess little experience with items and objects that are commonplace among older children and adults these can be effective learning tools. Consequently, the diversity and variety of objects available to teach and delight is almost limitless; here, new sights and sounds comprise a wonderland of source materials for pro-gram development. To illustrate, Table 9.7 offers the reader diverse exercises, using common materials, designed to expand the infant-tod-dler's sensory awareness.

Toys should facilitate development, including the child's explorations and discovery learnings, as well as his image of himself and others. The Public Action Coalition for Toys (PACT) offers the following guidelines for proper selection of good toys (1983):

1. Good toys are safe. Toys or items that are hazardous (for example, pins, objects with sharp edges, exposed nails, or protruding points) or unpredictable should be avoided.
2. Toys should be large enough to discourage swallowing.
3. Good toys are glued well so that small parts cannot be removed and swallowed.
4. Toys should be made of unbreakable materials.
5. Objects should be nontoxic.
6. Good toys do not contain parts that pinch fingers or toes or catch hair.
7. Acceptable toys do not have loose cords that can strangulate.
8. Good toys do not possess projectile parts that can inflict serious injury.
9. Toys designed for young children do not require the use of electricity.
10. A good toy can be used in different surroundings.
11. Appropriate toys are well labeled and contain clear instructions for their use.
12. Well-designed toys do not possess hidden hazards.
13. Good toys are easily cleaned.

**TABLE 9.7.   Common Objects as Sensory Exercises: Materials and
Activities Designed to Stimulate and Expand the Infant's
Awareness of Sights, Sounds, Tastes, Smells, and Feelings**

1. Wall mirrors and unbreakable hand mirrors
2. An old fashioned washboard with wavy ridges
3. Soap bubble solution, rings and pipes to make bubbles
4. Nontoxic finger paints from puddings, fruit pieces, etc
5. Plastic sifters and flour mixers
6. Pots and pans and varied wood spoons and spatulas
7. Fragrant plants and flowers in pots and boxes
8. A tub of warm water with sponges and bars of soap
9. Rocking chairs for infants and adults
10. Assorted brushes—soft and hard bristled, toothbrushes, hair brushes, crumbing brushes, and whisk brooms
11. Small nylon, orlon or cotton stretch gloves or mittens
12. Plastic bags filled with air and tied
13. Feelable materials such as plush, terrycloth, silk, yarns, leather scraps, fur pieces, metal link chains, and sponges
14. Soft receiving blankets for swaddling or cuddling babies
15. Music boxes, bells of different sizes and sounds, rattles, chimes
16. Similar items of different weights, a heavier metal cup and spoon, two beanbags or margarine containers with lids taped in place one packed lightly and the other densely with pebbles or beans, a linked metal necklace and a linked plastic necklace
17. Foods with distinctive odors: cut grapefruit, vanilla extract, ground cinnamon, fresh bread
18. Finger foods—Foods that can be picked up and eaten, such as bread or vegetable sticks, soft rolls, cut up fruits
19. Foods with different color and texture, such as most vegetables and fruits
20. Sand, snow, water alone or together

Adapted (with modification) from: Infant Caregiving: A Design for Training, Second ed., by A. S. Honig and R. Lally, Syracuse University Press, Syracuse, NY, 1981. Used by permission.

14. Toys designed for children should be age-appropriate. (That is, they should follow the developmental distinctions which roughly parallel the subdivisions of infancy, toddlerhood, preschool, and elementary school age childhood, suggested throughout this text.)

OBSERVING INFANTS AND TODDLERS

Formal assessment of infancy was initiated with the pioneering work of Arnold Gesell (1925). These initial efforts, which expanded to include several decades of research and data collection on infants and children, sought to provide normative guidelines surrounding the transition from early infancy to later childhood. However, Gesell was not only interested in plotting childrens' schedules of development. Nor did his work parallel that of Binet and others who were involved in categorizing individual abilities by chronological or mental age level.

Gesell's work was characterized by his concern for "infant welfare" and "infant hygiene," in an attempt to protect and enhance infant development. Moreover, age norms, while valuable, were nevertheless of secondary importance to his interest in the *process* of children's development. From these beginnings current means of formal assessment and evaluation of infant development emerged (Self and Horowitz, 1979; Yang, 1979).

Present assessment procedures involving infants range from techniques allowing for neurological and maturational evaluation to instruments designed for behavioral assessment. Patricia Self and Frances Horowitz (1979) offer an exceptional review of the present status of infant assessment, as well as descriptions and items associated with the most commonly employed infant assessment devices.

TABLE 9.8.   Neurological and Behavioral Assessment Procedures Used with Infants

Neurological

These tests are used to appraise the infant's reflexes and responsiveness to stimulation, her muscle tone, physical condition, and general state. They usually lead to a diagnosis concerning the infant's maturity and the status of the infants' central nervous system and capacity for sensory functioning. They include:

1. Dubowitz's assessment of gestational age
2. Prechtl and Beintema's neurological examination of the full-term newborn infant
3. Parmelee's newborn neurological examination

Behavioral

Behavioral assessment procedures appear more varied in their interests and concerns than standardized neurological assessment procedures. Tests in this category may, for example, differentiate between normal and abnormal infants, involve predictions of infant abilities and capabilities or may offer measures of individual differences among infants.

They include:

1. Gesell Developmental Schedules
2. Bayley Scales of Infant Development
3. Griffiths' Mental Development Scale
4. Graham Behavior Test for Neonates and the Graham/Rosenblith Test.
5. Brazelton Neonatal Behavioral Scale.

Children are serious as well as playful.

Many of the formal tests and measurement instruments for appraising the developmental status of infants demand special training and orientation for proper administation and scoring. However, the practioner may employ a variety of less formal, developmentally appropriate measures, either drawn from the assessment literature or from more formal procedures.

While informal assessment procedures should be used with caution, they may, nevertheless, provide the practioner with valuable information concerning the developmental status of those infants/toddlers in her care. Moreover, employed in a judicious manner, they may offer an informal appraisal of the child's rate of growth, and finally, used within the above framework and guidelines, may serve a valuable function in activity and program planning.

Two procedures for informal assessment are suggested for use by the interested reader. The first, designed at the Early Childhood Research Center, State University of New York at Buffalo (Cataldo, 1983), consists of a series of three early childhood competencies profiles with separate forms for use with 3-month- to 18-month-old infants, 1½- to 2½-year olds, and 2½- to 4½-year olds. Each form consists of topical categories representative of competencies associated with the age of the child being assessed. For example, 3-month- to 18-month-old categories include physical mastery, emotional well-being, social interaction; among 1½- to 2½-year olds, categories include physical mastery, emotional well-being, social interaction, language and communication, arts and creative expression; among 2½- to 4½-year-olds, categories include emotional well-being, social interaction, language, concepts, representation, general knowledge, independence, and preacademic cognitive skills). Each category, in turn, contains a variety of representative behaviors associated with developmental attainments characteristic of children within that age frame. For assessment purposes a simple scoring system is employed; each behavior is scored in terms of a three point system, wherein 1 indicates that the child may need assistance in the performance of that behavior, 2 indicates that the child is progressing toward the goal or behavior suggested, and 3 indicates that the child has attained that particular competency. Periodic assessment enables the teacher to appraise progress and plan activities leading to selected developmental outcomes.

An alternative procedure for assessment has been developed at Syracuse University by Honig and Lally (1981). This procedure, in contrast to that developed by Cataldo, does not focus on the infant-toddler-young child, but rather on *activities* that occur within infant-caregiver interactions. Moreover, assessment within this context concentrates on *caregiver behaviors*, which are performed on a regularly scheduled basis and therefore serve as a guide for events to be enacted. These activities, as indicated in Table 9.9, in which selected facets of the schedule are reproduced, are derived from Piaget's theory of development. The purpose of this checklist is to insure that infants, toddlers, and young children are provided the opportunity to engage in beneficial developmental activities as defined by Piaget. Moreover, the checklist offers caregivers informal feedback regarding their own relative effectiveness as caregivers. Planners may utilize both assessment procedures described here.

TABLE 9.9. Piaget Task Checklist

Please check the one(s) you did with the child today	NAME					BIRTHDATE				
	M	T	W	T	F	M	T	W	T	F
A. PREHENSION										
1. Reaching for toys	—	—	—	—	—	—	—	—	—	—
2. Shaking toys	—	—	—	—	—	—	—	—	—	—
3. Suspended toys—hitting	—	—	—	—	—	—	—	—	—	—
4. Suspended toys—pulling	—	—	—	—	—	—	—	—	—	—
5. Squeaking toys	—	—	—	—	—	—	—	—	—	—
B. OBJECT PERFORMANCE										
1. Peek-a-boo	—	—	—	—	—	—	—	—	—	—
2. Horizontal following of toy	—	—	—	—	—	—	—	—	—	—

328

3. Vertical screens—hidden object							
4. Horizontal screens—visible displacement							
5. Visible displacement—3 screens							
6. Invisible displacement—1 screen							
7. Invisible displacement—2 or 3 screens							
8. (a) Put things in containers							
(b) Nested boxes or bottles							

TABLE 9.9. Piaget Task Checklist (*Continued*)

Please check the one(s) you did with the child today	NAME					BIRTHDATE				
	M	T	W	T	F	M	T	W	T	F
C. MEANS AND ENDS										
1. Reaching over obstacles	—	—	—	—	—	—	—	—	—	—
2. Use of the support	—	—	—	—	—	—	—	—	—	—
3. Pull horizontal string to get toy	—	—	—	—	—	—	—	—	—	—
4. Pull vertical string to get toy	—	—	—	—	—	—	—	—	—	—
5. Bunch chain into box	—	—	—	—	—	—	—	—	—	—
6. Use stick to get object	—	—	—	—	—	—	—	—	—	—
7. Reject solid ring for stack	—	—	—	—	—	—	—	—	—	—

D. NEW SCHEMAS

1. Hitting two objects together
2. Tactile patting, scratching
3. Examining objects
4. Sliding objects, such as car
5. Show something to someone
6. Adorn self—put on necklace
7. Make doll or animal walk
8. Pull or stretch object
9. Attentive "listening" to songs

331

TABLE 9.9. Piaget Task Checklist (*Continued*)

Please check the one(s) you did with the child today	NAME					BIRTHDATE				
	M	*T*	*W*	*T*	*F*	*M*	*T*	*W*	*T*	*F*
E. CAUSALITY										
1. Bring unseen objects into sight	—	—	—	—	—	—	—	—	—	—
2. Ring bell to make sound	—	—	—	—	—	—	—	—	—	—
3. Wobble duck toy	—	—	—	—	—	—	—	—	—	—
4. Turn key to work toy	—	—	—	—	—	—	—	—	—	—
5. "Zoom" car to make it go	—	—	—	—	—	—	—	—	—	—
6. Work "Jack-in-the-box"	—	—	—	—	—	—	—	—	—	—
F. SPACE										
1. Glance alternately	—	—	—	—	—	—	—	—	—	—
2. Find object by its sound	—	—	—	—	—	—	—	—	—	—

332

3. Vertical trajectory following — — — — — — — ‖

4. Reversed objects — — — — — — — ‖

5. Roll objects down plane — — — — — — — ‖

6. Use detour to get toys — — — — — — — ‖

G. IMITATION

1. Familiar visible— "pat-a-cake" — — — — — — — ‖

2. Unfamiliar visible—crook a finger — — — — — — — ‖

3. Familiar invisible—wag head — — — — — — — ‖

4. Unfamiliar invisible—eye wink — — — — — — — ‖

333

TABLE 9.9. **Piaget Task Checklist (Continued)**

Please check the one(s) you did with the child today	NAME					BIRTHDATE									
	M	T	W	T	F	M	T	W	T	F	M	T	W	T	F
H. VERBAL LEARNING															
1. Imitation of baby sounds	—	—	—	—	—	—	—	—	—	—	—	—	—	—	—
2. Unfamiliar sounds "la-la"	—	—	—	—	—	—	—	—	—	—	—	—	—	—	—
3. Labeling															
(a) Objects	—	—	—	—	—	—	—	—	—	—	—	—	—	—	—
(b) People	—	—	—	—	—	—	—	—	—	—	—	—	—	—	—
(c) Feelings	—	—	—	—	—	—	—	—	—	—	—	—	—	—	—
(d) Actions	—	—	—	—	—	—	—	—	—	—	—	—	—	—	—
4. Read stories	—	—	—	—	—	—	—	—	—	—	—	—	—	—	—
5. Verbal decoding	—	—	—	—	—	—	—	—	—	—	—	—	—	—	—
I. BALLET AND EXERCISES															
1. Leg stretches	—	—	—	—	—	—	—	—	—	—	—	—	—	—	—
2. roll body into ball	—	—	—	—	—	—	—	—	—	—	—	—	—	—	—
3. Rocking on stomach	—	—	—	—	—	—	—	—	—	—	—	—	—	—	—
4. Somersaults	—	—	—	—	—	—	—	—	—	—	—	—	—	—	—

334

5. Arms and legs apart and together

6. Bounce body to music

7. Bend to pick up

J. SOUNDS

1. Play xylophone or piano

2. Taped sounds

3. Listening to records

DAILY COMMENTS

From: Alice S. Honig and J. Ronald Lally, *Infant Caregiving: A Design for Training*, 2nd. ed. Syracuse, N.Y.: Syracuse University Press, 1981. Reprinted by permission of the publisher.

335

SOME SELECT-SPECIAL PROGRAMS

Home-Based Programs

The Florida Parent Education Program

This program, under the direction of Ira Gordon (1969; Guinagh and Gordon, 1976) is one of the earliest parent-involvement, infant-based programs. The goals of this multidimensional effort are threefold: (1) to stimulate intellectual and personal growth in each child; (2) to create changes in maternal self-esteem through parent participation; and (3) to enhance better maternal child care by teaching caregivers tools and skills to be implemented during on-site training efforts.

This program was founded upon the use of community-based para-professionals, each trained and assigned to work as "parent educators" with 10 families. The workers received a five-week intensive training program prior to the inception of program efforts. Their training involved a brief introduction to principles of child development, the acquisition of interviewing skills, acquiring techniques for recording information, and the learning of specific exercises or games to be taught to their assigned families.

Gordon's targeted subjects were 275 indigent mothers and their children (a final sample of 193 families). The instructional program consisted of Piagetian concepts and selected activities representing cognitive-developmental principles. For example, the young infants played games which were sensorimotor, manipulative, and exploratory exercises (encouraging touching, picking up objects, examining means-ends relations) with later stages being represented by memory "activities" (object-person identification), followed by object identification using labeling (naming).

Each mother was visited weekly by her assigned parent-educator, at which time the parent-educator demonstrated activities that the mother was to carry out with her infant. As each activity was taught to the mother, it was emphasized that it was to be introduced to her child as a game. This latter instructional dimension ensured a more natural presentation of materials to the child and deemphasized formal teaching by the parent. In addition, minimizing academic concerns allowed the mother to present the learning activities sequentially and in a manner congruent with the child's developmental status. Activities could also be broken down into finer and simpler units, where warranted.

When the children turned two, a group experience was added to the home learning centers and new children were introduced to the group. The program continued with different mixes of enrichment being added (or, in some cases postponed) during the first three years of life for different assessment purposes. The intervention program terminated when the children reached three years of age, with assessment continuing until age six.

Continuous participation in this program over a two-year period during the first three years of life resulted in both academic and intellectual success over a six-to seven-year period. Long-term gains, however, were not demonstrated.

Gordon's model led to the current "Home Start" programs, which operate in some areas in conjunction with Head Start. In these programs teachers went into homes to demonstrate infant/toddler learning activities to families before youngsters were old enough to participate in Head Start.

The Milwaukee Model

The *Milwaukee Model* of Heber (Heber and Garber, 1975) represents one of the most dramatic and controversial of early infant-child intervention programs. This program consisted of 40 unusually high-risk black families (including 20 experimental and 20 control familes). (Each mother's WAIS I.Q. score was under 80 at the time the program began. In addition, the Milwaukee program began during early infancy when each of the infants was between three and six months of age. Moreover, the learning program consisted of intense and continuous instruction until the children reached their sixth birthdays.

The goals of this program involved children, as well as their mothers. For the children, an intensive instructional program was designed to teach academically related skills by professional and paraprofessional teachers through one-on-one tutorials. Maternal involvement was designed to enhance vocational success. Specifically, mothers received vocational training, assistance in remedial academic skills, group counseling, and employment counseling.

This demonstration program began when each infant was between three and six months old. The infants were involved in daily (five days a week) activities with the same assigned caregiver. The curriculum, which focused on perceptual, motor, cognitive, language, and socioemotional skill development, was adapted to the specific needs of each child as determined by developmental assessments. Each child's motivation was enhanced through the use of behavioral (positive reinforcement, continuous feedback) principles.

As indicated, the nature of learning was intimate; each child was assigned a specific teacher who remained with that child for the first 15 months of the program. At that time two infants shared two teachers. At 18 months a small group transitional phase was introduced, and at 20 months a preschool program was begun. Learning throughout the program was characterized by close child-caregiver interactions, individual attention, and low child-caregiver ratios. In addition, programs were specialized for each child and carefully coordinated to correspond with each child's developmental needs. Activities, moreover, were sequentially taught, with new elements being introduced gradually, and all learning interactions provided the target children numerous opportunities in experiencing success.

The results of this intense effort at early instruction were dramatic. Highly significant differences in intellectual gains and developmental learning were found in test score comparisons across the experimental and control groups. In each case, the findings were substantial, and in favor of the experimental group. On the Gesell Scale the performance of the experimental group at age 2 was clearly accelerated, whereas the performance of control subjects was below average or within the normal range. Between ages 2 and 5½ all the children were administered the Cattell and Stanford-Binet tests. The experimental group recorded an average IQ score of 122, whereas the control group showed an average IQ score of 91. These differences are substantial and highly impressive. However, these findings need to be followed to determine their long-term consequences, and the results need to be replicated by other investigators. Nevertheless, they demonstrate the dramatic importance of intense infant-caregiver interaction and individual instruction from early infancy through the preschool years.

Children's Centers: The Syracuse Model

One of the earliest center-based infant programs was initiated by Betty Caldwell (Caldwell and Richmond, 1964) at Syracuse University. The *Syracuse program*, which continues under the direction of Alice Honig (Honig and Brill, 1970), was initially designed to demonstrate that supplementary group care for infants can be valuable and will not result in developmental damage. Consequently, this program focused on affective (that is, emotional) rather than intellectual development, as described in the programs reviewed earlier. Another distinguishing facet of this program was its investment in providing supplementary, rather than substitute or surrogate infant caregiving. In the Syracuse program support for family-initiated interactions and functions assumed priority over center-based goals.

Two features of the Syracuse program underscored the above concerns. To ensure that the infant's separation from its mother did not interrupt or jeopardize their continuing relationship, routines resembling home care were introduced, and a continuous stable relationship with the same nurturant adult was established.

The curriculum focus and choice of activities to be used in this program were carefully selected with the above interests in mind. Events

that enhanced exploration, expression of individual interests, and discovery were of central interest. Different program elements also
allowed children to alternate between intimate (one-on-one) infant-
caregiver interactions and small group transactions (usually within a
4:1 ratio of infants to adult caregiver).

Participants in the program included 10 infants between 6 and 18
months of age and 15 infants between 18 and 36 months of age. Their
attendance varied from half to full days, five days a week.

Parental involvement in the program was a major concern and consisted of several components. These included a parent instructional orientation to infant development, monthly staff-parent conferences,
social services where needed, and the creation of opportunities for
mothers to participate as volunteers in ongoing programs.

As we noted earlier, one of the major concerns of the Syracuse study
was to demonstrate that such programs may enhance development
without causing serious detriment to normal child-family relations. The
results of this study indicate that there are no adverse social or intellec-

tual consequences associated with participation. Clear support for the Syracuse program was demonstrated by Caldwell (1970) in a comparison of social and intellectual growth among 23 home-reared infants and 18 infants who attended the children's center.

No serious effects were observed when the infants were separated from their mothers. Interestingly, this was true across social class (lower versus middle income) and racial affiliation (white versus black).

In terms of intellectual gains, Caldwell found that at 12 months of age the home-reared infants were significantly ahead of the center infants (as represented by their group performance) on the Cattell Infant Intelligence Scales. However, at retest at 30 months of age, the center-based infants were significantly ahead of the home-reared youngsters. This change was attributable to a decline in the developmental quotients of the home-reared children with a corresponding increase in the scores of the center-based infants, which occurred during the 18 month period between the first and second formal assessments. Although further evaluation is necessary to ascertain the long-term maintenance of these positive findings, it appears evident that this pioneering project supports the credibility and continuance of well-designed and appropriate group-based infant care programs.

SUMMARY

Economic and social conditions have created a need for infant/toddler care outside the home. Family day care and center-based infant care have developed to meet this need, and programs such as the Syracuse center have shown that not only are such experiences not detrimental to children, but they can even enhance development if well designed and carefully constructed.

Infants and toddlers have special needs, however, and low child-adult ratios, consistent, nurturing caregivers, and opportunities for appropriate developmental activities must be included in such programs. This is a growing area in early childhood education and will elicit much attention in the coming years.

Explorations

PERSONAL EXPLORATIONS

These exercises are designed to help you look at your own life—attitudes, experiences, dreams, myths, and realities.

1. If there is a photo album available with pictures of you as an infant and toddler, take an objective look at them, as if they were someone else. Note the physical changes, play activities, emotional expressions, etc. and then analyze these findings in relation to Tables 9.1 and 9.2. Write a short paragraph concerning your findings. (If these types of photos aren't available, see if a friend has some—that will make objectivity easier.)

2. What personal experiences have you had caring for very young children? How comfortable were you with them? What was it like to handle and play with a young child? Write a short synopsis of these experiences and bring it to class for small group discussion.

3. Lie down on the floor and look up at the world from an infant's perspective. What do furniture, walls, doors, people look like from down there? Close your eyes for a few moments and imagine someone large approaching you to pick you up or play with you. How would you like this giant to behave when he or she approaches you? Give yourself enough time to really feel what that would be like. Come to class prepared to share your experience.

INTELLECTUAL EXPLORATIONS

These exercises are designed to help you increase your depth of knowledge in some of the areas discussed in this chapter.

1. A variety of professional magazines for psychologists and educators have published research and opinions concerning family day care and center-based infant care programs. Find two articles that have different results and/or points of view. Bring a summary of the articles to class for a debate on infant care outside the home.

2. Several books and articles have been published concerning the education of infants to be "super-babies", that is, learning to read, early academic achievement, and so on. Find one book or article of this type and skim it to see what the author's approach is, then write a synopsis of what you read and your own personal opinion of the material.

3. Find a book about children's literature, or play activities or some other interest area. Find out what the recommendations are for working with infants and toddlers in this area. Write a number of the ideas down that you feel would be interesting to share in class.

FIELD EXPLORATIONS

These exercises are designed to take you out into the world to find real examples that illustrate and elucidate the material in this chapter.

1. Visit a family day care center, infant center, or cooperative play group that has children below the age of three (the younger the better). Observe the interactions between infant and caregiver, infant and infant, infant and other staff. Summarize your observations for discussion.
2. Go to a park or other area when young mothers and infants congregate or visit a friend or acquaintance who has a new baby or young child. Interview the mothers who are willing to talk concerning their experience as caregivers. Is it an easy or difficult job? What are their expectations of themselves, of their babies? Encourage them to talk, then later compare their comments with the table on the characteristics of competent caregivers. Be prepared to discuss your findings in class.
3. Find an infant to babysit or play with for an hour to two. Try some of the activities given in Table 9.9, the Piaget Task Checklist. Are some more "doable" than others? Which ones were relevant to the baby in your care? Bring the checksheet to class to discuss.

References

Caldwell, B. "Impact of interest in early cognitive stimulation." Paper presented at the meeting of the National Association for the Education of Young Children. Boston, 1970.

Caldwell, B. and Richmond, J. B. "Programmed day care for the very young child—A preliminary report." *Journal of Marriage and the Family*, 1964, 26: 481–88.

Cataldo, C. Z. *Infant and toddler programs: A guide to very early childhood education*. Reading, MA: Addison-Wesley, 1983

Clarke-Stewart, A. *Daycare*. Cambridge, MA: Harvard University Press, 1982.

Clarke-Stewart, A. and Fein, G. G. "Early childhood programs." In P. H. Mussen (Ed.), *Handbook of child psychology*. Fourth ed. (Vol. 2), New York: John Wiley & Sons, 1983.

Garvey, C. *Play*. Cambridge, MA: Harvard University Press, 1982.

Gesell, A. *The mental growth of the preschool child*. New York: Macmillan, 1925.

Gordon, I. J. "Early childhood stimulation through parent education." Final report to the Children's Bureau, Social and Rehabiliation Service, Department of Health, Education, and Welfare, Gainsville, Florida, University of Florida, Institute for the Development of Human Resources, 1969, ED 038 166.

Guinagh, B. J. and Gordon, I. J. "School performance as a function of early stimulation." Final Report to the Office of Child Development, 1976.

Heber, R. and Garber, H. "The Milwaukee Project: A study of the use of family intervention to prevent cultural-familial mental retardation." In B. Z. Friedlander, G. M. Sterrit, and G. E. Kirk (Eds.), *Exceptional infant*. New York: Brunner/Mazel, 1975.

Honig, A. S. "What are the needs of infants?" *Young Children*, 1981, 37: 3–10.

———. "Meeting the needs of infants." *Dimensions*, January 1983: 4–7.

———. "High quality infant/toddler care: Issues and dilemmas." *Young Children*, 1985, 41: 40–46.

Honig, A. S., and Brill, S. "A comparative analysis of the Piagetian development of twelve month old disadvantaged infants in an enrichment center with others not in such a center." Paper presented at the American Psychological Association meeting, Miami, 1970.

Honig, A. S., and Lally, R. *Infant caregiving: A design for training*. Second ed., Syracuse, NY: Syracuse University Press, 1981.

Jacobson, A. L. "Infant Day Care: Toward a more human environment." *Young Children*, 1978, 33, 14–21.

Jorn, M., Persky, B. and Huntington, D. S. "Staff Selection." In L. L. Dittman (Ed.), *The Infants we care for*. Washington, D. C.: National Association for the Education of Young Children, 1984.

Leavitt, R. L. and Eheart, B. K. *Toddler Day Care*. Lexington, MA: Lexington Books, 1985.

Public Action Coalition on Toys. "Guidelines for choosing toys." *Day Care & Early Education*, Fall, 1983: 6–8.

Self, P. A. and Horowitz, F. D. "The behavioral assessment of the neonate: An overview." In J. D. Osofsky (Ed.), *Handbook of infant development*. New York: John Wiley & Sons, 1979.

Yang, R. K. Early infant assessment: An overview. In J. D. Osofsky (Ed.), *Handbook of infant development*. New York: John Wiley & Sons, 1979.

Chapter 10

PRESCHOOL LEARNING
ENVIRONMENTS

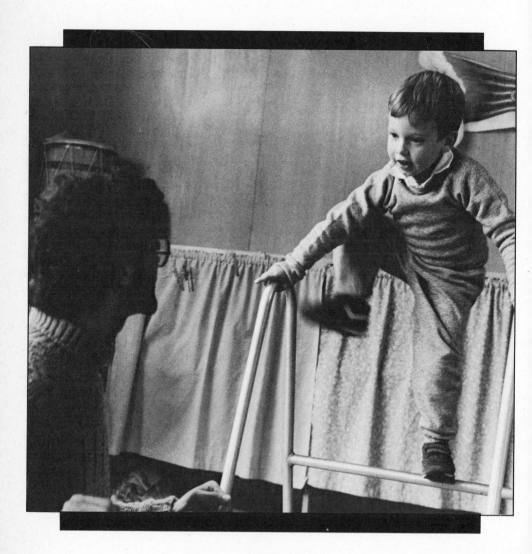

Objectives

After reading this chapter, the student should be able to:

1. Compare and contrast the characteristics of three-, four-, and five-year-old children.
2. List and define the findings from research concerning important components of child care settings.
3. Discuss the needs of the young child and their connection with caregiving as proposed by Katz.
4. Describe some of the basic concepts proposed by Piaget in relation to the thought processes of preoperational children.
5. List and define the 12 learning tasks of early childhood.
6. Compare and contrast two of the three programs of early childhood education described in this chapter.
7. Discuss the different research findings covered in various parts of this chapter and what they mean in practical terms for preschool settings.

Demographers predict that by 1990 the number of preschool-age children in the United States will reach approximately 23.3 million. It is further estimated that 10.4 million (about 45 percent) of these children will live in families where their parent or parents will be employed outside of the home (Verzaro-O'Brien, LeBlanc, and Hennon, 1982).

In the United States there are currently nearly eight million preschool children with working parents (Clarke-Stewart, 1982). Of these children, approximately two million are cared for in daycare centers. The majority of other preschool children with working parents are cared for through a variety of other caregiving arrangements. These include child care provided by a relative (grandmother, sibling, aunt) usually in the child's own home, or by a nonrelated caregiver in the caregiver's home (Clarke-Stewart and Fein, 1983).

Growth in the need for child care services in the United States reflects two phenomena: women at work and a continuing pattern of single parenting, which is partially attributable to the rising rates of divorce among parents of young children (see Chapter 13). These factors, of course, are not isolated, but interrelated, suggesting a spiraling pattern of continuing child care needs, particularly, among single-parent heads of households. However, these families are not alone in their child care needs. Intact households, including working class and dual career families, in increasing numbers, are requiring similar services. And, as new research findings on the effects of early experiences accumulate, particularly studies that suggest the potential benefical gains attributable to early learning opportunities, the demand for quality child care is likely to grow.

THE CHILDREN

Preschool environments typically serve a diverse population of children. The ages served by preschools usually range from three years to five years, although in some cases, late twos and early six year old youngsters may be included. The variations in experience and maturity characteristic of young children are often extensive and, as we have noted, more diverse than at any other period of life.

What is the average, three year old entering preschool like? Table 10.1 offers a thumbnail sketch of the characteristics that we observe in the three year old. There are some marked changes in interests and in maturity in the four year old. Some of these changes are suggested in descriptions of the characteristics of the four year old in Table 10.2. The five year old differs from her younger contemporaries. Aside from obvious chronologically linked differences, fives demonstrate a keen knowledge of events, reflecting, in part, an extended range of experiences with the physical world. Fives also possess significantly more useful information about others. In addition, fives have attained a perspective of themselves through the rehearsal of roles that fours, and some threes, are just newly experiencing. Finally, fives have matured to the point of anticipating (with some trepidation, as well as bravado) entrance into grade school (see Table 10.3).

Our refocused interest on the significance of the early childhood worker and teacher has come about, in part, through research findings from long-range studies documenting the important components of the early childhood environments that contribute to the quality of child care.

Supplementing research findings, various professional associations,

TABLE 10.1.   What Are Young Children Like?

Characteristics of Two Year Olds and Young Threes
Always on the go—prefer to run or climb
Beginning to develop a sense of danger
Easily frustrated—upset when events do not meet expectations
Developing independence—says, "Me do it" or "No" but are still dependent, too
Learning to be more helpful and responsible
Beginning to take care of dolls and act out familiar scenes
Experimenting with art materials
Developing control of finger and hand muscles
Acquiring interest in playing *with* other children
Learning language rapidly
Enjoy learning and using new skills

From: Public Action Coalition on Toys, "Guidelines for Choosing Toys." *Day Care & Early Education,* Fall, 1983:77–78. Reprinted by permission of the publisher.

TABLE 10.2.   What Are Young Children Like?

Characteristics of Older Threes and Four Year Olds

Test physical skills and courage—have some sense of caution
Like to play with others
Share and take turns sometimes—cannot wait long
Talk a lot—are silly, boisterous, use shocking language
Very interested in the world—ask lots of questions
Reveal feelings in dramatic play
Enjoy art materials—want to keep projects
Want to be grown up one day and a child the next
Developing a longer attention span
Want real adult things
Do not like to lose—may change rules or quit

From: Public Action Coalition on Toys, "Guidelines for Choosing Toys." *Day Care & Early Education*, Fall, 1983:77–78. Reprinted by permission of the publisher.

like the National Association for the Education of Young Children (NAEYC), have addressed licensure issues such as certification of early childhood educators with greater urgency (see Chapter 14). These efforts have contributed to a more comprehensive understanding of the needs of young children and the varied roles that adults serve in their lives.

One view of the role of the early childhood educator and caregiver was presented by Katz (1977) in a series of seven interlocking propositions concerning the needs of the young child. In the following paragraphs we cite each of these propositions and offer the reader a brief description and explanation of their role in fostering children's development.

TABLE 10.3.   What Are Young Children Like?

Characteristics of Five and Six Year Olds

Becoming more outgoing, sociable
Like to play cooperatively
More interested in making final product
More confident about physical skills
Able to use words to express feelings
Like grown-up activities
Still may need adult help to calm down
Take care of dressing and other personal needs
Prefer realistic working toys
Interested in numbers, letters, reading, and writing
Still need reassurance and affection
Curious about people and how the world works

From: Public Action Coalition on Toys, "Guidelines for Choosing Toys." *Day Care & Early Education*, Fall, 1983:77–78. Reprinted by permission of the publisher.

TABLE 10.4.   Evaluating Child Care Settings: Important Components Drawn from Research Findings

1. Gains in children's achievement, positive attitude, intellectual development, and constructive play are most likely in programs (in homes or centers) that offer children free choice combined with (a moderate number of) prescribed educational activities.

2. Sociability, cooperation, and self-motivated exploration are most likely to develop in programs that are "open" and focus their efforts on free play and social interactions among the children in a rich and varied environment.

3. High quality experience is less likely in a crowded and disorganized space (with less than 25 square feet per child and no separated activity areas).

4. An environment that offers a wide variety of materials and easy accessibility should be available: building construction materials (blocks, Legos); structured materials (puzzles, books); artistic materials (paints, musical instruments); manipulative materials (sand, buttons, water, dough, clay); social materials (games, cards, checkers, pickup sticks); fantasy or make-believe materials (dolls, dressups); active play equipment (slides, swings, tricycles); soft, cuddly materials (cushions, pillows, sofas).

5. A daycare setting in which the child is part of a small group of children, both boys and girls, with an age range of about two years, offers more positive, cooperative, complex, and sustained interactions with both other children and the caregiver and has benefits for social development.

6. The caregiver is the most important aspect of the daycare setting. The caregiver-child ratio is not as important as the kinds of behavior the caregiver exhibits. Behavior that indicates high quality includes active involvement by talking, teaching, and playing; providing interesting materials; responding to the child's interests, advances, and questions; positive encouragement and suggestions; no demands, threats, or punishment. Although the caregiver is actively involved, she also permits the child freedom, initiative, and exploration; she is not restrictive or critical. High quality caregiving in a daycare home or center is not indicated by an abundance of physical affection, constant praise, or strict discipline.

7. A caregiver in either a home or a center, who thinks of himself as a professional, has been trained in child development, has five to ten years of experience, and is part of a training and support network of educationally oriented centers, is more likely to offer involved, active, positive care and to have a positive influence on the child's development.

8. In general, center-based programs (daycare centers and nursery schools) are more likely than home-based programs (babysitters, childminders, daycare homes) to provide educational opportunities for children and to increase their social competence, maturity, and intellectual development.

9. In general, home-based care is more likely than center-based care to offer authoritative discipline, socialization training, and one-on-one adult-child interaction.

TABLE 10.4.   Evaluating Child Care Settings: Important Components Drawn from Research Findings (*Continued*)

10. Publicly funded daycare centers and nursery schools are the most likely form of group or center-based programs to offer care of high quality.

11. The best kind of care varies according to the individual needs of the child: for easy or average children, high quality is as described above; for slow-to-warm-up children, high quality care would be most evident in an unpressured, supportive atmosphere; for difficult children, greater consistency and structure is warranted; active children need more latitude and less physical restrictiveness; withdrawn children appear to benefit from sensitive and nurturant caregiving in a busy, cheerful environment; insecure children may experience difficulty in most forms of daycare.

Adapted from: Daycare by A. Clarke-Stewart. Harvard University Press, Cambridge, MA, 1982. Reprinted by permission.

Proposition One.   The young child has to have a sense of personal safety.

This idea refers to the child's need for psychological safety, that is, for interconnectedness with those about him. By this proposition, Katz suggests that the child needs to feel part of a larger configuration, to feel that she matters, that she is of significance to others. Rather than simply being acknowledged, or accepted, the child needs to be a part of her family, her school, and her community.

Proposition Two.   Every child has to have adequate self-esteem.

The acquisition of a sense of self-esteem or self-worth, as we have noted elsewhere, is central to development. Self-esteem, however, does not come about in the absence of values. Rather, it is a reflection of the beliefs about himself that are transmitted to the child through family interactions. In creating environments that enhance the child's self-esteem, we must therefore recognize and respect the primacy of the family in fostering the child's views and feelings about himself.

Proposition Three.   Every child has to feel, or experience, his life as worth living, reasonably satisfying, interesting, and authentic.

Kindness, warmth, and acceptance must underlie our interactions with children. However, we must also act with authenticity and genuineness. Young children easily perceive attempts to disguise real feelings, to conceal, or to perpetuate dishonesty.

Programs for young children must be equally real. Activities must be significant and intriguing to children. To solely amuse or to entertain, in itself is to trivialize, to devalue, and to demean childhood.

INSET 10.1   Children Learn What They Live

If a child lives with criticism, she learns to condemn.
  If a child lives with hostility, he learns to fight.
If a child lives with ridicule, she learns to be shy.
  If a child lives with shame, he learns to feel guilty.
If a child lives with tolerance, she learns to be patient.
  If a child lives with encouragement, he learns confidence.
If a child lives with praise, she learns to appreciate.
  If a child lives with fairness, he learns justice.
If a child lives with security, she learns faith.
  If a child lives with approval, he learns to like himself.
If a child lives with acceptance and friendship,
  She learns to find love in the world.

Proposition Four.   Young children need adults or older children who help them to make sense of their own experiences.

Young people seek to understand their world. As adults we can assist them in defining and extending this understanding, in correcting their misperceptions, and in enhancing their existing learning.

During the preschool years learning centers on one's self. As such, learning is personal and intimate. As the child enters the primary years, learning consists of understanding about the world of others. Both kinds of knowledge are important and remain so throughout life.

Proposition Five.   Young children have to have adults about them who accept the authority that is theirs by virtue of their greater experience, knowledge, and wisdom.

Children need adults who are not afraid to be adults. That is, children require *authoritative* persons about them. Such persons possess knowledge and understanding of their world that they are willing to teach with certainty, as well as compassion. Adults must encourage and support, as well as guide and lead, when appropriate.

Proposition Six.   Young children need optimum association with adults and older children who exemplify the personal qualities we want them to acquire.

Young people need good models. They need to be exposed to adults who strive to exhibit humane attitudes and proper behaviors toward others. In contrast, they need to be protected from attractive and glamorous counter-examples of improper, inappropriate, or inhumane behavior. Certainly, excessive exposure to violence, crime, adult sexuality, and transient fads or "heroes" needs to be discouraged.

Proposition Seven. Children need relationships and experiences with adults who are willing to take a stand on what is worth doing, worth having, worth knowing, and worth caring about.

Children need to be given clear signals concerning what we, the adults in their lives, believe in and care about. In a world of pluralistic values, multiculturalism, and increasingly technologically oriented

TABLE 10.5.   Criteria for High Quality Early Childhood Programs

1. *Interactions betwen Staff and Children:* Interactions between children and staff provide opportunities for children to develop an understanding of self and others and are characterized by warmth, personal respect, individuality, positive support, and responsiveness. Staff facilitate interactions among children to provide opportunities for development of social skills and intellectual growth.
2. *Curriculum:* The curriculum encourages children to be actively involved in the learning process, to experience a variety of developmentally appropriate activities and materials, and to pursue their own interests in the context of life in the community and the world.
3. *Staff-Parent Interaction:* Parents are well-informed about and welcome as observers and contributors to the program.
4. *Staff Qualifications and Development:* The program is staffed by adults who understand child development and who recognize and provide for children's needs.
5. *Administration:* The program is efficiently and effectively administered with attention to the needs and desires of children, parents, and staff.
6. *Staffing:* The program is sufficiently staffed to meet the needs of and promote the physical, social, emotional, and cognitive development of children.
7. *Physical Environment:* The indoor and outdoor physical environment foster optimal growth and development through opportunities for exploration and learning.
8. *Health and Safety:* The health and safety of children and adults are protected and enhanced.
9. *Nutrition and Food Service:* The nutritional needs of children and adults are met in a manner that promotes physical, social, emotional, and cognitive development.
10. *Evaluation:* Systematic assessment of the effectiveness of the program in meeting its goals for children, parents, and staff is conducted to ensure that good quality care and education are provided and maintained.

Adapted from: Accreditation Criteria and Procedures of the National Academy of Early Childhood Programs, National Association for the Education of Young Children, Washington, D.C., 1984.

solutions to human problems, children need to know where we, as professionals, stand. We need, therefore, to be aware of others, and to respect differing perspectives. Yet, we need also display the courage of our own convictions.

LEARNING AND THOUGHT

Preschool attendance occurs during Piaget's stage of *preoperational thought* (approximately two to seven years of age). This period covers considerable growth and change in how the young child thinks (the structure or form of thought), as well as how she processes information (uses ideas).

Between approximately two and four years of age the child enters the *preconceptual* phase of preoperational thought. During this period language emerges as a principal tool for processing ideas. At this time, for example, the child's ability to use words expands appreciably. Moreover, the child demonstrates an increasing capacity for organizing ideas and thoughts, which are readily expressed in descriptive sentences of moderate to complex structure.

Three year olds are exceptionally active, seeking out new personal challenges and activities involving others. For the three year old play is imaginative, is characterized by deferred imitation, and frequently involves others. Language now facilitates self-oriented explorations, as well as play with peers.

Between four and seven years of age children enter the *intuitive* phase of preoperational thought. At this time the child is engaged in the formation of concepts, the acquisition of classification skills, and the use of these newly emerging skills in an ever-widening series of applications. As Piaget observed, children at this stage can complete mental operations such as simple classification of objects into sets (name all the round things; give me all the yellow things). However, they are unable to explain how they arrived at these solutions. In addition, children at the intuitive phase of thought cannot demonstrate *reversibility*. To illustrate, the child can easily assemble a large container of liquid by adding together two or more small beakers of liquid. However, he will experience considerable difficulty if asked to then pour equal amounts of the liquid into two dissimilarly shaped containers or trays. The preoperational child is unable to focus on more than one physical dimension of a problem at the same time: a trait referred to as *centration*. This limitation in the child's ability to envision more than one dimension of an object or problem simultaneously is unrelated to the physical property of the object and is evident for different physical dimensions (such as shape, liquid, length, area, or volume). Consequently, the preoperational child could not name all the *small round* things represented in an array of items, or all the *big yellow* things from an alternative display.

Children during the intuitive phase of preoperational thought are also *egocentric*. This is not the same as being egotistic (self-centered or selfish) in attitude or behavior. Rather, it refers to the child's inability to consider another's viewpoint.

Egocentrism is characteristic of the child's thought and social interactions during this phase of development. The young child's view of the world is the only one possible for her. In her play, reality and fantasy are intertwined. In seeking information, she may engage in incessant questioning. For this child things don't just occur, but have an explanation, usually of questionable veracity. For example, a plane flys in the air because it has a round shape. Or, if the tricycle isn't moving, it must have run out of gas. Or, if the moon is out, the sun must be sleeping.

In social interactions, various facets of egocentrism may emerge. In telling a story to another person the young child often omits large segments of relevant dialogue, assuming that the listener already possesses knowledge of the tale. When talking *to* each other, young children tend to talk *at* each other. Pronouns are interchanged, often omitted, contradictions are introduced, and references are ignored. Piaget refers to these "conversations" as examples of the *collective monologue*. Fortunately, the amount of egocentric speech characteristic of the early phases of preoperational thought gradually decreases at the latter part of this stage.

ACTIVITIES AND INTERACTIONS

Orientation

The children's center is an active and busy community. For the child who attends a family daycare facility or a center-based program, her day is certain to be an active and intense series of happenings. For some children, particularly young threes, a full day of events may be too stressful or too taxing. For these children, a half-day nursery school program convening two or three mornings a week for several hours a day is often preferable to full-time care. The nursery school movement, as opposed to full-time day care, is still an active one in the United States, serving many children and providing activities and experiences that enhance children's social, emotional, and intellectual development.

For the child whose family needs require full-time care, a variety of orientation techniques may be useful in facilitating entrance to the preschool. These include:

1. Several brief meetings with the child's teacher in the accompaniment of a parent.
2. A short "private" meeting or two between the child and teacher.
3. Several opportunities for the child to walk around and explore the facilities with his teacher.
4. Opportunity for the child to observe the teacher with other children at *different times* of the day.
5. Introductory orientations to different activities through several limited participations.
6. Teacher-facilitated parent-child entrances and leave-takings.
7. Encouraging parent-child discussions of the day's events.
8. Arranging for the parent to share an occasional lunch with the group.
9. Ongoing teacher-parent assessment of the child's progress.

The Schedule

The day's activities are facilitated through an arrangement of time and events that ensure continuity and flow. Young children need to know

TABLE 10.6.   Sample Schedule for a Day Care Program

7:00–8:00	Greet children and parents
	Breakfast (as children arrive)
	Free play in block or housekeeping area (after breakfast)
8:00–9:00	Child-selected activities (alternate music, manipulative skills, and language with art, science, and dramatic play)
9:00–10:00	Outdoor play
10:00–10:30	Bathroom, clean up
	Morning snack
10:30–11:30	Small group (teacher-planned and directed) activities
11:30–12:00	Large group storytime
	Set tables and prepare for lunch
12:00–12:30	Lunch
12:30–12:45	Bathroom, cleanup, brush teeth, settle down for nap
12:45–2:00	Nap or quiet time
2:00–2:15	Bathroom, cleanup, comb hair
2:15–2:30	Snack
2:30–3:30	Child-selected activities (alternate art, science, and dramatic play with music, manipulative skills, and language, depending on what activities were done in the morning)
3:30–4:30	Outdoor play
4:30–4:45	Bathroom, clean up
4:45–6:00	Free play (stories, dry art, blocks or other manipulatives, music, or housekeeping—choice of at least two)

what is happening, who is in charge or responsible for them, and what to anticipate. The structure of events is usually facilitated by a schedule. Table 10.6 offers the reader a representative schedule for a full-day day care program.

Activities and Learning

The activities that we arrange for children should represent the *tasks of early childhood.* These tasks as a basis for curriculum decisions introduce the child to the cognitive, emotional, and social skills that are needed to order her environment. In turn, successful task completion will insure that each child will be able to effectively use these skills in the service of future learning.

There are twelve tasks that constitute the body of preschool learning which we find characteristic of early childhood environments (Honig, 1982).

Task 1 refers to learning that assists the child in her organization of different events and experiences through *grouping.* From sensory to physical phenomena, to common associations, children need to become aware of things that go together, that fit, that possess common or similar properties or characteristics. For example, all cars have wheels and all animals have legs. Wheels and legs help move things, propel objects, create motion. *Forming wholes* constitutes *task 1* learning.

Task 2 suggests the need to help the child sort out his world through the identification of those parts of elements that create groupings. In this task, the parts achieve major focus with the child learning to *create separate categories* from larger wholes. For example, there are different kinds of animals, including different kinds of dogs and different kinds of cats. Some are tame, others are wild; some are friendly, others are not.

Task 3 involves learning to *seriate,* that is, to *understand the order of arrangements and events* (by size, magnitude, or amount). Preschoolers are learning to form numerical concepts, and young children delight in assigning numerals to objects via counting. While learning to count is a relatively simple achievement, forming arrangements by order constitutes a more difficult and, thereby, significant accomplishment. Here the relative value of an object must be weighted and assessed first, then assigned some placement within an array of like objects. For example, apples might be arranged by size, or children may be assigned positions by height, weight, etc.

Task 4 concerns understanding *temporal arrangements.* Since schedules are determined by time, and events follow schedules, children need to learn what comes *before*, what occurs *after*, when *later* is, and certainly, how *soon* happenings will appear.

Task 5 involves helping children to organize places and spaces. As with *task 4*, *spatial learning* deals with the effective use of modifiers and descriptive terms that enhance our coordination of placements. For example, plates should be put on *top* of the table, *beside* the eating utensils, and *near* the glasses. Children sit *on* chairs, placed *behind* the table.

Task 6 refers to *counting skills*. According to Piaget, one of the first types of concrete operational learning to appear involves *conservation of number* (that is, the recognition that numerals form sums, not to be confused with size [big or little] or placements (rows or groupings of like sums). Enhancing such learning occurs when adults encourage children to count steps, to count out cups of juice, forks, and so on.

Task 7 refers to helping the child to learn how to distinguish between what *appears to be* from *what is*. A second form of concrete operational learning, as discussed by Piaget, is the child's attainment of *conservation of matter* (that is, the recognition that objects do not change

although appearances may be modified). Children are frequently fooled by what things *look like*. For example, a single item (a carrot stick) will be accepted as two if it is cut in half. Or, an apple cut into many pieces may be considered more than the sum of its parts. Adults may facilitate "reality learning" by encouraging children to weigh items, to count things, to sort, and to measure.

Task 8 involves helping the child to integrate varied body parts, to coordinate the use of arms and legs, and to create better flow of *body mechanics*. Activities ranging from assisting in clean up to the use of scissors in art projects help children regulate and use their bodies more effectively.

Task 9 refers to *learning to think and solve problems*. Here rudimentary reasoning may be enhanced by encouraging children to engage in "if-when," "because," "what-if," and "perhaps" explorations. Children who practice probabilistic, "problem solving" will seek better answers to complex issues, as well as be encouraged to ask "how."

Task 10 seeks to encourage the use of imagination with safety. As an extension of *task 9*, adults who are willing to foster "pretend-like" behaviors, also assist in the development of creative solutions. Safe explorations suggest that *fantasy and imagination* are valued.

Task 11 calls attention to assisting children in their use of language and in their development of attitudes that value books. Language facilitates children's communication and thinking. In fostering *language development* among children we need to encourage them to *speak*. And adults, in turn, need to be good listeners. *Listening* involves adult encouragement and patience.

Children enjoy stories and books tell stories. Books also encourage intimate child-adult interactions. Furthermore, books are facilitators of ideas and information, as well. Children, like adults, need to be encouraged to treasure books.

Task 12 directs our attention to the acquisition of *interpersonal skills*. As we have noted earlier, the preschool is a microcosm of the child's society. Here, often for the first time, children meet peers and adults within an organized institutional setting. What happens in the preschool is, therefore, of significant importance for latter adaptation, as well as of immediate interest. Emotional learning, in terms of personal interactions with others, is of particular importance to the preschool child. Children need to be helped to acquire *awareness* of their feelings. They need to be allowed to feel sad, afraid, joyous, and angry. Moreover, they need to develop an *acceptance* of difficult, often painful, and occasionally frightening, feelings. And finally, adults need to help children *express* their feelings in safe and constructive ways. Talking about feelings, using books that examine children's feelings, encouraging art and movement exercises all contribute to this process. Activities encouraging children's development are listed in Table 10.7.

TABLE 10.7. Some Good Toys and Play Materials for Young Children (All Ages Are Approximate. Most Suggestions for Younger Children Are Also Appropriate for Older Children.)

Sensory Materials	Active Play Equipment	Construction Materials	Manipulative Toys	Dolls and Dramatic Play	Books and Recordings	Art Materials
2 year olds and young 3's						
Water and sand toys; cups, shovels	Low climber	Unit blocks and accessories: animals, people, simple wood cars and trucks	Wooden puzzles with 4–20 large pieces	Washable dolls with a few clothes	Clear picture books, stories, and poems about things children know	Wide-tip watercolor markers
Modeling dough	Canvas swing	Interlocking construction set with large pieces	Pegboards	Doll bed	Records or tapes of classical music, folk music, or children's songs	Large sheets of paper, easel
Sound-matching games	Low slide	Wood train and track set	Big beads or spools to string	Child-sized table and chairs		Finger or tempura paint, ½" brushes
Bells, wood block triangle, drum	Wagon, cart, or wheelbarrow	Hammer (13 oz. steel shanked), soft wood, roofing nails, nailing block	Sewing cards	Dishes, pots, and pans		Blunt-nose scissors
Texture matching games, feel box	Large rubber balls		Stacking toys	Dress-up clothes: hats, shoes, shirts		White glue
	Low 3-wheeled, steerable vehicle with pedals		Picture lotto, picture dominoes	Hand puppets		
				Shopping cart		
Older 3's and 4 year olds						
Water toys: measuring cups, egg beaters	Larger 3-wheeled riding vehicle	More unit blocks, shapes, and accessories	Puzzles, pegboard, small beads to string	Dolls and accessories	Simple science books	Easel, narrower brushes
Sand toys:	Roller skates	Table blocks	Parquetry	Doll carriage	More detailed picture and story books	Thick crayons,
				Child-sized stove or sink		

358

muffin tins, vehicles	Climbing structure	Realistic model vehicles	blocks	More dress-up clothes	Sturdy record or tape player	chalk
Xylophone, maracas, tambourine	Rope or tire swing	Construction set with smaller pieces	Small objects to sort	Play food, cardboard cartons	Recordings of wider variety of music	Paste, tape with dispenser
Potter's clay	Plastic bats and balls	Woodworking bench, saw, sandpaper, nails	Marbles	Airport, doll house, or other settings with accessories	Book and recording sets	Collage materials
	Various sized rubber balls		Magnifying glass	Finger or stick puppets		
	Balance board		Simple card or board games			
	Planks, boxes, old tires		Flannel board with pictures, letters			
	Bowling pins, ring toss, bean bags and target		Sturdy letters and numbers			

5 and 6 year olds

Water toys: food coloring, pumps, funnels	Bicycle	More unit blocks shapes, and accessories	More complex puzzles	Cash register, play money, accessories, or props for other dramatic play settings: gas station, construction, office	Books on cultures	Watercolors, smaller paper, stapler, hole-puncher
Sand toys: containers, utensils	Outdoor games: bocce, tetherball, shuffleboard, jumprope, Frisbee	Props for roads, towns	Dominoes	Typewriter	Stories with chapters	Chalkboard
Harmonica, kazoo, guitar, recorder		Hollow blocks	More difficult board and card games		Favorite stories children can read	Oil crayons, paint crayons, charcoal
Tools for working with clay		Brace and bits, screwdrivers, screws, metric measure, accessories	Yarn, big needles, mesh fabric, weaving materials		Children's recipe books	Simple camera, film
			Magnets, balances			
			Attribute blocks			

From: ''Choosing good toys for young children'' by S. Feeney and M. Magarick, *Young Children*, 1984, 40(1), 21–25.

SOME SPECIAL/SELECT PROGRAMS

During the 1960s a variety of preschool programs were instituted for young children. Some represented modifications or extensions of previously established programs, while others were initiated through the support of new research findings or theoretical advancements concerning the nature of young children's learning and cognitive development. Many of these programs involved both university participation and federal sponsorship. Clearly, their rapid growth represented a highpoint of social interest and support of programs for young children. Today many of these programs continue to serve young children, some at a reduced level of support. Moreover, the ideas generated by these efforts have been widely disseminated and may be observed in programs.

Behavior Analysis in Early Childhood Education

One of the most controversial of early childhood programs initiated during this period was the *behavioral analysis model* of preschool education (Bereiter and Engelmann, 1966). This approach to teaching young children was originally designed to help compensate for learning deficits found among disadvantaged children, particularly black, youngsters residing in the inner city. In orientation and practice, this model is founded upon behavior theory and involves extensive structuring of both the child's classroom experiences and learning opportunities. A key aspect of the model is the idea of *structured learning*, which includes arranging the environment, specifying the behaviors to be acquired, and delineating what teachers do in assisting the acquisition and performance of selected behaviors. The logic of this approach, especially as applied to children with limited academic skills or learning difficulties, is suggested by Evans (1975). He notes,

> Aspects of the environment (e.g., physical equipment, teacher behavior, learning materials) are arranged to maximize the probability of desired behavior and to minimize the likelihood of incompatible behavior. In other words, the cues to which the child will respond must be structured so that positive reinforcement can be administered. Applied successfully, this principle has broad implications for the motivation of behavior (p.99).

By ensuring the occurrence of correct responses early in a learning sequence, success is fostered and the frustration of failure and error reduced.

Structure, involving the control of behavior, characterizes all facets of behaviorally oriented programing. For example, in a behavior modeled program, materials are carefully arranged or limited for specific use. To illustrate, play materials are not made readily available for children' use, particularly while the children are engaged in preacademic training activities. The logic for this procedure is that "play responses," particularly in an academic context, represent behaviors that are incompatible with desired academic responses. Hence, uncontrolled access to "play articles" would strengthen playful behavior and simultaneously weaken academic interests and motivation.

Activities and materials, as the reader may note, are clearly designed or arranged for specific use. Again, to illustrate, the learning of social responses, such as helping, cooperation, or sharing, involves learning acquired and maintained through teacher-initiated/directed behaviors, which guide the child toward desired outcomes. Hence, a teacher may ask a child to help distribute a musical instrument to each child in the group in preparation for a music activity, rather than to ask each child to select his own instrument (thereby avoiding grabbing and argument, as well). Or, on the playground children may be assigned specific tasks (for example, carrying out equipment, cleaning up the base paths, turn taking), which are subject to adult reinforcement and peer modeling influences. The role of the teacher in behaviorial programs is both active and directive.

The materials and learning advocated by this model are also characterized by order and structure. Learning is facilitated through the use of programmed materials usually directed by three interests. First, materials are arranged in a *graduated sequence—order of presentation* ranging from *simple to complex*. Learning is initially broken down into smaller parts, which are then acquired in an ordered prearranged sequence of presentations, whereby the child moves from one level of understanding to a slightly more difficult level of comprehension and so forth. Here, it is the *bits and pieces* that *form wholes*. A second feature of this approach is that the child is provided *immediate feedback* concerning correct or incorrect performance. A single bit of learning is achieved and confirmed; when a difficulty is encountered it is noted, and the child's efforts are redirected toward solution. A third facet of programmed instruction is that learning materials are "tailor-made," that is, *individuated*, with rate of progress determined by the child and her efforts rather than by group goals and achievements (Epstein and Skinner, 1982).

One of the innovative instrumental components of the behavioral model has been the development of the DISTAR Instructional System (Science Research Associates, 1972). This program consists of sequenced learning tasks in language, arithmetic, and reading. (Although this program was originally developed for disadvantaged preschoolers, it is currently being utilized for kindergarten and primary school children with academic and learning problems.) The central principle surrounding the DISTAR system is that instructional objectives may be arranged in a hierarchy of successive complexity and inclusiveness so that learning may proceed from one level of understanding to another. For example, one level of DISTAR language learning involves the ability to name positive and negative examples of different concept classes such as types of tools (for example, Is a hammer a tool? Is a dog a tool?), vehicles (for example, Tell me something that is a vehicle. Tell me something that is not a vehicle.), pieces of furniture, wild animals, and farm animals.

The main characteristics of the DISTAR method are:

1. Fast-paced instruction (drill)
2. Reduced off-task behavior
3. A strong emphasis on verbal responses
4. Carefully planned, small-step instructional units
5. Heavy work demands requiring high levels of concentration

The Cognitively Oriented Curriculum in Early Childhood Education

A second, highly innovative approach to preschool education emerging from the 1960s is the cognitively oriented curriculum (Weikart, Rogers, Adcock, and McClelland, 1971). This approach, based on the work of Piaget, takes a very different perspective from the behavioral model of early childhood education reviewed earlier. In this model educational focus is placed on *concept learning* rather than academic learning, favoring discovery and exploration over planned and structured curriculum. Teachers in this program are less directive than in behaviorally oriented programs.

> The main premise underlying the Cognitively Oriented Curiculum is that there cannot be a basic understanding of self and world without the ability to place the self in time and space and to classify and order objects and events. Within the Piagetian framework this means that two kinds of capabilities have to be developed by the child. First, the child must begin to make connections between objects, between events, and between objects and events; that is, he must construct relationships among the things in his environment and then expand his system of relationships into an organized way of dealing with the world. Second, the child must begin to construct mental representations in increasingly complex and abstract ways. The two are complementary: the ability to construct and make use of relationships goes hand in hand with the ability to construct meaningful representations (Weikart, Rogers, Adcock, and McClelland, 1971).

The cognitively oriented curriculum is based on Piaget's description of how children come to construct and arrange information. In essence two forms of organization are stressed: *logico-mathematical* and *spatio-temporal* relations. In logico-mathematical relations emphasis at the preschool level is placed upon grouping (classifying) information and ordering (seriating) objects. In *spatio-temporal* relations interest is focused on how objects are arranged in terms of their spatial and sequential relationship to each other. To illustrate, concepts such as *over/under, up/down,* and *inside/outside* are stressed in spatial learnings, whereas understanding *time, sequence,* and *cause and effect* relations occupy temporal learnings.

Using the above framework as a starting point, Weikart and his associates constructed a four part curriculum for preschool education. The four content areas consist of: classification, seriation, temporal relations, and spatial relations. Activities constructed by the teacher either focus on or include exercises in one or more of the four content areas, which serves as a basis for curriculum planning. A brief description, abstracted from Weikart and his associates, of each of these areas, with some illustrative activities follows:

1. Grouping or *classification*, is approached through having the child make relational or functional discriminations. Things go together because they are used for some activity (for example, a spoon and a fork go together because they are both used for eating), or because they derive their meaning from one another (for example, a hammer and a nail). More complex groupings are based on descriptive discriminations, that is, on certain attributes that can be perceived, such as *size, shape,* or *color.* The most abstract means of grouping is based on category discriminations or conceptual labeling (for example, vehicles, furniture, or other such general categories).

2. Ordering or *seriation*, is approached through having the child deal with objects in terms of their relationships in size, quantity, or quality (for example, big/little, more/less, rough/smooth). The preschool learning goal in this category is to help the child seriate four sizes, four quantities, and three qualities of objects or events.

3. *Spatial relations* are approached through expressions of the child's body orientation and her spatial orientation of objects apart from her body. Through motoric experiences at first, and later through verbal experience with concepts of *position* (for example, in/out), of *direction* (for example, to/from), and of *distance* (for example, near/far), the child is aided in her development of meaningful constructions of space and spatial relationships.

4. To understand and respond to *temporal relations*, children begin to deal with time in terms of periods having a beginning and an end; they begin to understand that events can be ordered chronologically, and that time periods can be of variable length (Weikart, Rogers, Adcock, and McClelland, 1971, p.7).

The curriculum component of the cognitively oriented program requires a unique teaching perspective. While the curriculum is implemented by the teacher, her role here is less tutorial than in other models; in the cognitively oriented curriculum the teacher guides learning rather than directly instructs.

In teaching, a threefold approach is taken with focus placed on the teacher's learning objectives for the children. First, the teacher proposes specific goals to be achieved within the four contextual learning areas (classification, seriation, temporal relations, and spatial relations) and what activities may best incorporate these goals. Second, using a hierarchy of representation at levels of understanding (ranging from object recognition to label identification), as derived from Piaget's theory, the teacher incorporates in his plans a sequence of activities that are arranged in terms of the child's current and projected level of understanding. Third, the teacher observes the mode of operation used by the child (whether motoric or verbal) in her completion of the activity. In this latter aspect of curriculum planning and implementation, he will encourage the child to use both motoric and verbal operational modes that range from simple to progressively more complex. For example, in a motoric mode of operation the child may progress from climbing up the ladder and sliding down the ramp to understanding such concepts as *up and down*. Similarly, in a verbal mode of operation the teacher may provide the initial verbal stimulus to the child (for example, "Jerry, tell me about. . . . "), leading the child to use self-verbalizations *while* on task, then later ask for verbalizations *after* the task is completed, and still sometime later, request the child to initiate self-verbalizations before the task's performance (e.g., "I am going to. . . . "). Such prompting in the use of verbal description and framing of behavior leads the child to the use of recollections from *memory*, and aids the child in her spontaneous discussions of her experiences.

In the cognitively oriented curriculum:

1. Activities are developmentally ordered.
2. Children are involved in the creation and implementation of activities.
3. Learning occurs as a function of active engagement.
4. Learning goals are open ended.

The Developmental-Interaction Viewpoint: The Bank Street Model

The development of new models of early childhood education during the 1960s also stimulated a *blending* of historical and contemporary views of human growth and learning. The developmental-interaction viewpoint, also known as the *Bank Street Model* (Biber, Shapiro, and Wickens, 1971), represents one of the more prominent attempts at the integration of intellectual and affective principles of development. This approach, which places primary emphasis on developmental processes (rather than developmental theory), consists of varied learning drawn together from ego psychology (most notably, Erickson and Anna Freud), Gestalt psychology, developmental psychology (primarily Piaget), and educational psychology and philosophy (especially Dewey).

The aims of the program are threefold. These include providing opportunities that: (1) enhance the child's ego strength (that is, the child's capacity for effective interactions with others); (2) foster her autonomy and creativity; and (3) maximize the child's integration of ideas, feelings, and behaviors.

In practice the developmental-interaction model seeks to encourage multifaceted learning in children, principally within a school environment that creates opportunities for self-growth, practical applications, and the extension of school learning into the community.

The theoretical underpinnings of the developmental-interaction model favor Piagetian principles. However, greater interest is placed on process variables (that is, articulating how we can foster learning outcomes, rather than focusing on how best to describe development), and how affective and cognitive development may best be integrated (rather than how simply to encourage their parallel development). Agreement with the cognitive-developmental ideas of Piaget is evident in their mutual recognition of the need for children to engage in active interactions with the physical and social environment and in their common acceptance of development as founded upon stage-determined principles. Yet, it is in their differences that departures in emphasis and practice are suggested. As Shapiro and Biber (1972) declare, the developmental-interaction model seeks to provide children opportunities, "to try out, shift backward as well as forward, to create where necessary the opportunities for the kind of interaction that is essential for the assimilation of experience, the achievement of new integrations, and the resolution of conflict—in both the cognitive and emotional realms." (p.68).

The developmental-interaction model, as advocated by the Bank Street School, has led to the development of a variety of educational activities and learning materials, including readers, language stimulation and discovery learning materials, and mathematical learning kits. However, learning opportunities for children are neither restricted to nor inclusive of such activities. Rather, cognitive skills are considered best acquired through a "total life experience" approach. For example, conversational language activities such as reading to children, directing their attention to pictorial images, encouraging discussions of major themes and examinations of how they are depicted, all constitute important avenues for learning. Similarly, school learning focusing on

Water play allows for discovery learning.

a specific theme (water) begins with concrete school-related experiences (the use of water in caring for plants, for drinking, and for food preparation) and extend to larger external ideas (to aid in the growth of fruits and vegetables that we eat, to denote seasonal changes, for seafaring transportation and commerce).

In the developmental interactional model:

1. Priority is placed on the development of a positive attitude about learning.

2. Learning occurs within a flexible and varied format of child-centered activities.
3. Children learn to trust in the predictability of the school environment.
4. "Support-guided play" (that is, active explorations within a nurturant, safe, and varied environment) are encouraged.
5. Acceptance of the child and avoidance of pressure are considered necessary conditions for encouraging constructive teacher-child relations.

Some Program Comparisons

Each of the three programs that we have reviewed offers different perspectives and approaches to preschool education. It may, therefore, be asked which of these varied perspectives meets the needs of young children, and how?

A variety of inquiries have been directed toward evaluating the three programs reviewed here. Peters, Neisworth and Yawkey (1985) offer the reader a well-balanced, comparative survey of these and related findings derived from representative studies of early childhood intervention projects. From their review several conclusions concerning the relative value and strengths of these differing programs emerges.

For *behaviorally oriented programs* in early childhood education, as the reader might suspect, we find academic gains closely associated with the advocacy and stress that such programs place on learning. For these programs, skills such as numerical readiness, arithmetic achievement, reading achievement, language usage, task persistence, and test-taking behaviors, are enhanced. Current evidence does not suggest that these programs are affiliated with gains in social, emotional, or cognitively defined (for example, problem solving, curiosity oriented) developmental outcomes.

Among *cognitive-discovery programs*, such as the cognitive-oriented curriculum, current evidence suggests benefits congruent with the aims of such approaches. Here, varied studies support gains in childrens' inventiveness and curiosity, verbal expression and social interactions, practice play, and problem-solving ability.

In the case of *maturational-socialization programs*, such as the developmental-interaction viewpoint (as advocated by the Bank Street model of preschool education), the programmatic goals of this approach appear to be well reflected by research findings derived from programmatic evaluations. Discovery learning programs appear to be associated with enhanced problem-solving skills and higher IQ gains, as well as independence and cooperative peer play. Children enrolled in these programs also appear somewhat more creative and responsible (that is, they assume greater responsibility for their own successes and failures, as well as ability to monitor their own behavior).

Children learn through creation.

JUDY'S DAY: SAGA OF A HEAD-TEACHER

"On my way to school, I think about the various activities that I will be setting up as soon as I arrive, and I focus upon any information about the day I will be giving to the staff teachers.

"When I enter the classroom I feel a sense of energy. My adrenaline and anticipation mount as I begin to set up the physical space and to take care of the daily administrative duties.

"The tone that we try to set each morning is one of warmth and of support. We try to make the classroom look cheerful and try to design activities that are inviting. We personally greet each child and parent to ensure that they feel welcomed.

"Specific children that attract my attention are those who appear withdrawn or sad upon arrival or at times throughout the day. I also pay close attention to children whose families are going through changes, such as the birth of a new baby or the death of a relative. In addition, I work closely with children who are very active or who may have trouble with school routines or in interactions with peers.

"In planning I strive for a balance of structured and nonstructured activities that are done alone versus in groups. We concentrate on promoting learning through play. In the course of a week I plan involvement for each child in activities in each of the many curriculum areas. General objectives throughout the week include fostering attention span, creativity, initiative, large and small muscle coordination and most of all, a love of school, and a love of learning.

"Preschool schedules are very routine-oriented. Because children at this age cannot tell time, they feel secure in knowing what comes next by the routines that they follow. For example, after outdoor time, they know to wash their hands and be seated for snack. This relieves the teachers of constantly directing their actions.

"Unanticipated events in a preschool range from a surprise visit from a child's puppy, to wet pants, to head lice, to a fall off the climber. If a school is well staffed, one teacher can get bandaids or be with a sick child while other teachers are with the rest of a class. Because we've all been through it before, usually you just take a deep breath, smile, and cope with whatever situation comes along. It is a larger problem when, on a particular day, some of your teachers and teacher aides call in sick. In that case, you quickly redesign the day to include activities that do not require a lot of adult supervision.

"During a day I have contact with one or both parents of each child, and occasionally with children's babysitters, grandparents, or siblings. Being a preschool teacher is unique since you see parents both at the beginning and at the end of each day. I interact with the director, other teachers, teachers' aides, university students, volunteers (including senior citizens), a custodian, and a secretary. On certain occasions I see speech therapists and physical therapists. I also occasionally see salespersons from equipment and supply companies.

"I greet parents daily. I try hard not to use a generic greeting but I speak to each parent by name and smile at each child. I usually have a brief conversation with the parent about the child or something happening in the parent's life, such as her job. Here I try to create a continuity between school and home, as well as letting parent and child know I care.

"I meet with parents for a formal parent conference about twice each

year. We also have about four family events each year where we social-
ize with children and their parents.

"At the end of each day I reflect on the overall tone of the day's events
and happenings. Did the children seem content and involved today? Did
the lessons go the way I expected? Are there any administrative loose
ends to take care of tomorrow?"

Analysis

Judy functions as the head-teacher of a preschool. Therefore, her duties
require administrative expertise, as well as the conventional teacher
attributes. This dual role is difficult to perform and requires a person of
high energy level and stamina. For some teachers the details of planning, supervising, *and* teaching are too stressful or too demanding. It is
important to respect those who choose to teach as well as the person
who can effectively wear several "hats."

Parent involvement and connection are obviously two of Judy's
strengths. Being aware of the total family picture of the child is an
immense aid in relating to the child's needs, but it also requires a little
something extra in time and attention. Judy's dedication to these extra
facets of her job are part of or what make her an outstanding preschool
teacher and administrator.

SUMMARY

In this chapter we have described some of the characteristics of preschool children and the tasks they must meet as they engage in the various activities of preschool learning environments. While children who
do not attend preschool programs will also acquire these abilities, the
rate and variability with which these tasks will be met and achieved
will be less predictable.

Different preschool environments also vary considerably. We have
described three programs, which emphasize different goals and procedures. Which program, behaviorally-oriented, cognitive-discovery,
or maturational-socialization, a parent chooses to send their child to
will, to a large extent, depend on the values of the parent, as well as the
local availability of these programs.

Children grow and learn because of, and often, in spite of their home
and school environments. Parents and teachers share the responsibility
in choosing and guiding children in their learning. Experience and
research suggest that a well-articulated, child-oriented preschool program with professional, trained child caregivers/teachers can be an
asset to the future learning of every child (Schweinhart and Weikart,
1986).

Explorations

PERSONAL EXPLORATIONS

These exercises are designed to help you look at your own life—attitudes, experiences, dreams, myths, and realities.

1. What was your own personal experience with out-of-home care from two years to five years of age? Do you remember this period or have you "heard" this from family members? What memories stand out for you? Write a list of some of the things you remember to discuss in class.
2. What were your favorite games before you began regular school? With whom did you play? What kind of places did you play in, that is, school, backyard, park? Draw a sketch of your best friend and where you used to play.
3. Who were the significant adults in your preschool life? What kind of relationships did you have with them? How well did they help you complete the 12 tasks discussed in this chapter? Write your evaluation of the interactions you had with caregiving adults during this preschool period.

INTELLECTUAL EXPLORATIONS

These exercises are designed to help you increase your depth of knowledge in some of the areas discussed in this chapter.

1. Find several early childhood education texts that describe toys and materials for preschool children. What major themes do they share? What major discrepancies exist? Write a brief paragraph on your findings.
2. What model of preschool education do you feel is most appropriate for preschoolers? Find some research evidence to back up your opinion and bring a summary of these data to class to debate with your classmates.
3. Look at the advertisements in several early childhood periodicals for teachers. What kinds of materials and learning activities are companies trying to sell? How do these stack up with your research on materials and toys for preschoolers? Write a critique of the marketplace offerings for early childhood settings and bring it to class for discussion.

FIELD EXPLORATIONS

These exercises are designed to take you out into the world to find real examples that illustrate and elucidate the material in this chapter.

1. Watch a Saturday morning cartoon show for children. Pay special attention to the themes of the stories and cartoons and the advertisements. Are there any connections in style, in content? What do you think children are learning by viewing these programs?
2. Try to observe a preschool in which the children are divided into age groupings, that is, three-year-old group, four year olds, five year olds. Take notes as you watch. Compare the behaviors observed with Tables 1–3 on the characteristics of different age children. How well do your observations match the tables? What differences are there? Can you postulate any possible reasons for the differences? Write your findings on one page and bring to class.
3. Attend a library preschool story hour and observe the children as they are listening to the story teller. Can you tell how old the children are from watching their expressions, attention spans, hearing their questions and comments, seeing how they relate to their parent or other adult? If possible, check out your guesses at the end of the hour and be prepared to discuss the experience in class.

References

Bereiter, C. and Englemann, S. *Teaching the culturally disadvantaged child in the preschool.* Englewood Cliffs, NJ: Prentice-Hall, 1966.

Biber, B., Shapiro, E. and Wickens, D. *Promoting cognitive growth: A developmental-interaction point of view.* Washington, D.C.: National Association for the Education of Young Children, 1971.

Clarke-Stewart, A. *Daycare.* Cambridge, MA: Harvard University Press, 1982.

Clarke-Stewart, A. and Fein, G. G. "Early childhood programs." In P. H. Mussen (Ed.), *Handbook of child psychology.* Fourth ed. (Vol. 2), New York: John Wiley, 1983.

Endsley, R. C. and Bradbard, M. R. *Quality day care.* Englewood Cliffs, NJ: Prentice-Hall, 1981.

Epstein, R. and Skinner, B. F. *Skinner for the classroom.* Champaign, IL: Research Press, 1982.

Evans, E. D. *Contemporary influences in early childhood education.* Second ed. NY: Holt, Rinehart and Winston, 1975.

Feeney, S. and Magarick, M. "Choosing good toys for young children." *Young Children.* 1984, 40, 21–5.

Honig, A. S. *Playtime learning games for young children.* Syracuse, NY: Syracuse University Press, 1982.

Katz, L. G. "What is basic for young children?" *Childhood Education.* October, 1977, 16–19.

National Association for the Education of Young Children Governing Board. "Criteria for high quality early childhood programs." Washington, D.C.: National Association for the Education of Young Children, 1984.

Peters, D. L., Neisworth, J. T. and Yawkey, T. D. *Early childhood education from theory to practice.* Monterey, CA: Brooks, Cole, 1985.

Schweinhart, L. J. and Weikart, D. P. "What do we know so far? A review of the Head Start synthesis project." *Young Children.* 1986, 41: 49–55.

Science Research Associates, Inc. *DISTAR.* Chicago: Science Research Associates, Inc., 1972.

Shapiro, E. and Biber, B. "The education of young children: A developmental-interactionist approach." *Teachers College Record*, 1972, 74: 55–79.

Verzaro-O'Brien, M., LeBlanc, D. and Hennon, C. "Industry-related day care: Trends and options." *Young Children*, 1982, 37: 2.

Weikart, D. L., Rogers, C., Adcock, C. and McClelland, D. *The cognitively oriented curriculum: A framework for preschool teachers.* Washington, D.C.: National Association for the Education of Young Children, 1971.

Chapter 11

KINDERGARTEN

Objectives

After reading this chapter the student should be able to:

1. Describe the major characteristics of a kindergarten age child.
2. Identify and describe differences between preschool and kindergarten environments.
3. Compare and contrast the facilitative and directive teaching approaches in kindergarten programs.
4. Describe the major components of a typical kindergarten day in relation to children's learning and write a sample daily schedule.
5. Define, describe, and illustrate the use of "behavioral objectives" in the kindergarten.
6. Define the term "readiness" and show the skill progression for one of the major subject matter areas illustrated in this chapter.
7. List several teacher attributes in each of the following areas:
   a. professional competencies
   b. classroom management
   c. understanding children and adults
   d. personal qualities

THE CHILDREN

Going, Coming, Moving, Knowing: Laughter and Learning

A step into the contemporary kindergarten reveals a wealth of active bodies, curious minds, and eager social contacts. Kindergarten is one of the most important and critical transitions the individual child will make in her educational career. For many children it is their first step into a school-like environment. For others, especially the increasing number of children who have had various preschool experiences, kindergarten remains an educational landmark. Never again will she be totally free of the world external to her immediate family. The expectations and demands of the "real" world have begun in earnest. The children's success or failure in this environment will shape their image of themselves as a competent "I can do it" learner or as a struggling, not quite competent individual. The developmental task of the school age child centers on "Industry vs. Inferiority," (Erikson, 1950). The child seeks to become competent and productive in this new world. Kindergarten, then, is the beginning of a long, exciting, stimulating, and often arduous road.

The Participants

Kindergarten typically begins at five years. Most public schools accept a four year old if the child's birthday will occur sometime before the end of the calendar year. The age range of a typical kindergarten therefore can be from four years, eight months to five years, nine months if the cut off date in a particular school system is December 31. Private schools may, in contrast, accept children as much as a full year earlier. This age span does not take the child's developmental level into account, however. Rather it is chronologically ordered, ignoring evidence suggesting that the range of developmental differences between individual children increases with age. The five year old whose social behavior is more like that of a three year old child is just as common an occurrence as the five year old whose verbal ability matches that of

TABLE 11.1. Developmental Expectations for Five Year Old Children (Kindergarten)

Psychomotor Skills	Language Skills
Gross Motor	*Language Recognition*
Can hop on each foot about five times	Can recognize differences in 20 minimal pairs
Can walk a straight line—toe to heel	Can identify objects by descriptions
Can catch a ball with two hands	Can remember and follow three verbal directions
Can gallop	Can place three objects in order given
Spatial Concepts	Can repeat five words in a sentence
Names objects from left to right	Understands verbal analogies
Understands up, down, beside, behind, over, under, in, out	Understands opposites
Visual Perception	Can use 25 to 50 words to describe a picture
Can identify body parts	Can use plurals, possessives, and comparisons
Can find objects hidden in a picture	Can tell three events in sequence
Can match shapes, letters, and words	
Fine Motor	
Can use scissors	
Can copy a circle and square	
Cognitive Skills	Beginning Academic Skills
Can recognize objects from pictures	Can listen to a five minute story
Can pantomime use of objects	Can identify primary colors
Can identify words as standing for objects	Can recognize rhyming words
Can group objects by shape, size, or color	Can recognize 10 capital letters
Can use two qualities in grouping objects	Can recognize five small letters
Can place objects in graduated order	Can count to 10
Can repeat a pattern of four objects	Can recognize numerals 1 to 10
Can anticipate next item in a pattern	Can match numerals one to five to sets
Can put together an 8- to 10-piece puzzle	Can identify quantities as "greater-than" or "lesser-than"
Can group objects by class, i.e., tools, toys	Can identify hour on clock

the typical seven year old. The kindergarten teacher must deal with these developmental differences in his classroom as well as those differences that reflect chronological age level. Some public school systems now use developmental screening (Gesell Developmental Screening Test is a typical example) in order to place their kindergarten children in roughly homogeneous groupings. However, this is usually possible only where the system has made the commitment to a "transition" grade between the kindergarten and the regular first grade program. For many public schools this option is not possible and the teacher must adapt her program to all levels of developmental ability and achievement.

Private schools vary greatly in the exercise of placement options. Some programs are highly flexible whereas others are extremely structured. Some programs exercise strict correspondence to age while others allow entrance based on academic or other criteria. Multiple age groupings for primary grades such as the British Infant School model place their kindergarten children into a larger social and academic matrix with the philosophy that children will work with their academic peers, as well as with their chronological age mates. Thus we see that date of birth, developmental level, program parameters, and institutional framework all affect the child's entrance into the formal educational process.

Child/Adult Ratio

The standard public school kindergarten program usually involves 25 children with one teacher. Most state educational codes place a maximum limit of 29 children in a primary classroom and a recommended number is usually 20 children. Once more, it is obvious that there is wide variation in even the most regular of our classroom types.

Starting in the 1960s with the introduction of compensatory education programs, schools across the nation began adding teacher aides and volunteer parent-participants to the classroom. By lowering the pupil-teacher ratio these changes created more opportunities for individualized instruction. Subsequently, many special education and creative programs now require these additional positions.

In California, the State Department of Education financed a program that provided school districts more funds per each kindergarten pupil if the local educational agency lengthened the school day from two and a half to three hours and hired two kindergarten teachers per classroom. In this arrangement one teacher is placed in charge of the morning session and during half of the session the afternoon teacher acts as an aide. The other half of the second teacher's morning is spent on preparation and planning for herself and her aide—the morning teacher. Such cooperative efforts have occurred under special funding and occasionally in the absence of such funding.

Many schools have been innovative in exploring ideas and developing techniques for encouraging or attracting additional classroom support. Senior citizen programs, service clubs, and individuals with special expertise (such as foreign language proficiencies) have all been used extensively in primary classrooms.

Schools that offer college training programs have used student teachers and varied observer/participants as a regular part of their staff. Even some high school and middle school programs provide opportunities that bring young people into the classroom to learn about young children and career choices while providing some valuable "helping hands."

Peer-tutors are "upper grade" children who spend some time each week helping a younger child with some difficulty (for example, learning the alphabet). These programs require additional administrative skills on the part of the teacher as well as the school staff, but are seen as extremely valuable for both the child and the volunteer. (Research on peer-tutoring programs has shown greater gains academically for the tutor herself than for the student tutored.)

In private schools the pupil-teacher ratio is often considerably lower than the public school student-teacher ratio. Generally, we find a 15-to-1 ratio as the norm, and occassionally, even lower ratios.

Oddly enough, a class of less than 12 pupils may actually lose some of the very qualities of group dynamics that enhance different kinds of learning. As the reader will recall, Piaget, among others, notes that this is a period of life where children learn from their peers, particularly as they move from the egocentric patterns of early childhood, and the narrow, singular perspective of events evoked during this period, to less confined, multidimensional, sociocentric approaches to the world. Too small a group can hinder learning by offering fewer opportunities for experimentation, modeling, and exchange of reciprocal role relations. Kindergarten teachers report an "ideal" class size of 15 to 20 as adequate in allowing for frequent interaction, but not too great to impede individualized and small group work with the teacher and others.

Length of Care

The length of the kindergarten day is probably one of the most frequently discussed, and often controversial subjects, in contemporary school programming. At present a two and a half hour period is the standard kindergarten day in the public schools. Variations include a three hour day and a "full" five hour day (for example, 9–12 A.M. and 1–3 P.M.). Why is there controversy? As the public school program increases its emphasis on formal directed teaching programs, particularly in reading and mathematics, more and more schools are beginning to turn to workbook-oriented curriculums in the kindergarten program. Such instruction (for example in the alphabet, both recognition and printing, sound-symbol correspondence and recognition, writing and computation with numbers) requires time for practice and

TABLE 11.2.   Sample Daily Schedule—Kindergarten Session A.M.

9:00–9:15	Arrival
	Attendance
	Opening exercises
	Flag salute
	Calendar
	Daily news
9:15–9:30	Concept lesson—whole group participation
	Examples:
	Colors
	Letter name
	Social studies concept
9:30–9:50	Small group lesson—expansion of concept lesson: primary colors
	Examples:
	Group 1—Children construct color collages
	Group 2—Children draw "red," "blue," "yellow" items on prepared sheet with color words written at top
	Group 3—Children dictate stories to aide or teacher using color identifications, e.g., my favorite red thing is ___
9:50–10:30	Free play activities
10:30–10:40	Snack time
10:45–11:00	Whole group lesson
	Examples:
	Art
	Music
	Literature
	Outdoor
11:00–11:20	Whole group concept lesson
	Examples:
	Number concept
	Health
	Self-image
11:20–11:35	Lesson learning review
11:25–11:30	Dismissal

expression. By incorporating social and emotional growth experiences, (for example, "show and tell," music, literature, social studies, and science lessons and even a snack time, as well as "free play" with the traditional block, puzzle, or puppet activities) we find that the traditional period alloted creates a monumental problem of time management. Add to this issue the fact that most kindergarten teachers teach two sessions per day (namely, 9–11:30 A.M. and 12:30–3:00 P.M.) and work with approximately 50 children in this period, and we can see problems of "burn out" quickly approaching.

If, as in some states, the nature of the kindergarten program continues to move into this more formal course of study it seems inevitable that the length of the school day will be increased. What effects this change will have on those five year olds who are not developmentally ready for the demands of a more complex, extended day of activities will be an issue of ongoing concern and advocacy for the professional educator in the near future.

PROGRAMS

The majority of programs serving young children are eclectic, that is, drawing ideas and techniques from different models and sources as the school and communities deem appropriate. We note, for example, that most kindergartens follow this general pattern to a significant degree. Yet, as we saw in reviewing the history of early childhood education, several distinct models of education have arisen. In the last few years we have witnessed an increased demand for more cognitive learning in the kindergarten program. Since public school kindergartens are especially sensitive to the desires of parents, school boards, and taxpayers, a host of factors calling for more academic requirements have arisen. With these demands we see an increased demarcation between two distinct teaching approaches: *facilitative teaching* and *directive teaching*. Each model offers different ideas concerning the learning process, suggesting different conceptions of how children learn and what methods are most appropriate and meaningful for young learners.

Facilitative and Directed Teaching

Facilitative teaching is primarily developmental in orientation. It sees the child as active and internally motivated with the teacher serving to guide, mediate, and organize. In *directive teaching* specific skills and competencies are taught, which are considered necessary in our modern technological culture. Here the child is expected to be receptive to new information via teacher motivated processes, that is, lessons pre-

TABLE 11.3.   Facilitative and Directed Teaching in Kindergarten Education: Characteristics and Contrasts

Dimension	Facilitative	Directive
Orientation	Maturational	Learning
View of child	Active	Receptive
Motivation	Internal	External
Curriculum	Flexible	Structured
Activities	Emergent	Planned
View of adult	Supportive	Didactic
Role of adult	To guide	To teach

sented in a manner that catches the child's curiosity and builds interest but are paced by teacher directed goals. Specifically, the teacher's role is to plan lessons that will help the child to learn curriculum material that is considered appropriate at specified points in the educational ladder (see Table 11.3).

In fact, neither view delineated here, facilitative or directive, would be considered appropriate by most modern educators if taught alone or used for all children. Rather, these two approaches can be viewed as the ends of a continuum, with most programs occupying some midpoint between these extremes. Certainly, the child left totally to his own choices might decide he only wants to learn *some* of the skills we believe are needed in modern society. Nor will directed external control ensure experience in the creative thinking skills necessary for adaptive growth and change. In an eclectic approach the degree and amount of directive and facilitative teaching varies from school to school, from teacher to teacher, and often from subject to subject. Yet differenes in choice of basic approach can, and do, produce strikingly different classroom environments. What degree of balance between these positions will provide the best learning environment for young children while still meeting the demands of our society remains one of the important and pressing issues in early childhood education.

In illustrating these approaches we turn our attention to an example of the well-known facilitative approach, namely, the *open classroom* model and alternatively to a public school kindergarten program that might serve as an example of directive programming. We caution the reader that it is important to realize that how one views these different approaches is often a reflection of one's own philosophy of education and beliefs about human nature and individual personal experiences. As teachers we note that choosing an appropriate balance between these perspectives entails a carefully defined range of options based on a broad understanding of the learning process and the individual learner. We will discuss each of these programs describing their unique and central characteristics. We also note that the application of these approaches varies greatly in practice and that any particular classroom will differ somewhat from our description.

The Open Classroom

This facilitative model of teaching is frequently referred to as a form of unstructured or informal education. It is based on the English Infant School, and its American counterpart is generally referred to as the Open Classroom or open corridor (Weber, 1971). In concept and practice the open educational model represents an educational experience quite different from the practices of more traditional U.S. primary school programs. In theory and application, the open education classroom views the child as an active and inquisitive learner who asks her own questions and is innately motivated to interact with the environment. Resting heavily on the work of Rousseau, Froebel, and Piaget, this program emphasizes the special distinctiveness of the individual learner and the individuality inherent in her learning style. Here learning is personally defined and individually practiced. Further, the learning process is neither predictable nor controlled. It is anticipated that the child's development will be uneven in both pace and pattern, reflecting both the learner's unique experiences, as well as her capacity for the integration of disparate events. Using the Piagetian concept of learning as stemming from assimilation-accommodative processes, the child's inner needs are viewed as being inextricably linked to her outer adaptations.

In the classroom Open Education translates into a program focusing on creative interest centers, individually independent and often spontaneous, learning where adults serve as unobtrusive guides. Specifically, the adult plays a supportive rather than didactic role here, with emphasis placed on creating both situations and opportunities for the child to learn. A facilitative teacher in the Open Classroom is expected to be knowledgeable in the theoretical framework of Piaget and to be able to accurately assess the child's cognitive functioning level so that the centers and materials created will stimulate the *natural* accommodations of the child. One such form of learning is reflected in social development, which is fostered through multiple and diverse peer interactions. In the original English model the classroom was typically ungraded, with ages ranging from four or five to seven or eight years. Similarly, the U.S. counterpart of the Open Classroom may be ungraded with children ranging in age from five to seven years interacting at various points during the course of the full school day.

The physical arrangement of the Open Classroom, as its name

implies, is neither self-contained nor closed. Rather, it is a working environment that spills into the corridors and throughout the primary learning areas. Children may be located anywhere in the total space, perhaps reading, writing, cooking, building, weighing and measuring, or discussing their experiences with others. There is no set plan of the day and few organized or fixed periods. Opening exercises, music and movement, lunch and snack times, are usually the only times of the school day structured to enable the large group to come together as a single interacting body. Clearly, skills are taught. Yet, a skills period may typically involve a number of different groupings each working simultaneously on a related, but different aspect of some larger activity. While some children may be writing, others will be reading or involved in numerical tasks, each at his own level of understanding, with all activities linked to a central, integrating project. Thus, a reading group might be dictating stories on the new guinea pig in the animal corner, while another group is writing their own animal stories and poems with a teacher's guidance, while still a third group of children may be weighing the food or the guinea pigs themselves. Other children might be working independently in a group of two or three or might be reading to each other from a factual book about animals. Purposeful involvement is the keynote of such an approach. The child's use of the environment cuts across subject areas as each pursues interests leading to an integration of experience and learning.

The teacher in the Open Classroom moves from child to group to activity, offering suggestions, supplying information, guiding new investigations, and participating in various learning endeavors. When new materials are introduced or a new center set up, the purpose is to stimulate curious minds, and few directed lessons are planned. Above all, the general mode of teacher behavior is characterized by her availability, flexibility, mobility, and nonjudgemental posture. She is a vital, if unobtrusive part, of the children's activities.

On first glance the teaching style portrayed in the Open Education classroom may look easy. In fact, it requires intense awareness, continuous involvement, and a great deal of stamina. The teacher must be aware of each child: his interests, his skill level, his learning pace, and his social and emotional needs. She must be aware of what comes next for this child, this group, this unit and what will be the best way to provide the necessary experiences and materials to ensure appropriate learning outcomes. In her work, she must be moving, interacting, planning, discussing, reassuring, stimulting, and doing—a process that requires enthusiasm, as well as sustained effort. Facilitative teaching as a primary mode of interaction is a complex and demanding role, and the Open Classroom represents a special approach to learning. Certainly, it is not for all schools, all teachers, or all learners. Program participants in this approach see the child as the center of learning, trusting the learner to follow self-directed paths of knowing. Correspondingly, the teacher is seen as a less central figure in the learning process. She motivates through gentle control and suggestion. She teaches through creating opportunities for learning. For those who believe in the Open Classroom concept, school is an exciting and stimulating place—a challenge and an adventure.

The Public School Kindergarten

In contrast to the above approach, in the United States the kindergarten has established a slowly evolving tradition of viewing learning through readiness. The notion of "readiness" refers to the body of pre- and beginning academic skills, which will prepare the child for the acquisition of reading, writing, and mathematical competencies. This concern with preparation for the "grades,'" that is, first through sixth grade, requires a more directive teaching approach and a more structured curriculum. While the precise curriculum of the school program varies, as does the teaching approach, common experiences may be anticipated. For example, we find activities based on individual and small group interacton, with "free play" integrated into the environment and programs where the total class is engaged in workbook directed exercises.

Certain academic learning and skills are deemed necessary by the culture in which the school is embedded. A child needs to learn how to read and, therefore, the letters of the alphabet, the letter-sound relationships (for example, the sound of *r* in bar, rubber, scrub, and so on), the associations of word and print, and left-to-right eye patterning are included in the curriculum. Writing skills dictate adequate fine-motor control so that the use of scissors, crayons, and pencils will be included in a variety of activities. For mathematics, lessons in counting, recognizing, matching, and writing numerals and experiences with time, temperature, and measurement will be introduced. Directive teaching is a necessary basic mode for the teacher in a readiness curriculum. It is the teacher who motivates student involvement. She is the key to the success of the program. Her knowledge of child development is reflected in her ability to assess and plan activities suitable to the child. She must coordinate activities to reflect the child's present level of skill in those academic areas suggested, and direct attention to such important social and emotional growth indexes as attention span, cooperation, persistence, and peer interaction.

Within the guidelines of academic criteria established by educational policy and method of instruction, the teacher plans lessons, establishes learning centers, and creates activities that will interest and motivate the child to learn needed skills. Most teachers attempt to create a balance in their program by including periods of "free play" where children choose their own activities from the many available in the environment. Some types of centers or lessons may also be more exploratory, such as working with magnets or experimenting with colors in finger painting. However, the need to meet stated achievements by the end of the school year requires that the teacher keep the overall goals of the curriculum progressing. It is the teacher's job to blend the children, the methods, and the materials into an exciting, meaninfgul, and productive learning environment. Furthermore, the learning that occurs must offer a positive experience for the individual child since his basic attitudes about his ability to learn in school will be shaped by this foundation of experience. A positive sense of self, a belief that "I can do it," and a feeling of personal worth are essential components in success or failure in any school environment.

The responsibility for learning is clearly centered on the teacher in this type of public school program. Most kindergarten teachers provide this learning environment for 2 classes a day, each containing approximately 20 to 30 children. Planning, interacting, teaching, nurturing, disciplining, each create a constant flow as the children move from large group activities, to small group lessons, to individually chosen or assigned tasks. As the child creates a fall collage with leaves, twigs, and moss she is engaged in a formal art project. For the teacher the child's activity also sets the stage for a science lesson created by the use of changing fall colors, as well as a physical growth exercise allowing the child an opportunity to practice fine-motor skills as the child clips, places, and pastes objects, and a writing activity as the child laboriously prints her name on her piece of construction paper. Each activity is planned to meet one or more of the readiness objectives of the program.

TABLE 11.4. Kindergarten Materials: Outdoor Apparatus

Swings, trees (for climbing, shade)	Storage sheds
Slide	Large hollow blocks
Climbing gym	Walking boards
Climbing rope	Large cubes/blocks
Sandbox and assorted toys and pails	Logs and culverts
Garden with assorted tools	Wooden mazes/tunnels
Seesaws (teeter-totter)	Play house
Rocking boat	Tree house
Outdoor trampoline	Puppet theatre
Bikes and wagons	Open areas for organized games, e.g., softball, kick ball, circle games, etc.
Roller skates	Pool
Skate boards	
Traffic controls (signs, traffic lights, play garages, etc.)	

TABLE 11.5.   Kindergarten Materials: Music

Piano	Assorted drums	Kazoos
Autoharp	Triangles	Rattles
Record player	Tone blocks	Tambourines
Records	Rhythm instruments	Xylophones
Tape recorder	Cymbals	Maracas
Assorted bells	Gongs	Shakers

TABLE 11.6.   Kindergarten Materials: Housekeeping

Table and chairs	Floor mirror—full length
Chest of drawers	Broom, mop, dust pan
Cupboard	Dishes, tea set
Sink	Clothes line, basket, clothes pins
Stove	Telephone
Ironing board and iron	Doctor's kit
Refrigerator	Cooking utensils—pots, pans, cutlery
Tea table and chairs	Dress-up clothes
Rocking chair	Bed or cot
Doll carriage	Pillows, quilts, blankets
Dolls and doll beds	Food containers
Push-me carriage	

TABLE 11.7.   Kindergarten Materials: Water Play Center

Large water container	Tubes
Pails	Funnels
Cans	Straws
Water Wheel	Food coloring
Corks	Hand mixers
Sponges	Egg beaters
Soap	Squeeze bottles
Floating toys (boats, inflatables)	Alternative use materials (sand, rice,
Strainers	snow, shaving cream, etc.)
Buckets	

This approach is just as demanding as the facilitative approach explored earlier. The teacher must be able to meet the needs of the child and the requirements of the school community. The task is exacting, sometimes frustrating, and often enormously rewarding as the child grows and learns.

TEACHER-SCHOOL ACCOUNTABILITY. The multifaceted directive learning approach sketched above has become characteristic of the modern kindergarten program. It is, in part, a response to recent demands from

TABLE 11.8.   Kindergarten Materials: Manipulatives

Blocks	Puzzles
Airplanes	Shape sorters
Boats	Pounding benches
Barges	Large and small dominoes
Cash register	Lacing and tying boot
Gasoline pump	Geometric forms
Train, bus, fire engine	Tinkertoys
Giant floor truck, tractor, dump truck, trailer	Erector sets
Interlocking wood trains	Stringing materials
Farm, zoo animals	Lincoln logs
Miniature wooden or plastic animals	Tiles
Small wooden cars, trucks, buses	Abacus
Wheelbarrow	Stack puzzles
Lotto games	Nesting toys
Commercial games	Lock box
Pegboards and pegs	Weaving frame

public interest groups which have stressed teacher-school accountability. This demand for accountability means that the teacher is expected to show parents, his principal, the local school board, and the community that the children are learning. Methods used to measure this learning include behavioral objectives, individually designed programs, and testing and evaluation measures. All are part of the press for accountability.

THE PUBLIC KINDERGARTEN AND BEHAVIORAL OBJECTIVES.   Behavioral objectives are specific goals or learning outcomes, which in many areas have become the focus of public accountability. In part, such objectives

TABLE 11.9.   Kindergarten Materials: Woodworking/Construction

Workbench	Sandpaper
Large table	Assorted materials (sticks, ceramic tiles, hinges, latches, wooden spools, etc.)
Hammers	
Screwdrivers	
Saws	Rulers
Pliers	Yardstick
Vise	T square
Wrenches	Compass
Nails	Protractors
Nuts and bolts	Paint
Screws	Glue
Assorted containers	Paint brushes
Scrap lumber	Closet and rack for tools

TABLE 11.10.   Kindergarten Materials: Art

Paper—butcher, fingerpaint, drawing, newsprint, brown paper	Paint brushes
Pencils	Stamp pads and ink pad
Pens	Erasers
Crayons	Staplers
Chalkboards	Paper clips
Paints	Chalk—white and colored
Easels	Pipe cleaners
Aprons, old shirts for smocks	Assorted sticks (for mixing and construction)
Drying racks	Different tape—masking, clear
Baby food jars, assorted containers	Thumbtacks
Clay	Yarn and string
Tissue paper	Toothpicks
Wax paper	Toothbrushes
Tinfoil	Sponges
Tagboard	Tongue depressors
Cotton	Buttons
Magic markers	Macaroni
Aluminum foil	Bits of cloth and ribbon
Clay	

TABLE 11.11.   Kindergarten Materials: Language Arts

Favorite story books	Writing materials—paper, pencils, crayons
Picture books	Magnetic board
ABC books	Sound-symbol games
Mother Goose books	Picture-word games
Children's magazines	Felt, magnetic, sandpaper, letters
Flannel board stories	Typewriter
Photographs	Record player
Filmstrips	Pictures

TABLE 11.12.   Kindergarten Materials: Science

Magnifying glass	Books
Aquarium	Microscope
Magnet, filings	Stethoscope
Scale	Balance
Thermometer	Prisms
Pulley	Kaleidoscope
Measuring things—ruler, compass, tape measure, timer	Abacus
Discovery box	Old machines and gadgets
Weather instruments	Containers
Theme box—"things that move"	Flashlight
"things that grow"	
"things to cook and eat"	

TABLE 11.13. The Kindergarten Curriculum

1. *Curriculum areas for kindergarten*
   - 1.1. Social skills
   - 1.2. Motor skills—gross and fine motor
   - 1.3. Music
   - 1.4. Art
   - 1.5. Language arts—listening and speaking
   - 1.6. Social studies
   - 1.7. Science
   - 1.8. Readiness skills-mathematics and reading
2. *Objectives for all areas*
   - 2.1. Motor and perceptual skill (eye-hand coordination)
   - 2.2. Kinesthetic and tactile awareness
   - 2.3. Spatial relations (body awareness in relation to environment)
   - 2.4. Auditory skills (discrimination and memory)
   - 2.5. Visual skills (discrimination and memory-sequence, patterning)
   - 2.6. Expressive and receptive language
   - 2.7. Logical thinking
   - 2.8. Social development
3. *Components of curriculum areas*
   - 3.1. Social skills
     - 3.1.1. Following directions
     - 3.1.2. Attending and concentrating
     - 3.1.3. Working independently
     - 3.1.4. Controlling impulsiveness
     - 3.1.5. Completing tasks
     - 3.1.6. Cooperation
   - 3.2. Motor Skills
     - 3.2.1. Gross motor
       Basic rhythmic activities—hopping, skipping, Jumping, etc.
       Catching and throwing
       Correct use of playground equipment—safety
       Group games and relays
       Good sportsmanship
       Exercise and fitness
     - 3.2.2. Fine motor
       Puzzles and manipulative materials
       Cutting and pasting, use of scissors
       Use of writing implements
   - 3.3. Music
     - 3.3.1. Materials
       Rhythm instruments
       Autoharp and songbells
       Records
     - 3.3.2. Content
       Seasonal songs
       Songs for enjoyment
       Songs from other cultures and countries
       Body movement and dance

TABLE 11.13.   The Kindergarten Curriculum (*Continued*)

3.3.2.   Content (*cont.*)
Music for listening
Live musical performances

3.3.3.   Concepts
Beats and time
Ascending and descending scales
Loud and soft
Appreciation

3.4.   Art

3.4.1.   Materials
Crayons and chalk
Tempera paint, poster and finger paint
Watercolors
Play dough and clay
Papers—construction, tissue, foil, etc.
Wood, wire, paper mache, and other construction materials

3.4.2.   Methods
Painting with brushes, sponges
Making murals, dioramas, mosaics
Drawing and designing
Modeling and constructing

3.4.3.   Concepts
Line and pattern
Texture and dimension
Mixing and blending
Appreciation

3.5.   Language Arts

3.5.1.   Listening
To follow directions
To find specific information: who? what? when?
For enjoyment

3.5.2.   Speaking
Show and tell
Relating experiences
Giving explanations
Reporting messages
Giving descriptions
Contributing to group discussions
Discussing poems and stories
Building vocabulary
Improving enunciation and pronunciation
Participating in creative dramatics
Pantomime
Puppetry
Dramatization
Finger plays
Choral speaking

3.5.3.   Creative Writing—Dictating messages
Language experience stories
Imaginative stories

TABLE 11.13.   The Kindergarten Curriculum (*Continued*)

3.5 Language Arts (*cont.*)

    3.5.4. Children's Literature

        3.5.4.1. Bringing children and books together

                Presenting literary forms—stories, poems, fables

                Reading aloud

                Story telling

                Flannel board stories

                Dramatizations

                Choral reading

        3.5.4.2. Activities to stimulate interest in

                Independent reading

                Trips to library

                Child selection of appropriate books

                Child sharing ideas about books

        3.5.4.3. Story interpretation through questioning at various levels of thinking

                Memory

                Translation

                Interpretation

                Application

                Analysis

                Synthesis

                Judgement

    3.5.5. Language Patterns and Usage

        Sentence sense

        Simple grammatical devices—periods, capitals

        Kernel sentence—noun, verb

3.6. Social Studies

    3.6.1. Family—functions and patterns in relation to child's self-esteem

        Different types of families

        Comparison and differences of families

        Families at work

        Families at play

        How all family members help

        Child's own place in family

    3.6.2. School

        What we do in school

        Parts of the school (library, cafeteria, etc.)

        School workers

        Duties of workers

    3.6.3. Community

        3.6.3.1. Major concepts

                What is community

                Who and what live in a community

                Organizations that benefit a community

        3.6.3.2. Where we live

                City

                    Urban living

                    Suburban living

TABLE 11.13. The Kindergarten Curriculum (*Continued*)

3.6.3.2. Where we live (*cont.*)
Country
Town
State
3.6.3.3. Homes and other buildings
Types of homes
Other buildings in a community (hospital, fire station, post office, stores, etc.)
3.6.3.4. Work people do
Community helpers
Police
Firefighters—fire prevention
Other community service
Other occupations in a community
3.6.4. Transportation and communication
Types of transportation
Types of communication
3.6.5. Maps and globes
3.6.6. Holidays—As U.S. traditions
Seasonal holidays (Christmas, Channukah, Valentine's Day, St. Patrick's Day) with attention to holidays of different religious and ethnic groups.
Patriotic holidays (Columbus Day, Memorial Day, etc.)
Comparison with other countries
4. Science—Often studied in units
4.1. Basic methods
Observing
Experimenting
Hypothesizing
Recording and charting
4.2. Living things
4.2.1. Animals
Care
Homes
Sounds
4.2.2. People
Healthful living
Bodies
Parts
Functions
Care
Basic four food groups
Drugs—use and abuse
4.2.3. Plants
Parts
Functions
Difference in growing
Soils
Care
Uses

TABLE 11.13. The Kindergarten Curriculum (*Continued*)

4. Science (*cont.*)
    4.3.   The earth and the universe
          4.3.1. Weather
                 Types of weather
                 Clothing and weather
                 Seasons
                 Weather instruments
          4.3.2. The universe
                 Moon
                 Sun
                 Planets
                 Stars
          4.3.3. Ecology
                 Inter-dependence of all systems
                 Personal involvement in a clean world
    4.4.   Matter and energy
             Change in state of matter—cooking
             Heat, fire, fuels
             Light
             Machines and frictions
             Magnetism and electricity
5. Readiness skills—mathematics and reading
    5.1.   Mathematics
          5.1.1. Level I concepts—prenumber concepts
                   Size (big-little, small-large, etc.)
                   Amount (more-less, greater than-less than)
                   Shapes
                   Seriation
                   Counting from 1 to 10
          5.1.2. Level II concepts—number concepts
                 One-to-one correspondence of sets
                 Equivalent and nonequivalent sets
                 Number-numeral recognition
                 Order of numbers 1–9 (numberline)
                 Ordinal numbers—1st, 2nd, 3rd
                 Addition and subtraction as concepts
                 Money—pennies, nickles, dimes
                   Counting
                   Simple word problems
                 Counting and number order through 99
                 Time
                   Recognizes hour and half hour
                   Uses yesterday and tomorrow
                 Calendar and seasons
                   Days of week
                   Four seasons
                 Numerical reporduction 0-9
                 Oral word problems

TABLE 11.13. The Kindergarten Curriculum (*Continued*)

5. Readiness skills-mathematics and reading (*cont.*)
    5.2. Reading readiness
        5.2.1. Level I
            Concepts
                Opposites
                Colors
                Relationships (milk-cow, letter-postman)
            Visual discrimination
                Matches similar objects and pictures
                Matches small and capital letters
                Classifies by one attribute
            Auditory discrimination
                Recognizes environmental sounds
                Recognizes rhyming words
            Auditory memory
                Remembers details
                Remembers sequence for poems and stories
        5.2.2. Level II
            Alphabet
                Identifies and recalls letter names
                Recalls and produces letters
                Symbol correspondence (phonics)
                    Recognizes beginning sounds
                    Associates sound with letter name
                    Identifies ending sounds
                    Recognizes and produces minimal pairs (rap-tap-map; look-loot-loop)
            Comprehension
                Literal
                    Identifies details from a story or event
                    Identifies main ideas from a story or event
                Interpretive
                    Is able to summarize
                    Is able to arrange story events in sequence
                    Is able to understand cause and effect relationships
                    Is able to identify problems and evaluate solutions
                    Is able to discriminate between fact and opinion
                    Is able to draw conclusions from story facts
        5.2.3. Level III—language experience approach
            1. Child or group dictates story, reads together from chart, reads individually from chart, duplicates story and puts in child's reading book.
            2. Reads story together from chart, reads story individually and underlines words child knows; child illustrates story.
            3. Child reads story and underlines words he know, does a word matching game.

TABLE 11.13.   The Kindergarten Curriculum (*Continued*)

5.2.3.		Level III—language experience approach (*cont.*)
	4.	As a group activity have children work on a word recognition game (card games using story's vocabulary). Have sentences reproduced; child arranges in order, cuts up individual words, puts words in word box.
	5.	Isolate known words and keep a list of words child knows.
		If a child knows 80 percent of words in the story, start over again with a new subject matter.
	6.	Phonics and word skill activities based on words in individual word boxes.

replace vaguely stated goals for educational programs, which were difficult, if not impossible, to document. For example, how can one show that a child has learned to "appreciate" art or "knows" the alphabet? In addition, as we have shown, an activity such as making a collage or feeding the rabbits does not provide an observer with an obvious, discernible, or measurable learning product unless she understands the relationship between the activity and the skills the child employs in the process of its performance. By stating specific objectives, which are written in behavioral terms, the teacher can establish the learning relationship of an activity relative to its performance and the specific outcome that may be expected. This approach allows the teacher to "check" her own goals against the reality of the child's performance and to modify and augment her planning as the feedback from the child's actual learning becomes apparent. This attention to actual learning as behaviors that can be sampled is also known as a *criterion referenced* approach. The concept of criterion referenced tasks implies that there is a specific behavior for which we can set a specific criterion and this will show us if mastery of learning has occurred. For example, if I want to know if a child has learned the alphabet letters I can listen to him sing the ABC song. But will that really show me he has mastered his letters? What if I show him a letter out of order, will he know it by sight? Will he know both the capital and small letter? What if it is presented in cursive style? Could he write the letter? As the reader can see there are many criteria we could choose from in determining if a particular child knew this information. Also, depending on the criteria chosen we would, in fact, tap different levels of knowledge in the child. Developmentally, certain kinds of learnings are "easier," that is, it is easier to find a letter if the teacher asks, "Which is the 'L'?" (the identification level) than if the child must independently recall the name of the letter; writing the letter is even more difficult.

Writing exercises foster children's self-expression.

Attention to appropriate criteria can provide both a clear means of ascertaining if the child has learned something and information as to what type of curriculum lessons would be appropriate for learning. For example, the child in our previous example who could identify a letter at the teacher's request but could not recall it independently, can use a flash card game, "Go Fish," and other activities to practice independent letter naming. Conversely, a child who could not yet identify letters would benefit from making a collage of a particular letter with examples cut from magazines, which show many different styles for writing and printing that letter, or from learning rhymes and tongue twisters which stress a particular letter, for example, "Billy Button bought a buttered biscuit."

Behavioral objectives that are appropriately designed with a criterion referenced approach allow both proof of learning and guidelines for teaching. However, behavioral objectives are not the only use of criterion referenced measurement. Developmental testing and diagnosis always have been rooted in this approach. Teachers have frequently used criterion referenced tasks as a useful diagnostic measure. Criterion referenced measurement clearly has a variety of applications and can be used whether or not a behavioral objective approach is desired. It is an important asset in maintaining relevant teaching and learning.

Two examples of criterion referenced behavioral objectives will serve to illustrate this approach.

1. LESSON: Making fall collages.

General objective: Children will learn about fall colors and practice fine motor skills by making a collage of leaves and other natural materials.

Behavioral objective: Each child will paste and place a minimum of four items on a collage using scissors and paste and will make one statement to the class naming the items and their relationship to the fall season.

2. LESSON: Distinguishing between the letters B, S, and T (most common English consonants).

General objectives: Each child will review the sounds of B, S, and T and be able to discriminate among them.

Behavioral objectives: Each child in the class will place nine pictures, three beginning with each sound, under the appropriate letter on the pocket chart by naming the picture and identifying the sound the object begins with (for example, bat, ball, base, cat, can, car, and so on) with 90 percent accuracy.

In stating her learning goals in these specific measurable terms, the teacher may assess objectively whether or not the child has performed as expected. If the lesson is appropriate to the child's level of understanding, the child can be successful and the teacher's program will

TABLE 11.14.   Writing Behavioral Objectives

1. *General Objectives*
    1.1.   A general objective is a general statement of intent which is:
        1.1.1.   Broad, having wide scope
        1.1.2.   Often intangible; may never be attained
        1.1.3.   Designed to provide educators with long-range direction
    1.2.   Sample general objective—The school shall help every child master the basic communication skills to the fullest extent possible for that child.

2. *Behavioral Objectives*
    2.1.   A behavioral objective is a specific statement of intent which is:
        2.1.1.   Precisely stated
        2.1.2.   Tangible; may be fully attained
        2.1.3.   Measureable; can be verified
        2.1.4.   Involves some form of human behavior
        2.1.5.   Directly related to goals
        2.1.6.   May be written for one lesson or for a unit (group of lessons centering on a common theme)
    2.2.   Sample behavioral objective—The students in my classroom who now read at a preprimer instructional level will master two additional levels by the end of the school year, as determined by administering the Spache Diagnostic Reading Scales on a pre/post basis.

3. *Basic Elements of a Behavioral Objective*
    3.1.   *Who* is going to perform
    3.2.   *What* they are specifically expected to do
    3.3.   *When* they are to achieve goal
    3.4.   *How* measured—how will you know if they attained the objective

4. *Steps in Constructing Behavioral Objectives*
    4.1.   Decide who is to do what
        4.1.1.   Common terms are learner, student, child, 80 percent of the class, the highest reading group.
        4.1.2.   Example—"The students in my classroom who now read at a preprimer instructional level . . ."
    4.2.   Decide what specific thing the learner is to do as clearly and precisely as possible with as few words as possible
        4.2.1.   Behavioral terms include words such as point, match, identify, make, state, sort.
        4.2.2.   Example—" . . . will master two additional levels . . ."
    4.3.   Decide when the behavior is to be accomplished
        4.3.1.   Time can be short or long range such as "by the end of lesson" or "after hearing the story"
        4.3.2.   Example—" . . . by the end of the school year . . ."
    4.4.   Decide how well the behavior is to be performed
        4.4.1.   In some cases the performance should be qualified. The writer may wish the behavior to be performed with a specific degree of accuracy, but this is not always included.
        4.4.2.   Examples—"with 80 percent accuracy," or "three out of four times"

TABLE 11.14.   Writing Behavioral Objectives (*Continued*)

4. *Steps in Constructing Behavioral Objectives (cont.)*
   4.5.   Decide how the writer will know if the objective has been reached
      4.5.1.   This step is most important. The method of determining will depend on the type of behavior being asked for. Most objectives are verified by a student product such as a worksheet, by a test, with a survey checklist, or by teacher observation.
      4.5.2.   Example—" . . . as determined by administering the Spache Diagnostic Reading Scales on a pre/post basis."

TABLE 11.15.   Useful Words for Expressing Objective in Behavioral Terms (The student should be able to:)

Level I (simple)	*Level II (requires application of more complex mental operations)*
Find	
Gather data	Prove
Investigate	Organize data
Describe	Analyze
Make	Apply
Do	Distinguish between
Compute	Construct
Measure	Devise a method
Prepare	Plot a graph
Manipulate apparatus	State a problem
Recognize	Contrast
Examine	Identify the variables
Identify	Compare
Recognize and site evidence for	Suggest
Classify	Differentiate
Illustrate	Relate
	Discriminate
Level III (shows student has firm grasp of major concept or shows original thought)	Justify
	Interpret
Generalize from data	
Synthesize	
Infer	
Predict	
Deduce	
Integrate	
Propose reasons for and defend them	
Formulate hypotheses	
Reorganize	
Discover	

TABLE 11.16. Sample Unit Outline: "The Ocean and You." Unit: "Our Five Senses and the Ocean" (An introductory primary unit to acquaint children with concepts and vocabulary about the ocean.)

1. General objectives
   1.1. To relate through personal experience to the concept of "ocean" or "sea."
   1.2. To promote an understanding of the ocean environment as containing plants and animals living together.
   1.3. To appreciate the ocean as a recreational and food producing source.
2. Behavioral Objectives
   2.1. After lessons in this unit students will be able to classify a minimum of 10 items of the ocean according to the 5 senses.
   2.2. After lessons in this unit students will be able to identify a minimum of five plants and animals of the ocean.
   2.3. After lessons in this unit students will be able to name a minimum of three recreational activities and three occupations associated with the ocean.
   2.4. After lessons in this unit students will demonstrate an affective appreciation of the ocean by reciting poems, songs, and stories introduced in this unit.
3. Possible Unit Experiences
   3.1. Language Arts
      3.1.1. Five senses classification charts
      3.1.2. Language experience charts—develop after trip or simulated trip to ocean; cooking; science activities
      3.1.3. Description and identification of shells from feel
      3.1.4. Dictated stories
      3.1.5. Flannel board poem, "The Fish with the Deep Sea Smile"
      3.1.6. Individual or class books, "Our Trip to the Ocean," "Our Five Senses and the Ocean"
   3.2. Science
      3.2.1. Field trip or simulated field trip to ocean—associating to each of five senses
      3.2.2. Evaporation of salt water and fresh water—How is ocean water different from regular "fresh" water?
      3.2.3. Constructing a sea water aquarium
      3.2.4. Classifying plants and animals of the sea
      3.2.5. Cooking—fish chowder
   3.3. Social Studies
      3.3.1. Role playing of occupations relating to the ocean recreations
      3.3.2. Classifying "work" and "play" activities at the ocean.
   3.4. Mathematics
      3.4.1. Comparison and contrast of
         3.4.1.1. Shell sizes—large-small; big-little, round-pointed, etc.
         3.4.1.2. Shell numbers—counting; one-to-one correspondence; pairs; more-less; odd-even, etc.
      3.4.2. Placing shells in graduated sizes
      3.4.3. Weighing shells

TABLE 11.16   Sample Unit Outline: "The Ocean and You." (*Continued*)

3.4 Mathematics (*cont.*)

        3.4.4. Identifying and matching shapes of sea items—triangle of sail on sailboat, round of sand dollar, etc.

   3.5. Reading

        3.5.1. Prereading experiences

             3.5.1.1. Sequence—Field trip, making fish chowder

             3.5.1.2. Auditory and Visual association—Picture/word cards

             3.5.1.3. Visual memory—Concentration card game with shell pictures

        3.5.2. Beginning reading experiences

             3.5.2.1. Language experience charts

             3.5.2.2. Class and individual stories and books

        3.5.3. Music

             3.5.3.1. Learn songs of the ocean

             3.5.3.2. Creative movement—*Dance-A-Story "At the Beach"*

             3.5.3.3. Movement to classical music—Debussey's *La Mer*

        3.5.4. Creative Dramatics

             3.5.4.1. Acting out flannel board poem "The Fish with the Deep Sea Smile"

             3.5.4.2. Choral verse with poems from unit kit

             3.5.4.3. Acting out stories from unit kit or other books about the ocean

        3.5.5. Art

             3.5.5.1. Sand painting

             3.5.5.2. Fish mobiles, sea shell mobiles

             3.5.5.3. Sea weed collages

             3.5.5.4. Crayon resist—ocean in water color wash over crayon boat outline

             3.5.5.5. Sea pebble mosaics or paper weights

   3.6. Suggested Order of Included Lessons

        3.6.1. Introductory lessons

             3.6.1.1. Field trip or simulated field trip to ocean

             3.6.1.2. Five sense classification charts with picture/word cards

        3.6.2. Ongoing lessons

             3.6.2.1. Art—sand painting

             3.6.2.2. Science—evaporation of salt and fresh water

             3.6.2.3. Music—dance-a-story

             3.6.2.4. Science—classifying plants and animals of the sea

             3.6.2.5. Language arts—describing and identifying shells from feel

             3.6.2.6. Reading—concentration card shell game

             3.6.2.7. Mathematics—graduated shell sizes

             3.6.2.8. Language arts—flannel board poem

        3.6.3. Culminating activities

             3.6.3.1. Social studies—role playing occupations and recreations

             3.6.3.2. Science—cooking fish chowder

TABLE 11.17. Sample Lesson Plan: Unit I—"Our Five Senses and the Ocean," Lesson #1—Science, A Field Trip to the Ocean.

1. General Objective: To provide a direct experience with the ocean environment.
2. Behavioral Objective: Each child will contribute one item from the ocean/beach to bring back to the classroom.
3. Materials: A bag (preferably plastic) for each child with his name on tape. Small shovels and pails. Several paper boxes, jars with lids. A clipboard with paper and pencil or other method of recording children's observations.
4. Procedure
   4.1. Introduction—children should be prepared for trip in advance. Class rules, clothing needs, transportations, etc. will vary with class.
   4.2. Pretrip discussion—what can be found at the beach? What items can be brought back to class? Introduce concept of being a "beachcomber."
   4.3. At beach
      4.3.1. Keep a record of what children observe and any special comments they make.
      4.3.2. Guide children to experience beach and ocean through the five senses
         4.3.2.1. What do you see? (waves, white caps, rocks, boats, etc.)
         4.3.2.2. How does the beach, the seaweed, the shells, smell?
         4.3.2.3. Touch the water, the sand, the seaweed, the barnacles. How do they feel?
         4.3.2.4. How does the ocean/sea water taste? Is there anything else to taste?
         4.3.2.5. Close your eyes. What sounds can you hear?
      4.3.3. Bring back to class
         4.3.3.1. Jars of sea water
         4.3.3.2. Live animals in sea water if available
         4.3.3.3. Sand—a boxfull would be good
         4.3.3.4. Seaweed—some in water and some not
         4.3.3.5. Shells, skeletons, driftwood, rocks, and other items of interest
   4.4. After trip
      4.4.1. Write a class language experience story (for very young children use rebus style)
      4.4.2. Children draw or paint individual pictures of trip
      4.4.3. Items from beach are set up in an "Ocean Corner" with a large picture or poster for further exploration.
      4.4.4. Discussion of items seen or brought back as appropriate to level of children
5. Follow through: Additional activities of unit will provide integration of concepts and vocabulary from trip.

move ahead. If the child experiences difficulty with the lesson, the teacher can reteach or otherwise redesign her plans to more effectively reach the particular children involved.

Behavioral objectives and criterion referenced testing, then, can be seen as providing ongoing evaluation of the teacher's success in reaching students. They are easily monitored and can serve as a device for communicating the various aspects of the curriculum to others interested in the program, including the child's parents. Most importantly, they serve the teacher in her primary mission. The responsibility for the children's learning clearly rests squarely on his shoulders. In many ways the teacher's primary role is one of decision maker. His decisions are what make the program effective and are the essential ingredient in the public schools' conceptual frame. The kindergarten is the beginning and the foundation of the school program. And the kindergarten teacher is the key in insuring its success for every child.

TEACHERS AND TEACHING

As the child matures, passing various developmental milestones, the environment and the challenges of learning change. Coupled with the acquisition of well-defined motor, social, and cognitive competencies, the tasks of learning within a formal, institutionalized setting now present the child with a new adult role model—her kindergarten teacher. In Table 11.18 we have summarized changes associated with the tasks and expectations of child and teacher in the preschool as contrasted with the directive kindergarten environment.

TABLE 11.18.   Characteristics of Preschool and Directive Kindergarten Settings

Preschool	Kindergarten
Informal	Formal
Play-oriented learning	Task-oriented learning
Stimulate	Motivate
Define	Instruct
Care	Teach
Concrete/object learning	Abstract/sign learning
Developmental	Pedagogical
Sensory/perceptual	Intellectual
Guidance	Education
Initiation	Direction

State Regulations

As defined by prevailing state laws, the requirements for teaching in the public school are set by official regulatory bodies. Usually, the state department of education serves this role, setting state-wide standards for formal educational training and criteria for accredited field experience. Although many preschool educators obtain training similar to their kindergarten colleagues, and a few states do have early childhood teaching certificates, the formal requirements and training for preschool positions are usually determined locally with standards set by a local board of directors. One important variation to this pattern is accreditation of the Child Development Associate (C.D.A.). This two-year degree program, which has recently produced its ten thousandth graduate, is a nationally established, hence, standardized program of studies and supervised field experiences for day care workers (see chapter 14). The growth of this program has created impetus for the standardization of national criteria for preschool educators, an important goal in ensuring quality care and development of young children. This degree is not, however, uniformly required for preschool positions.

As a part of the public school system the kindergarten teacher is formally accountable to established governing bodies. In her teaching she is usually responsible for enacting plans of study that follow established

TABLE 11.19.   Teacher Attributes: Professional Competencies

1. Participants in school, faculty, parent, and professional meetings.
2. Shows knowledge of community environment and utilizes resources.
3. Is able to develop and execute learning experiences in the following areas:
   a. language development
   b. math and science concepts
   c. pre- and beginning reading concepts
   d. music and art activities
   e. free choice activities such as block building, carpentry, and dramatic play
4. Can formulate learning/behavior objectives.
5. Is able to enact objectives effectively.
6. Exercises creativity and originality in the performance of tasks.
7. Shows ability to analyze own strengths and weaknesses and make appropriate instructional changes.
8. Shows ability to pace teaching activities.
9. Can evaluate children's progress and recognize areas of need.
10. Can gather observations of behavior into cogent statements concerning a child.
11. Can use appropriate diagnostic tools.
12. Maintains a balanced curriculum leading to children's social, emotional, and intellectual growth.

TABLE 11.20.   Teacher Attributes: Classroom Management

1. Organizes classroom for efficient use:
    a.   of space
    b.   of time
    c.   of resources
2. Is able to organize transitions successfully.
3. Shows appropriate attention to cleanliness and order of classroom.
4. Encourages children to maintain an orderly classroom.
5. Maintains a cheerful, educationally appropriate environment.
6. Is able to maintain control:
    a.   consistent with developmental level of children
    b.   of small groups
    c.   of whole groups
7. Encourages children to build self-discipline.
8. Utilizes additional classroom workers such as aides or parents in an efficient and effective manner.

curriculum guidelines, leading to specified learning outcomes. These outcomes, of course, are determined by local and/or state boards of education.

The parameters of the kindergarten teachers' duties, including the number of students to be taught, the number of classrooms to be served, as well as the length of her day, vacation periods, and salary schedules are established collectively through negotiated contracts in many school districts. This procedure guarantees the teacher's rights, as well as establishes her obligations to the educational system she serves.

Teacher Competencies

Our study and work with children and their teachers suggest the importance of four areas of professionalism, each critical to achieving teaching excellence. They include professional competencies, applied understanding of children and adults, behavioral/classroom management skills, and the execution/demonstration of related personal qualities. The varied facets of these competencies appear in tables 11.19 to 11.22.

A Teacher's Perspective

The attributes offered in the preceding tables represent formal characteristics that have been identified with good teaching. These interlocking aspects of teaching clearly define for us the form and, in part, the objectives of teaching. Moreover, they suggest a set of standards and expectations that the teacher must be attuned to in meeting her professional obligations. Yet, what of teaching itself? Every student needs to

TABLE 11.21.   Teacher Attributes: Understanding Children and Adults

1. Shows positive attitude when working with children.
2. Is sensitive to needs of individual children.
3. Shows positive attitude when working with adults.
4. Shows ability to analyze and evaluate the developmental level of children.
5. Is able to communicate with parents in an effective and supportive manner.
6. Works effectively with other teachers and paraprofessionals in a "team" managerial approach.
7. Works with administrators and school personnel in a professional manner.
8. Communicates a nonjudgemental approach towards children and adults.

TABLE 11.22.   Teacher Attributes: Personal Qualities

1. Exhibits poise and self-confidence.
2. Respects attitudes and opinions of others.
3. Accepts and uses criticism and analysis.
4. Has appropriate voice quality.
5. Shows growth in self-awareness.
6. Engages in learning activities to enhance professional growth.
7. Demonstrates competence in basic communication skills, including:
   a. listener skills
   b. speaker skills
8. Shows responsibility in:
   a. being on time
   b. submitting assignments and reports
   c. respecting confidentiality
   d. having materials ready and available

ask, "Is it for me?" The following narrative offers the reader a representative, and somewhat individualized, perspective on kindergarten teaching. It is a composite of one teacher's day.

Wendy's Day

"I am a morning person. I usually get up early, sometimes around 5 o'clock. As I get ready for school, I try to organize my day. I write out bills, clean up, put things in place. One of the things that I have learned in teaching is that once you go into a classroom you don't have time to plan other parts of your life.

"As I drive to school in the morning I try to run through the day, reviewing the day's planned activities and lessons. Everything has been prepared the day before, so I'm able to run through the day's events, ensuring that the children and I will be able to concentrate on the tasks ahead.

"As I enter the classroom the first thing that I hear are the guinea pigs screaming to be fed, the rabbit jumping around in his cage, the plants calling out to be watered. These are the routine things that need to be done. Paper has to be ordered, and supplies secured. Once the children arrive there is no time to attend to such matters. My planning helps to create an atmosphere of preparedness. Now I can enjoy the children because I have organized my personal space and the events that will affect the next several critical hours of their lives.

"When the children arrive around 9 o'clock, I am ready. This is important to me. I want the children to be sure of me. To know that I am ready to meet and learn with them. School is a pleasant experience, created by the atmosphere I have been able to provide for the children.

"As the children arrive, they are eager to come in. I want to support this energy, creating an emotional context that they can look forward to, one that is positive and predictable. I am an important role model for them, and I try to make sure this image is a good one.

"As the children enter the classroom I try to make contact with each

child, not just the noisy child or the one seeking attention, but each child. It's like meeting an old friend, establishing rapport with them, ensuring them that I know that they are here. Through facial expressions, body language, puffy or sad eyes, sometimes bruises, each child will speak to me. Sometimes, I am a counselor, as well as a teacher, often a mother to their varied needs. At times a child will need some special attention, a hug, some assurance that I am there. And I am.

"The day begins with opening exercises. These activities tell the children that *school is starting*. We first meet as a group, greeting each child, noting who is here and, especially, who is absent. Children need to know that they are accounted for and missed. After attendance, new events and happenings are briefly discussed. We then move to classroom routines. We discuss what day it is, where we are in the week, the month, and the season. Temperature and weather conditions are also noted. Then we have the salute to the flag, followed by "collections." There are notes from home, milk money, trip money, picture money, and a variety of other forms of exchange. Sometimes I feel like an accountant.

"After opening exercises, since it's Tuesday, we break into reading groups. Reading groups occur on Tuesday and Thursday. Other mornings consist of gym or music. During reading groups I will try to work with one group, directing my student teachers in their work with the other two groups. The student teachers are very important, and part of my attention is given over to them to ensure, like the children, that they too know that I am aware of them.

"After reading, we have a creative art activity, for example, the creation of a theme collage. This is followed by free play. Usually the children will paint, play with clay or blocks, engage in water play or doll play. I give the children the responsibility of choosing their own activity. When rules are ignored or conflicts arise, I will intervene and select an activity. Since I teach in a double classroom, I will alert the children that free play is over by flicking the lights, and they will start their cleanup. Again, cleanup becomes another opportunity for them to assume responsibility for their activities and to establish an organized working environment.

"At this time, we will begin either a group math or writing activity. A typical math activity may consist of numeral identification, in which the children will be asked to match various numerals with a corresponding series of objects such as oranges or hats. In writing, we set one day aside for learning the letter of the week. Also, the children will practice writing their names or copy a small sentence or their alphabet letters.

As some children finish before others, we may sing a little song or recite a quiet poem while waiting for the rest of the group to join us. This is often a familiar, seasonal song or poem that alerts the children to finish their activity. As the others join in, we complete our song and the children wait quietly. I will then suggest that all the children whose name begins with, perhaps the letter J, or all the children who are wearing the color green get the snack that they brought from home and quietly take a chair and sit at one of the four tables we set up for snack time. During snack time I will return the children's papers, discussing their individual efforts and my corrections or suggestions for further work. After clean up there is quiet time. Each of the children may get a book, puzzle, or quiet game to bring back to their table to engage their attention.

"We follow quiet time with a group story. Our stories are usually seasonal (fall, winter), topical (Thanksgiving, Hannukah, Christmas), or informational (planting, harvesting), or related to trips or activities that we may be pursuing currently. The stories are selected to reinforce past learning, as well as to motivate future activities.

"Outside activities, weather permitting, follow. During inclement weather we stay indoors. Then a marching band or creative movement activity might occur within the classroom.

"At this time, approximately 11:15, the children start to prepare for departure. The morning session begins at 9:00 and ends at 11:30, while the afternoon session begins at 12:30 and ends at 3:00. During the colder months, this means getting 22 children into snowsuits, buttoned and zippered, and ready to go. As the children line up in the hall, in anticipation of the bus ride home, I pass out notices and papers to be taken home to parents.

Between the morning session and the beginning of the afternoon group, I usually meet with a parent, who may have come to take his child home, and, particularly, with the student teachers in order to offer feedback on their work and to review the next day's activities. I then run to the bathroom, followed by a quick dash to the central office to pick up my mail and notices. At this time I have about 15 minutes for lunch or personal time. Sometimes, I might take a short ride, getting that needed respite from an active and busy morning of learning. I find this short rest period very important if I am to maintain enthusiasm for the afternoon group.

"I am now ready for the afternoon group.

"A lot of things happen in the course of the day, some planned for, many unanticipated. There is the nitty-gritty of having to deal with sickness, the children's primarily, but my own as well. And there are accidents that require my attention. In the middle of a lesson, there might be a firedrill. That's frustrating. Particularly, after I've put all this preparation into a lesson. Then I need to be able to step back and realize that there is a tomorrow. Many unanticipated events involve people. A father, under a court restraining order, wants to take his child home. Or a distraught mother may come in to demand that her child be put into another class or taken out of school. Sometimes I can help. Sometimes I can't. I feel that both the parent and child should receive the best help. That might mean being able to make an effective recommendation to help them feel better about themselves. But even when I can't solve the problem, they leave with the feeling that I care.

"My day is filled with many interactions, involving children, parents, colleagues, administrators, support personnel, and others. In each of these I need to say things in a positive way, so that parents, teachers, and other persons feel positive about themselves. Other teachers are often important here. They are people I can go to for assistance and comfort. Three of my students have Individual Educational Programs (I.E.P.s). As such, I need to coordinate my teaching with other teachers and specialists. In other interactions we will discuss the progress of "old" students, comparing notes, sharing our learning about the children.

"Having a good principal is also important. She needs to be someone I feel comfortable with, whom I can go to with a problem. A good principal, through her support and encouragement, creates good teachers. And support personnel are critical. Our janitorial help not only cleans, but becomes a hidden resource in locating an incubator for children to use in special projects. Good secretarial help sets up parent-teacher conferences, locates parents in times of need, checks up on delivery dates, and ensures that supplies and materials are ordered on time. Teaching is a complicated enterprise. It involves the cooperative efforts of a lot of people and it demands coordination of effort.

"Work with parents is especially important. Frequently, I am a counselor, especially a person that listens. One parent's husband has recently left, and she is alone and struggling. I need to know when to refer, how to listen, how to assist. Another parent feels that his child should be achieving more. He is dissatisfied and argumentative. How do I explain individual differences and developmental lags in a manner that he can understand? It's been a long day. As it draws to an end, I ask, have I ensured the day's learning? Also, have I received feedback? Have I been an effective teacher? Do we need to emphasize further work and for which children?

"I feel good. It was fun. With hugs and kisses, the children reaffirm me. They understood my limits and my love. They will miss me. And they will come back. What I do in kindergarten will effect each child. Their future academic career will be changed, but also who they are as people, how they will learn, and what they will believe. We are setting up their entire school experience. Learning should be a joy and it is my responsibility to make that happen."

As Wendy's narrative highlights, the role of the kindergarten teacher is both demanding and fulfilling. The classsroom where Wendy teaches is a large double room shared with another kindergarten class. The two groups work separately and periodically together during the various portions of the school day. The myriad details and interactions require constant alertness and an ability to meet the emergencies of the moment with flexibility and good humor. The energy and enthusiasm Wendy brings to her classroom are met and matched by the exuberance of the children. Her attention to each child and the ebb and flow of the entire class speak eloquently of her patience, caring, and the years of experience and training she brings to her task. The complex meshing of mother and mentor, teacher and trouble shooter, coordinator and counselor is not for everyone. Clearly, Wendy loves her job and conveys this to her children in a variety of ways. She has her periods of discouragement, her "off" days, but the prevailing impression is that of a competent and professional person, doing her best and encouraging the children and her colleagues to do the same.

OBSERVING THE KINDERGARTEN CLASSROOM

Because of the enormous numbers of children, teachers, and schools across the United States, the variety and differences in kindergarten education are considerable. The balance between individual style and experience as reflected in the teacher's role and the realities of the needs of diverse children and community requirements make evaluation difficult. Do any of us really know what is the *best* route for the child to take on her road to growing up? We have some knowledge and many "educated" guesses.

Yet there are some guidelines that can provide helpful clues to the educational value of a particular setting and whether the classroom observed is providing an appropriate environment for all the children attending. Calm, busy, articulate children working with a friendly and encouraging teacher can occur in facilitative classrooms, directive classrooms, and anywhere in between. The key is the attention that is given to the developmental needs of the children, the feelings of success in the children, and the style of interaction between the teacher and the children. The child who is lost and confused in a facilitative open classroom or the child who is frustrated and failing in a directive lesson are testimonies to a poorly executed program. As parents and educators we can ill afford any child to suffer from poor teaching or misdirected curriculum decisions.

SUMMARY

The beginning of the formal educational process starts for most children with their kindergarten experience. The quality and success of that experience rest on a complex interaction of factors including the developmental readiness of the child, the programmatic demands of the particular school environment, and the competence and charisma of the teacher herself. It is the teacher whose decisions and assessments control learning. The use of criterion referenced objectives are measureable and systematic aids capable of aiding in planning, but ultimately the professional competence of the teacher is the variable that determines the pattern of learning and the child's sense of success or failure.

As parents, professional educators, and individuals who are concerned with children, it is our obligation to be aware of the policies and directions of our public schools and to provide input and, when necessary, political pressure to maintain and increase the standards of excellence for the teaching of young children.

Explorations

Do one or two explorations in each category to extend and enrich your understanding of this chapter.

PERSONAL EXPLORATIONS

These exercises are designed to help you look at your own life—attitudes, experiences, dreams, myths, and realities.

1. Think about your first school experience. Using a child's crayon draw a picture of your kindergarten teacher. In a paragraph or two, describe your drawing.
2. Write a short paragraph describing your most vivid recollections of your first teacher. What three attributes stand out most clearly? In what ways, positive or negative, did these experiences influence your attitudes toward school?
3. How would you describe your kindergarten experience to a younger brother or sister attending kindergarten for the first time.

INTELLECTUAL EXPLORATIONS

These experiences are designed to increase your depth of knowledge in some of the areas discussed in this chapter.

1. Do some library research on the current status of the readiness concept. Find two articles with different perspectives and compare and contrast their viewpoints. Write a short paper stating your views on this issue, and indicate the support or lack of support for your opinions.
2. Using the sample lesson plan, "A Field Trip to the Ocean," as a model, design a science lesson appropriate for the kindergarten level, for example, planting seeds, experimenting with magnets, what sinks and floats, and so on. Be sure and use all the components shown in the model. (You will need to check some curriculum guides and other appropriate resources).
3. Is teaching an art or a science? Drawing from an empirical study or inquiry you have found in an educational research journal, write a one-page reaction to this question. In response be aware of teacher attributes versus technique or method. Some examples of appropriate journals are *The Journal of Educational Research*, *Review of Educational Policy*, *Developmental Psychology*, and *Child Development*.

FIELD EXPLORATIONS

These exercises are designed to take you out into the world to find real examples that will illustrate and elucidate the material in this chapter.

Visit a school in your community that has a kindergarten program. Be sure to call first for permission and to find out when it is convenient for the teacher. Check in with the office when you first arrive. Most schools require strangers to check in. Then complete as many of the following activities as feasible.

1. Visit a kindergarten program and write a short description and summary of the activities and lessons associated with children's learning that you were able to observe. Be sure to discuss the balance between facilitative and directive teaching.
2. Draw a sketch of the indoor and outdoor kindergarten classroom environment illustrating:
   a. The various learning centers
   b. The major equipment present
   c. The children's principal traffic patterns.
3. Using the following interview protocol, interview the kindergarten teacher and summarize the data elicited through your inquiries.

Teacher Interview

1. As you drive to school, what do you think about the coming day?
2. Upon entering your classroom, what thoughts and feelings do you experience?

3. As the children enter the classroom, what emotional tone do you want to establish? How will you help this happen?
4. What specific children attract your attention? Why?
5. What activities might you have planned? What objective might you hold?
6. What routines will help your day flow smoothly? What unanticipated events might occur?
7. What adults will you see during the course of your day: teachers, aides, specialists, principal, janitor?
8. What type of interaction might you have with parents?
9. As the children prepare to leave, what learning from the day will you emphasize with them?
10. How will you evaluate your day? Did you meet your learning objectives? Were you able to set an appropriate emotional tone? What specific interactions with children and adults were most special?
11. As you look back on this day, what is your perspective on the importance of kindergarten programs for children, and how do you see yourself and your personal contribution as a teacher in meeting these objectives?

References

Erickson, E. H. *Childhood and society*. New York: Norton, 1950.
Weber, L. *Open education: The English infant school and informal education*. Englewood Cliffs, N.J.: Prentice-Hall, 1971.

Chapter 12

SPECIAL CHILDREN/SPECIAL NEEDS

Objectives

After reading this chapter the student should be able to:

1. Name and identify the three major provisions of legislation enacted to ensure the educational rights of the handicapped.
2. Identify five handicapping conditions established by P.L. 94–142, and discuss their central characteristics.
3. Define the concept of assessment and discuss basic principles of behavioral-developmental assessment.
4. Define and discuss the following concepts:
    a. Individual education program (IEP)
    b. Mainstreaming
    c. Least restrictive environment
5. List and discuss how the teacher of a mainstreamed classroom would assist in the special-needs child's general developmental progress and in addressing his special requirements for adaptation to the classroom.
6. Identify four handicapping conditions and discuss specific guidelines for the teaching of these special-needs children.

The first knowledge I had of Laura's existence was from reading an account of her case written by Dr. Mussey, then resident at Hanover. It struck me at once that here was an opportunity of assisting an unfortunate child, and, moreover, of deciding the question so often asked, whether a blind-mute could be taught to use an arbitrary language. I had concluded, after closely watching Julia Brace, the well-known blind-mute in the American Asylum at Hartford, that the trail should not be abandoned, though it had failed in her case, as well as in all that had been recorded before.

From the journals of Samuel Gridley Howe, M.D.

Within the last several decades, both in spirit and deed we have begun to address the developmental-learning needs of all of our children. Separate facilities set aside in the past for the disabled and the handicapped were often inferior and further disabling. Presently, through vigorous effort and commitment among proponents for equal education, the rights of the handicapped have been formally addressed and mandated in federal and state legislation. Past attitudes of neglect and indifference, expectations of underachievement and lifelong dependency are gradually being replaced.

The U.S. Office of Education estimates that there are approximately 7.8–9 million handicapped persons between the ages of 3 and 21. Until relatively recently only half of these persons were in adequate educational programs, and approximately one million persons received no education at all.

LEGISLATION FOR THE HANDICAPPED

In the mid 1970s a landmark piece of legislation entitled *The Education for All Handicapped Children Act of 1975* (P.L. 94–142) was passed by Congress and signed into law. This act created federal funds to be made available to each state that initiated "free and appropriate" education for all handicapped persons between the ages of 3 and 18 no later than September 1, 1978, and for persons between 3 and 21 no later than September 1, 1980. Incentive grants were also made available to those states providing preschool educational services for handicapped children between the ages of three and five.

   P.L. 94–142 was the culmination of several decades of change in the treatment of infants and preschool handicapped children. While existing special education programs often created opportunities for care and training, guidelines for the *identification* of special needs children, procedures for their *assessment*, and a process for the effective planning and monitoring of *intervention* strategies were frequently random, lacked consistency or uniformity, and were haphazard in application. Moreover, efforts in addressing the developmental needs of handicapped children were usually separated from parent and family concerns. The school could, and often would, implement programs with little or no parental input. P.L. 94–142 created a mandate which viewed the handicapped person's access to an appropriate educational experience as a civil right. Moreover, its provisions offered, for the first time, guidelines for application, as well as opportunity for appeal.

The Participants

The handicapped represent a diverse group of people characterized by one or more areas of *developmental delay* or *impairment*. These conditions typically *distort* or *restrict* a child's growth and development and create *negative* and *inhibiting* restraints on her adjustment and adaptation to the environment. Moreover, depending upon the nature and severity of the handicapping condition, the child has often strained available family and educational support systems. According to P.L. 94–142 the term "handicapped children" refers to participants who are "mentally retarded, hard of hearing, deaf, speech impaired, visually handicapped, seriously emotionally disturbed, orthopedically impaired, other health impaired, deaf-blind, multihandicapped, or as having specific learning disabilities, who because of those impairments need special education and related services." (See Table 12.1.)

TABLE 12.1. Handicapped Children

Condition	Description
Deaf	A hearing impairment that is so severe that the child is impaired in processing linguistic information through hearing, with or without amplification, which adversely affects educational performance
Deaf-blind	Concurrent hearing and visual impairments, the combination of which causes such severe communication and other developmental and educational problems that the child cannot be accommodated in special education programs solely for deaf or blind children
Hard-of-hearing	A hearing impairment, whether permanent or fluctuating, which adversely affects a child's educational performance but which is not included under the definition of deaf in this section
Mentally retarded	Significantly subaverage general intellectual functioning existing concurrently with deficits in adaptive behavior and manifested during the developmental period, which adversely affects a child's educational performance
Multihandicapped	Concurrent impairments (such as mentally retarded-blind, mentally retarded-orthopedically impaired), the combination of which causes such severe educational problems that they cannot be accommodated in special education programs solely for one of the impairments. The term does not include deaf-blind children
Orthopedically impaired	A severe orthopedic impairment that adversely affects a child's educational performance. The term includes impairments caused by congenital anomaly (for example, clubfoot, absence of some member) impairments caused by disease (for example, poliomyelitis, bone tuberculosis), and impairments from other causes (for example, cerebral palsy, amputations, and fractures or burns that cause contractures)
Other health impaired	Limited strength, vitality, or alertness, due to chronic or acute health problems such as a heart condition, tuberculosis, rheumatic fever, nephritis, asthma, sickle-cell anemia, hemophelia, epilepsy, lead poisoning, leukemia, or diabetes, which adversely affects a child's educational performance
Seriously emotionally disturbed	A condition exhibiting one or more of the following characteristics over a long period of time and to a marked degree, which adversely affects educational performance including: a) An inability to build or maintain satisfactory

TABLE 12.1.   Handicapped Children (*Continued*)

Condition	Description
	interpersonal relationships with peers and teachers
	b) A learning difficulty that cannot be explained by intellectual, sensory, or health factors
	c) Inappropriate types of behavior or feelings under normal circumstances
	d) A general pervasive mood of unhappiness or depression
	e) A tendency to develop physical symptoms or fears associated with personal or school problems
	f) Children who are schizophrenic or autistic
Specific learning disability	A disorder in one or more of the basic psychological processes involved in understanding or in using language spoken or written, which may manifest itself in an imperfect ability to listen, think, speak, read, write, spell, or to do mathematical calculations. The term includes such conditions as perceptual handicaps, brain injury, minimal brain dysfunction, dyslexia, and developmental aphasia. The term does not include children who have learning problems that are primarily the result of visual, hearing, or motor handicaps, of mental retardation, or the result of environmental, cultural, or economic disadvantage.
Speech impaired	A communication disorder, such as stuttering, impaired articulation, a language impairment, or a voice impairment, which adversely affects a child's educational performance.
Visually handicapped	A visual impairment which, even with correction, adversely affects a child's educational performance, including both partially seeing and blind children.

Assessment of the Handicapped Child

The assessment of disability is the second phase of working with the handicapped. Through assessment the nature, magnitude, and degree of disability may be known. Moreover, assessment allows for effective intervention by highlighting areas of strength and potential growth. Neisworth and Bagnato (1981) note that assessment allows us "to determine *where* the child stands within the development sequence, *what* the child's capacities and deficits are, and *how* and *under what conditions* the child learns best" (p.41). Principles which underscore this approach are presented in Table 12.2.

TABLE 12.2.   Principles of a Developmental-Behavioral Approach to Assessment of the Handicapped

1. Developmental sequences are similar for all children, wherein each child progresses at his own rate.
2. Individual variations in development occur early and show consistency as the child ages.
3. Development proceeds in a hierarchical fashion where rudimentary skills are acquired before the acquisition of complex skills.
4. Development proceeds in a cephalocaudal (head to foot), proximodistal (body midline to extremities) direction and reflects a progression from general to more specific functioning.
5. Individual progress in development is highly variable and is marked by accelerations, regressions, and plateaus.
6. Development is multidimensional and occurs simultaneously across different behavioral domains.
7. Development is a function of the interaction between individual maturation and environmental stimulation.
8. Early skills are primarily sensorimotor in nature while later skills reflect verbally mediated behaviors.
9. Infant development and assessment is a dynamic, continuous, multidimensional, and individual process.

Adapted from: Linking Developmental Assessment and Curricula, by J. T. Neisworth and S. J. Bagnato, Aspen Publications, Rockville, MD, 1981.

Intervention/Implementation of Special Programs

The third provision of P.L. 94–142 was to specify procedures for effective intervention and implementation of programs for the handicapped. This prescription was established by the creation of three criteria, namely, the *individual educational program* (IEP), the concept of *mainstreaming*, and the principle of the *least restrictive environment*.

The Individual Educational Program (IEP)

The concept of the IEP was created in order to ensure that each handicapped child would receive the best possible educational experience available, based on her present functional capacity, prognosis for continued growth, and resources accessible to the school. In practice, the IEP represents a team effort, involving the child, the special education director, the child's teacher(s), and the child's parents. According to federal and state law the local school district is responsible for initiating, developing, and implementing the IEP for each of its handicapped children. This process should follow specific guidelines detailing the role of the school and the rights of the child and her parents.

INSET 12.1   INDIVIDUALIZED EDUCATION PROGRAM

NAME __John Michaels__   DOB __/   /__

AGE __5–6__   GRADE _____

SCHOOL __Southport Preschool__

PARENTS/GUARDIANS __Wm. and Joan Michaels__

ADDRESS _____

PHONE _____

On _____, the IPRD Committee
    (Date)
met to review all current data and
recommends Level _____ placement.

Date of next review _____

Exceptionality: __Downs Syndrome__

Present at meeting:

Parents __Mr. & Mrs. M__

Others: Name/Position __Ms. R., speech therapist__

CURRENT TEST DATA

TEST/DATA/RESULTS

Psych.	/	Wechsler Intelligence Scale for Children
Sp. & Lang.	/	Uses 3–4 word phrases; identifies common
	/	nouns and expressions
OT/PT	/	Ongoing treatment

Recommended Special Services (Hrs/Wk):

Speech and language therapy	/	1 hr./wk.
Occupation/physical therapy	/	1 hr./wk.
	/	

Total Hours/Week:

Special Education Classroom __2__

Regular Classroom __4__

Representative of District/Agency __Mrs. D., preschool head teacher__
__Mr. L., occupational and physical therapist__   /

The committee has determined the following strengths and needs to be reflected in the IEP:

STRENGTHS	NEEDS
Socialization skills	To improve articulation of sounds
Some expressive language	Improve auditory processing
	Improve expressive language skills
	Continue to improve balance
	Continue strengthening knees, hips, and ankles
	Continue to improve visual-motor skills
	Continue to improve proximal joint stability

Inset 12.1 Individualized Education Program (Continued)

Annual Goal	Specific Objectives	Methods	Comments
Expressive language	Encourage conversational interchange in spontaneous speech. Expand use of adjectives in phrases and sentences. Establish appropriate use of *is* and *are*. Increase expressive vocabulary. Reinforce appropriate use of pronouns (*he, she, they*) in sentences. Expand length of utterances in sentences to an average of 5 and 6 words. Establish the use of *who, what,* and *where* questions. Establish appropriate reversals of words in questions.		
Articulation	Reinforce correct production of /p/ /b/ /w/ /h/ in conjunction with clinician at Community Language Clinic.		
Auditory processing	Recall a four stage command. Listen to questions and respond appropriately. Verbally relay incidents of the previous day and week. Comprehend categorization of items (food, clothing, animals, etc.).		
Improve balance	Balance on L or R foot, eyes open for 5 sec.	Ball gymnastics Seated bounce Roll hips forward/back; Roll hips L & R Hop on 1 foot Walk straight line; various patterns	

422

Increase muscle strength		Ball gymnastics: prone—airplanes
Hip extension & abduction	Do 10 hip extensions and 10 hip abductions L and R	Side-lying leg lifts.
Knee extension	Use 2# weight on ankle; do 10 extensions L and R seated, feet unsupported	Floor exercises—prone and seated, feet unsupported—leg extensions.
Gross motor		Trike riding Jumping Jacks Angels in the snow Run & kick ball Jump down from height
Eye/hand coordination	Catch ball independently in various situations	Ball handling (bounce, catch). Catch ball bounced 1' to either side. Catch ball thrown 2–3' above head. Imitate clapping—regular and irregular rhythms.

423

PARENTAL RIGHTS. It is mandated that parents be notified of a meeting, that meetings be scheduled at parental convenience at mutually agreed upon times and settings, and that all data or information collected regarding their child be made available to the parents. Moreover, as a member of the planning team the parent must consent to the IEP in order to ensure its implementation. In cases where parental rights have not been adequately represented, the child's parents, under law, may obtain an independent evaluation of their child. Parents may obtain an impartial hearing pertaining to perceived failures of the school or its officials in fulfilling the mandate or spirit of the law.

COMPONENTS OF IEP. The individual education program shall include:

1. A statement of the child's present level(s) of educational performance.
2. A statement of annual goals, including short-term instructional objectives.
3. A statement of how the specific special education and related services will meet the needs identified in the evaluation report and the extent to which the child will be able to participate in regular educational programs.
4. The projected dates for initiation of services, the anticipated duration of the services to be performed, and the location where these services will occur.
5. Appropriate objective criteria, evaluation and reevaluation procedures, and schedules for determining, on an annual basis, whether the short-term instructional objectives are being achieved.

Mainstreaming

Mainstreaming refers to the full and complete integration of all children within the normal classroom. This idea, applied to the handicapped youngster, argues that each child has the right to participate in an educational setting most like, and representative of, experiences of his peers. Clearly, this idea recognizes that children need opportunities to interact and learn with each other. In practice, mainstreaming involves the following components:

1. Maximum opportunity for exposure to participation in normal classroom activities and interactions.
2. Creating special educational opportunities that might be administered in the classroom.
3. Incorporating regular classroom personnel in the implementation of special educational efforts.

4. Providing peer group educational opportunities that facilitate learning among both handicapped and unimpaired children.

Mainstreaming creates both special opportunities and challenges for the school. It is not simply, nor should be construed, as a financial alternative to providing needed special services. The haphazard mixing of children with diverse needs without regard to how or by whom such needs will be met can do disservice to those in need, as well as the nonhandicapped. Mainstreaming suggests that children with special needs can remain within the classroom with supportive services. Moreover, it argues in favor of the idea that special-needs children can participate effectively in regular classrooms. Finally, it recognizes that the presence of the special-needs child offers special opportunity to others, namely, that the special-needs child will contribute to the development of the

nonhandicapped child. Again, this reciprocity of interests is a relatively new idea.

The Least Restrictive Environment

The third facet in the implementation of special programs is the concept of the least restrictive environment. This idea stems from reactions to previous practices designed to hide or inhibit both awareness and attention to the special needs of the handicapped child. Historically, as the opening vignette to this chapter indicates, special needs children were traditionally considered different, often tainted or cursed, frequently feared. Their associations were restricted, and their freedom of movement in society was curtailed. Often they were inappropriately institutionalized.

The implementation of the concept of the least restricted environment was a response, in part, by the authors of P.L. 94–142 to ensure that past practices directed toward special-needs children would not be continued. The provisions of this concept include:

1. Access to equal educational opportunity within acknowledged and established public educational settings
2. Opportunity to use all the facilities that may maximize the handicapped child's capacity for educational advancement
3. Emphasis on the toal development of the child, including opportunities for growth that do not reflect the child's present handicapping condition.

Integrating and Teaching Special-Needs Children

The concept of mainstreaming, as discussed in the previous section, has created both a mechanism for classroom integration of the special-needs child, as well as a number of challenges to its proper implementation. In developing an effective strategy for integration, familiar and new elements of the classroom must be addressed, including the roles of many of the persons we have met in other chapters, namely, the children and the teachers, as well as new people such as educational specialists who will work with the special-needs child. In addition, special curriculum and activities, as well as modifications of available learning spaces, may be required. Finally, the integration of these people and resources must be accomplished to the mutual benefit of the special-needs child and her peers.

The teacher can aid a handicapped child's successful classroom integration in a variety of ways. These include active involvement in the development and modification of the child's IEP by acquiring knowledge and special skills in the instruction of the special-needs child, and by developing sensitivity to, acceptance of, and understanding and communication with the special-needs child. This latter task may be accomplished in several ways, both directly and indirectly.

First, and most directly, the teacher can focus on the child's strengths and assets. The enhancement of a child's self-image, and her image among others, is highly dependent upon the child and her peers' perceptions of competence. Emphasis on what the child can do is of critical importance to successful adaptation. What can only be accomplished with difficulty needs attention but not emphasis. Second, the teacher, based on his understanding of the child's handicapping condition, must constantly encourage independent growth and development. The central idea behind the IEP is that behavioral objectives can be assembled, targeted, and met as a function of proper encouragement and instruction. Certainly, the teacher plays a major role here. Third, when evaluating pupil progress, the teacher must be aware of the nuances in the learning style of the special-needs child, as well as the nature of his developmental gains. Small incremental steps in learning must be acknowledged, as well as larger, more dramatic changes that may be achieved on special occasions. Fourth, the teacher must guard against unwarranted, and unwanted indulgence or sympathy.

The teacher may aid the accomplishments of the special-needs child more indirectly, by regulating, modifying, and directing the interactions of others, both child and adult, who share the classroom. Among the children, he must share with sensitivity, openness, and honesty the nature of the handicapped child's disability, as well as suggesting her strengths. The teacher must also guard against other children's discriminations and fears and their indulgence or patronizing of the special-needs child. Instead, cooperative activities involving all the children must be planned and effectively incorporated into the curriculum. Encouraging a buddy system consisting of a disabled and nonhandicapped peer may facilitate learning and development in each child. This appears especially true where the nonhandicapped peer is of similar developmental, rather than similar chronological age, to her disabled partner. Formal modeling may also be facilitated through encouragement of peer tutoring activities. Here, the modeled peer may provide valuable instruction for a disabled child. In turn, she may improve her own academic skills, through practice, while acquiring an appreciation and understanding of handicapping disabilities.

Teachers influence other adults as well as children. The role and value of colleagues in helping meet the needs of the disabled youngster must be recognized and welcomed. Plans with specialists, aides, and

INSET 12.2   Areas in Which Young Peers Can Function as Tutors

Teaching appropriate social behavior
Teaching initiation of positive social interactions
Teaching appropriate use of classroom materials
Teaching play behaviors
Teaching identification, discrimination, and labeling of colors, shapes,
  and simple quantities
Teaching speech patterns
Teaching basic letter-sound associations
Teaching a simple sight vocabulary
Teaching appropriate responses to oral reading
Teaching spelling of simple words
Teaching basic computational facts

From: Mainstreaming Young Children by B. Spodek, O. N. Saracho, and R. C. Lee, Wadsworth, Belmont, CA, 1984. Reprinted by permission of the publisher.

other teachers must be coordinated. In addition, the flexibility of the classroom schedule may need to be enlarged; activities may need to be rearranged; areas may need to be restructured and, at times, modified for special projects and needs. In her interactions with other professionals the teacher may need to champion the disabled youngster, as she might advance the interests of all the children. Finally, the parents of the disabled child will require special time, as well as additional patience. They will require information pertaining to their special-needs child, and at times, instructional assistance in the implementation of special programs to be conducted at home. Lastly, they will need to be encouraged in becoming active advocates and contributors to other classroom activities and events. As the parents of special-needs children become successfully involved and active participants in classroom proceedings, the interest of parents of nonhandicapped children must also be addressed. Occasional planned educational meetings for these parents need to be arranged. Topics leading to a better understanding of the disabled youngster may be addressed, and fears pertaining to the concept of mainstreaming can be openly discussed and reviewed. These become equally important goals for the successful education of all of our children.

SOME SPECIAL CHILDREN

The Mentally Retarded

Marty is mentally retarded. He is an eight year old who has been diagnosed as a Down's Syndrome child. Marty is a happy child. He smiles readily and is easily approachable. Yet his behavior is appropriate to that of a younger child. He plays with toys usually chosen by younger children and in a manner more characteristic of his younger peers. Characteristically, his behavior resembles that of a three to four year old. An observer may notice Marty sitting at a work table manipulating a set of different sized cones, involved in parallel play. As a peer approaches, Marty maintains interest in the task at hand. When an adult enters the work area, Marty turns to greet her and smiles. He is affectionate, particularly with adults. He likes to be touched and hugged. In verbal interactions, his speech often appears garbled, but he is understandable. Above all, he is eager to please and participates readily in planned activities.

According to the American Association of Mental Deficiency (AAMD), intellectual impairment may be characterized by one of four levels of functioning, each representative of differing performance scores obtained on standardized intelligence tests. Table 12.3 summarizes the AAMD classification system of mental impairment relative to a child's performance on the two most frequently administered and best standardized measures of intellectual ability, the Stanford-Binet and the Wechsler Intelligence Scale for Children.

TABLE 12.3.   Classification and Characteristics of Mental Retardation by Level of Functioning

Level	Stanford-Binet (Score)	Wechsler (Score)	Characteristics
Mild	68–52	69–55	Can function normally in most respects, but will develop skills more slowly. Requires slow pace in learning activities. Developmental level two or more years below chronological age.
Moderate	51–36	54–40	Functioning in school setting limited, but possible. Body self-care and rudimentary signal recognition can be mastered.
Severe	35–20	39–25*	Limited self-care with careful instruction.
Profound	19–below	24–below*	Requires custodial care at all levels.

*Extrapolated score

The needs of mentally retarded children present special challenges to the classroom teacher. These may be met through a variety of teaching strategies.

Guidelines for the effective classroom integration of the mentally retarded child include:

1. Individual program planning that emphasizes incremental step-by-step achievements
2. Planning educational experiences in terms of the child's developmental level rather than his chronological age
3. Frequent evaluation of accomplishments and modification of program objectives where appropriate
4. Creation of concrete learning opportunities, use of manipulative learning materials, and employment of objects that enhance perceptual awareness (sight, sound, touch, movement, taste, smell)
5. Repetition, use of simple instruction, temporal spacing, and patience in the assignment of activities
6. Use of praise, including behavioral modification principles, where appropriate
7. Encourage verbalization of interests, problems, and achievements
8. Avoid comparisons and competition with other children

The Physically Handicapped

Debbie is a physically handicapped child. She is six years old and attends kindergarten. Children with physical disabilities such as Debbie, are usually referred to as "orthopedically impaired," suggesting the existence of one or more prevailing physical disabilities (see Table 12.1). Debbie is an alert, actively involved child. She moves about, often quite rapidly, in a specially built wheelchair. She is a determined, persistent, and frequently assertive child. She is peer oriented, having been attended by parents and other adults much of her life. With peers, Debbie plays an active role in most activities. Among adults, particularly those seeking to help, she may appear impatient. She exhibits "grit" and determination, and above all the attitude "I can do it myself." Yet, occasionally, her determination may give way to tears of frustration. Then, caring adults become especially important in her life.

An "orthopedically impaired" child is a youngster of normal intelligence who is physically handicapped through congenital or acquired defect. Here, locomotion or bodily activity is limited, disallowing the child access to normal classroom opportunities and children of similar age or grade level expectancy, without special conditions. In cases of "orthopedically impaired" children special sitting or activity devices, often including wheelchairs, must be provided to ensure access to the

Sometimes an adult's hand is needed in helping a child grow.

classroom itself. Frequently, building modifications are necessary in accommodating these children and their special needs. Table 12.4 lists some common physical handicaps among preschool children.

As with other special-needs children, the "orthopedically impaired" child may suffer a variety of difficulties specific to her special handicap. These include: (1) a multitude of frustrations that may be encountered due to the combination of impaired mobility and an adult size world; (2) being subject to the insensitive behaviors of nonimpaired children; and (3) experiencing the negative attitudes of a society that offers both pity and rejection of physical differences.

TABLE 12.4.   Common Physical Handicaps Among Preschool Children

Condition/Disability	Major Characteristics
Cerebral palsy	A degenerative disorder of the central nervous system resulting from brain damage, especially before or during birth, and characterized by spastic paralysis, defective motor ability, and so on
Poliomyelitis	A degenerative infectious disease caused by a viral inflammation of the gray matter of the spinal cord usually accompanied by paralysis of various muscle groups that sometimes atrophy, often with resulting permanent deformities
Amputation	Loss of any limbs
Spina bifida	A disorder caused by malformation of the spinal cord, resulting in severely impaired mobility, usually accompanied by paralysis of the legs. Complicating handicapping conditions may include mental retardation and/or lack of bladder and bowel control

Guidelines for the effective classroom integration of the "orthopedically impaired" child include:

1. Modification of classroom structures limiting or restricting child's access
2. Incorporation of special programmative elements into the classroom, specifically, those designed to aid, modify, exercise, and allow for practice of physical disabilities.
3. Creating opportunities for achieving independence or minimal reliance upon others
4. Focus upon areas of attainment and classroom contributions
5. Developing the child's network of social contacts and her acceptance by peers

The Visually Impaired

Amy is a visually impaired child. She is four years old and attends nursery school. Her appearance is dominated by heavy, obtrusive glasses. When walking she occasionally stumbles, seeking support. She reaches out to other people, often impulsively, a characteristic that may produce some confusion and nervous reactions in others. Amy is an eager learner, but avoids tasks which require fine eye-hand coordination. Gross motor play is eagerly entered but occasionally proves frustrating. Noisy tears may accompany her participation in a game in which she must keep up with her quickly moving, sighted peers. The teacher must help the group "slow down" to allow Amy to keep up with them.

A visual handicap is defined as a visual impairment that is sufficiently severe to restrict the child's ability to learn through normal visual channels (see Table 12.1).

Visually handicapped children include:

1. The *blind* whose vision indicates a central visual acuity of 20/200 or less in the better eye after refraction (that is, the ability to perceive objects at approximately 20 feet as if they appeared at a distance of 200 feet). A blind person may or may not perceive light, dark, color, or other dimensions of sightedness. Specifically, they are unable to use sight to negotiate through the world.
2. The *partially-sighted* whose vision indicates a central visual acuity range of from 20/70 to 20/200 in the better eye after refraction. Some of these children may have sufficient sight for ordinary mobility but will be unable to do academic tasks such as reading or writing. The least severely disabled child in this category may be able to use special books or viewing instruments in these areas.

The problems of the visually impaired child include learning to maximize her limited visual perceptions, developing nonimpaired, alternative sensory capacities, and acquiring favorable attitudes toward learning and herself.

Guidelines for the effective classroom integration of the visually handicapped child include:

1. Incorporation of special visual management programs including orientation and mobility training
2. Providing speech, language, and hearing training to all blind and partially sighted children in need of such services
3. Providing special reader and tutorial services for blind and partially sighted children whose educational development can be significantly assisted by the provision of such services
4. Teaching effective use of auditory, olfactory, tactile, and kinesthetic sensory modalities
5. Incorporation of alternative learning strategies such as the use of braille reading and typing to facilitate each child's educational development.

The Hearing Impaired

Jody suffers from a severe hearing disability. He is five years old and attends kindergarten. Luckily, Jody's impairment was discovered early in life. Frequently, this is not the case. Many children suffering from hearing loss grow up unaware of their disability, with such impairment likely to be discovered when accompanied by other, usually emotional or behavioral, difficulties. Jody is an active five year old. He enjoys gross motor games and likes physical activities. He wears a hearing aid which assists his active involvement in peer initiated activities. However, his hearing difficulties become evident to the observer as he engages in tasks characterized by high verbal interaction. Here he may experience difficulty or confusion as instructions are offered or in carrying out teacher-directed assignments. Special difficulties are encountered in tasks that are verbally sequenced. In his one-on-one interactions with others, Jody is less hampered, particularly in situations allowing for face-to-face contact and immediate feedback. He enjoys these contacts and seeks them out among his peers.

A hearing disability is one evidenced by a loss of auditory sensitivity severe enough to affect the child's ability to communicate with others (see Table 12.1).

Hearing disordered children include:

1. The *deaf* whose hearing impairment is so severe that they do not learn primarily through the auditory channel, even with a hearing aid, and who require extensive special instruction to develop communication and learning skills.
2. The *hard-of-hearing* whose hearing level for speech is adequate to allow the child to acquire speech and to learn by auditory means although they may experience difficulty, under some circumstances, in verbal communication with or without a hearing aid or other amplification device.

The hearing-impaired child will experience, depending on the degree of his handicapping condition, a variety of learning problems. A hearing impairment may affect the child's acquisition of speech and language, his patterns of communication, his general intellectual development, and his concepts of self.

Guidelines for the effective classroom integration of the hearing-disordered child include:

1. Encouraging active use of special hearing aids or devices
2. Teaching effective use of visual, olfactory, tactile, and kinesthetic sensory modalities
3. Providing recommended instruction in communication by teacher and peers, that is, sign language
4. Encourage the development of alternative learning strategies such as the use of lip reading, the "reading" of facial expressions, and the interpretation of nonverbal communications

The Learning Disabled

Paul is five years old. He too attends kindergarten. Recently, he was assessed as a learning-disabled child. Paul is young in appearance and in behavior. He is restless, highly distractable, and often appears confused. He moves about the room, avoiding tasks requiring prolonged attention or persistence. Impetuous, he rushes ahead before waiting for directions. Frequently, he makes many mistakes. This leads to frustration and occasionally, bursts of anger. Paul creates an impression of immaturity and emotional instability. He is not favored by peers, often becoming a loner or, conversely, the ring leader or class clown.

Learning disabilities, relative to other handicapping conditions we have discussed are, perhaps, the most difficult to define. In part, this problem stems from imprecise descriptions and methods of measurement and, in part, from the fact that the degree of severity demonstrated may show considerable variation and complication. Children with a specific learning disability often display symptoms that are confused with allied disorders, particularly emotional disabilities.

A "specific learning disability" refers to disorders involved in the understanding or use of language. According to the guidelines of P.L. 94–142, such disorders involve "using language, spoken or written, which may mainfest itself in an imperfect ability to listen, think, speak, read, write, spell, or to do mathematical calculations." (see Table 12.1).

The symptoms of a learning-disabled child may involve one or more of the following:

1.   An inability to follow simple instructions
2.   An inability to repeat orders or directions
3.   Levels of cognitive functioning below the child's actual intelligence
4.   Poor gross and/or fine motor control and coordination
5.   Confusion in understanding spatial arrangements or locations
6.   Absence of established right-left-handed preference
7.   Difficulties in communicating thoughts, needs, or wants.

Guidelines for the effective classroom integration of the child with a specific learning disability include:

1.   Use of frequent repetition
2.   Awareness of the pace and tempo of learning
3.   Allowing for frequent one-on-one sessions
4.   Limiting work sessions to short, intensive periods of activity, rather than intervals of extended action or inaction
5.   Ensuring that the child has mastered one level of accomplishment before moving on to the next task
6.   Use of opportunities for offering praise at frequent intervals

7. Ensuring that the child listens to you as you speak, and using feedback and requests for information as safeguards of effective communication
8. Use of concrete, rather than abstract, learning materials and strategies of learning
9. Use of program packets and routines in order to ensure structure and regularity

TEACHING SPECIAL NEEDS CHILDREN

A Teacher's Day: Pat's Day

"Some days I wonder if I was made to be in the bathroom all day long. And then there are other days when you see a kid do something for the first time that she has never done before, when you see a child that has a lot going cognitively, *finally*, lift a switch or operate the lever of a wheelchair for the first time in his life. Or, see the idea behind a concept you have been working on with a child click. That makes you feel like you've done something.

"Then there are the days when you run around because you are short staffed, or just about get all the children fed or changed and you say to yourself, 'I went to school to get a Master's degree for this?' But, if you acknowledge that it was just a bad day, and don't dwell on it, you can forget about it until the next day. Then you try to figure out what went wrong and try to find ways to change it so that it won't happen again."

So ends Pat's day as a teacher of multihandicapped children. Pat and her colleague, Janice, who helped us compile this narrative, teach handicapped preschool children. Their students, whose primary assessment reflects orthopedic impairment, attend a special school for the physically disabled. This school focuses on orthopedic and related disabilities, and in contrast with other programs for the handicapped, represents a special multidisciplinary approach to work with one special segment of the special-needs population. Pat and Janice's story reflect themes and issues that are representative of people working with special-needs children. Who are the children they work with? What is a school day like for these children? What roles do Pat and Janice and others play in their lives? In this narrative we attempt to explore these questions.

The children that Pat and Janice teach are multihandicapped. Most are physically disabled with other complications associated with their primary disability. Some are also deaf, others are cognitively impaired as well. Some demonstrate gross motor delay, with known or unknown specific etiology. All exhibit some form of orthopedic disability usually in conjunction with other developmentally distressing symptoms. Aside from their differences in orthopedic handicap, these special-needs children also differ, as all children do, in personality and temperament, as well. Pat acknowledges that she likes to work with the chronically ill child, usually the child with limited prognosis. She also likes to work with children who exhibit behavior problems such as hyperactivity or aggressive acting out. For Pat, these children represent a challenge. As she notes, "I tend to shy away from the passive child. I like to work with the more active child. Especially, the multi-handicapped child. I think the more difficult the disability, the more I am attracted to working with that child."

The setting that supports the work of Pat and Janice reflects the homogeneity of their special target population, the special developmental demands of their children, and the need for multidimensional approaches to teaching special-needs children.

Both Pat and Janice teach in the preschool program. This component of the school runs as a unit which operates out of 5 subunits of classrooms of approximately seven children each. The children are initially grouped chronologically, then with regard to level of disability. Each classroom consists of one teacher and one paraprofessional who serves as a teacher's aide. As Pat explains, "Our work is team based. At the beginning of the school year we sit down as an organizing and planning team and develop our program. The team includes the teachers, the aides, various therapists, the psychologist, and the social worker. First we review the children. Then the team decides what our goals will be for the year. Then we plan the year. This planning will provide for self-contained classroom activities as well as whole group work. The latter is team taught. This year, because the children are chronologically younger and are having more difficulty with relating to the large group, we have pursued more self-contained classroom activities. Here, each teacher develops his own daily schedule of activities with his assistant, creating an agenda of planned interventions and goals to be achieved in conjunction with each child's IEP. "With my group, which is the youngest, I try to integrate organized, structured activities with less structured experiences.

"Most days, in our classroom, we try to follow a consistent pattern. The staff arrrives at 8:00 in the morning to get out activities and materials for the day's events. I try to analyze what kinds of things I need to focus on today, what goals I need to accomplish with the children, what I will be looking for in each child. I may meet with the social worker or other teachers to gain new information on the status of a specific child. For example, with an ill child who is just returning to school, I have to know what I will need to do in order to get that child back into the classroom. In the beginning of the year, as here, I ask myself how am I going to get each child through the day safely. As the term progresses, I will shift from emotional to social and cognitive concerns.

"The children arrive at about 8:30 in the morning. It has been a very long ride on the school bus for many of them. As they enter the classroom I try to be low key. This is why coming in prepared is so important. Some of the children will line up to be unbraced, splints may have to be put on, some may have soiled themselves and need to be changed. I try to greet each child in a nonharried way, to create a slow, smooth pace. It is a very confusing time for many of the children. I need to be organized and to interact in a friendly manner, to establish a trusting atmosphere. We all engage in fitting and applying new bracing to the children. It is a nice role to play, in which you get to deal with the children on a different level.

"It is important in working with my children to emphasize flexibility. Activities and schedules often need to be modified in line with changing needs and unplanned-for events. With the children I work with, the flexibility of the teacher is critical.

"The school day for these children is five and a half hours. It begins with arrival and greeting, unbracing, bathrooming, special or specific bracing, and the formation of a good morning circle. We then break for specific work on individual goals, usually activities involving physical or motor behavior, such as balancing, sitting in adaptive or therapeutic equipment for specific needs. This is followed by snack, the introduction of new bracing or equipment (that is, prone standers) and further motor coordination tasks. As we progress through the morning we will break for recess, followed by a language activity, perhaps a music activity, a library activity, or a cooking class. It is important to note here that each activity involves continuous task analysis. For example, language is very important in our program, and we try to emphasize receptive and communication skills. Yet during a specific language period, each child will be learning at his own pace. Thereby, a specific language activity might be conducted on four or five different levels reflecting the different abilities of each child, as well as their specific level of disability. Also, each child's progress must be individually recorded for future planning.

"Next, programmatically, we may provide some form of sensory play such as sand play or water play. An hour lunch period will then follow. Here we teach, as well as care for the nutritional needs of the children. Many of the children will have to be fed. And others are just starting to care for themselves. There is an awful lot of spilling and clean up. But they have to learn to do it for themselves, so patience is important here. At one o'clock we have a rest time, with some of the children sleeping or resting for up to an hour. At this time parent communications, which are necessary, will be written in notebooks for parents to read when their child returns from school. When the children awake I usually introduce a social interactive game that stresses communication skills. Preparations are then made for departure.

"It has been a long day."

As indicated by Pat's narrative, the teaching of handicapped children is a special challenge. It involves considerably more than just teaching. Pat is a highly trained professional, with considerable expertise and experience in working with special-needs children. Yet, as her story indicates, her involvement with these children includes many phases of teaching and, frequently, caregiving, beyond that taught or anticipated by her training. The difficulties in teaching posed by her children are considerable. They involve the normal aspects of teaching that we have reviewed earlier and the many complications of working with children with special needs, as well.

Pat succeeds in her role as a teacher of multihandicapped children for many reasons. Her training certainly helps. But, as the opening paragraph of her narrative reveals, it is only one attribute that she brings to her job. It is also important to note that Pat works in a highly visible, well-supported, multidisciplinary setting. This factor ensures program continuity, instructional support, and sustained advocacy for the goals and efforts of Pat and her colleagues.

Yet it is Pat and her co-workers who make the program work. As she observed during the interview, how she approaches her work, both objectively and subjectively, seriously affects performance, including her ability to meet obstacles and seek effective solutions. Pat knows who she is as a professional, particularly how to apply her skills in an effective manner. And she knows, perhaps most critically, who she is as a person. She recognizes that patience and flexibility are critical, if untaught, attributes of her work. Moreover, she knows where the challenges in working with special-needs children lie. This maturity and understanding characterize her work and its success.

SUMMARY

We began this chapter with a brief description of a special-needs child, indicating some of her special difficulties and her unique challenges. We end this chapter by reviewing the role of a special-needs teacher in helping children to adapt to their handicapping conditions and to learn and develop as children.

As we have indicated in tracing the provisions of legislation affecting special-needs populations, the treatment of the disabled youngster has come a long way. Through P.L. 94–142 and such concepts as mainstreaming, least restrictive environment, and the individual educational program, the handicapped child has achieved, in principle, significant gains in attaining access to normal educational opportunities. These accomplishments will aid the handicapped child in pursuing and leading a more effective life. Yet the tasks of identification, assessment, and continued program development with concomitant implementation constitute an ongoing process. Certainly, it is one that cannot be abandoned and must be ensured for future generations of all children with special needs.

Explorations

Do one or two explorations in each category to extend and enrich your understanding of this chapter.

PERSONAL EXPLORATIONS

These exercises are designed to help you look at your own life—attitudes, experiences, dreams, myths, and realities.

1. Are you (or have you known someone) who has shared with you his experience of being a handicapped child? What is (was) your reaction? What is (would it be like) to be a handicapped child? Write your personal feelings about having experienced (directly or indirectly) being handicapped.
2. Think back on your early school experiences. Have you encountered a special-needs child as your classmate? How was he treated by the class, by the teacher? To your knowledge, what special provisions for his handicap were made? Write a paragraph recalling or describing your experience with a special-needs classmate.
3. Imagine what it would be like to have a handicapped child. How would you feel about having a special-needs child? What resources would the family need to care for this child? What would your hopes be for this child? Write a paragraph discussing your thoughts, ideas, and reactions to these questions.

INTELLECTUAL EXPLORATIONS

These exercises are designed to increase your depth of knowledge in some of the areas discussed in this chapter.

1. Find a historical account of how mentally retarded children were treated 50 years ago. What were the prevailing practices of the time? How did they differ from contemporary practices? Write a brief

account summarizing your research and be prepared to discuss your reactions in class.

2. Go to the library and read two research articles that further define the learning capacities of a special-needs child with a "specific learning disability." Write a short report indicating how this information may be translated into educational practices or policies that may influence the educational growth and development of children experiencing the handicapping condition under consideration. (See Table 12.1 for representative conditions).

3. Consult the directory of special services of the Department of Health, the Department of Social and Rehabilitative Services, or the Department of Education in your state. For any of these agencies indicate what special services are available, how comprehensive these services appear to be, which handicaps are represented, and whether these services extend to families. Using this information, prepare an analysis of your state's provisions for handicapped persons and offer any recommendations that you feel are appropriate.

FIELD EXPLORATIONS

These exercises are designed to take you out into the world to find real examples that will illustrate and elucidate the material in this chapter.

1. Talk to a parent of a special-needs child. What special problems has she encountered in obtaining help for her child? What agencies have been especially responsive to the needs of this child? What improvement in services may be forthcoming?

2. The treatment of special-needs children has changed dramatically since the enactment of P.L. 94–142.
   a. Visit a school in your neighborhood and talk with the special education director or person responsible for implementation of this statute. What changes have been instituted in his school in response to P.L. 94–142? What difficulties or problems have been encountered in reaction to these changes? Have they involved the use of financial, personnel, or capital resources? What successes have been achieved? Write your impressions and data for class discussion.
   b. For this exercise follow the general guidelines and questions suggested in the preceding explorations. However, for this inquiry, interview either a school administrator (principal, vice-principal) or a classroom teacher. Compare and contrast the reactions elicited by these queries for those school personnel you have interviewed. What similarities are evident among respondents? What differences appear? Write a reaction paper based on data you were able to gather through your inquiries.

3. Visit a library. Browse through the children's book section. Look at a minimum of 15 books written for young children. Note whether hand-

icapped persons are represented in these books. Note the particular handicap represented. How are special-needs persons depicted? Look at the publication dates of the books reviewed. What conclusions can you draw from this exploration regarding the formation of children's attitudes toward the handicapped?

References

Neisworth, J. T. and Bagnato, S. J. *Linking Developmental Assessment and Curricula*, Rockville, MD: Aspen Publications, 1981.

SECTION FOUR

The Child in Society

Chapter 13

PAST AND CONTEMPORARY WORLDS OF CHILDHOOD

Objectives

After reading this chapter the student should be able to:

1. Discuss two major interpretations of the historical treatment of children.
2. Describe and discuss three historical types of child abuse.
3. Briefly describe two historical approaches to child care outside of the family.
4. Discuss three factors that affect the pattern of life in the modern U.S. family.
5. List five specific problems faced by the United States' "other" children.
6. Discuss five of the contemporary myths concerning children and their families.
7. Discuss three suggested policies for improving the lives of children and families.

Childhood offers a variety of images to us. For the young expectant parent it is a period bursting with promise and joy. For the single head of a household it is a period of struggle and perseverance. For the parents of a special-needs child, childhood is alternatively a time of personal sacrifice and special accomplishment.

These varying images change through experience and opportunity. Yet, each suggest a contemporary portrait of childhood in the United States. However, they offer only part of our vision of childhood.

PAST IMAGES OF CHILDHOOD

Until recently, we knew little of childhood in previous eras. However, through the tireless efforts of historians, varied images of childhood have begun to emerge. In part, through such efforts we are finding that the historical legacy of childhood is one far darker and more difficult to decipher than any contemporary portrait may project.

The history of childhood deserves retelling for several reasons. First, how children were viewed and treated represents an important source of information to us. Such knowledge may serve as important data for appraising and evaluating the historical sociocultural context of childhood, including the bearing, rearing, and educating of children. Second, it may serve as a source for examining our current attitudes toward children. And, finally, it can shed light upon our choice of various contemporary child rearing practices, as well as our present treatment of children.

The Legacy

Like many aspects of development itself, the history of childhood from antiquity to the present is neither clearly charted nor precisely known. What is obvious is that children, in historical context, have been perceived as of little importance or value to adults, a revelation evident, in part, by the dearth of established or available historical records. In part, children were largely unrecognized because the vast majority did not live beyond age five. Historical records, where and when they have been kept, usually have been found to be incomplete, sometimes incomprehensible, and, occasionally, self serving. As such, the pursuit of information and discovery of what childhood was like across different historical periods is both a painstaking search, and one susceptible to varied interpretation.

Two major perspectives have arisen regarding the history of childhood. The first of these, as represented by Aries (1962), portrays childhood as a historical accident, namely, as a relatively recent discovery from which modern ideas and attitudes about children emerges. This perspective encompasses the Medieval view of the child as a *homunculus* (or miniature adult). Medieval art depicts children as adult-like and there was an absence of special treatment or protection of children, allowing their full participation in all facets of society's rites of passage. Children during the Middle Ages were privy to all aspects of human experiences, bearing witness to the birth of their peers, as well as being provided ample opportunity to view the proceedings surrounding natural and induced death. According to Aries (1962), the child was a natural creature, attune to, in full participation with, and, in large part, supported by his society.

However, with the emergence of industrialization this portrait changed. Now the child became a tool of production, being viewed as capable of contributing to her own and her family's maintenance. Over time this condition worsened; the use and exploitation of children grew to such enormous proportions that the interest of moralists and the labor movement itself were alerted to the demanding need to seek change (Shaftesbury, 1868). While many changes were often self-serving (for example to control the flow of inexpensive juvenile labor), they were frequently well warranted. As Kessen (1965) notes in his citation of the passage of one such law in 1833, "the statute prohibited night work to persons under 18 in cotton, woolen and other factories, and provided that children from 9 to 13 were not to work more than 48 hours a week and from 13 to 18 not more than 68 hours a week. Children under 9 were not to be employed at all" (pp. 43–44).

With the enactment of this and similar statutes, the child's role in the labor movement was more humanely defined and increasingly restricted. These changes, coupled with the growth of compulsory education, as in the United States, redefined the child's role in adult society, and placed the child under the protective custody of the State (Rosenheim, 1973).

More recently, an alternative, far bleaker portrait of the child in history has been presented by deMause and his associates (1975a,1975b). This thesis is that the child, from antiquity to the present, has been the unwitting victim of adult mistreatment and exploitation. In scope and frequency of expression, de Mause states that these abuses extend beyond those experienced by any contemporary minority and have existed throughout history, constituting the rule, rather than its exception. He writes, "The history of childhood is a nightmare from which we have only recently begun to awaken. The further back in history one goes, the lower the level of child care, the more likely children are to be killed, abandoned, beaten, terrorized, and sexually abused" (1975a, p.1). While direct, comparative data remain unavailable, deMause (1975a), using historical documents, argues that a significant number of children born prior to the eighteenth century were, using current terminology, "battered children." In fact, deMause's review of historical records of children's home, school, and related environments suggests

TABLE 13.1.   Past Images of Childhood

Spare the rod and spoil the child.

Children should be seen and not heard.

I have been assured by a very knowing American of my acquaintance in London, that a young healthy child well Nursed is at one year Old a most delicious, nourishing, and wholesome Food, whether Stewed, Roasted, Baked, or Boyled, and I make no doubt that it will equally serve in a Fricasis, or a Ragoust.

The abandonment of babies continued; in the mid-eighteenth century, for every three births registered in Paris, one foundling was left at the Hospice. It was too heavy a load for the understaffed institutions to carry; the foundling homes varied widely during the eighteenth century but came to tragic excess in Dublin during the last quarter of the century when, of 10,272 infants admitted to the foundling home, only 45 survived.

There was an old woman who lived in a shoe,
  She had so many children she didn't know what to do;
  She gave them some broth without any bread.
  She whipped them soundly and put them to bed.

Come away, O human child!
  To the waters and the wild
  With a faery, hand in hand,
  For the world's more full of weeping
  than you can understand.

that the "the child's life prior to modern times was uniformly bleak" (1975b, p.85).

Historical Modes of Child Rearing

Infanticide

The practice of *infanticide* was widespread among many ancient people, including the Irish Celts, the Gauls, the Scandinavians, the Egyptians, the Phoenicians, the Moabites, the Ammonites, and, at times, the Israelites. Moreover, in some cases, according to historians, such civilizations as the ancient Roman Empire could count infanticide and its resulting decimation of the Roman population as a principal cause of its decline.

Changes in the practice of infanticide did not occur until the fourth century A.D. These changes were, in part, prompted by the Catholic Church (Lyman, 1975). However, the pressures of the Church were only partially successful, and historical records indicate that the incidence of infanticide extended well into the eighteenth century in every "civilized" country in Europe.

Abandonment

A second form of treatment to emerge was that of *abandonment*. As the systematic recording of public health data affecting children (birth and death certification) began to be kept, it became apparent that well into the eighteenth century, in Europe, the likelihood of survival was extraordinarily poor. As Kesson writes,

> The century had almost closed before children born in London had an even break on surviving until their fifth birthday, and before 1750 the odds were three-to-one against a child completing five years of life. Aside from the dangers of infection and disease in an age not notable for cleanliness, children of the time were subjected to the graver threat of abandonment (1965, p.8).

THE WET NURSE. In response to the plight of children subject to infanticide, two forms of child care emerged. The first, the *wet nurse*, can be traced to Biblical references, the Code of Hammurabi, the Egyptian papyri, and Greek and Roman literature. While the practice of wet-nursing appears to have been initiated originally in order to ensure adequate nutrition and to decrease infant mortality, as most modern references to pediatric nursing suggest, its popularity quickly extended to include surrogate child rearing, as well. Indeed, the widespread publication of tracts advising parents on the correct choice of a wet nurse attest to the importance of choice of caregiver, particularly as pertains to the character and temperament of the wet nurse. Caldwell (1964) cites one such guide suggested by Thomas Phaer in 1545 in *The Boke of Children.* He writes,

> Wherfore as it is agreing to nature, so is it also necessary & comly for the own mother to nourse the child. Wiche if it maye be done, it shal be most commendable and holsome, yf not ye must be well advised in taking of a nourse, not of yll complexion and of worse manners; but such as shal be sobre, honeste and chase, well fourmed, amyable and chearfull, so that she maye accustome the infant unto myrth, no dronkard, vycyous nor slut-tysshe, for suche corrupte the nature of the chylde (p. 158).

The practice of wet nursing continued from antiquity through much of the nineteenth century, growing in both popularity and excess. As late as 1780, the police chief of Paris, decrying the incidence of this practice (through its institutionalization of abandonment) estimated that of the 21,000 children born each year in Paris, 17,000 were sent into the country to be wet nursed, 2,000 to 3,000 were placed in nursery homes, 700 were wet nursed at home, and only 700 were nursed by their mothers.

THE ASYLUM.   A second form of institutionalized child care was the *asylum.* This vehicle of care, which arose in response to humane concern over continued and widespread infanticide in Europe, was initiated in Milan in 787 A.D. Shortly thereafter, the asylum became a prominent form of child care for abandoned waifs throughout Europe. Yet so widespread were the practices of abandonment and negligence that, even with the founding of asylums for unwanted children in every major city and capital in Europe, efforts to care for abandoned children were insufficient in curbing the tide; as each home was opened, babies poured in from all over the cities and countryside resulting in the closing of asylum doors for want of more space. As Kessen (1965) writes, in describing the prevailing conditions,

> It was too heavy a load for the understaffed institutions to carry; the found-ling homes replaced the streets as a locus of death. The mortality rate [in] foundling homes varied widely during the eighteenth century but came to tragic excess in Dublin during the last quarter of the century when, of 10,277 infants admitted to the foundling home, only 45 survived (p. 8).

Abandonment showed other faces during different periods of history, including the use of children in the bartering of services and the actual sale of children. This latter practice was prevalent in ancient Babylonian times, in Athens during the height of the Golden Age, and continued to more modern times (as in Russia, well into the nineteenth century). In addition, we find that children have been used throughout history as political prisoners, as indentured servants, or as security or payment of debts. Those children who survived such practices were often subject to the whims, amusements, or interests of the adults with whom they resided.

TABLE 13.2.   Chronology of Historical Modes of Child Rearing

Mode	Period	Characteristics
Infanticidal (Antiquity)	Antiquity–Fourth Century A.D.	Widespread practice of infanticide; severe physical and sexual abuse of children.
Abandonment (Medieval)	Fourth–Thirteenth Century	Acceptance of the child's right to life, paradoxically coupled with a denial of parental responsibility (i.e., neglect) through abandonment of child care to others (viz., wet nurses and asylums); continued practice of physical abuse.
Ambivalent (Renaissance)	Fourteenth–Seventeenth Century	Era of instruction and salvation of the child; development of the madonna-child theme; continued acceptance of the use of physical control to mold, shape or construct the child
Intrusive	Eighteenth Century	Emphasis on training through child management; compliance attained through threat/guilt; reduction in the use of physical punishment.
Socialization	Nineteenth–Mid-Twentieth Century	Predominant models of child rearing practice with emphasis on channeling of impulses (psychoanalysis) and behavior control (behavior theory)
Helping	Mid-Twentieth Century	Belief that the child's needs are best determined by the child (cognitive-developmental theory); parents serve to assist the child in its growth through emphasis placed on independence and training in responsibility

Adapted, with modification, from: "The Evolution of Childhood" by L. DeMause, In *The History of Childhood*, L. deMause (Ed.), Harper Torchbooks, New York, 1975.

Ambivalence

The disciplinary practices of adults toward children have usually been harsh, and often cruel, throughout recorded history. According to deMause (1975a), "Beating instruments included whips of all kinds, including the cat-o-nine tails, shovels, canes, iron and wooden rods, bundles of sticks, the discipline (a whip of small chains), and special school instruments like the flapper which had a pear shaped end and a round hole to raise blisters" (p.4). Children were especially likely to be the recipents of such aversive controls during the *ambivalent* mode of child rearing.

Other practices directed toward children were more benign but potentially harmful in other ways. The practice of *swaddling* (that is binding) young infants, for example, has been universally evident thoughout history. In addition, children have been subjected to a variety of practices advocated among adults to purify, to limit, or to instill obedience. Evil was curtailed through a variety of instructional lessons which threatened harsh adult retribution in response to any misbehavior or disobedience. The use of fairy tales of varied horror, books describing the tormented souls of sinners, and evil demons and devils of every sort in song and poem appear evident in the lessons prepared for children among almost all cultures and civilizations. Moreover, the lessons of evil and its consequences were more than passively taught. Wet nurses, parents, and teachers alike actively terrorized children into submission and compliance by forcing them to inspect rotting corpses cast aside following public executions in an effort to instruct children on the inevitable punishments following transgression. Sometimes children were required to bear witness to public hangings, whereupon their parents would whip them afterward to impress upon their offspring the harsh lessons of their observations.

Aversive practices and cruel treatment toward children have not simply disappeared. Centuries of brutality involving children are still evident in the perpetuation of similar behaviors in contemporary times, namely, the physical abuse of children, the sexual exploitation of children, and various forms of neglect or misuse (Pogrebin, 1983). Changes in the frequency and unacceptability of these practices have occurred gradually, with some still evolving. Others have followed legislative action or have reflected the efforts of educators and moralists seeking revision in our beliefs and attitudes toward children. While we may note better treatment of children in modern times, other issues and concerns affecting children have arisen. A look at the U.S. family of the last several decades highlights these modern concerns, and provides us with a contemporary perspective to complement our historic journey.

PRESENT ISSUES FACING CHILDREN

The American family has changed substantially since the founding of our Republic. In general, these changes, as Keniston (1977) has noted, have mirrored the gradual movements and shifts of U.S. society, most importantly, the United States' slow emergence from a rural, agrarian society to an urban, industrial one. However, since the last world war, the pace of socioeconomic change has quickened.

The American Family: A Contemporary Portrait

Bronfenbrenner (1975), in viewing U.S. family life patterns over the last 25 years, observed that rapidly accelerated changes have affected the traditional structural composition of the family and, subsequently, its varied functional roles. Of this somewhat recent past, Bronfenbrenner (1976) wrote,

> There was a kind of family stability in the late 1940s and early 1950s. The extended family still existed in places; one out of 10 families had another relative living under its roof . . . the divorce rate was quite low, especially among families with young children. Only one mother in four was working outside the home. And fewer than four percent of all children were illegitimate. Parents fought for a better education for their children, kicking off a school and college building boom. Television, which became commercially available to households in 1948, was almost unknown. Mass magazines wrote of "togetherness" and radio soap operas featured families. Hollywood made films about young Andy Hardy, Shirley Temple, and young Dorothy from Kansas, who went to see the Wizard of Oz but longed to return to her family (p.425).

The portrait of American family life depicted above has changed radically. Moreover, these changes have been neither accidental nor isolated occurrences. Rather, they represent consistent, changing trends in the nature of U.S. family life, supported by census data compiled by Keniston and others (Bronfenbrenner, 1973, 1975, 1976). Most importantly, they appear to represent only the tip of the proverbial iceberg, forecasting substantially deeper and, perhaps, more pervasive changes in the future of U.S. family life.

Changes in the structure of family life in the contemporary United States have led to dramatic alterations in the environments within which children live and grow. As Keniston (1977) writes,

> Some children in this country have no contact with adults for extended periods of every day. They are either locked up alone in empty apartments or left for hours out on the streets, more prone than other children to get-

Swings provide children with opportunities for guided fantasy.

ting into trouble. No one knows how many "latchkey" children there are, but the fact that they exist at all contributes to the general feeling that American families are in real difficulty (p.7).

Who then is rearing the children? Clearly not the parents, as some critics contend, who, in increasing numbers, are more apt to respond to the demands of jobs, commuting, entertaining, and meeting community commitments, than spending time playing, reading, and listening to their children. Nor it is likely, with declining birth rates, to find older brothers and sisters still living at home, able or willing to share child rearing responsibilities. Because of extensive changes in the nature of the extended family, children's access to grandparents, aunts, and uncles has decreased. Distance from relatives reduces children's alternative sources of emotional support, sources of child rearing information and assistance, and the sharing of child care philosophies (Stinnett and Birdsong, 1978).

Depopulation/Reconstitution of the Family

Three specific factors, among a host of other conditions, contribute to the above picture. They include the partial dissolution of the traditional family unit through separation, divorce, and desertion, the rising rate of out-of-wedlock births, and the precipitous growth of full-time employment among mothers of young children.

Divorce rates, as Keniston (1977) reports, have risen more than 700 percent in the last century. Moreover, as Bronfenbrenner (1976) indicates, nearly 40 percent of all marriages now end in divorce, with 3 out of every 10 women separating from their husbands before the age of 30.

Supplementing these figures, we find a rising rate in the number of both men and women disregarding divorce in favor of desertion. Although historically desertion has been used primarily as a male prerogative, more recently, women have chosen to abandon husbands and children in ever increasing numbers. The incidence rate for the runaway wife now joins that of deserting husbands as a major contributing factor in the creation of new single parent families.

Teenage Motherhood

In the last 25 years the illegitimacy rate has more than doubled, from 4 percent of 100 recorded live births to 10 percent of 100 recorded live births. Current data indicate that this approximates three-quarters of a million births each year. Most critically, a preponderence of these

TABLE 13.3.   Babies Having Babies: Adolescent Motherhood

About 523,000 babies are born annually to teen mothers. Over 50 percent of
these young women are single. These young female-headed families are
four times as likely to be poor and five times as likely to stay poor than two-
parent families.

Whether black or white, young mothers under 25 heading families are very
likely to be poor. In 1983, the poverty rates for young black female-headed
families was 85.2 percent; for young white female-headed families, it was
72.1 percent.

Today 12.1 million children or 1 in 5 are living in female-headed households.
7.2 million are white. By 1990, 1 in 4 children will live in a female-headed
household.

Fifty-seven percent of all black babies born today are born to unmarried
mothers, a trend that will lock hundreds of thousands of children into
poverty and dependency.

From: Children's Defense Fund, 1985.

births, an estimated 500,000 to 600,000 infants, represent unplanned-for
pregancies among school age people (Ogg, 1976; Nye, 1976; National
Center for Health Statistics, 1981). In all, 80 percent of all of all children
born out of wedlock are born to women under 25 years of age (Bronfenbrenner, 1976).

Cross nationally, data cited by Belsky, Lerner and Spanier (1984) indicate that the teenage birthrate in the United States is among the world's
highest. Specifically, teenage births in the United States are twice that
reported by Sweden, Spain, and France, 3 times that reported for the
Soviet Union, and 17 times that found among teens in Japan. Present
data indicate that in the United States there are now about 1.3 million
children living with 1.1 million teenage mothers. Of these children,
more than half have mothers who are unmarried, while two thirds of
the children were born to mothers aged seventeen or younger (Alan
Guttmacher Institute, 1981).

Single Parenthoood

The number of children living in single parent families is presently
twice to three times that of a decade ago. Moreover, this pattern is most
dramatically witnessed among children under 6 years of age. By the
mid 1970s, 13 percent of all children under 3 years of age, nearly a million children, were living with only 1 parent (Brofenbrenner, 1976). By
comparison, in 1948, 1 out of every 14 children (.07 percent) under 6
years of age lived in a single parent household. (Yet, by 1973 that figure
doubled to include 1 out of every 7 children.) Moreover, current predictions forecast a continually increasing pattern of children living in

single parent (or reconsituted) families. Hetherington (1979) states that
40 to 50 percent of all children born during the 1970s will spend some
time in a single parent household. Furthermore, she estimates that the
average length of time of assignment within a single parent family will
average six or more years. Currently, more than 18 percent of all
children in the United States live in a single parent family (Edelman,
1981).

Working Women

Perhaps the most influential change in parent-child relations stems
from rises in the rate of female employment, especially among women
with school age children. As of 1978, 51 percent of all mothers of school-
age children were working. Moreover, of these, approximately 33 percent had preschoolers or children under 6 years of age. These figures
represent a 500 percent increase over 1940 (Tetenbaum, Lighter, Travis,
and Rabinor, 1980).

In its annual report of activities, the *United States House of Representatives' Select Committee on Children, Youth and Families* describes
demographic changes that have altered family living patterns in the following manner:

> Today's children are being raised in conditions far different than those of
> past generations. Women now comprise 44% of the workforce, and over
> 50% of all children are now raised in families where both parents, or the
> only parent present, works. Twenty-two percent of all U.S. children now
> live in single parent families, and 1 out of 3 white children and 3 out of 4
> black children can expect to spend some of their childhood in a single par-
> ent household. These changes in the workplace and in family composition
> have developed over many years and show every sign of continuing for
> the forseeable future
>
> p. xi

At present the numbers of both working mothers and their preschool
children needing child care outside the family setting represents an
enormous and largely unanswered problem. There were 6.9 million
children under 6 whose mothers participated in the labor force in 1975,
and it is projected that there will be 10.4 million children of working
mothers by 1990. These figures mandate that careful attention be given
to child care needs outside the family.

Current family living arrangements and working patterns, as these
data indicate, serve to belie the "Dick and Jane" myth of the U.S. family.
Presently, only 1 family in 17, less than 6 percent of all American families, includes a working father, a full-time homemaker mother, and

children facing other than normal developmental problems (Edelman, 1981).

The "Other" Children

For many children life is unfair and inequitable. For the poor, black, and other minority children, the learning disabled, and the handicapped child, the chances of achieving a decent life are often beyond the grim realities of daily survival. Approximately, *one-quarter* to *one-third* of all U.S. children live among poor families who face financial deprivations for part or all of their lives. According to the *United States House of Representatives' Select Committee on Children, Youth, and Families:*

> A combination of recession, unemployment, and changed budget priorities has shaken the economic stability of American families. Collectively, American families lost $171 billion in income between 1980–1982, an average of over $2,000 per family, with low income and minority families suffering disproportionately high losses. The number of poor children increased by 2,000,000 between 1980–1982. Today, 1 out of 5 children, and 1 out of 2 black children, live in poverty

> p. xi

For these children life will consist of less food, more crowding, poor schooling (when available), little privacy, few toys and books, and less chance of surviving the very first year of life. As Tulkin (1972) observed, in America the poor are less than poor. They are poor while others are rich. They must endure the glaring contrast of life styles, knowing that the grass is really greener elsewhere, but having little power to demand a more equitable share.

Approximately one-half million children do not live in any family at all, while 10 million, about 17 percent, live in a family at or below the poverty level (Edelman, 1981). Moreover, it has been estimated that 40 million children receive inadequate medical attention and 10 million receive no health care at all.

As Edelman (1981) has observed, "children are the easiest people to ignore" (p.111). Moreover, efforts to improve the world of the child are not likely to be popular at this time. It has been noted that the U.S. climate toward children has become inhospitable. And prospects for the furture may appear even less encouraging (Lindner, 1986).

The status of minority and handicapped children is more problematic. Being nonwhite increases both the probability of facing marginal economic status and the likelihood of remaining poor. For among nonwhites, both poverty and lack of opportunity and discrimination work

"IS IT SAFE TO COME OUT YET?"

hand in hand to prevent or discourage upward mobility. Moreover, these disadvantages continue throughout the lives of minority children. According to the *United States House of Representatives' Select Committee on Children, Youth and Families:*

> In many states and communities, black and Hispanic students are twice as likely to drop out of high school than are white students. Minority students are also over-represented in rates of suspension, expulsion, and non-promotion. This over- representation of minorities continues into the juvenile justice system. In adulthood, the disparities continue. In 1982, the median income for white families was $24,603, compared to $13,598 for black families and $16,227 for families of Spanish origin. Among black and Hispanic families headed by women, 70% of all children are growing up poor
>
> p. xii

Among the learning disabled and the handicapped, prejudice, discrimination, and often simply lack of acceptance, prevail. For these children, the stigma of being different is often sufficient to ensure failure.

Other children, including those not classified as poor, nonwhite, or disabled, face a growing plethora of hazards in daily living. Some defy single causation, ready explanation, or immediate remedy. Others reflect lack of concern or neglect by adult society, a legacy from earlier historical roots. They include children caught in the nightmare of child abuse and neglect, the increasing numbers of young suicides, the growing numbers of juvenile criminals, and the increasing ranks of academic failures (Bronfenbrenner, 1975).

Childhood Today

Our observations of changes in the child's familial and external worlds offer serious challenges to our concern for the quality of children's lives. Moreover, they signal a growing awareness of related difficulties affecting children. We know that for many children life is far too hazardous and opportunities for misguided development far too frequent an occurrence. For these children, the freedom and joy of youth has been replaced by anger and sadness. For these children, darkness and despair characterize much of their lives.

The uncertainties and ills of our time affect millions of children, those who currently live among us, and those to come. These problems also affect millions of adults, including those who choose to bear children, as well as those who nurture, teach, or serve the needs of children. Certainly, the quality of these lives has been, and will continue to be, influenced by our commitment, or lack thereof, to improving the climates and environments in which children grow and learn.

FUTURE DIRECTIONS

Clearly, the future of childhood has yet to be determined. In part, the form and substance of future worlds of childhood will depend upon our ability to maintain those positive changes derived from the past. Indeed, we are not wedded to the traditions or follies of less enlightened times. Yet, how shall any gains be preserved? And, even more importantly, how shall they be extended to incorporate the new problems and dangers children face?

Our description of the past and contemporary worlds of childhood suggest that the rights of children need be pursued through several avenues of expression. These include support for children, support for families, and support for those who teach and care for children. The National Academy of Sciences (1976), in addressing this issue, found that the development of a significant proportion of the nation's children is inadequate, and by the time these children begin school they already lag behind in their potential to become competent adults. Most programs aimed at compensating for differences in preschool cognitive development, moreover, have failed to demonstrate lasting effects, once such programs have been discontinued after the preschool period. They report further that the experience of Head Start and other early intervention programs indicates that it is substantially more difficult than expected to remedy developmental deficiencies that stem from the continuing impoverishment in which some children and their families live. Much of what happens (good and bad) to shape the development of children occurs in the home and the surrounding environment of their early years (Berns, 1985).

INSET 13.1 Contemporary Preschool Programs: Some Findings

Bronfenbrenner (1974) has argued that preschool compensatory educational efforts demand "ecological intervention" planning. This approach links high quality preschool programs within the framework of parent-child relations, utilizing parents as teachers and support/maintenance providers of intellectual achievment. More recently, Lazar and Darlington (1982) report the collaborative findings of 11 preschool compensatory intervention programs initiated in the early 1960s. Their findings indicate that children who attended these high quality programs were significantly more likely to meet basic school requirements than controls who did not attend or receive comparable preschool training. One of these programs, the Perry Preschool Project in Ypsilanti, Michigan, recently reported some ongoing effects of its early efforts at preschool education among three-year-olds. Participants, who have now reached 19 years-of-age, have demonstrated significant success in early adulthood as they shift from school to real-world indicators of vocational, employment, and career development. Specifically, at age 19, the rates of employment and participation in college or vocational training after high school for the preschool group were nearly double those of youths without preschool education; teen-age pregancies in the group were approximately half those of non-preschool girls; preschool graduates were involved in 10 percent fewer arrests and detentions and approximately 20 percent fewer had dropped out of high school (Berrueta-Clement et al., 1984).

As suggested, the obstacles to the development of sound environments for children and their families are complex and multifaceted. They reflect economic interests, health- related concerns, and social values. Moreover, they demand vigorous action and commitment.

Marian Wright Edelman, executive director of the The Children's Defense Fund, offers several guidelines in marshalling energies in support of children and their families. Edelman (1981) argues for the need to extend the rights of children, as well as the need to challenge contemporary myths that impede effective legislative and social action.

Contemporary Myths

Samples of contemporary "myths" affecting the treatment of children and families include:

Myth 1: "Only other people's children have problems."
Myth 2: "Families are self sufficient; they should take care of their own children."

**TABLE 13.4.   Contemporary/Future Images of Children and Families;
Tenets for the Development of a National Policy**

Area: Family Economic Resources
1.   To ensure that families have the minimum income necessary to provide adequate food, shelter, and care for their children.
2.   To allow for one (or the only) parent to remain in direct and full-time care of a child under six without being deprived of adequate income.

Area: Health and Health Care of Children
3.   To place emphasis on a child and family health program providing health maintenance and preventative services of demonstrable quality.
4.   To promote a national system for continuous epidemologic and demographic monitoring of children's health care services.
5.   To place children's health problems resulting from social causes in high priority in research and demonstration effects.

Area: Child Care
6.   To offer families, where needed, substitute care for their children, including such alternative care arrangements as prekindergarten, kindergarten and nursery school, inhome care, family day care, and center-based day care programs.
7.   To ensure that alternative child care arrangements meet national and state standards, to include continuity of care, adequate child/adult caretaker ratios, cleanliness and nutritional adequacy, health services, safety, and stimulating environments.

Area: Special Services
8.   To provide programs for children in need which do not presume family breakup or inadequacy.
9.   To minimize, when unavoidable, family separation or breakup.
10. To ensure that all programs for children with special needs be based on the principle of maximum exposure of the child to normal, developmental relationships. In particular, large, congregate, custodial children's institutions should be abolished, and residential care of diverse types, rich in educational, developmental, and treatment resources, should be provided when own-family or substitute-family care is not appropriate.

From: "A National Agenda for Change" by National Academy of Science, Washington, D.C., 1976.

Myth 3: "No one should take responsibility for children except their parents".

Myth 4: "Helping children whose families cannot fully provide for them condones and rewards failure and erodes U.S. family values".

Myth 5: "Child advocates want the government to take control over families' and children's lives."

Myth 6: "Meeting children's needs and protecting their rights will divide families and pit parents and children against each other.

Myth 7: "Children's issues should be above the political process."

Myth 8: "Providing needed services is too expensive."

The above "myths," as we have seen, in their varied guises and forms have served as both historical and contemporary impediments to the recognition of children, their need for preservation and care, and their right to adequate developmental environments. We have traveled many miles in hazardous journeys, over many lands and great distances in examining the worlds of childhood. And the journey continues.

Last year, over two and a half million children were born in the United States. How they will develop, what form future patterns of growth will assume, and under what social conditions they will mature form the unanswered questions of this chapter. Historically, we have noted the horrors in care and treatment that children have been exposed to in the adult world. Today, we look at broad patterns in order to delineate the difficulties children still face. And specifically, we must ask, what quality of life will our children experience; what hopes may they aspire toward; what realities must they face and resolve; and what are we willing to do to assist them?

Explorations

Do one or two explorations in each category to extend and enrich your understanding of this chapter.

PERSONAL EXPLORATIONS

These exercises are designed to help you look at your own life—attitudes, experiences, dreams, myths, and realities.

1. Think back on your own life history. What form of discipline did you grow up with? What was its purpose? How did you feel about the methods used? What alternatives may have been employed? What form of discipline would you use with your children? Write a paragraph describing your most vivid memory of being "punished."
2. Have you known anyone who was a battered or abused child (including victims of incest)? What was your reaction? What would it be like to be treated cruelly by the adults in your life? Write your personal feelings about this kind of treatment.
3. Write a page about your personal concerns of having a family of your own, given the data discussed in this chapter. How could you balance your needs to work, entertain, be active in the community, and so on with those of a young child? How is this the same or different from how you were brought up?

INTELLECTUAL EXPLORATIONS

These exercises are designed to increase your depth of knowledge in some of the areas discussed in this chapter.

1. Do some library research on the current status of family law in this country or in the state you live in. Law, family counseling, and social work journals are all good places in which to examine this issue. Find two articles that have information in them that surprises or contradicts your expectations and write a paragraph on one to bring to class for discussion.
2. Scan the newspapers for several days. Clip out articles concerning children. Divide them into two groups, those reporting negative news and those reporting positive news. Either mount selected ones on a poster or in a notebook. Write a short reaction paper to your findings.
3. Find a book or article that proposes solutions to one or more of the dilemmas of the modern American family. Write a critical evaluation of these solutions both in terms of their practicality and their potential effect on children.

FIELD EXPLORATIONS

These exercises are designed to take you out into the world to find real examples that will illustrate and elucidate the material in this chapter.

1. Visit a local health center or well-baby clinic. Call first and make an appointment or find out when is the best time to allow you to see the clientele and get a chance to talk to a nurse or other personnel at the center. What do they see as the primary health problems of young families? What are the clinic's resources? What did you observe? Write your impressions for discussion, incorporating information you obtained from the clinic's resource personnel.
2. Take a trip to family court. While cases involving children directly are often closed, divorce cases and other domestic matters are usually open to the public. Talk to a clerk or judge. What are their opinions concerning the issues that appear in court? What do you observe? Write a reaction paper based on data you were able to gather through your inquiries.
3. Visit a day care center that serves low income families or a facility that cares for handicapped children. As you observe and talk to child and staff, think about the potential problems one of these children could face in "making it" in our society. What resources do these children have? List 5 to 10 potential problems which these children might face in the future. For each problem enumerated think of as many solutions as you can. Which list is longer? Are your solutions feasible? Write your reactions to this process for class discussion.

References

Allan Guttmacher Institute. *Teenage pregnancy: The Problem that hasn't gone away.* New York: The Alan Guttmacher Institute, 1981.

Aries, P. *Centuries of childhood.* New York: Vintage Books, 1962.

Belsky, J., Lerner, R. M. and Spanier, G. B. *The child in the family.* Reading, Mass.: Addison Wesley, 1984.

Berns, R. M. *Child, family, community.* New York: Holt, Rinehart and Winston, 1985.

Berrueta-Clement, J., Schweinhart, L. J., Barnett, W. S., Epstein, A. S., and Weikart, D. P. *Changed lives: The effects of the Perry preschool program on youths through age 19.* Ypsilanti, Mich.: High/Scope Press, 1984.

Bronfenbrenner, U. "Who cares for America's children? Problems and proposals." Unpublished manuscript, 1973.

———. "Is early intervention effective?" Washington, D.C.: Department of Health, Education and Welfare, Office of Child Development, 1974.

———. "The next generation of Americans." Paper presented at annual meeting of the American Association of Advertising Agencies, Dorado, Puerto Rico, March, 1975.

———. "The disturbing changes in the American Family" *Search*, 1976, 2: 4–10.

Caldwell, B. M. "The effects of infant care." In M. L. Hoffman and L. W. Hoffman (Eds.), *Review of child development research*, Vol. I. New York: Russell Sage Foundation, 1964.

Children's Defense Fund. "Adolescent and single-parent families: An action agenda for the 1980s." Washington, D.C.: February, 1985.

deMause, L. "The evolution of childhood." In L. deMause (Ed.), *The history of childhood.* New York: Harper Torchbooks, 1975(a).

———. "Our forebearers made childhood a nightmare." *Psychology Today*, 1975(b): 85–88.

Edelman, M. W. "Who is for the children?" *American Psychologist*, 1981, 36: 109–16.

Hetherington, E. M. "Divorce: A child's perspective." *American Psychologist*, 1979, 34: 851–58.

Keniston, K. "Do Americans really like children:" *Childhood Education*, 1975, 52: 9–12.

———. *All our children.* New York: Harcourt, Brace, Jovanovich, 1977.

Kessen, W. *The child.* New York: John Wiley, 1965.

Lazar, I. and Darlington, R. "Lasting effects of early education: A report from the consortium for longitudinal studies." *Monographs of the Society for Research in Child Development*, 1982, 47: Nos. 2–3.

Lindner, E. W. "Danger: Our national policy of child carelessness." *Young Children*, 1986, 41: 3–9.

Lyman, Jr, R. B. "Barbarism and religion: Late Roman and early Medieval childhood." In L. deMause (Ed.), *The history of childhood.* New York: Harper Torchbooks, 1975.

National Academy of Science. "A national agenda for change." Washington, D.C.: *United States Government Printing Office, 1976.*

Nye, F. I. *School-age parenthood: Consequence for babies, mothers, fathers, grandparents, and others.* Extension Bulletin 667, Pullman Washington, Cooperative Extension Service, Washington State University, 1976.

Ogg, E. *Preparing tomorrow's parents.* Public Affairs Pamphlet 520, New York: Public Affairs Pamphlets, 1976.

Pogrebin, L. C. "Do Americans hate children?" *Ms.*, November, 1983.

Rosenheim, M. K. "The child and the law." In B. Caldwell and H.N. Ricciuti (Eds.) *Review of child development research.* Vol. III. Chicago: University of Chicago Press, 1973.

Shaftesbury, A. A. Cooper, Earl of. "A speech on moving for leave to bring in a bill to make regulations respecting the age and sex of children and young persons employed in the mines and collieries of the United Kingdom." *In speeches of the Earl of Shaftesbury.* London: Chapmen and Hall, 1868, pp. 31–58.

Stinnet, N. and Birdsong, C. W. *The family and alternate life styles.* Chicago: Nelson Hall, 1978.

Tetenbaum. T., Lighter, J. R. Travis, M. and Rabinor, J. R. "The revolution in maternal employment: Implications for school psychologists." Paper presented at the 12th Annual Convention of the National Association of School Psychologists, Washington, D.C.: April, 1980.

Tulkin, S. "An analysis of the concept of cultural deprivation." *Developmental Psychology*, 1972, 6 (2).

United States House of Representatives' Select Committee on Children, Youth, and Families. *Children, youth and families: 1983: A year-end report.* Washington D.C.: United States Government Printing Office. 1984.

Chapter 14

THE CUTTING EDGE—TEACHING AS A PROFESSION

The field of early childhood education has attracted varying interest and enthusiasm over time. In the 1960s, as we discussed in Chapter 1, Head Start grew out of new research information and the recognition of the learning gap between children in middle-class homes and the children of poverty. Then in the 1970s this interest waned because many of the initial gains achieved through the Head Start and Follow-Through programs did not appear to be sustained over time. These gains, unfortunately, were measured in term of scores and I.Q. points attained through standardized testing. Now in the 1980s the field of early childhood education is once more receiving favorable publicity as long-term follow-up results show that these federally funded programs have made a difference in the lives of the children who attended them. This difference is not translated into I.Q. points or other achievement test scores but rather in terms of fewer school failures, lower juvenile arrest rates, and increasing college attendance. The societal benefits from such outcomes are enormous. Because of early childhood education opportunities, a larger segment of U.S. citizens have a greater stake in education and are participating more fully in society as a whole. This type of result could only be demonstrated over time.

This renewed interest in the value of early childhood programs accompanies changes arising from the large increase in working mothers and single parents. In a recent paper, the National Association for the Education of Young Children (1984) reports that:

> In response to the tremendous need for care which supplements and complements that which the family provides, Early Childhood programs are expected to expand and multiply. As such programs increase in number, it is equally important that they reflect the knowledge that exists concerning how best to provide optimal care and education for young children.
>
> Research clearly shows that a major factor in the quality and effectiveness of programs for young children is the specialized education of the staff (p. 59).

Increased need for care, then, is another factor contributing to a growth in programs and positions in the ECE field.

THE STATUS OF THE EARLY CHILDHOOD PROFESSION

In its concern for quality programs and education for ECE staff, NAEYC outlines a four-level teaching hierarchy that reflects the training, experience, and specialized roles possible within early childhood education settings (see Figure 14.1)

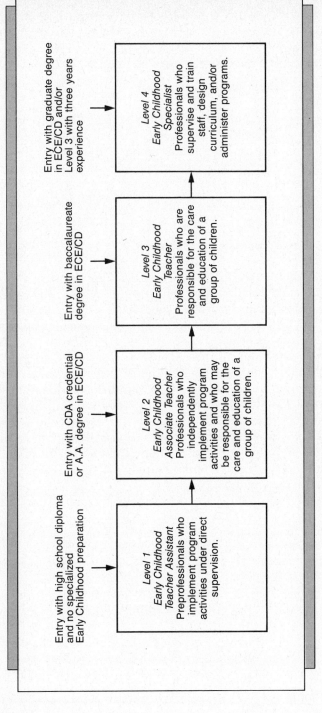

FIGURE 14.1 Four-level teaching hierarchy.
Adapted from: Guidelines established by the National Association for the Education of Young Children (1984).

Differences in the roles affiliated with each level of training are as follows:

Levels of Professional Involvement in Teaching

Level I: Early Childhood Teaching Assistant

Individuals who work under direct supervision and have at least a high school diploma are teaching assistants. This level of preprofessional must be reliable, healthy, able to get along with adults and children, and able to follow the directions of the teachers with whom they work. Many young people who start at this level go on to complete more training and move into teacher positions. This level usually pays a minimum hourly wage.

Level II: Early Childhood Associate Teacher

At this level, individuals usually work in a setting that has at least one fully qualified, state certified teacher present. While they are able to implement a program and be responsible for the care and education of a group of children, they are still limited in their planning and devising of programs and their in-depth knowledge. Qualifications at this level are either the completion of the competency-based CDA (Child Development Associate)—National Credentialing Program or an associate degree in early childhood education or child development. The CDA program allows individuals to show they have the skills necessary to teach at this level through documentation of experience and course work from a variety of sources. People who have worked in the field without formal training can "prove" their capabilities in this manner. Two-year training programs in many junior colleges also lead to a CDA credential or the associate degree.

Six basic goals outline the areas of competency included at this level:

1. To establish and maintain a safe, healthy learning environment.
2. To advance physical and intellectual competence of children.
3. To support social and emotional development and provide positive guidance and discipline.
4. To establish positive and productive relationships with families.
5. To ensure a well-run purposeful program responsive to participant needs.
6. To maintain a commitment to professionalism.

Level III: Early Childhood Teacher

While individuals at levels II and III may both be responsible for the care and education of a group of children, Level III teachers have a baccalaureate degree in early childhood education or child development from an accredited college or university and are expected to have both the competencies of a level I or II person and theoretical knowledge and in-depth understanding of children, in planning and implementing programs. The following list of competencies is suggested by NAEYC, as appropriate at this level:

1. Human development through the life-span, with special emphasis on cognitive, language, physical, social, and emotional development, both typical and atypical, from birth through age eight.
2. Historical, philosophical, psychological, and social foundations of early childhood education.
3. Curriculum for young children, including goal setting and development of appropriate content and methodology.
4. Observation and recording of children's behaviors for purposes of assistance in achieving goals, providing for individual needs, and appropriately guiding children.
5. Preparation for working in settings that include atypical children: understanding the needs of developmentally diverse children and recognizing conditions requiring assistance from other professionals.
6. Communication and conference techniques, interpersonal and intergroup relations, and techniques for working with staff as an instructional team.
7. Family and community relations, including communication with parents and parent involvement.
8. Awareness of value issues and the existence of codes of ethics in professional life.
9. Comprehension of cultural diversity and its implications.
10. Knowledge of legislation and public policy as it affects children, families, and programs for children.

Teachers who attain these competencies usually complete a formal student-teaching experience as well as a variety of course work and experiences in various ECE settings.

Level IV: Early Childhood Specialist

At this level, individuals have both training and experience and are expected to supervise and train staff, design curricula, and/or administer programs. The director or master teacher in an early childhood setting usually operates in this type of capacity and should have the additional competencies of:

1. Designing and supervising the implementation of developmentally appropriate program content and curricula.
2. Designing and implementing appropriate staff development activities and adequate supervision of personnel and volunteers.

Specialists can also serve as resource and referral specialists, parent educators, researchers, or policy analysts.

These varying roles within ECE settings allow for a high ratio of adult to child supervision, which is of utmost importance in programs for very young children. For example, it would be prohibitively expensive to attempt to provide fully trained four-year educated teachers at a ratio of three to one as required for infant-toddler programs. This system also allows interested workers to gain training and experience while they pursue further educational goals. As such, this proposal by NAEYC deserves careful consideration by federal and state agencies who license schools for young children (Brown, 1984).

State Certification

Another trend that affects staff education and career potentials within this field is the growing number of states that are adopting Early Childhood Education Teaching Certificates. This is often coupled with state-funded mandates creating full-day kindergartens and other specialist positions focusing on early childhood education needs. In February of 1984, for example, the state of Georgia passed a $231 million dollar legislative bill, which includes full-day kindergarten programs in all public schools by 1987–88. Such legislation is a growing trend nation-wide and some states are even contemplating adding programs for four year old children to the public school. Certificates for such teachers conform to the Level III NAEYC guidelines. Many also require an additional 36 college credits or a master's degree to be acquired during the first seven years of teaching. Thus the profession as a whole is up-grading the requirements for teaching young children as the need for such programs and the understanding of their importance grows.

Rising standards are likely to affect the field in several ways. More private and state-funded positions mean more jobs. Higher standards of education will create higher salaries. Both of these changes make the entire field more viable and should help increase the quality of candidates and the quality of programs offered.

THE EXPERIENCE OF TEACHING

The variety of models and types of early childhood programs are considerable. What type of setting will appeal to a particular individual is, of course, determined by his own personality and interests, as well as his experiences. In a good training program, students will have a variety of different and challenging opportunities. These involvements can help a student decide the age of child and the type of program that will be most appropriate and of greatest personal interest.

Basic Guidelines for Evaluating Children's Programs

It is helpful to be aware of how to evaluate programs and facilities both as a potential teacher and as a parent. Some of the things to look for are obvious: clean, comfortable spaces; reasonable safety precautions; a lively, aware staff; good food; and regular naps. At a more subtle level other factors are important (Collins, 1983, Collins and Deloria, 1983). Some concerns include:

1. The stability of the staff, that is, how long they have been in their positions, how regular their hours are.
2. The size of the group: federal guidelines set one adult to three children for infant care, one to four for two year olds, and one to eight for three to six year olds in day care settings; and one to five children under two and one to six for children from two to six for home care.
3. Appropriate kinds of attention, that is, face-to-face interaction with infants, naming objects and singing songs with the one year old, helping the two year old learn to pull up his own pants, etc.;
4. The right kind of activities, that is, developmentally appropriate games, walks, toys, etc., *no* television watching for the very young, *no* extended periods of sitting
5. The role of parents: Day care facilities should welcome parent involvement and allow "drop-in" visits; there should never be a feeling of "us," the experts, and "them," the parents

All of these factors *must* be present in a facility for young children and can be observed and discussed with the center staff.

ECE Curriculum

Another area of evaluation concerns the particular curriculum model used. Both day care and school settings may profess a "curriculum" and the degree to which a particular model is followed is an indicator of the type of experience the child will receive. This is the portion of the program which may be the most difficult to assess for several reasons:

1. The center or school may not have a thought-out model and each teacher may follow her own ideas.
2. The staff may consider themselves eclectic, that is, using a variety of models or techniques.
3. The school or center may espouse a particular approach but only partially monitor their staff's willingness and ability to follow the program.
4. A model may be referred to in promotional literature for the school or center, that is, "Piagetian curriculum," "Montessori school," but the execution of that program may differ greatly from other schools with the same claims or from the original model being credited.

TABLE 14.1.　Evaluating Models in Early Childhood Education

1.0.　*Assumptions*—The basic "givens" of a program.

　　1.1.　*Assumptions about the client.* How does the program conceive of the child and childhood? Are parents considered clients as well?

　　1.2.　*Assumptions about the educative process.* Are there specific theories of learning or of instruction underlying the program? Are they related?

　　1.3.　*Assumptions about the school.* Is the school conceived of as a broad social agency or as narrowly concerned with limited learning?

　　1.4.　*Assumptions about the teacher.* Is the teacher considered as an instrument of the program or is she a major decision maker?

2.0.　*Goals of the program*—The purposes of the program.

　　2.1.　*Long-range goals.* What long-range objectives are to be achieved?

　　2.2.　*Short-term objectives.* Are immediate objectives stated?

　　2.3.　*Relationship between the two.* Are long- and short-range goals consistent?

　　2.4.　*Degree of specificity of objectives.* Are objectives stated as observable behavior? Are objectives stated in other ways?

3.0.　*Curriculum*—The content of the program.

　　3.1.　*Range of content of the program.* Is the program broadly or narrowly conceived?

　　3.2.　*Sequence of learning or experiences.* Is a specific sequence prescribed?

4.0.　*Method*—The teaching strategies used.

　　4.1.　*Child-child transactions.* What is the nature of the child-and-child transaction behavior?

　　4.2.　*Child-teacher transactions.* What is the nature of the child-and-teacher transaction behavior?

　　4.3.　*Child-materials transactions.* What is the nature of the child-and-material transaction behavior?

　　4.4.　*Explicitness of prescriptions.* How explicitly are these transactions prescribed?

5.0.　*Style*—The degree of personalization allowed in teaching the program.

6.0.　*Organization*—The way in which elements are put together.

　　6.1.　*Scheduling.* How is time used?

　　6.2.　*Spatial organization.* How are resources deployed?

　　6.3.　*Grouping of children.* Are children grouped in some specific manner in the program?

　　6.4.　*Use of staff.* What kinds of staffing patterns are suggested?

7.0.　*Effectiveness*

　　7.1　*Achievement of goals.* Is there information about the degree to which the program can achieve its goals?

　　7.2　*Comparisons with other programs.* How does the program compare with other available programs?

8.0　*Practicality*

　　8.1.　*Cost of program.* How much does the program cost to implement?

　　8.2.　*Staff requirements.* How many staff members are needed? What sorts of qualifications are required?

TABLE 14.1.   Evaluating Models in Early Childhood Education (*Continued*)

8.3.   *Space requirements.* How much space is needed?

8.4.   *Materials requirements.* What kinds and quantities of materials must be used in the program?

8.5.   *Availability of supportive resources.* Are the necessary materials available? Are resource materials and persons available to support the program?

From: Teaching in the Early Years by Bernard Spodek, Prentice-Hall, Inc., Englewood Cliffs, NJ, 1972, pp. 317–18. Reprinted by permission.

Evaluating Programs

Because of these difficulties, a framework for gathering information about a curriculum model is essential. Knowing what questions to ask and what factors to observe can simplify evaluation and make it possible to compare different programs. In Table 14.1 *Evaluating Curriculum Models in Early Childhood Education* (Spodek, 1972), eight areas of concern are delineated.

The philosophy of a program is stated in its *assumptions.* How one views human development, learning, and the educational experience all contribute to our conceptualization of the curriculum. A view that the child is a "tabula rasa," blank slate, will lead to a different kind of curriculum from one that views the child as capable of organizing his own learning. The *goals* are an outgrowth of the assumptions and are derived from the purposes ascribed to education by the developer. For example, we may wish to train cognitive skills or provide opportunities for growth in social cooperation. While both might be possible, the main focus will tend to shape the choices of content. Next, we can view the *curriculum* as the range of encounters and activities that the child is given and the sequence in which these encounters take place. Does the child learn the alphabet letters before beginning to read words or is initial letter learning based on familiar or interesting words the child can recognize? Is learning to play a simple instrument an available experience as well as singing songs or using records? Most of these decisions are based upon our assumptions and goals.

The "how" of teaching is what we call *methods.* Presentation of learning sequences, whether they involve the teacher, other children, or materials are usually dictated by the model. Some behavioral programs, for example, have a specific monitored script a teacher is required to use. The degree of explicitness of teaching methods and the training of the teachers in following the stated procedures will determine the *consistency* of a curriculum. Where a model is unclear in this regard, teachers must use their own judgment and training. Programs where this is the case tend to be more variable.

Children often teach one another.

Style is a highly subjective aspect of teaching. The personality, train-ing, and level of understanding of the model being used all contribute to the style of presentation in a given curriculum. The manner in which personnel, materials, space, and time are put together and used to reflect the ideas and concepts of the program becomes the *organi-zation* of the model.

The final elements in this framework concern how we judge the appropriateness of our information. Both *effectiveness* and *practicality* may prove elusive dimensions. If a particular center or school has not

operated for very long or has not kept efficient records, it will be difficult to assess its effectiveness. Sometimes a curriculum model has been
used in other settings and it is possible to compare the present program
with the original. At other times only an approximate sense of effectiveness can be gained, limited to observations and discussions with
staff and parents. The practicality of a program can be translated into
both monetary figures and tangible lists of resources. However, monetary considerations alone can be misleading. The effectiveness of a program and its practicality match goals and resources in appropriate
combinations.

It should be apparent that evaluating a curriculum model within an
applied setting is a complicated task. The amount of time spent on such
an endeavor should be determined by the reasons for the evaluation. A
research team, a potential teacher, a student in training, or a parent will
each have different purposes and, therefore, will use different means
and standards for appraisal.

Becoming a Good Teacher

Teaching is a skill that can be learned from observation, practice, and
intellectual understanding. This is a principal assumption of teacher
training programs and is evident throughout this text. How good a
teacher one becomes, however, is based on factors within the individual as well as the effectiveness of the particular program the student
attends. Some excellent teachers have learned their skills on the job,
through personal readings, and through self-evaluation. Other teachers
just don't "make it" in spite of extensive training. Individual motivation,
personality, level of maturity, and life experience all enter into the
question of "good" teaching.

While we cannot claim absolute success in teacher training programs, we do know that the likelihood of success is greater when there
is extensive interaction with children, sufficient feedback on student
progress, and a reasonable sequence of learning activities which allow
for increased levels of independence in teaching responsibility. Teachers who learn to monitor their own effectiveness can learn and grow
in a variety of educational settings. As we have seen, written objectives
help one become aware of the success of a particular lesson, but this is
only one way to measure performance. Having an outside observer
who gives honest and helpful feedback is also highly valuable. Unfortunately, in the real day-to-day world of the ECE setting, this kind of
evaluation is hard to secure after the student's supervised teaching
experience is past. What other methods are available?

Several kinds of self-evaluation can be used, and some combination
of them is most helpful. Keeping a diary or journal over time is a very

It's fun to share a silly moment together.

useful device. Record keeping allows us to remember past levels of performance, frustration, and success. A journal assures personal and private feedback. A checklist of teacher skills may also be used. If a colleague or head-teacher does such an evaluation as well, results may be compared. Comparisons show the amount of agreement and discrepancy between how we see ourself and how we are perceived by others. Periodic appraisals can help us gauge our objectivity, as well as our skill level. Table 14.2 offers some important areas of evaluation.

Two other valuable methods of self-monitoring are the audio tape and the video tape. Naturally, the video tape is the best possible vehicle

TABLE 14.2. Teacher Skills Checklist

Directions:

Check items that are performed regularly. Put question mark on items you do not understand. Leave all other items blank.

1. Safety
   - _____ Promotes common safety practices within each activity area
   - _____ Encourages children to follow common safety practices
   - _____ Stops or redirects unsafe child behavior

2. Health
   - _____ Encourages children to follow common health and nutrition practices
   - _____ Provides and uses materials to ensure children's health and cleanliness
   - _____ Recognizes unusual behavior or symptoms of children who may be ill and provides for them

3. Learning environment
   - _____ Determines what activity areas can and should be included in the classroom on the basis of program goals, space available, and number of children
   - _____ Separates activity areas and places them in appropriate spaces
   - _____ Changes equipment and materials so that children can make choices easily and independently

4. Physical
   - _____ Assesses physical needs of individual children and makes appropriate plans to promote their development
   - _____ Provides equipment and activities to promote large and small motor skills in and out of the classroom
   - _____ Provides opportunities for children to move their bodies in a variety of ways

5. Cognitive
   - _____ Helps children use all of their senses to explore their world
   - _____ Helps children develop such concepts as shape, color, size, classification, seriation, number
   - _____ Interacts with children in ways which encourage them to think and solve problems

6. Communication
   - _____ Interacts with children in ways to encourage them to communicate their thoughts and feelings verbally
   - _____ Provides materials and activities to promote language development
   - _____ Uses books and stories with children to motivate listening and speaking

7. Creative
   - _____ Arranges a variety of art materials for children to explore on their own
   - _____ Accepts children's creative products without placing a value judgment on them
   - _____ Gives children the opportunity to have fun with music

479

TABLE 14.2.   Teacher Skills Checklist (*Continued*)

8. Self
    - _____ Accepts every child as a worthy human being and lets him or her know this with nonverbal cues
    - _____ Helps children to accept and appreciate themselves and each other
    - _____ Provides many activities and opportunities for individual children to experience success

9. Social
    - _____ Provides opportunities for children to work and play cooperatively
    - _____ Helps, but doesn't pressure, the shy child to interact with others
    - _____ Provides experiences that help children respect the rights and understand the feelings of others

10. Guidance and discipline
    - _____ Uses a variety of positive guidance methods to help children control their negative behavior
    - _____ Helps children establish limits for their behavior
    - _____ Helps children handle negative feelings through acceptable outlets

11. Family
    - _____ Involves parents in planning and participating in children's programs
    - _____ Communicates frequently with parents
    - _____ Treats information about children and families confidentially

12. Program management
    - _____ Uses a team approach to plan a flexible classroom schedule
    - _____ Uses transitions and small group activities to accomplish the goals of the program
    - _____ Plans for individual needs based on child observation and the interpretation of data obtained

13. Professionalism
    - _____ Is able to assess own teaching skills and those of others
    - _____ Can demonstrate competence in each of the skill areas included in this text
    - _____ Takes every opportunity to continue own professional growth

14. Special needs
    - _____ Helps bilingual children become fluent in both languages
    - _____ Helps bicultural children to appreciate their cultural heritage
    - _____ Helps handicapped children develop their strengths

From: *Skills for Preschool Teachers* by J. J. Beaty, Merrill, Columbus, OH, 1984.

for both seeing and hearing one's interactions. Video equipment is not always available, however, and may also be too awkward to use without help. An audio tape is a useful, though more limited, substitute. Listening to interactions and objectively recording the types and frequency of teacher and child statement may offer a clearer picture of

HERE THEY COME!

SCHOOL HOUSE

the appropriateness and value of a given lesson. (See Table 14.3 for a recording scheme.) Making a tally mark every three to five seconds in one of the categories and then adding up the total amount of time in the lesson and the percentage of that time in each indicates the degree of balance between child-teacher interactions and the amount of involvement in the lesson. Many other nuances of the lesson and its effectiveness can also be derived depending on the type of lesson and the creativeness of the person analyzing the material.

The trials and rewards of teaching are many and varied. Only actual involvement can tell you whether this is the right path for you. The strain of a day in which everything seems to go wrong must be balanced against the magic moment in which a child learns something for the first time or the shy youngster who has not talked all year suddenly decides to discuss some class project. Vast amounts of energy and persistence are required when working with the young child; and when

TABLE 14.3.   Tape Recording Analysis Form

			Tally	Total
Teacher Talk	1.	Lectures___		
	2.	Questions___		
	3.	Gives directions___		
	4.	Praises or encourages___		
	5.	Criticizes, negative comments___		
Student Talk	1.	Responds to teachers___		
	2.	Initiates new idea on topic___		
	3.	Talks to others off topic___		
Silence___				
Confusion				

From: *Developing Teacher Competencies* by J. E. Weigand, (Ed.), Prentice-Hall, Englewood Cliffs, NJ: 1971.

one is overtired or coming down with the latest flu, it may be difficult to remember what prompted you to take on a group of highly charged, busy little individuals. Then, suddenly, a child takes your hand and smiles or gives you a hug as she heads out the door and your memory returns. Maybe it's worth it after all!

ALTERNATIVE INTERACTIONS WITH CHILDREN

Other Professional Paths

Being a teacher in a nursery, day care center, or school setting is not the only career path for someone interested in working with young children. More and more alternative careers are available for people with the type of training an early childhood education program can offer. Some of the related careers include:

1. Hospital play center worker or teacher
2. Foster care placement worker
3. Group home worker for special-needs children
4. Playgound director or afterschool program worker
5. Home Start teacher demonstrator
6. Parent educator

These are just a few of the possible alternatives. In addition, there is an even greater variety of settings which conduct ECE programs. These include:

1. Company day care
2. Athletic center drop in care
3. Shopping center drop in care

4.   After school activity centers at YMCAs or other community facilities.
5.   Vacation resort child care facility

The possibilites seem only limited by one's imagination and willingness to try something new. Many of these alternatives are private businesses that are run within a company or center by an individual. Being willing to risk one's own time and energy to get the service started is often the only requisite for such ventures.

Becoming a Parent

Even if the career path of someone with early childhood training progresses in an alternative direction, there is great value in the knowledge and expertise gained from such experience as one becomes a parent. Naturally, parenting is a more complicated commitment than teaching. Yet, the training and objectivity of the teacher can be a valuable asset in raising one's own children. Knowing the normal development of a child and what to expect at different ages can be valuable. Techniques that promote growth and learning are also useful. And the experience of relating to children will provide confidence and increased understanding. Because so very few people actually learn to parent in our society, many new parents are confused and nervous about the parenting experience. This is one place where education is an especially valuable resource. However, the wealth of books published each year for parents is often overwhelming and contradictory. Having some concrete practice in ECE settings along with the academic understanding such training provides, offers a viable way to prepare one's self for raising a family.

Becoming a "Growing" Adult

A final and subtle advantage to education in the early childhood field is its boost to one's own developing self. Understanding growth and development, and learning to appreciate young children give us the opportunity to meet the child within us. Through this process we can come to terms with our own unique constellation of experiences, our limitations and our strengths, our own profound and funny piece of the human comedy. As we see ourselves in the children we nurture and teach, we can gain greater perspective on our successes and failures and can, finally, give up the egocentric view which insists that *our* mistakes and *our* problems are so very different from those of our fellows. We can decide to become a "growing" adult, one who is dedicated to self-understanding as a road to human understanding. Our training and interactions with children can show us where we have been and give us a window into what we can become.

Explorations

PERSONAL EXPLORATIONS

These exercises are designed to help you look at your own life—attitudes, experiences, dreams, myths, and realities.

1. Think back to your early school days. Who was your favorite teacher? What was she/he like? How would she rate on the Teacher's Skills Checklist (Table 14.2). Write one page summarizing your findings.
2. Whether you choose to work with young children in a teaching capacity, you are still likely to become a parent (if you are not one now). What skills and attributes of teachers would also be helpful as a parent? Are there any that would not be relevant? Make an outline of your ideas.
3. Look back at the present semester's course. What are some things you have learned about young children that are important or meaningful to you? What have you learned about the field of early childhood education? About teaching? About yourself? Bring a list of these learnings to class for a discussion?

INTELLECTUAL EXPLORATIONS

These exercises are designed to help you increase your depth of knowledge in some of the areas discussed in this chapter.

1. The four-level teaching hierarchy produced by the NAEYC is a goal but not a reality in early childhood education. Look up the state requirements for settings for young children (the library should have a copy). How do they compare with the goal? Write a paragraph analyzing the similarities and differences between the two.
2. Examine two teacher-practioner journals (*Learning, Young Children, Day Care, Childhood Education*). What type of articles do they include? What do these journals tell you about the teaching profession? Be prepared to discuss your findings in class.

FIELD EXPLORATIONS

These exercises are designed to take you out into the world to find real examples that illustrate and elucidate the material in this chapter.

1. Ask a teacher if you may tape record a brief lesson she conducts with a small group of children. Take it home and later compare your find-

ings with the recording scheme in Table 14.3. After you do the tally and count up the categories, ask yourself questions like:

Is the amount of teacher-talk and child-talk reasonably balanced? Could you tell if the children were involved? How did the teacher respond to divergent thinking? descriptions? confusion? silence? Write a summary of your conclusions.

2. Look through several newspapers in your area (big city, little city, local). Are there jobs listed for working with young children (up to seven years of age). What types of jobs? What are the requirements? How many different jobs? Bring your findings to class for discussion.
3. What are people's attitudes toward teachers of young children in the area in which you live? Ask some neighbors. Look in the newspaper. Ask some local politicians. What do those attitudes mean to you? Be prepared to discuss your feelings in class.

References

Beaty, J. J. *Skills for preschool teachers*. Columbus, OH.: Merrill, 1984

Brown, J. F. (Ed.), *Administering programs for young children*. Washington, D.C.: National Association for the Education of Young Children, 1984.

Collins, R. C. "Child care and the states: The comparative licensing study." *Young Children*, 1983, 38, 5: 3–11.

Collins, R. C. and Deloria, D. "Head start research: A new chapter." *Children Today*, July/August, 1983: 15–19.

Spodek, B. *Teaching in the early years*. Englewood Cliffs, NJ: Prentice-Hall, 1972.

Weigand, J. E. (Ed.), *Developing teacher competencies*. Englewood Cliffs, NJ: Prentice-Hall, 1971.

Index